CONSCIENCE AND ITS PROBLEMS

Conscience and Its Problems

An Introduction to Casuistry

Kenneth E. Kirk

Introduction by
David H. Smith

 Westminster John Knox Press
Louisville, Kentucky

First published in 1927 by Longmans, Green and Co. Ltd. Reissue with additions published in 1933; new editions published in 1936 and 1948. Introduction © 1999 Westminster John Knox Press.

Published by Westminster John Knox Press
Louisville, Kentucky

This book is printed on acid-free paper that meets the American National Standards Institute Z39.48 standard. ∞

PRINTED IN THE UNITED STATES OF AMERICA

99 00 01 02 03 04 05 06 07 08 — 10 9 8 7 6 5 4 3 2 1

Library of Congress Cataloging-in-Publication Data

Kirk, Kenneth E. (Kenneth Escott), 1886-1954.
    Conscience and its problems : an introduction to casuistry /
Kenneth E. Kirk, ; introduction by David. H. Smith.
        p.   cm —(Library of theological ethics)
    Originally published: London : Longmans, Green, 1927.
    Includes bibliographical references and index.
    ISBN 0-664-25578-7 (alk. paper)
    1. Conscience.   2. Casuistry.   I. Title.   II. Series.
    BJ1471.K5   1999
    171'.6—dc21   98-44982

To my wife

CONTENTS

PART I.—CONSCIENCE AND CASUISTRY

PART II.—PROBLEMS OF CONSCIENCE

LIBRARY OF THEOLOGICAL ETHICS

General Editors' Introduction

The field of theological ethics possesses in its literature an abundant inheritance concerning religious convictions and the moral life, critical issues, methods, and moral problems. The Library of Theological Ethics is designed to present a selection of important texts that would otherwise be unavailable for scholarly purposes and classroom use. The series engages the question of what it means to think theologically and ethically. It is offered in the conviction that sustained dialogue with our predecessors serves the interests of responsible contemporary reflection. Our more immediate aim in offering it, however, is to enable scholars and teachers to make more extensive use of classic texts as they train new generations of theologians, ethicists, and ministers.

The volumes included in the Library comprise a variety of types. Some make available English-language texts and translations that have fallen out of print; others present new translations of texts previously unavailable in English. Still others offer anthologies or collections of significant statements about problems and themes of special importance. We hope that each volume will encourage contemporary theological ethicists to remain in conversation with the rich and diverse heritage of their discipline.

ROBIN W. LOVIN
DOUGLAS F. OTTATI
WILLIAM SCHWEIKER

INTRODUCTION

Consider these situations:

A psychologist wants to study the impact of family dynamics on a form of mental illness that is thought to have both genetic and social causes. The research is relevant to development of forms of care for persons suffering from this disability, but it cannot be done if the research subjects recognize the goals of the research. Experimentation on persons without their consent is widely held to be immoral. Must this research be forbidden? Must policy proceed in ignorance?

Mary and Bill, married for five years, have been unable to conceive a child. Testing has shown that Bill is sterile. They contemplate use of artificial insemination by donor.

I have an aged and infirm friend who is not expected to survive another month. I learn that her beloved son has been killed in an automobile accident. She asks me what I have recently heard from her son. What should I tell her?

The church to which I belong opposes the remarriage of divorced persons. A member of the church has separated from his wife and lived with another woman for fifteen years. They have children and are loving and faithful. Should he participate in the eucharist? If his priest knows the situation, should he refuse to give him communion?

These are examples of the kinds of problems with which Kenneth Kirk is concerned in *Conscience and Its Problems*.[1] They are problems that call for casuistry—the disciplined resolution of challenging moral situations. In Kirk's terms the first and last are problems of *error* (either the community or the individual must be wrong); the second is an issue of *doubt* (the community's expectations are unclear); and the third is an issue of *perplexity* (clear and relevant principles are in conflict).

Casuistry as a form of moral reasoning was pilloried by Pascal, and much of the moral literature written since has avoided the term "casuistry." But casuistical practices never died in the Catholic tradition of moral theology; much of traditional Jewish ethics is casuistic; and a large fraction of modern moral philosophy takes the form of sophisticated analysis of real and imagined cases. In the post-modern mode, foundation-based system building is out of fashion. One option is to insist that serious moral discussion must fall back on case-by-case resolution of issues. Kirk anticipated this development, and his viewpoint remains profound and provocative.

Kenneth Escott Kirk (1886-1954) was born into a Wesleyan Methodist middle-class family that joined the Church of England when he was twelve. Kirk attended public schools and Oxford, was ordained a priest in the Church of England, and served as a chaplain in World War I. After the war, Kirk returned to Oxford as a university don, and he never left. His scholarly reputation rests on the books he published in the 1920s and 1930s. Elected Bishop of Oxford in 1937, Kirk continued to be an active member of the academic community; he became a leader of the Anglo-Catholic party of the Church of England. He argued strongly for the validity of Anglican orders within a broader Catholic community and for the importance of apostolic succession in ensuring that validity; he was a critic of the plan to develop an ecumenical Church of South India. This ecclesiologically conservative side was the most widely recognized part of Kirk's intellectual persona throughout the '50s, '60s, '70s and '80s. In this introduction, however, my more narrow focus will be on Kirk the moralist.

WHAT IS CASUISTRY?

Casuistry, most broadly understood, is a process of reasoning that focuses upon specific cases or moral problems, as opposed to a general study of ethical theories or concepts. The root of the English word is the Latin *casus* or case. In this sense, almost every serious moralist has been a casuist, in at least part of his or her writing. Thus, casuistry is a perennial element in the study of ethics or moral theology.

But in more precise attempts to differentiate among writers on Christian ethics, casuistry has a narrower denotation. Most narrowly it refers to the work of a group of moralists of the sixteenth and seventeenth centuries who had heirs within Catholic, Protestant, and Anglican traditions. And it has been given a new, not necessarily religious formulation in the late twentieth century in the work of Albert Jonsen and Stephen Toulmin, John Arras, Richard B. Miller and others.[2]

Conscience and Its Problems remains one of the landmark statements of twentieth-century casuistry. To see its significance, we need to know a little more about casuistry in general.

If I say that something is a work of casuistry, I imply that it has four attributes. First, I suggest that the center of gravity or focus of the work is on the resolution of a specific case or problem, rather than on the conceptual, doctrinal, or theoretical field in which a case arises. Simply making this claim points up the difficulty of the point, for many problems arise precisely because of the conceptual or emotional worlds we inhabit. One simply cannot radically separate case from intellectual context.[3] Nevertheless, differences of emphasis are important, and the casuist's emphasis is heavily on the case itself.

The casuist begins with the case, identifies the moral presumptions that make the situation a problem[4] and then questions those presumptions. In contrast, some noncasuists concentrate their attention on a more general level, investing much more intellectual capital in issues like the meaning of love or justice, or the relationship between God and the world, or the role of character in the moral life. Casuists need not dismiss those concerns; to the contrary. But a true casuist is someone for whom those general issues come up secondarily or derivatively; the casuist is pushed to them by the difficulties encountered in discussing cases, and general principles must cohere with insight into the cases.

Something is not made a work of casuistry by the inclusion of some discussion of specific problems; it is not disqualified as casuistry because its author has made some abstract or general commitments. But to call it casuistry tells us something about priorities in ethical reasoning.

Second, casuistry displays serious concern with responsibility or accountability. Works of casuistry may deal with hypothetical as well as real cases; they may deploy sophisticated arguments; the issues may confront individuals or groups. But they are always in answer to a question like "What is it permissible (or forbidden or obligatory) for me (or us) to do, in order for X to happen (or be avoided)?"

Casuistical moral reasoning always presupposes an answer—perhaps a complex and sophisticated answer—to the question "Why be moral?" Why shouldn't I lie to my son? Because I would be unhappy, or lose my self-respect, or depart from Torah, or betray Christ. A casuist does not allow the rationale for leading a moral life to slip very far into the background.

The casuist begins with the idea that the agent is responsible to something or someone and then asks what counts as a default on—or fulfillment of—that responsibility. "What is my (or our) responsibility in this situation?" "Was that result my fault?" or "Can she take credit for that achievement?" There is always an agent referent in casuistry.

To sort out these issues of responsibility, casuistry characteristically makes use of a set of distinctions that have been used in analyzing responsibility.[5] They may include distinctions between the intended and unintended consequences of an action, between negligence and innocent carelessness, or between lying and studied ambiguity. Few, if any, casuists use the whole menu of distinctions that casuists have employed over the years. They seek tools that fit the task at hand and the hand of the craftsman. Thus, Paul Ramsey, a heavily casuistical writer, extensively used the distinction between direct and indirect killing in his writing on war. In his discussions of care for the dying, however, he began by using the distinction but later displaced it. He wrote little about complicity or mental reservation. I don't mean to canonize any of these distinctions here, only to note that they and others are an inevitable element in casuistry, in contrast with moral inquiry that is less focused on agency and responsibility.

Third, casuistical reasoning makes heavy use of precedents, analogies, or paradigm cases. Casuists have some comparative certainties or fixed reference points for their arguments, but those certainties or reference points characteristically are judgments about specific events or situations, rather than general or abstract principles or rules.

The casuistical method works on a schema that may be easier to illustrate than to explain:[6] Suppose I believe that I should not lie to my wife about my plans for the evening. On the other hand, I realize that I don't owe strangers an account of my plans. But I am uncertain as to what level of explanation or disclosure is owed to siblings, or children, or coworkers. Assuming the verdict on spouse and strangers is clear, the casuist's question is: How is my relationship—and therefore my obligation—to a neighbor, a parent, or a child *like* one of those other relationships? One reasons from the more certain to the less certain situation, and the intellectual task consists of comparative analysis, e.g., are coworkers more like family or more like strangers? Verdicts are often in doubt or problematical. Knockdown certainty will be rare.

Of course, as the reasoning proceeds to a new situation, the relevance of one of the existing precedents, or even the verdict on it, may be called into question. There *may* be times when it is right to lie to my wife—for example, if my plan is to shop for her birthday present. Thus the whole intellectual web of cases will constantly flex as new cases are decided and old ones are rethought or refined. Occasionally, a key paradigm may change, requiring significant rethinking. Universal values or principles may be called upon. But the dominant mode of reasoning is from a more or less settled case to a vexing one.

Finally, consistent with these themes, casuistry occurs within the context of an identifiable tradition with some specificity to its moral life. There is an intellectual reason for this requirement: To get the moral reasoning process up and running, one needs an ongoing community that agrees on the resolutions of at least a few key cases. There doubtless are some resolutions on which all humankind could agree, but they won't take casuistry very far. There must be a group that treats some cases as provisionally settled.

Thus, casuistry is a process associated with some historical group that takes seriously the authority of certain texts, documents, or decisions; it is natural to refer to Jewish, Puritan, Catholic, or Anglican casuistry. Although the existence of the adjective is essential, the community of casuistry need not be religious. The case method in Anglo-American common law is distinctly casuistical, and professional or other occupational groups may develop distinctive forms of casuistry in the process of self-regulation. But casuistry entails an appeal to something that a community treats as authoritative.

All of these examples suggest that the tradition-based nature of casuistry relates to publicly acknowledged processes of decision making. Whether the mechanism

be the rabbinic *responsum*, the confessional, the jury, or the medical ethics committee, casuistry entails some kind of social institution that renders a verdict.
While the web of cases grows and shifts, individual cases must be settled, and any
given casuistical tradition must specify how that settlement will occur and note
that it has occurred at least as far as this particular case is concerned. If there were
no public resolution, everyone would always start from scratch; that would be inef-
ficient and would not be conducive to the development of habit and custom that
rightly simplify the moral life.

Kirk's casuistry stakes out a position under each of these headings. It is case-
centered, concerned with accountability and rationale for moral action, makes
heavy use of a comparative case analysis, and is rooted in an identifiable religious
and cultural tradition. To do his views justice, I will take them in a different order
and begin with the idea that casuistry focuses on responsibility or accountability
and thus presupposes an answer to the question of why we should be moral.

CASUISTRY FOR THE VISION OF GOD

In *Some Principles of Moral Theology*, his first book, Kirk argued that happiness
or "perfection" was the goal of the moral life. His mature discussion of the issue
is in *The Vision of God*, where he argued that happiness cannot be sought directly
because the ideal character is disinterested and unselfish. Preoccupation with
myself—even with my own moral progress—is simply a sophisticated form of selfishness. How can I be both unselfish and happy? The only way, according to Kirk,
is through worship that "lifts the soul out of its preoccupation with itself and its
activities, and centres its aspirations entirely on God."[7] Worship is the necessary
premoral condition for a moral life; it reorients the self away from preoccupation
with itself. When that reorientation occurs, the individual acts morally so as to
worship better and so as to make the world more closely conform to the ideals that
are glimpsed in worship.[8]

This exalted role for worship may seem strange to persons accustomed to hard
pews, boring sermons, or moralistic harangues. More searchingly, Oliver
O'Donovan has suggested that Kirk's thesis amounts to a "project of oblivion" in
which the self is asked to have affection for an abstraction.[9] The commonsense view
is that worship or devotion cannot play the role in a life that Kirk's theory requires
it to play; O'Donovan's view may be that it should not. And, perhaps because the
best connections are indirect, perhaps because many people are impatient with the
time demands of serious worship, many religiously observant persons see little connection between worship and their moral lives.

Kirk's theory, however, does not require any uncritical assumptions about altruism or the effectiveness of worship. He thought that the crucial component in all
worship was reorienting the self toward God, which entailed the discovery of a
good beyond the self. He believed that experiences of the discovery of and engage-

ment with a good beyond the self might come in many forms and were not rare but "at once the commonest and greatest of human accidents."[10] Kirk, who made extensive use of the work of William James, had an understanding of worship that was broader than one might suppose.

Kirk's own major concern, of course, was with Christian tradition and Christian worship. Formal Christian worship, he thought, could consistently provide a reorientation of the self. Moreover, he stressed the necessity for Christians to supplement communal worship with study of the life of Jesus and daily meditations based on the Gospels.[11]

One way of seeing the significance of Kirk's claim is by laying it alongside the work of another of this century's major writers on Christian ethics. In *Ethics,* Dietrich Bonhoeffer argued that so long as moral reasoning refers only to a set of self-created standards, individuals are caught in an egoistic circle. From the point of view of morality, he continued, "the great change takes place at the moment when the unity of human existence ceases to consist in its autonomy and is found, through the miracle of faith, beyond the man's own ego and its law, in Jesus Christ."[12] Christ becomes the center around which the transformed life now revolves. Bonhoeffer develops an antitype with the role of Hitler in the life of a Nazi, and he suggests that ego-redeeming release from self-centered moralism enables one to "bear guilt" for the sake of others, as one takes responsibility for one's actions before Christ.

As other portions of *Ethics* make clear, Bonhoeffer did not mean these claims to justify permissiveness. The verdicts of autonomous conscience remain relevant, and there are limits on what anyone can conscientiously do in the service of others. "The extent of the guilt which may be accepted in the pursuit of responsible action is on each occasion concretely limited by the requirement of the man's unity with himself, that is to say, by his carrying power."[13] I retain a specific and particular identity that limits what I can responsibly do with integrity. But true ethics is impossible without the transformation of the self in faith.

In effect, Kirk is explaining how this transformation of self occurs: in worship. His notion of the importance of decentering the self is very much like Bonhoeffer's. A main difference is that Kirk specifies how this decentering may occur and then talks about the connection between the process of self-transformation and ethics. In *The Vision of God,* he contends that behavior should reflect and will inevitably be informed by most fundamental commitments or loyalties, as in the case of the Nazi or Bonhoeffer's Christian. Therefore, any group of persons who share a common object of worship will require some forms of behavior or discipline of each other, but the motive for discipline should be to assist group members as they struggle to sustain their loyalty, not to exclude others to ensure the purity of the community.

Indeed, discipline requires the formulation of general rules of conduct, for the sake of efficiency and security. But subscription to those moral rules should be "forced upon" someone "by the exigencies of worship" rather than imposed by external authority.[14] A moral rule should genuinely assist in achieving the reorientation of self. Thus, the test of a good rule is not its formal clarity or consistency but its effectiveness in sustaining a Christian life.

Of course, following rules will require some renunciation of the self's interests or causes. Historically, entry into the rigorous discipline of a monastic community was an important way for Christians to live out that renunciation, and one could imagine a revision of Bonhoeffer in which transformation of the self by Christ meant that all other standards and considerations, including the particularities of the self, were ignored. But Kirk was very clear that withdrawal from the world is not necessary. Self-discipline may take many forms, including lay asceticism.

Kirk's whole intellectual project was driven by a distinctive set of religious ideas: that selves seek happiness, that happiness can be found only when the self is reoriented to God, that this reorientation happens through worship, that someone so transformed will want to be loyal to the community, and that the community of reoriented persons may make legitimate demands on its members. The effect is to create an intellectual core around which he built his casuistry.

CASUISTRY IN THE CHURCH

Kirk specified the group in and for which he spoke; his casuistry was self-consciously Catholic and Anglican. "I find myself to be a member of a particular community," he says in effect. "Now, what does loyalty to this community require of me?" Kirk's discussion of loyalty demonstrates his conviction that selves are social; persons are not alone; individuals are members of communities to which they owe allegiance. The social character of the self is intrinsic, a gift to be thankful for. Among other things, our social nature helps us to recognize duties beyond those we would otherwise see, and it compels us to avoid harming others. Membership in any community entails legitimate claims upon its members.

Kirk's discussions of specific issues of church discipline are difficult to appreciate unless one remembers just how seriously he takes the idea of loyalty. He assumes that a member of a community will be uncomfortable betraying its core values, that no one would want to be a Christian while ignoring the discipline of the tangible and real Christian community of which he or she is a part. The whole problematic and pathos of *Conscience* is lost if this assumption of identification and loyalty on the part of the moral agent is forgotten.

Consider a secular analogy. Two people have learned that it is destructive to smoke. One of them believes the conclusion is scientifically correct, then asks herself how often she can indulge her habit with safety. Is the rule certainly proven? Does it apply to cigars after dinner? What if the diplomacy of the nation is affected by my refusal to smoke with a foreign diplomat? Those sound like Kirkian questions, and in a formal sense they are. But this person, as I have described her so far, has not really entered the moral problematic as Kirk sees it.

Contrast her with her friend, who says many of the same things about smoking but whose opposition to smoking is rooted in her membership in a community of nonsmokers—perhaps her family of origin, influenced by the death of a relative from lung cancer. For this second person, the questions take the form of what her loyalty to her family requires of her in this situation. Were we right to give up smoking? Always? Can I, as a loyal member of this family, accept that cigar? The moral question for the loyal person does not only concern the rightness or wrongness of a general rule but also the requirements of loyalty to a tangible and particular community.

Of course, knowing just what loyalty required was particularly difficult in a large and heterogeneous "family" such as the Church of England. Kirk was deeply ambivalent about the issue of diffuse and uncertain moral authority. On the one hand, he resented the state's heavy influence on the church, and he recognized that reliance on many different standards leaves the individual feeling rudderless. He could understand why the Roman Catholic Church had stressed its autonomy and claimed authority formally to clarify its moral teaching, i.e., stressed promulgated law.[15] On the other hand, Kirk celebrated the rejection of a juridical model and confidence in a more pragmatic, pluralistic, and commonsensical style in the Church of England.

Some of the standards of the community are written and lawlike; some are habitual; some are local or regional. Kirk's idea was that this plurality of standards should be taken seriously by loyal Christians. So when it comes to working through a moral issue, they will find themselves appealing to a range of norms found in juridical and theological writing, social practice, and in literature that stretches the moral imagination. The fact that no general rule clearly applies to a situation is instructive, but that scarcely means that there are no relevant normative considerations to be brought to bear.

Kirk's understanding of the role of tradition was shaped by his convictions about invincible ignorance. *Ignorance, Faith and Conformity* is, to a significant degree, a restatement and defense of the principle that an erring conscience binds. I have a responsibility to learn all I can and to be open to new sources of insight; irresponsible ignorance is intolerable. But once I have reasoned a matter through, I must follow my conscience.

That will inevitably lead to conscientious disagreement within the community, or the problem of error taken up in *Conscience and Its Problems*. Error occurs when a clear conflict arises between what the community affirms and what the individual is convinced is correct. For there to be error, in the technical sense, both positions must be clearly articulated—as in the first and last situations mentioned at the beginning of this introduction. The last, Kirk's own example, concerns the issue of divorce, a hotly debated topic in the Church of England of his day; I have offered a case from research ethics. The point to note regarding error is that someone must be wrong: Either the Church is wrong to deny the possibility of the remarriage of divorced persons, or the couple is wrong to think of themselves as married; either the consensus on experimentation without consent is wrong, or the important experiments should not be performed.

The striking thing about Kirk's discussion of error is his unequivocal affirmation that the community, not just the individual, may well be wrong. This conclusion, of course, is consistent with his understanding of the role of custom and moral argument. The individual must reason the matter through; once that is done, her or his conscience binds. A harder issue for Kirk is whether the dissenting individual must call the attention of the community to the fact of nonconformity (for instance, by telling the parish priest of the previous marriage, or flagging the imperfect consents for the institutional review board that is responsible for enforcing research ethics requirements). Kirk thinks that disclosure is the right course, but his community's practices do not require it. In any case, it is not the business of the priest to refuse communion; the issue of continuing to receive communion concerns the "bearing power" of the individual's conscience. Can she or he stand the dissonance between the standard of the community and her or his own formed conviction?

Over time and through discussion, the standards of the church as a community change. Kirk envisioned the church as a community of moral deliberation. Uncritical appeals to authority will lead to "moral indolence" or "stagnation" and "to a life which may by accident remain superficially respectable, but is bound to collapse in any serious moral crisis."[16] He considers the dilemma of an Anglo-Catholic priest who is uncertain whether marriage is compatible with his ordination vows. The priest should not simply suffer or agonize in silence but should enter serious discussion in the church.

> [I]f he has her welfare at heart, he must play his part in the process of selecting from among a vast number of competing practices and opinions the dominant laws and customs of the future. He will play a part in that process anyhow, if in no other way than by an indolent and prejudiced adherence to tradition, or an unregulated and unreflective acceptance of each new idea.[17]

Through serious moral discussion, the church's code gets the constant revision it requires.[18]

All Christians must engage in moral reasoning so as to shape custom, for custom or social habit is the foundation for operative morality. Kirk thought that because the Church of England had a very minimal process for establishing moral standards, custom had the force of law; it could "introduce, interpret, or abrogate" law. "There are practically no limits to the action of custom and desuetude in the introduction and abrogation of claims upon loyalty, provided always that the tacit consent of authority can be assumed."[19] Christians "individually and collectively" have "the right and the duty of reflecting upon all these incipient customs, ideas and opinions—some of them destined to failure, others to success—and of coming to conscientious decision for and against them."[20]

Kirk's appeal to individual conscience is differentiated from individualism by his assumption that the individual wants to be loyal to the community, that she or he means to be a member of the community who has some integrity. But there is another way in which Kirk's views of tradition are not individualistic, and that is in his reliance on the confessional. He thought that confession to a priest was an important part of the Christian moral life. While the driving force behind much of Kirk's argument is a desire to criticize priests who were rigorist in the use of their authority, he nevertheless assumed that serious Christians took confessional discipline seriously.

For example, at the time Kirk wrote, the Church of England opposed the use of contraceptives in most circumstances. He thought conscientious Christians might dissent from this judgment, but even if good arguments for the use of contraceptives could be advanced—if the case for using condoms were, in his terms, "probable"—Kirk rejected the idea that in this case of moral doubt it was acceptable simply to proceed to use condoms. In the first two editions of *Conscience*, he argued that conscientious Christians should rely on the counsel of "official penitentiary advisers"[21] and would not, for example, be free to use a condom until they had "received the authority of the church, speaking through the accredited channel of the priesthood, for [their] . . . own particular case."[22]

Between the second and third editions, the 1930 Lambeth Conference of Anglican Bishops from around the world passed a resolution slightly more open to the use of contraceptives. Kirk revised the section so as to make the role of a confessor less essential. Now "[w]e should attempt to persuade the conscience of the Church of England that in a matter of such urgency her members should at least take the opinion of responsible authority before making their decisions."[23]

Kirk's understanding of the role of the church in Christian ethics has recently been seriously criticized by one of his successors at Oxford, Oliver O'Donovan. For O'Donovan, Kirk's views are "historicist"; they have the effect of domesticating the teachings of Jesus and replacing them with tradition. On Kirk's terms, revelation cannot serve as a basis for moral thought, nor can morality offer stringent criticism of social practice or custom.[24] Most particularly, on O'Donovan's reading, Kirk denies that the church is a moral agent that must be concerned with its own integrity and faithfulness to God. Rather, Kirk's church sees itself as somehow above the responsibilities and ambiguities of the real world.

O'Donovan, in contrast, wants the church to acknowledge its public responsibility to bear a witness of integrity; among other things, that means a revival of the practice of excommunication as a sign of God's final judgment. The church is not merely a community of individuals on pilgrimage; in its corporate life, it should be a community of witness. O'Donovan does not argue for a busybody church intruding in all sorts of decisions. Most of the church's teaching to assure integrity can take the form of "counsel" directed to the "inner life of thought, attitude, and motive, and the response to individual vocation."[25] Nevertheless, there are occasions when it is important for the church to command.

When should the church move from counsel to command? When the individual has done something that is a "refusal of God's word" rather than a departure from the "church-political order."[26] For example, we should not excommunicate a layman for celebrating communion, but we probably should excommunicate someone who "publicly advocates and practices violent intimidation for monetary gain."[27] Between these extremes lie some hard cases, e.g., euthanasia.

This perspective is not unique to O'Donovan. Stanley Hauerwas has written that the church does not have a social ethic; it *is* a social ethic.[28] Among other things, Hauerwas means by this assertion that the church should not primarily be a teacher but that it should embody the Christian way of life in its practices, in worship, and in the lives of its members. Kirk, perhaps because he was always identified with an established church in a diverse society, was tentative about just exactly what it might mean for the church to "be" an ethic. The real world of the church community is too diverse and complex to be identified with any highly particularized ethic. The ambiguity of the moral problems he considered in *Conscience* was never far from his mind.

O'Donovan's and Hauerwas's conception of the church is very different from Kirk's. It is both more evangelical or Protestant and more clearly set in contrast with the larger culture. Unfortunately, the contrasts O'Donovan draws rest on a reading of Kirk that is largely off target. To begin with, there is the obvious epistemological point. Kirk's tone was pastoral and modest in its claims to know the will of God for diverse persons in diverse places. He would never have surrendered the possibility of excommunication on principle, but the whole force of *Conscience* is toward a recognition of diversity and legitimate, conscientious moral disagreement. O'Donovan's church is not modest in its claims for itself. In contrast, Kirk's vision of the church includes reckoning with the authority of custom, practice, and individual conscience. Those things are not to be overridden lightly. The track record of saints who have been sure of their own rightness is not encouraging.

Most fundamentally, however, to characterize Kirk's conception of the church as an entity above the fray, unconcerned with its own integrity and faithfulness to God, is quite misleading. Kirk's whole project is to sort out the demands of loyalty to an institution that stands for something. If it stood for nothing, there would be no problem of loyalty to consider. To be sure, Kirk's understanding of what the Church should stand for was largely conventional, and when he does acknowledge that problem—as in his brief discussion of what the Church of England should say about birth control (p. 305 of the present edition)—the result is frustrating. He might well make more use of scriptural metaphor and principle. But Kirk seems to take the plausible view that it is not difficult to map the basic outline of Christianity's requirements; as a community, Christians have learned something about that. Now they must talk together to shape their own lives and the future of their community.

In fact, Kirk was ambivalent about the importance and the significance of the church, as such, taking a stand. On the one hand, he could say the substantive teachings of Anglicanism were disappointing.

> A tendency to vague generalizations, to pious platitude, to compromise with conventional standards, to the avoidance of pronouncements which may prove unpalatable to public opinion, results in an almost complete absence of any attempt to deal with the immediate detailed problems of the moral life in a healthy and bracing manner.[29]

Against this prophetic blast stands the whole argument of *Conscience* for recognition of diversity within the church and, indeed, a celebration of the stress on custom and case-based analysis. It is not easy to get people to rally around a strong public stand for the acceptance of ambiguity.

PRIORITIES IN CASUISTICAL REASONING

So far, we have explored two key ingredients in Kirk's casuistry: its religious motivation and its home in the Christian community. This discussion brings us to the casuistical process per se. For Kirk, casuistry is the development of "rules of procedure" for dealing with intuitions and "rules (if any there be) by which the relevant laws of conduct can be discovered in particular cases and the irrelevant recognized as such and set aside; as well as a knowledge of the truest definitions of justice, truth and the like."[30] For example, the fact that an erring conscience binds, discussed above, is one important casuistical rule.

Casuistry got a bad name because of its association with rationalization and laxity. Kirk believed that those faults occurred because many earlier casuists engaged in over-general and sweeping moral rigorism, painting themselves into a corner. To avoid their mistake, Kirk needed a way to explain the relationship between general moral considerations and particular judgments. What is needed is a casuistical process that entails "extension of wise general principles to fit new problems and circumstances" rather than "the dangerous though inevitable whittling away of laws too sweepingly laid down, in the interests of particular exigencies."[31]

He clearly rejected the idea of working out a detailed set of abstract norms and then applying them to cases. In fact, he seems to favor what Henry Richardson has more recently called "specification," where one is willing to "revise one's normative commitments so as to make at least one of them more specific."[32] Kirk could say with Richardson that a "pure model of application depends upon an ideal achievement of moral theory that is beyond our grasp."[33] One should not begin the moral reasoning process with a set of clearly defined rules; rather, the initial generalities are refined and made more nuanced and specific as reasoning proceeds. In Richardson's model of specification, the key idea is that the basic set of relevant norms cannot be thought of as fixed in content in every detail; instead "the exact extent and nature" of the things they oblige us to have some "latitude" about them.[34]

Similarly, on Kirk's view, when the principles of morality are applied to new cases "each extension of a law must involve some modification of it."[35] Our under-standing of the law of God is "progressive."[36] Or, as Richardson says, "specification is genuinely distinct from the model of application, since a specification will in general not follow deductively from what it specifies."[37]

For Kirk and Richardson, the alternative view, beginning with a fully specified rule such as "Never tell a lie," discredits moral reasoning. Every generalization has its exceptions, but where will the list of exceptions stop? The process of accumu-lating exceptions has the effect of discrediting the original rule. Therefore, one should be more circumspect at the outset.

> The only proper procedure is to labor towards the understanding of the law until we are able to state it in a form which will exclude whoever [or what-ever] merits exclusion, without emphasizing the device of ethical exception. Anything else is not an "adaptation," but only an emasculation of the law.[38]

If the exception-making strategy fails, some rigorist may try splitting hairs. Take the issue of lying. One way to make the universal prohibition palatable is excep-tions; another is to offer a refined definition of what constitutes a lie. Kirk refers to this strategy as "the exact scrutiny of the formula in which the law is expressed in order to find some means of escape from its severity."[39] In the history of moral dis-cussion of truth telling, various moralists have held that studied ambiguity, equiv-ocation, or mental reservation, although admittedly misleading, are not lies.

For Kirk, that is much too subtle; he wants to take the bull by the horns and say that reasoning obviously designed to save the reputation of clearly stated and rig-orous but in fact incredible rules leads to the development of a corrupt casuistry that defensively lines up behind the undefensible. A rule's original lack of speci-ficity and limitations should be admitted up front.

To appreciate the casuistic principles that Kirk defends (in addition to the stress on the integrity of conscience that characterizes his discussion of error), we need to realize that the crisp disagreement between individual and community that char-acterizes error is comparatively rare, certainly in a community that takes custom as seriously as Kirk means to. Often the community's expectations are unclear; some of its authorities say one thing and others something different. This disparity creates the situation of doubt: What I want to do may be clear, but what is expect-ed of me is not. My illustration of the use of artificial insemination by donor illus-trates this situation; Kirk's examples include the requirement of clerical celibacy, abstinence from alcohol, or adoption of a vegetarian lifestyle, and—the issue he discusses most thoroughly—use of birth-control devices.

The basic maxim that underlies Kirk's discussion of doubt is that when the moral stakes are less than ultimate, when "vital interests" such as life and salvation are not at issue, a law of doubtful relevance does not bind. As Kirk sees it, the issue arises when branches of Catholic Christianity differ, or when a serious reform movement within the church suggests a raising of standards. Which set of puta-tive Christian standards should I follow?

Kirk runs through the types of answer that have been offered for dealing with this problem. He never explicitly considers *laxism*, which holds that individuals can do whatever they wish if there is any doubt whatsoever about the pertinence of a moral guideline. Rather, he begins with *tutiorism*, the view that the morally safest option should always be chosen: no insemination using donor sperm, no alcohol, no animal products in the diet, no contraceptives.

This mind-set dictates that one should follow every conscientious suggestion or the most demanding option. Kirk found it to be impossible, an example of precisely the kind of scrupulosity that has tended to discredit serious moral reasoning. The Anglican casuists of the seventeenth century also rejected it, opting instead for *probabiliorism*, which held that one must follow the most reasonable viewpoint and could reject out of hand views that were unreasonable. From Kirk's point of view, this approach is well intentioned but not helpful, because identifying *the* most reasonable solution is virtually never possible. One simply does not have time to sum up and comparatively assess all the possibly relevant arguments in a way that would allow saying, "This alternative is the most probable conclusion."

Therefore Kirk follows the seventeenth-century Jesuits and their preferred system of *probabilism*: Reasonable doubt as to a law's validity is sufficient to discredit its claim. One might use artificial insemination by donor, drink alcohol, eat meat, or use condoms—if the arguments for the more rigorous positions can be shown to have "internal" inconsistencies, that is, if they are unsound on their own premises. The issue for Kirk is not whether I am resourceful enough to find an authority to defend the option I want to choose. That was the charge of the seventeenth-century Anglicans against the Catholics—that they concluded it was permissible to do anything approved by some authority or other. Kirk means his point to be a matter of logic, not politics. I am not bound by a logically problematic rule, and I may follow a reasonable one, even if I can't show that it is the "safest" option. In other words, there must be serious moral problems with the rule I reject, and the course I follow must be arguably better—but not provably best, as the probabiliorists would require.

Kirk was aware of the extent to which probabilism opened the door to what a later generation would call "situation ethics." Nor would he have rejected all of what was argued under that heading.[40] But he insisted that, for probabilism to come into play, doubt about the right thing to do must be real—meaning presumably that serious persons would acknowledge it as an issue of doubt. Nor would he allow the following of a merely probable course when vital issues are at stake.[41]

But the core of the difference between Kirk and a situationist like Joseph Fletcher has another basis. Earlier, I noted the parallels between Kirk's argument and a philosophical proposal by Henry Richardson. One risk of strategies like those of Kirk and Richardson is that they seem to leave the core of morality with little firm content.[42] It may appear that "anything goes." Richardson resolves this problem by an appeal to a "coherence standard" in which the reasonableness of a particular specification is assessed with reference to the rest of the accepted principles or elements of the system.[43]

Kirk could find some of this strategy attractive, but for him the problem of insufficient moral content is mitigated by the fact that he situates morality in the context of a specific institution and tradition. Kirk believed that persons should try to act according to God's will, that there was a real institution (the church) that knew something (not everything!) about that will and a practice—confession—for listening, confiding, and giving advice. His trust in those institutions and processes stood behind his conviction that people should be very modest in their statements of general moral rules; he meant to defend diversity and flexibility, not permissiveness.

The final type of casuistical situation Kirk considers is that I may find myself in a situation in which I am perplexed because I confront a genuine dilemma: Two obligations of unquestioned validity bear on my situation, and they require different courses of action. An example is the third case mentioned in the Introduction, taken from Kirk, in which the obligation to tell a friend the truth conflicts with the obligation not to harm her.

To see the pathos of perplexity, it is important to remember that, for Kirk, moral claims are issues of loyalty to individuals or groups. Thus, when claims or obligations conflict, we confront a conflict of loyalties. The issue of perplexity presents the question of how I will betray a trust or loyalty. This betrayal can happen in any one of three ways.

First, I may find myself in a situation in which betrayal of some normally powerful claim is actually expected. Kirk's example is lying to the enemy in war. Here I find myself torn between the claim to tell the truth, rooted in my loyalty to the Christian community that stands for truth, and the claim of my nation on my allegiance. One claim must be betrayed. Kirk argues that lying to the enemy may be justified because that is what is expected in the context of war, and the enemy—who does not expect the truth from me—cannot really be betrayed by the lie. The general point is that some situations establish accepted priorities among obligations.

Second, I may be perplexed because my action will amount to a betrayal of the very person to whom I am attempting to be loyal, as in the case of the infirm friend. Kirk's way of resolving these situations is to appeal to "the distinctive mentality of the patient" and the "exact relationship existing between her and the speaker."[44] By the first, he means both the extent to which the patient will feel betrayed if a lie is discovered, and the exact risk that truth telling poses for her. He considers these the relevant variables, and their assessment calls for skills of accurate perception and judgment in each situation.

Kirk's reference to the "exact relationship" is more schematic. He argues that a family member has a strong obligation to run the risk of telling the truth because of the distancing and alienation that lying entails in an intimate relationship; physicians, whose appropriate focus of concern is physical health, might be more pardonable in a lie; priests "peculiarly commissioned to safeguard the credit of truthfulness"[45] have a very strong obligation to tell her the truth. No one's obligations are absolute in such a case, but the type of relationship between the speaker and the patient is of great moral relevance.

Third, I may be perplexed because my lie will discredit the community of which I am a part, betraying something at the heart of what the community stands for. For example, I might be tempted to lie to save someone threatened by an outlaw. At this point, Kirk's reasoning becomes quite utilitarian: He considers the action's consequences to society, the action's motivation (it is one thing to save myself, another to save someone else). Harms to the threatener, to the agent's character, and to social practices are all relevant. Not all factors in moral reasoning are justified on utilitarian grounds, but utilitarian assessments are the only reasonable course in some situations.

From Kirk's point of view, the casuist's objective is to minimize the number of situations that must be settled on utilitarian grounds. Seeing an issue as a problem of error or of doubt is a means to that end. If a morally uncertain situation is a situation of error, the issue becomes one of strain on the individual conscience, the need for change in the community's standard, or possible resignation from the community. The issue is one of politics or process, not of the merits of the case, for coming to agreement on the merits of the case is impossible in instances of error.

Kirk concedes that situations of doubt can be redescribed as issues of perplexity in which some other obligation conflicts with "the assertion of freedom," i.e., a duty to be free.[46] But the effect of that maneuver is to "elaborate a wholly trivial problem, easily decided on probabilist lines, into a crisis of conscientious scruples."[47] We see symptoms of this mistake in the late twentieth century when people recast every want of the self into an issue of obligation. Then—when normal moral obligations conflict with those wants—resolution of the competing "obligations" is made in terms of utilitarian balancing.

For example, a man may find his marriage less than completely fulfilling; he could reason that he faces a conflict of obligations between his duty to himself and the promises he made to his wife. Thus, he would see the situation as one of perplexity, to be resolved on balancing terms. "How will we all be better off in the long run?" That is the kind of redescription that Kirk means to discourage. He would insist that this situation is more accurately described as one of doubt about the implications of marital vows. Arguing that these situations are better described as doubt has the effect of focusing on the stringency of an obligation of obvious pertinence and cuts through some disingenuous rationalization.

A third way of avoiding the appeal to balancing judgments is compromise, which Kirk sees as "deferring the issue."[48] Kirk's ambivalence about compromise is palpable. On the one hand "the purpose of compromise . . . is merely to stave off the evil day in the hope that some *deus ex machina* will emerge to avert its threatened catastrophe."[49] Or, ". . . a moral issue has been evaded; a judgment of conscience which should have been made deliberately has gone by default."[50]

Nevertheless, "it may prove better to delay the issue rather than to force it."[51] The dangers of compromise are that convenience and inertia will take over; furthermore, living with ambivalence takes its own toll on a thoughtful person.

All of those considerations are true, but if moral tension is neither gravely diminished nor increased, "we need not be too anxious about the duration of a compromise; its limits are set by psychological and moral rather than by temporal calculations."[52] Kirk finds it a little hard fully to embrace the pastoral side of his intellectual persona and his celebration of custom and the imagination. Instead, he seems to think that right decisions in cases of perplexity *must* be made by a concerted act of will. The thought that the passage of time might allow one to recast the problem by seeing it in a new light, or that a right decision is something that somehow emerges in the mind—rather than being ordered to appear—is not stressed.

PRECEDENT AND AUTHORITY

The final dimension of casuistry in general is a heavy reliance on precedent cases and analogical reasoning. The casuistical process requires the identification of these key reference points. The striking thing about Kirk's casuistry at this point is his use of Christian scripture and tradition. As any reader of a few pages of this book will realize, he was steeped in that tradition, but one finds remarkably little use of scripture, in particular of the teachings of Jesus, as sources of moral insight. It is a mistake, however, to draw the inference that Kirk found the New Testament irrelevant to moral reasoning. Rather, Jesus was "the greatest of casuists."[53] The parables are examples of casuistic reasoning, and Jesus was "severely technical and scientific"[54] in his handling of the moral traditions he inherited.

Jesus, the prototypical and exemplary casuist, defended two basic principles. The first was an appeal to consistency and a rejection of hypocrisy: Arbitrary and self-serving distinction should be eliminated. The second is a use of analogy: Similar cases must be decided in similar ways. Thus, a key component of moral reasoning is discriminating judgment about which cases are most alike. Jesus was particularly good at this art, and the Gospels show "the astonishing deftness of Christ in His moral solutions."[55] He not only came to an insightful resolution but he displayed an unparalleled "*moral tact*, the discovery of the *best* way of doing the right or allowable thing," a "genius for the appropriate."[56]

Kirk did not extract a general rule or principle, such as *agape* or the deliverance of the oppressed, from the Bible. He wrote a commentary on the Epistle to the Romans, and he spent much of his academic career teaching the New Testament, but in his work in ethics he did not substitute some theological or historical theory for the diversity and richness of the biblical case material. Jesus' main substantive relevance to morality was as an object of worship, a source of consolation, a source of power and grace—not as someone who announced a full set of moral principles. The principles are there, to be sure, but the main thing the Christian learns from Christ is how to use them, how to reason and live amid ambiguity. Kirk maintains that we should reason about cases as Jesus reasoned about cases.

Thus, although the Bible was important in Kirk's concept of the Christian life and is the medium through which we see the casuistic method most clearly illustrated, he makes remarkably little use of biblical stories or teachings as a trump suit of cases to which appeal can be made in moral argument. Nor are the resolutions of church authorities or theologians—even great figures to whom Kirk is heavily indebted, such as Aquinas—treated as necessarily decisive. The Bible and Christian tradition are his conversation partners; they are sources of insight, norms and principles that require specification, and distinctions. But the real treasure they pass on is the casuistical method embodied in the teachings of Jesus. Kirk does not begin with a biblical rule or story and then inquire into its moral implications; he begins with what he conceives to be the plight of someone who wants to be a loyal Christian and then asks what Christian casuistry requires of that person.

For these reasons, Kirk directly confronts an issue that writers on morality often dodge: their own expertise at practical advice; the appropriate qualifications for the role they play. Understandably, many moralists are cautious about taking on the role of moral adviser, but Kirk thought the burden was inescapable. In particular, he thought the character of the moralist was a vital part of casuistical reasoning. To perform the task of casuistry well, the casuist must be someone of good character, the kind of person who will recognize a moral claim for what it is. "None but the morally earnest are safe guides in casuistry; nor can it be a profitable subject of study for any but the morally earnest." Someone who is not trying to be moral will have trouble with discernment; "no one who is *not* trying to live the Christian life has any right to attempt to weigh up its moral niceties."[57]

Moreover, he was clear that moral advisers need to make serious efforts to learn what they are talking about. When dealing with an issue of perplexity, for example, the priest or adviser should "obtain the experience and the disposition which will enable him to enter with sympathy into the inner meaning of the claims on either side . . . by a deliberate, devoted and prayerful effort to extend his range of sympathies in every direction."[58] Kirk calls on moralists to master as much of the factual material necessary to understand a problem as possible. More than that, he stresses the importance of empathy. Being a serious casuist is intellectually and emotionally difficult.

CONCLUSION

Seventy-five years after its composition, *Conscience and Its Problems* remains a pertinent, original, and insightful essay. Kirk addressed issues of the rationale for moral thought, the role of the church as a moral community, and of the handling of problematical moral situations in ways that remain helpful and current at the end of the century. His appreciation for the role of loyalty in the moral life complements the work of American writers such as Josiah Royce, H. R. Niebuhr, and Paul Ramsey. A later generation has been more self-conscious about the differences between the demands of the Gospel and those of any given culture, but Kirk's combination of moral seriousness and renunciation of dogmatism, his respect for the diverse consciences of serious Christians, and his sense of responsibility as someone speaking not just for himself but for a group or community of fallible human beings remain powerfully instructive.

NOTE ON THE TEXT

Conscience and Its Problems, first published in 1927, was revised twice in Kirk's lifetime. The first revision concerned the Lambeth Conference's statement on birth control in 1930, and I refer to those changes earlier in the introduction. A second revision, much later, also reflected Kirk's response to the changing rules about marriage and divorce in the Church of England; it consisted of deleting Note C: "Marriage with a Deceased Wife's Sister, and Re-marriage of Divorced Persons." Kirk explained his reason for dropping this Note, and we retain that short argument.

ACKNOWLEDGMENTS

I presented an early draft of this introduction at a meeting of the Guild of Scholars of the Episcopal Church at the General Theological Seminary in November 1996, and I remain grateful to the Guild and its president, Charles Forker, for their attention. Drafts have been helpfully read by Philip Turner, Timothy Sedgwick, Thomas Breidenthal, Gilbert Meilaender, Richard B. Miller, and Catherine Cookson. Professor Cookson also helped me dig out facts about Kirk's life, thought, and publications; she was a fine conversation partner over many months. Professor Gordon Dunstan, who knew Kirk well, kindly took time to offer extended pertinent commentary. Judith Granbois exercised a characteristically judicious editorial hand, and Beverly Davis produced some great copy. I am grateful to all these friends for their help and support.

David H. Smith

NOTES

1. Kenneth E. Kirk, *Conscience and Its Problems* (London: Longman's Green and Co. Ltd., 1927).

2. Albert R. Jonsen, "Casuistry and Clinical Ethics," *Theoretical Medicine* 7 (1986): 65–74; Albert R. Jonsen, "The Confessor as Experienced Physician: Casuistry and Clinical Ethics," in Paul F. Camenisch, ed., *Religious Methods and Resources in Bioethics* (Dordrecht: Kluwer Academic Publishers, 1994), 165–79. Albert R. Jonsen, "Casuistry: An Alternative or Complement to Principles?" *Kennedy Institute of Ethics Journal* 5 (September 1995) 237–51; Albert R. Jonsen and Stephen Toulmin, *The Abuse of Casuistry: A History of Moral Reasoning* (Berkeley: University of California Press, 1988); Albert R. Jonsen, "Casuistry" in Warren T. Reich, ed., *Encyclopedia of Bioethics*, 2d ed., vol. 1 (New York: The Macmillan Company, 1995), 344–50; John D. Arras, "Getting Down to Cases: The Recovery of Casuistry in Bioethics," *Journal of Medicine and Philosophy* 16 (1991): 29–51; John D. Arras, "Principles and Particularity: The Role of Cases in Bioethics," *Indiana Law Journal* 69 (No. 4, 1994): 983–1014; Richard B. Miller, *Casuistry and Modern Ethics: A Poetics of Practical Reasoning* (Chicago: The University of Chicago Press, 1996); Nigel Biggar, "A Case for Casuistry in the Church," *Modern Theology* 6 (1989): 29–51; James F. S. J. Keenan and Thomas A. Shannon, eds., *The Context of Casuistry* (Washington, D.C.: Georgetown University Press, 1995); Edmund Leites, ed., *Conscience and Casuistry in Early Modern Europe* (Cambridge: Cambridge University Press, 1988).

3. James M. Gustafson, "Context Versus Principles: A Misplaced Debate in Christian Ethics," Charles M. Sweezey, ed., *Christian Ethics and the Community* (Philadelphia: Pilgrim Press, 1971); James F. Childress, "Moral Norms in Practical Ethical Reflection," Lisa Sowle Cahill and James F. Childress, eds., *Christian Ethics: Problems and Prospects* (Cleveland: The Pilgrim Press, 1996).

4. Miller, *Casuistry and Modern Ethics*, 25–26.

5. Ibid., 32–37.

6. For a helpful description in schematic form, see Albert R. Jonsen and Stephen Toulmin, *The Abuse of Casuistry: A History of Moral Reasoning* (Berkeley: University of California Press, 1988), Chapter 16.

7. Kenneth E. Kirk, *The Vision of God: The Christian Doctrine of the Summum Bonum*, 2d ed. (London: Longman's, Green and Co., 1931), xii.

8. Ibid., xiii.

9. Oliver O'Donovan, *Resurrection and Moral Order: An Outline for Evangelical Ethics* (Grand Rapids, Mich.: William B. Eerdmans Publishing Co., 1986), 252.

10. Kirk, *Vision of God*, 464.

11. For example, ibid., 471f.

12. Dietrich Bonhoeffer, *Ethics*, 1955 ed. (New York: The Macmillan Company, 1962), 212. Although I am grateful to Thomas Breidenthal for this reference, he cannot be accountable for my use of it.

13. Ibid., 215.

14. Kirk, *Vision of God*, 469.

15. Kenneth E. Kirk, *Ignorance, Faith and Conformity: Studies in Moral Theology*, 2d ed. (London: Longman's, Green and Co., 1925), Chapter 5.

16. Kirk, *Conscience and Its Problems*, 101.

17. Ibid.

18. Ibid., 81.

19. The last phrase is puzzling; it may refer to consent by the Convocation of the Church of England, or by the Crown, or perhaps by the Magisterium of the larger Catholic Church. In any case, the qualification plays no operative part in Kirk's reasoning about specific questions.

20. Kirk, *Conscience and Its Problems*, 86.

21. Ibid., 302. [Note that this and following note refer to an earlier edition, not the one reprinted here.]

22. Ibid., 302 and 303.

23. Ibid., 302 in this edition.

24. O'Donovan, *Resurrection and Moral Order*, 167.

25. Ibid., 171.

26. Ibid., 174.

27. Ibid.

28. Stanley M. Hauerwas, *The Peaceable Kingdom* (Notre Dame, Ind.: University of Notre Dame Press, 1983), 96-115.

29. Kirk, *Conscience and Its Problems*, 88.

30. Ibid., 37.

31. Ibid., 178.

32. Henry S. Richardson, "Specifying Norms as a Way to Resolve Concrete Ethical Problems," *Philosophy and Public Affairs* 19 (1990): 283; James F. Childress, "Moral Norms in Practical Ethical Reflection," in Lisa Sowle Cahill and James F. Childress, eds., *Christian Ethics: Problems and Prospects* (Cleveland: The Pilgrim Press, 1996); Gilbert Meilaender, *Body, Soul, and Bioethics* (Notre Dame, Ind.: University of Notre Dame Press, 1995).

33. Richardson, "Specifying Norms," 286.

34. Ibid., 293; "latitude" is Kant's term.

35. Kirk, *Conscience and Its Problems*, 125.

36. Ibid., 130f.

37. Richardson, "Specifying Norms," 299.

38. Kirk, *Conscience and Its Problems*, 124.

39. For a helpful discussion of the classical casuists on lying, see Jonsen and Toulmin, *Abuse of Casuistry*, Chapter 10.

40. The best-known exponent of situation ethics was a man whose sensibility was shaped in the Anglican communion and who regularly cited Kirk's work. See Joseph Fletcher, *Situation Ethics: The New Morality* (Philadelphia: Westminster Press, 1966).

41. Kirk, *Conscience and Its Problems*, 273.

42. Richardson, "Specifying Norms," 292.

43. Ibid., 300-302.
44. Kirk, *Conscience and Its Problems*, 347.
45. Ibid.
46. Ibid., 399.
47. Ibid. See the whole of Supplementary Note F for Kirk's own example.
48. Ibid., 363.
49. Ibid., 364.
50. Ibid., 365.
51. Ibid., 364 and 368.
52. Ibid., 368.
53. Ibid., 150.
54. Ibid., 157.
55. Ibid., 161.
56. Ibid., 161f.
57. Ibid., 115.
58. Ibid., 376.

BIBLIOGRAPHY

Arras, John D. "Getting Down to Cases: The Recovery of Casuistry in Bioethics." *Journal of Medicine and Philosophy* 16 (1991): 29-51.

————. "Principles and Particularity: The Role of Cases in Bioethics." *Indiana Law Journal* 69 (No. 4, 1994): 983-1014.

Beauchamp, Tom L. "Principles and Other Emerging Paradigms in Bioethics." *Indiana Law Journal* 69 (No. 4, 1994): 955-972.

Biggar, Nigel. "A Case for Casuistry in the Church." *Modern Theology* 6 (1989): 29-51.

Bonhoeffer, Dietrich. *Ethics*. 1955 ed. New York: The Macmillan Company, 1962.

Brody, Baruch. *Life and Death Decision Making*. New York: Oxford University Press, 1988.

Childress, James F. "Moral Norms in Practical Ethical Reflection." In *Christian Ethics: Problems and Prospects*, edited by Lisa Sowle Cahill and James F. Childress, 196-217. Cleveland: The Pilgrim Press, 1996.

Fletcher, Joseph. *Situation Ethics: The New Morality*. Philadelphia: Westminster Press, 1966.

Gustafson, James M. "Context Versus Principles: A Misplaced Debate in Christian Ethics." In *Christian Ethics and the Community*, edited by Charles M. Sweezey, 101-126. Philadelphia: Pilgrim Press, 1971.

Hauerwas, Stanley M. *The Peaceable Kingdom*. Notre Dame, Ind.: University of Notre Dame Press, 1983.

Jonsen, Albert R. "Casuistry and Clinical Ethics." *Theoretical Medicine* 7 (1986): 65-74.

————. "The Confessor as Experienced Physician: Casuistry and Clinical Ethics." In *Religious Methods and Resources in Bioethics*, edited by Paul F. Camenisch, 165-179. Dordrecht: Kluwer Academic Publishers, 1994.

————. "Casuistry." In Warren T. Reich, ed. *Encyclopedia of Bioethics*, 344–350. 2d ed. Vol. 1. New York: The Macmillan Company, York, 1995.

————. "Casuistry: An Alternative or Complement to Principles?" *Kennedy Institute of Ethics Journal* 5 (September 1995): 237-51.

———— and Toulmin, Stephen. *The Abuse of Casuistry: A History of Moral Reasoning*. Berkeley: University of California Press, 1988.

Keenan, James F. S. J., and Shannon, Thomas A., eds. *The Context of Casuistry*. Washington, D. C.: Georgetown University Press, 1995.

Kemp, Eric Waldram. *The Life and Letters of Kenneth Escott Kirk: Bishop of Oxford 1937-1954*. London: Hodder and Stoughton, 1959.

————. "Kenneth Kirk." *The Compact Edition of the Dictionary of National Biography*, Vol. 2, Oxford: Oxford University Press, 1975.

Kirk Kenneth E. *Some Principles of Moral Theology and Their Application.* London: Longman's, Green and Co., 1921.

————. *Ignorance, Faith and Conformity: Studies in Moral Theology.* 2d ed. London: Longman's, Green and Co., 1925.

————. *Conscience and Its Problems.* London: Longman's Green and Co. Ltd., 1927.

————. *The Vision of God: The Christian Doctrine of the Summum Bonum.* 2d ed. London: Longman's, Green and Co., 1931.

————. *The Threshold of Ethics.* London: Skeffington & Son Limited, 1933.

————, ed. *The Apostolic Ministry: Essays on the History and Doctrine of Episcopacy.* 2d ed. London: Hodder and Stoughton, 1946.

Leites, Edmund, ed. *Conscience and Casuistry in Early Modern Europe.* Cambridge: Cambridge University Press, 1988.

Maurice, Frederick Denison. *Reconstructing Christian Ethics: Selected Writings.* Edited by Ellen K. Wondra. Louisville: Westminster John Knox Press, 1995.

Meilaender, Gilbert. *Body, Soul, and Bioethics.* Notre Dame, Ind.: University of Notre Dame Press, 1995.

Miller, Richard B. *Casuistry and Modern Ethics: A Poetics of Practical Reasoning.* Chicago: The University of Chicago Press, 1996.

O'Donovan, Oliver. *Resurrection and Moral Order: An Outline for Evangelical Ethics.* Grand Rapids, Mich.: William B. Eerdmans Publishing Co., 1986.

Preston, Ronald F. "Re-Review: Kenneth Kirk's The Vision of God." *The Modern Churchman* 22 (1980): 36-39.

Richardson, Henry S. "Specifying Norms as a Way to Resolve Concrete Ethical Problems." *Philosophy and Public Affairs* 19 (1990): 279-310.

Sedgwick, Timothy F. "Revisioning Anglican Moral Theology." *Anglican Theological Review* 63 (1981): 1, 1-20.

————. "The New Shape of Anglican Identity." *Anglican Theological Review* 77 (1995): 2, 187-97.

Thornton, Martin. "Re-Review: Kenneth Kirk's Some Principles of Moral Theology". *The Modern Churchman* 29 (1987): 2, 54-57.

Tomlinson, Tom. "Casuistry in Medical Ethics: Rehabilitated, or Repeat Offender?" *Theoretical Medicine* 15 (1994): 5-20.

AUTHOR'S NOTE TO 1948 EDITION

The entire stock of this book was destroyed by enemy action during the late war, and the opportunity for revision and reissue has only now presented itself. When I came to consider the degree to which rewriting might be desirable, I found that my mind had moved on to a new plane, and that the book seemed to me at least to have 'dated.' This was not surprising. It was first written twenty-one years ago, and at that time, as also when the second and third editions were produced (1933 and 1936), I was fully engaged in teaching Theology, Moral Philosophy and the Philosophy of Religion. This meant that the original moulds in which the book was cast were those of traditional and (if I may use the phrase) classical ethical discussion. Since those days, however, circumstances have taken me out of the academic into the pastoral and administrative spheres, and the modes of thought which were familiar to me between 1927 and 1937 have been superseded by others more appropriate to my present activities. The process of transition was to be seen at work, by myself at all events, in its early stage in a book called *The Threshold of Ethics* which I wrote in 1933, and much more definitely in an essay on 'Moral Theology' in *The Study of Theology* (1939).

My first instinct, therefore, was to rewrite *Conscience and its Problems* very extensively before republishing it. On reflection, however, I decided (rightly or wrongly) that the principles I had tried to set out in the book were at once sound and adequately stated, and that although I might derive some personal satisfaction from presenting them in a new dress, there was no reason to suppose that the reading public would find such a presentation more to its taste than the existing one. No doubt the experiences of the past ten years and our present perplexities have brought to the fore new aspects of the time-honoured problems of ethics which call urgently for extended treatment. Thus, in this country at least, the 'general strike' is not at the moment a live issue; its place has been taken by such problems as those of 'restrictive practices' in industry, propaganda by means of 'cells' and 'committees of action,' controls, single-party elections, and the like. But the basic tension is still the same—the tension between democratic government and free institutions on the one hand and organised bodies of dissidents on the other. On the principles which should guide discussion of that tension *in whatever form it shows itself* I have said what I desire to say in the section on 'general strikes' (*infra* pp. 354-62). Were I to substitute a discussion of Communistic methods of subversive infiltration (for example) as being more appropriate to the present situation in England, I should be found merely to be enunciating the same principles in a different context. I never intended in this book to discuss casuistical problems except as illustrations of the proper application of general principles to particular cases.

For these reasons I have left the main body of the book untouched. One major change, however, must be pointed out. In the earlier editions of the book there appeared at the end an appended Note C, on 'Marriage with a Deceased Wife's Sister, and Re-Marriage of Divorced Persons.' The first of these two matters is no longer a problem in the Church of England since the promulgation of a new version of Canon 99 by the Convocations in 1946. This Canon revised the Table of Kindred and Affinity and removed "wife's sister" and "husband's brother" from the list of prohibited degrees. The second question has now an entirely new setting as the result of the section 12 of the Matrimonial Causes Act of 1937, whereby a parish priest is legally empowered to refuse the use of his Church for the marriage of two persons either of whom has a previous partner living. I have therefore suppressed this note in its entirety, and the book is re-paged from page 383 forward. For convenience of reference, however, I have refrained from re-lettering the remaining Additional Notes (D-H). What has to be said about the discipline of re-married divorced persons will now be found at some length in the last chapter of the new edition (1948) of my *Marriage and Divorce*.

Oxford, *May* 1948.   K.O.

AUTHOR'S NOTE TO 1936 EDITION

In a revision of this book, issued in September 1933, the section on Birth Control was considerably rewritten, in view of the resolutions of the 1930 Lambeth Conference on the subject. In the present impression this section is retained in its revised form.

Various corrections on points of detail have been made, including those of three *errata* mentioned in the Author's Note of the 1933 impression. Most of these corrections have been designed to clear up an ambiguity in the words 'necessary to salvation' and their equivalents on pages 271, 282, 284, (285 in this impression) and 288. The point at issue, which affected the arguments but not the conclusions on those pages, is indicated in footnote 4 of page 271 of this impression, and more fully discussed in a new Additional Note (Note H).

Some rearrangement of material has taken place, and a few sentences of no particular importance have been omitted between pages 270 and 290.

K.E.K.

Oxford, *November* 1935.

PRINCIPAL ABBREVIATIONS

Alph. Lig. : (St.) Alphonso M. de Ligorio, *Theologia Moralis* (first published 1755 ; edition used, *editio omnium accuratior*, Turin, 1879). Cited by book and paragraph.

C.J.C. : *Corpus Juris Canonici* (Paris, 1500 ; Rome, 1582, and later editions ; the best that of E. Friedberg, Leipsig, 1879–81, 2 vols.). Contains the *Decretum* of Gratian, *Decretals* of Gregory IX, the *Sext*, *Clementines*, *Extravagantes Joannis XXII* and *Extravagantes Communes*. Cited according to the usual formulæ.

Cod. Jur. Can. : *Codex Juris Canonici*, Benedicti Papæ XV auctoritate promulgatus, Rome, 1918.

Denz.-Bann. : H. Denzinger and C. Bannwart, *Enchiridion Symbolorum, Definitionum et Declarationum*, edd. 14 and 15 (revised J. B. Lemberg). Friburg, 1922.

Döllinger-Reusch : I. von Döllinger and H. Reusch, *Geschichte der Moral streitigkeiten in der römisch-Katholischen Kirche seit dem sechzehnten Jahrhundert* (Nördlingen, 1889), 2 vols.

Duct. Dub. : Jeremy Taylor (Bishop of Down and Connor), *Ductor Dubitantium, or the Rule of Conscience* (first published, 1660 ; later editions and reprints). Cited by book and chapter.

Gibson : E. Gibson (Bishop of London), *Codex Juris Ecclesiastici Anglicani*, London, 1713.

Gury : J. P. Gury (S.J.), *Compendium Theologiæ Moralis*, 2 vols. (many editions ; first published 1857 ; edition used, 5th German, Ratisbon, 1874). Cited by vol. and paragraph.

Gury-Ferreres : J. B. Ferreres (S.J.), *Compendium Theologiæ Moralis J. P. Gury, multis additionibus auctum* (6th edition, Barcelona, 1913), 2 vols.

Hauck-Hertzog : J. J. Hertzog, *Realencyclopädie für protestantische Theologie und Kirche*; 3rd edition, revised by A. Hauck, Leipzig, 1896–1913.

Johnson : J. Johnson, *Laws and Canons of the Church of England* (London, 1720 ; reprinted with annotations, Oxford, 1850). Cited by year.

Lehmkuhl : A. Lehmkuhl (S.J.), *Theologia Moralis* (9th edn., Friburg, 1898), 2 vols.

Lyndwood : W. Lyndwood (Bp. of St. David's), *Provinciale seu Constitutiones Angliæ* (c. 1433 ; edition used, Oxford, 1679).

Prümmer : M. Prümmer (O.P.), *Manuale Theologiæ Moralis*, Friburg, 1915 (3 vols.).

S.T. : (St.) Thomas Aquinas, *Summa Theologica* (*c.* 1270 ; many editions).
The parts are cited i. ; i. 2 ; ii. 2 ; iii. ; Suppl.

Tanquerey : A. Tanquerey, *Synopsis Theologiæ Moralis*, 5th and 7th
editions (Rome, Tournai, Paris, 1919, 1920), 3 vols. There is some
confusion in the volumes, pagination and indexing of this conflate
edition. The tractates on *Penance, Matrimony and Order*, some
parts of which are also incorporated in the author's *Synopsis Theologiæ
Dogmaticæ*, form the first volume ; the introduction to moral theology
proper opens the second volume.

Wilkins : D. Wilkins, *Concilia Magnæ Britanniæ et Hiberniæ* (London,
1737), 4 vols.

INTRODUCTORY

I

THE origin and purpose of the present book can best be explained by reference to its two predecessors. In ' Some Principles of Moral Theology ' I ventured to put forward a tentative scheme for the development and teaching of moral theology in the Church of England. The scheme was in the barest of outlines only ; but it was an attempt to divide up the whole ground to be covered on a systematic plan, and thus to suggest a general background upon which clergy, and others whose vocation, interests or ideals led them to a study of Christian moral problems, might co-ordinate their thought and reading. Naturally enough, I hoped myself to find opportunity to think and read along the lines thus suggested ; and perhaps to advance in subsequent books or essays a more detailed treatment of what I had so far suggested in outline only.

At the outset of this more detailed consideration, however, there arose a problem which I had only partially foreseen. ' Some Principles of Moral Theology ' had borrowed its ground-plan (if that expression may be allowed) in the main from two sources—the ' Summa Theologica ' of St. Thomas Aquinas and that adaptation of Thomist principles to the needs of the Church of England which underlies the writings of Bishops Sanderson and Jeremy Taylor. The question at once presented itself : Do not the present circumstances and the probable future of the Church of England make all such borrowing illegitimate or misguided ? The catholicism both of St. Thomas and the Caroline divines envisaged a Church clear in definition, authoritative in command, highly organised in administration and strict in discipline. The Church of England as we see it to-day, on the other hand, reveals a freedom of thought on the part of the individual, and a tolerance of that freedom on the part of authority, which would have startled both St. Thomas and his Anglican disciples. Is it fair, wise or profitable to attempt to adapt the principles of a closely-knit organism such as the Church which produced the moral theology of the past, to a loosely-knit association like the Church of England of the present ? Is it not an attempt to pour new wine back into old bottles ? The Church of England may still be ' catholic ' in a sense, and that no doubt a true sense ; but does it not differ so widely from the catholicism of the past on this fundamental question of authority and the individual as to separate it wholly from the traditional moral system, and to demand an entirely new construction based upon principles more in accordance with its distinctive character ?

It was obvious that this question would have to be answered before any further progress could be made ; and that if the answer showed a radical difference between the Church of to-day and the Church of yesterday in this matter, a wholly new foundation would have to be laid for that modern Anglican moral theology which seems so much in demand. If our system of authority and freedom is wholly different from that of the past—if it has rejected elements which the past treated as essential, or introduced elements which the past would have disallowed—then we must abandon the attempt on any large scale to draw upon the experience of the past ; and must confine ourselves to the needs and affirmations of the present, using the past no longer as an organic system capable of adaptation, expansion and renewal, but only as a storehouse from which here or there a valuable but isolated illustration or suggestion can be drawn. The enquiry thus opened up presented a good many difficulties, but in the end it reached conclusions which, with the evidence in their support, were embodied in a book called ' Ignorance, Faith and Conformity.'

Briefly, the conclusions in question were as follows. On the one hand, the Church of England has not abandoned any of the fundamental principles of the moral theology and canon law of the past, though some of them she has interpreted with a wise discretion ; and others she holds, for the moment at all events, very much in reserve. And, on the other hand, the two factors of liberty of thought and of tolerance, which specially characterise contemporary Anglicanism, are not new phenomena in organised Christianity, though perhaps they have never before been seen in the same proportionate combination as to-day. Both factors were anticipated, recognised and provided for by the two principles of ' invincible ignorance ' and of ' custom ' which Christian experience has for centuries fully allowed and understood. It seemed right and justifiable, therefore, to speak of Anglicanism, as we know it, as ' within the limits of a legitimate development of the principles of Western Christendom as a whole,' or as an ' experiment initiated within the legitimate bounds of true catholicism.'[1] It remains to be added only that, in the writer's opinion, this ' development ' or ' experiment,' however strange and confused the circumstances which have conditioned it, is wholly providential, and has brought to light new aspects of Christian truth of infinite value for the Church, which might otherwise have remained partly if not wholly unnoticed.

II

On the conclusions thus reached, of which more is said in the second and fifth chapters of the present book, depend certain obvious corollaries.

(1) The Church of England even as it is to-day is not a mere disorganised chaos, but an organism on lines which Christian thought has always recognised as valid. Its moral code, though expressed in a manner superficially novel and disconcerting, is none the less continuous with the code of the Church's past ; and amenable to interpretation, understanding and application by methods whose reliability has been tested and endorsed in history. We may hope for more definite and methodical guidance for conduct from our Church in the future, but it would be ungrateful to ignore the fact that such guidance is already offered to us in the present ; and it is open to argument that the methods and forms in which it is offered may yet—for all their perplexing elusiveness, and with all their faults and lacunæ—prove

[1] *Ignorance, etc.*, pp. vi., 162.

to be as much akin to the mind of Christ as the methods of other communions and centuries.

The Church of England has not deserted her children in their journey from this world to the world to come. She has chosen, or had forced upon her—it matters little which— modes of dealing with their problems so baffling that at first sight they appear to be nebulous and even non-existent. But patient enquiry and a reverent attempt to understand will show, we may well believe, that baffling though these methods are, they are designed in God's providence to produce a type of Christian character, at once highly individualised and yet truly loyal, as beautiful, saintly and effective as any type in history. To decry the Church of England and the help she offers is poor courtesy to a society which has mediated to us all that is central in our apprehension of the love of God and the grace of the Lord Jesus. Though we do not ignore her defects, we should try to understand her genius, and to discover how far (and indeed it seems to be much further than we sometimes think) she is able to guide and direct her children's lives.

(2) Even without any further development of Christian ethics or moral theology, Anglicanism can guide us no little distance. If it does not often speak with the authoritative voice of canonical enactment, there is no lack of general agreement as to Christian morality which is very near the surface of its public utterances, and is endorsed by the unanimous acceptance of its members. Any one of us could without a moment's difficulty set down an impressive array of moral precepts of the most far-reaching significance to whose validity no Anglican would for a moment demur. Nor is this all. That wide tolerance of conscientious divergence of view, which is both the peculiar genius and the crowning glory of Anglicanism, enables the Church to endow with some degree of authority — now more, now less — many other principles for the guidance of conduct. Some of them are of long standing, others novel and experimental. Some have at least the authority of canonical promulgation in other ages or by other Christian bodies, others are customary only. Some have the full support and encouragement of individual members of the episcopate or of groups of clergy and laity ;

others, though they seem to be the private possession of individuals only, are at all events not forbidden by the body. No one can complain of any lack of general principles for his guidance.

(3) But it is when we come to enquire of the Church for guidance in special questions and difficulties that we find ourselves at a loss. We admit readily enough those general principles which have the undoubted sanction of the Church—truth, honesty, sobriety, unselfishness and the like ; but what particular duties do they involve ? When, for example, if ever, is a departure from strict truth allowable ? At what point are we to draw the line between ' shrewd business methods ' and dishonesty ? Does sobriety imply total abstinence ? Is a due regard for one's own legitimate needs compatible with Christian unselfishness ? Or, where a principle of the second and less official category noted above appears to be supported not by the full authority of the Church, but by some partial encouragement or mere toleration alone, what degree of deference towards it is required of us ? Or, if any two of these principles, each of them perhaps enforced by a different weight of authority, come into conflict in a particular case, how are their conflicting claims to be adjusted ? It is easy enough and true enough to say that each man's conscience must decide for him ; but if conscience does not give its verdict spontaneously and *proprio motu,* along what lines should it be encouraged to move in order to secure one ?

The difficulty is not, as the last paragraph may perhaps have suggested, a difficulty of the individual Christian and his special problems alone. It is one in which the whole Church of England is involved. That the tolerance which she shows towards individual divergences of opinion is a healthy condition for the promotion of conscientious thought about moral questions is an obvious truth ; and in all probability her organisation—that novel and providential experiment ' within the legitimate bounds of a true catholicism '—is more adapted than any other to secure this desirable result. But the object of conscientious thought is after all to secure unanimity. Truth, though it has many facets, is really one ; and we can only interpret the demand for ' more moral

theology ' in the Church of England as a demand for a degree
of unanimity on the subordinate requirements of Christian
morality akin to that which already exists, at all events
informally, on its main principles. To approve of this
demand as laudable and legitimate is not in any way to
commit ourselves to another and very different demand—the
demand, namely, for a rabbinic code of ethics which will not
leave the smallest corner of conduct open to the free
determination of the individual conscience, but insists on
legislating down to the utmost conceivable minutiæ. The
cry for more unanimity is a very different thing from a
demand for complete uniformity ; unanimity is, as the name
implies, of the spirit, whereas uniformity insists upon the
letter as well.

III

This greater unanimity which most churchmen agree to
be desirable will only be secured if thought moves along
disciplined and well-tested lines in its progress from the
general to the more detailed. We are driven back to the
need for a sane casuistry ; for the first duty of casuistry
(assuming ourselves to be in sure possession of the general
principles of morality) is to determine the lines along which
the advance from the general to the particular can best
be made. To make the advance is also its duty ; but it is
a secondary duty which can only be successfully performed
as the first is successfully completed. Rules of procedure
must come before actual procedure itself, even though they
cannot finally be tested except in the crucible of procedure.
The Anglicanism of the 17th century was fully aware of this
fact ; Sanderson, Taylor, Hall (and, it may be mentioned,
Richard Baxter as well) moved so securely among the difficult
problems of their time for no other reason than that they
were employing the soundest principles of mediæval casuistry.
It is one of the curiosities of history, to which we shall have
to devote a moment's passing attention, that with the dawn
of the 18th century not Anglicanism alone, but all the Reformed Churches, lost their grasp upon these time-honoured
rules of procedure. To that fact (whatever its cause or

causes may have been) may be attributed, in part at least, the steady and ever-increasing failure of these societies to guide their members in the recurring particular problems of the Christian life in any manner which the ordinary man could appreciate ; and from that moment dates the super-session of ' moral theology' in the Reformed Churches by a ' Christian ethics ' which contents itself with the statement of general principles and evades the problem of their detailed application.

It would seem therefore, for all these reasons, that the recovery of sound rules of procedure for the task of reaching such unanimity as is desirable on the subordinate principles or detailed problems of Christian morality is a need second to none in the Church of England to-day. Such a recovery will not be the work of one generation, still less of a single writer or a single book ; and the chapters which follow represent at best a very fragmentary and tentative contribu-tion to the task. They do not hesitate to draw upon the traditional moral theology and canon law of the past, which, rightly regarded, are no more than the formulated experience of the Christian centuries. The legitimacy of such an appeal to tradition is vindicated by the conclusion we have previously noticed, that there is nothing in the constitution of contem-porary Anglicanism which was not envisaged, in some measure, by that moral theology and canon law. If our Church has simply, under the providence of God, adapted old principles to meet new needs, and has done so, if not with complete success, at all events not without many encourage-ments and rewards, we can scarcely be wrong in attempting a similar adaptation in that branch of theology which during the last two centuries she has most neglected. In this way, without ignoring the special problems of the modern world, we shall not run the risk of losing anything of the secure achievements of Christianity in the past.

IV

The first chapter of this book treats therefore of conscience —its duties, privileges, limitations and dangers. The second considers the deference which loyalty demands that conscience should pay to principles commended by authority of varying degrees. The third and fourth chapters deal with the nature and history of casuistry, and attempt to show the stages by which Christian experience evolved sound principles of dealing with the various problems produced by this interaction of conscience and loyalty in the changing circumstances of the centuries. In the remaining chapters these problems are classified under the three main headings of Error, Doubt and Perplexity ; rules of procedure which have at least the sanction of long recognition by the Church behind them are propounded as a help to their solution ; and the validity of such rules is subjected to a preliminary examination by applying them to questions of immediate interest or of special value as test cases.

Readers familiar with the admirable text-books in use in the Roman communion will recognise that the ground here covered is more or less co-terminous with that of the tractates *de legibus* and *de conscientia* which always form part of their introductory material. There is no one recognised arrangement of this material, and each writer follows his own bent ; but in general it comprises at least two other tractates in addition to the discussions of law and conscience. One of these deals with the goal of human life (*de ultimo fine hominis*), the other with human acts (*de actibus humanis*) The first, as its name suggests, puts forward and defends some ultimate guiding principle of a Christian code of morality, and might well go on to show (as it often does) how that principle—usually expressed as the ' Vision of God '—flowers and articulates itself into the various Christian virtues. The second deals with problems of human psychology, of responsibility and freedom, of the various intellectual and psychological causes—error, fear, compulsion, temperament, weakness of will and the like—which sometimes appear to limit freedom and diminish responsibility. The nature and growth of sin usually forms the subject of a separate section ; but there would be nothing inappropriate if it also were included in this treatise *de actibus humanis*.

For reasons which have already been suggested, the present book addresses itself at once to the problems of law, conscience and casuistry. It might perhaps have been more logical to have started the detailed approach to moral theology by a discussion of the purpose of life ; and to have developed an ideal code of Christian ethics co-ordinated round one central principle—be it the vision of God, the proclamation of the Kingdom, the brotherhood of mankind or the imitation of Christ. But about the main principles of Christian conduct, as applicable to a civilisation like our own, there is little controversy. Difficulties only begin with the discussion of the subordinate precepts dependent upon these main principles ; and such subordinate precepts can only be reached with any degree of assurance and unanimity if the rules of procedure adopted are both wise and commonly accepted. Here, therefore, at the point where controversy presses, a prior study of casuistry is all-essential.

Nor does it seem true that a psychological enquiry into freedom and responsibility should take first place. There is ample and urgent need for such an enquiry, it is true ; not least of all because modern developments of psychological theory go far to suggest that man is wholly the creature and plaything of subconscious forces over which he has little if any control. But in general the Christian conscience rejects this suggestion, and clings firmly to the conviction that human nature is endowed with some measure, at least, of freedom ; and therefore may be treated as in some degree responsible for its actions. This psychological treatment, therefore, is also postponed for the time being ; not because it is unimportant or alien to the subject, but rather because, important though it is, agreement upon the principles of casuistry to be employed by Anglican thought on ethics seems to be of even greater importance.

v

The last few paragraphs have perhaps pressed the question of the contents and arrangement of the prolegomena to moral theology to undue lengths. They may serve, however, not merely as a partial vindication for the choice of subject which occasioned this book, but also as an indication of the vast extent of the questions which must be covered and discussed before anything approaching a systematic Anglican text-book on moral theology can be produced. We are still in our pre-scientific stage, exploring the possibilities, noting the phenomena and comparing results, not merely one with another, but also with the data provided by history and by other Christian systems of the present day. And some measure of agreement on the prolegomena is a necessary preliminary to that detailed scientific treatment of Christian duty and sin, apart from which a text-book (unless it were to be a mere *ex parte* statement) could do no more than repeat the generalised aspirations of conventional ethics.

There is another reason why we should hesitate to comply with the demand for text-books too hurriedly. When all has been said that can be said in praise of the wise combination of freedom and authority which characterises the Church of England, it would be foolish to assert that it is incapable of improvement or adjustment. Not only is the practice of some groups, at all events, within the Church already promoting such adjustment—witness the growth of the practice of private confession ; the demand for adjustment by canonical authority is raised on all sides. More discipline is asked for in some quarters, more definition in others ; sometimes both discipline and definition are desired by the same persons. Some would have us develop along post-Reformation lines, others would prefer a reversion to particular mediæval practices or institutions. It would be easy to produce a text-book in harmony with one or other of these varied demands ; and the task would not be wholly futile—for it would show how the claims of one group or another would work out in detail in so far as they were concerned with conduct, and so would enable the Church to form a better judgment upon the merits of those claims. But the ideal Anglican text-book would run on very different lines. It would be no partisan statement of limited outlook ; but would attempt, after an examination of the various claims put forward by different voices in the Church, to combine all that was good in them (however varied) in a single harmonised system, and on that basis to outline the moral code, together with the appropriate methods by which it should be expressed, commended and defended, of the renewed Church of England which is to be.

Whoever undertook the preparation of such a text-book would have to carry out an even wider preliminary examination than that already suggested. He would recognise that the exact proportions in which liberty and authority are at present combined in the Church of England need not be the ideal proportions; and he would consider, on the basis not merely of principle but also of history, whether what is required is (as some say) more authority or (as others) more freedom. And having achieved such a canon he would apply it in all his determinations of moral problems; saying, for example, 'Here is a duty so imperative that no one who refuses to conform to it can properly claim the privileges of Church membership as well'; or again, 'Here is a principle which, while it admits of exceptions in rare cases, is nevertheless of such serious obligation that the decision as to when any exception is to be made should be reserved to the judgment of authorised experts only'; or again, 'Here is a principle which, though we regard it as generally desirable, we cannot lay down as a peremptory obligation upon our members—we treat it not so much in the light of a precept, as in that of a counsel of perfection.' It is possible, of course, to lay down distinctions such as these on canons borrowed wholesale from other communions or other ages; but unless every such distinction has been tested by reference to the special ideal of Christian constitutionalism which animates the Church of England, much of the labour involved may have been wasted. We have no guarantee that the book which results will be the book that Anglicanism needs; it may, on the contrary, prove to be the very book that is needed least of all.

The prolegomena therefore to an Anglican text-book would have to include not merely those studies in casuistry, psychology and general moral principles to which we have alluded; but also some detailed enquiry into the ideal system of Church legislation and discipline, and the extent to which 'indifferent acts' and 'counsels of perfection,' as distinct from authoritative precepts, may be allowed in such a system. Here are matters, again, on which the widest differences of opinion

exist. Greater agreement upon them is needed before our
moral theology can progress far ; and such agreement will
only be secured when all the arguments and evidence have
been made available, and submitted to wise and careful
scrutiny. On all these subjects what is most needed at the
moment is the painstaking collection of evidence over a
wide field, till we have at our disposal a knowledge, both in
principle and in detail, of the main variations of moral code
and discipline within organised Christianity, and of the results
to which they severally lead. There is work enough here to
occupy many students over a considerable period ; but the
labour involved will not be wasted. It will end by putting
the Church of England in possession of a thought-out code
of morality adequate both to her high ideal and also to her
delicate task of finding that adjustment of liberty to authority
which, at all events for the modern world, shall prove most
fertile in upright and Christ-like lives.

VI

Of the present book little more need be said. That it
does not aspire to be a text-book will be sufficiently obvious
from the preceding paragraphs. But in applying the principles discussed I have in the main tried to select such
problems as present themselves to the ordinary priest or
layman, in the hope that, if the methods employed commend
themselves to him, he will be able with these examples before
him to apply them to problems of a similar kind as they arise
in practice. On this point, however, I feel bound to make a
personal request. However much a practical interest may
dominate the reader's mind, I would ask him to recognise that
in the present state of the Church of England the eliciting
of the true principles of casuistry is as practical and urgent
a matter as the solution of particular cases. He may very
well hesitate to accept—he may even flatly reject—some of
the solutions here suggested. If this is the case it is neither
very surprising nor very important ; what is important is
to discover *why* the solutions are wrong. Is there an
obvious fallacy in the argument, or are the principles along

which it moves falsely stated ?   If the solutions in question merely excite the judgment, 'I don't agree with this,' the purpose of the book will remain unfulfilled ; whereas if the critic can expose the cause of his disagreement, he will put us in the way of recognising some of the pitfalls which Anglican casuistry must avoid.   It is to elicit criticism and discussion of this character—and that not merely from technical theologians, but from all whose business it is to handle moral problems in the concrete — that the book has been written.

With the same hope of securing the interest of others than professed theologians, I have relegated to footnotes or to the Additional Notes at the end such theoretical or technical considerations as seemed necessary to meet criticism or justify statements, but might merely irritate the reader whose interests are mainly practical.   In the same way, while it was not possible altogether to avoid one or two ventures into the sphere of general ethics in Chapter I, I have kept them within the smallest practicable limits   They must not be taken as in any way an attempt at a detailed philosophical statement, nor do they do more than summarise what appears to be the ordinary Christian view of conscience. They are necessary for even such a moderate degree of completeness as the subject seems to demand at this stage ; but they can be rapidly passed over or wholly ignored by readers whom they fail to interest.

A great part of the book has been delivered in the form of lectures to various audiences during the past four or five years.   A course of four lectures to the St. Paul's Lecture Society, in February 1926, was reported by the 'Church Times,' and I am indebted to the editor for his permission to reproduce some parts of the report in an expanded form.   Other passages have appeared in 'Theology,' as parts of articles entitled 'Four Cases of Conscience,' and in this case also I gratefully acknowledge the editor's courtesy in allowing me to reprint them.   Members of Clergy Schools at Oxford, Worcester, York, Scarborough and Ely will recognise here and there fragments of lectures to which they listened with exemplary patience ; they may even discover how much I owe to their criticisms and questions.   For their help and encouragement, also, I feel bound to express my sincerest gratitude.

To Mr. H. H. Price, Fellow of Trinity College, Oxford, I am indebted for most valuable criticism and advice in connection with Chapter I, as well as other parts of the book. Dr. Darwell Stone discharged a similar kind office with regard to Chapter V ; the Rev. Francis Underhill, Warden of Liddon House, with regard to the section on birth-control in Chapter VI ; and Professor Ogilvie, Professor of Economics at Edinburgh University, with regard to the section on strikes in Chapter VII. The greatest obligation of all was laid upon me by the Rev. F. H. Brabant, Fellow of Wadham, who read the whole of the manuscript before it went to press ; and the Rev. B. E. Butler, Tutor of Keble College, who revised the proofs. There are few sections of the book which have not been materially improved as the result of their suggestions. In deference to all these advisers, numerous passages have been re-written, sometimes more than once, and many fallacies and ineptitudes eliminated. It must not be thought, however, that they are in any way responsible for the opinions and arguments here expressed, nor that they agree with them ; and I do not wish for a moment to use their authority as a cloak for the many blemishes which must remain. But the very real gratitude I feel for their help and advice makes it incumbent upon me not merely to mention their names, but also to credit them with a large share in whatever value the following pages may have.

K. E. K.

OXFORD,
January 1927.

PART I

CONSCIENCE AND CASUISTRY

CONSCIENCE AND ITS PROBLEMS

PART I—CONSCIENCE AND CASUISTRY

CHAPTER I

CONSCIENCE

1. *Moral Judgments*

CONSCIENCE is a phenomenon which may be studied from
many points of view. The philosopher devotes himself to
considering whether conscience is an emotion or a function
of the reason. The psychologist directs our attention to
its association with particular instincts characteristic of the
human species. The anthropologist traces its emergence
from the group-morality of the primitive tribe. The historian
elaborates the theme of the growth of liberty of conscience
in western civilisation. At some of these questions we shall
find ourselves forced to glance, but for our main purpose—
which is to consider a few of the actual problems with which
the Christian conscience has to deal in the world as it now
is—it will be enough to follow the great scholastic tradition
maintained by St. Thomas Aquinas, and to define conscience
as ' the mind of man passing moral judgments.' [1]

The human mind passes all kinds of judgments upon the
material presented to it by experience and by imagination.
There are its scientific judgments, as when it says, ' This
is the cause of that.' There are its aesthetic judgments, as
when it says, ' This is beautiful ' or ' That is ugly.'
We may subdivide more narrowly still, and speak of

---

[1] See Additional Note A : *Definitions of Conscience*, p. 379.

'commercial' judgments, as when we say, 'This is a good bargain,' or 'That isn't worth the money'; or judgments of health, as, for example, 'This food is indigestible,' or, quite generally, 'Bread is nutritious.' Moral judgments, or the judgments of conscience, are judgments which employ such words as 'right' and 'wrong,' 'ought' and 'ought not,' 'virtue' and 'vice,' 'duty' and 'sin'; judgments such as 'It is right, or my duty, to do so-and-so'; 'I have behaved wrongly, or left undone what I ought to have done.' No human being, however degraded, seems to be wholly destitute of moral judgments of this character; even the villainous skipper in Stevenson's 'Ebb Tide,' though he had no objection whatever to murder, regarded the use of vitriol for the purpose as morally out of the question.[1]

To investigate problems which belong to the sphere of general ethics is foreign to the purpose of this book. But it will not be wholly unprofitable to tabulate, very roughly, the characteristics which seem to belong to moral judgments in ordinary Christian thought. (1) They may be spoken of, in the first place, as either particular or general. When they are general (as, for example, 'It is always wrong to lie') they are sometimes called 'laws'[2] or 'principles' of morality. When they are particular (as, 'Such-and-such an action is your duty here and now'), they are often called 'dictates' or 'precepts.' And just as it is the aim of every intelligent person to make, let us say, his scientific judgments as general as possible—just as he is not content with saying,

[1] Compare also Ribot's argument based upon the objection to cannibalism manifested even by the most primitive races, *Psychology of the Emotions* (E.T.), pp. 295, 296.

[2] The use of the word 'law' in ethics is often objected to, both on the ground that (by analogy with 'human law') it might seem to imply an anthropomorphic and arbitrary legislator, and a system of pains and penalties ('sanctions'); and on the ground that (by analogy with 'economic law,' 'laws of health,' etc.) it might be thought merely conditional (e.g. 'If you wish to be healthy, keep regular hours'). Nevertheless it would seem a mistake to discard the use of the word on these grounds; we require something imperative or preceptive (and this is given by the analogy with 'human law'); and also something invariable (which is given by the analogy with 'economic law,' or the so-called 'laws of nature'). The undesirable implications of the word noticed above can easily be guarded against in using it. See also *Ignorance, Faith and Conformity*, pp. 37, 38.

' This particular event happened after that particular action,' but aims at a knowledge of universal relations which are always true, irrespective of the circumstances of the moment—so it is, or should be, the aim at least of the moral man to bring the particular dictates of conscience under more general laws or principles ; to discover the moral principles or laws upon which he can base his conduct throughout life.

(2) Every type of judgment has its own proper sphere, and outside that sphere it is either nonsensical (as though a man should try to estimate the morality of cheese, or the colour of thought) or irrelevant. Irrelevant judgments are common enough in ordinary life. Ann Veronica's father, in Mr. Wells' novel of that name, selected the fiction he read entirely on the principle that a book with a ' chromatic ' title (such as ' The Yellow Man ' or ' The Blue Umbrella ' or ' The Green Monster ') must be a book worth reading. In making this his test of literary excellence he was applying a particular kind of aesthetic judgment to a subject with which it had nothing whatever to do. Similarly, the profiteer or *nouveau riche* who is alleged to judge the merits of his pictures entirely according to their cost per square foot is introducing into aesthetics a type of judgment—the ' financial ' judgment—which is in fact foreign to the subject. In each case, it is clear, the deciding factor in a choice is a judgment which, beyond all doubt, is wholly irrelevant to the matter in hand.

The primary sphere of moral judgments is that of voluntary or responsible action. It is true that we pass moral judgments about other phenomena of human life besides actions. We can judge (for example) motives or intentions, as when we say ' Revenge is a wrongful motive ' ; we can judge desires, as in saying ' No man ought to covet another's property.' Especially do we pass moral judgments upon character as a whole, and say ' He is a virtuous man,' or ' He is not the sort of character he ought to be.' But it seems true that all these other judgments are only possible because we can refer them to prior judgments about actions or types of actions. We call a desire or a motive virtuous or vicious when it will lead (if unchecked) to actions of the

B

kind we recognise as right or wrong ; and a ' just ' man is
a man who will act justly in all circumstances which demand
and admit of just action.

This is not to say of course that any or all of these
judgments are really identical with one another. In calling
a man ' just ' we may mean more than that he merely performs or will perform ' just ' actions ; in calling an action
' right ' we may not perhaps imply that it sprang from a
moral motive, or we may imply that and something more
besides. Nor does it follow from what has been said that
the principal business, or the only business, of the moralist
is the judgment of actions ; indeed it is clear that morality
took a great stride forward when men began to realise,
as we say, that motives matter as well as actions, and that
character matters most of all. But with problems such as
these we are not at present concerned. In saying that
actions are the primary sphere of moral judgments we only
mean that we could scarcely hope to pass valid moral judgments upon character or desire or motive unless we had
already passed similar judgments upon actions ; unless,
that is to say, we had some conception of what kinds of actions
were right and what kinds were wrong.

Voluntary action being therefore the primary (though not
necessarily the only or the most important) sphere of moral
judgments, no such judgment is irrelevant within that
sphere. Nothing that we choose to do is necessarily and in
itself exempt from a possible judgment of conscience which
has an immediate bearing upon the question whether we
are to do it or not, or (if it has occurred) upon the question
whether we ought to have done it or not. There are,
indeed, plenty of choices in which as a matter of fact conscience utters no such judgment, and in which—if it were
uttered—it would come as a surprise. Questions such as that
of phrasing a sentence in this way or in that, or of choosing
between a blue and a red carpet in a shop, are questions
with which conscience normally has no concern. For that
reason we should be surprised if it intervened in the choice,
nor do we usually make such matters the subject of moral
scrutiny. But this does not mean that we should be sharing
in the absurdity of Ann Veronica's father if we *did* look

at questions of this character from the point of view of right or wrong. We might be guilty of a morbid scrupulosity in thus forcing the moral issue, but no one could brand the course as wholly illegitimate. To use one particular phrase rather than another may, after all, scandalise honest readers ; to choose the blue carpet rather than the red may give pain to your wife. In such circumstances conscience would be perfectly justified in intervening with the judgment, ' You are about to embark on a course which will give pain, and to give pain unnecessarily is always wrong ' ; and it would be immoral of us to stifle these qualms without consideration, on the ground that the matter was one exempt from the jurisdiction of conscience in which questions of right and wrong could not possibly arise. Good sense demands that we should not agonise over the rightness or wrongness of matters which in fact are indifferent ; but common morality insists that we should never bolt and bar the door against the possible intervention of conscience.[1]

(3) All our judgments are in the end judgments of fact ; they fall into the form, ' This is . . . .' or ' This is not . . . .' But many of them imply in addition some kind of a claim or obligation upon us to suit our actions to the fact, to conform to it. Thus if we judge, ' That is a beautiful picture,' there is implied a claim upon us :—' Do not injure it in any way.' If we judge of a man that he is unreliable, common-sense claims of us that we should not entrust important affairs to his care. Often enough, indeed, the claim involved is of the very slightest ; it is difficult to see what obligation, if any, the judgment that the earth goes round the sun imposes upon the ordinary man. Moral judgments, however, are always judgments of claim as much as of fact, and this we express by throwing them into a form which is unique, by the use of the words ' ought ' and ' ought not.'[2]

---

[1] More of this question *infra* pp. 38 ff.

[2] The words ' must,' ' should ' and ' ought ' are commonly used as interchangeable. This however is both careless and misleading, and a clear apprehension of their difference is essential for all thought about morality. ' Should ' is conditional, and always implies an ' if ' or ' unless.' ' Must ' is absolute, but implies the exercise of irresistible compulsion by an outside force upon the person of whom it is predicated. ' Ought,' while implying that the subject of the verb is a free agent, is absolute

' This is my duty ' means exactly the same as ' I ought to
do this,' and the word ' ought ' implies a claim upon us to
which conscience demands that we should conform in all
cases, except of course when a claim even more imperative
intervenes.

(4) The claims or obligations upon us, asserted by
conscience in its use of the word ' ought,' are sometimes
spoken of as ' categorical,' ' unconditional ' or ' absolute.'
An important truth is contained in these adjectives, but we
must not allow them to lead us into extremes.[1] They do
not by themselves imply that any moral obligation expressed
in general terms, such as ' Thou shalt not lie,' must necessarily be obeyed in any and every case in which at first
sight it seems to apply. There is always the possibility, in
any given set of circumstances, that another and even more
urgent claim may intervene ; how to decide between two
such claims when they conflict is one of the problems with
which we have to deal. Nor do the words necessarily imply,
as has sometimes been supposed, that conscience is free to
reach valid decisions for conduct in individual cases without
considering the consequences of the act proposed. We
are responsible for the foreseen consequences of our actions,
as much as for the actions themselves ; and the consequences
might well, in certain cases, involve the disregard of a claim
even more pressing than that which the action would satisfy.
Nor, finally, does the idea of an ' absolute ' obligation mean
necessarily that the desires and interests of the agent
can have no bearing upon a problem of conscience ; we
have yet to consider whether the fulfilment of a desire may

also, though in cases where it refers to the means by which a moral end
will be secured it may be explained by a ' because ' introducing another
' ought.' Thus ' You should go to bed now ' implies, for example, ' if
you wish to rise early,' without suggesting whether the early rising is desired
on moral or merely interested grounds. ' You must go to bed ' implies
strictly ' I am going to put you into bed whether you are willing or not '
(the true sense of the word being indicated, for example, by the sentence
' All men must die '—where both ' should ' and ' ought ' would be inappropriate). ' You ought to go to bed ' implies a duty, which can of
course be evaded, and which is seen to be absolute either in itself or because
it is the only way of securing an admittedly moral end—e.g. the keeping of
a promised appointment in the morning.

[1] Cp. on this H. Rashdall, *Theory of Good and Evil*, i. pp. 57-89.

not in certain cases be itself an obligation as absolute as any other.[1]

What the words we are considering seem to imply is rather that, once conscience has reached its judgment (after consideration of desire and interest if necessary), it has a claim to obedience which takes precedence of any claim that desire or interest can *then* put forward. Once we have reached the judgment (rightly or wrongly) 'Never tell a lie,' we are not free any longer to tell the truth only when it suits our convenience. 'You ought to respect life and property' does not mean 'You ought to do so unless your own interests conflict' or 'if you wish other people to respect yours'—it means, 'You ought to do so whatever your interests and wishes in the matter may be.' Honesty is no doubt the best policy, but the verdict 'Always be strictly honest' implies that honesty has an unalterable claim upon us even when knavery appears, on all ordinary showing, to be the only 'politic' course.

(5) The last paragraph has brought us within sight of what is often called the 'conflict of duty and desire,' a problem which will occupy our attention at a later stage. At the moment all we need do is to take it as a reminder that moral judgments are often (though not always) framed in an atmosphere of considerable emotional unrest. In this, indeed, they do not stand alone. Aesthetic judgments, for example, are usually accompanied, if not actually preceded, by an emotional stirring of the profoundest character. The reason of this is not far to seek. An aesthetic judgment is necessarily a judgment that such-and-such an object of experience is calculated to arouse a particular emotion (though there may be more in it than that), and it would be hard to reach such a judgment unless we were at the same time stirred, or had at some time been stirred, by the appropriate emotion. So, too, there are facts which rouse distressing emotions simply because they exhibit the impossibility of realising a desire; other facts which heighten our pleasure because they show that an object of desire is within reach; and we call these 'unpleasant' and 'pleasant' facts respectively. Further, we may remind ourselves that many

[1] On the last two points see *infra* pp. 324 ff.; on the first point, *infra* pp. 318 ff.

judgments of facts involve some element of claim ; and in so far as they do this, they are not without effect upon the emotions, even though they cannot be called either aesthetic, or pleasant or unpleasant.

At the same time it seems true that the majority of our everyday judgments, through our familiarity with them or their like, arouse in us very little emotion. The judgment that two and two make four, for example, is a judgment with which we have grown up from infancy. We do not remember any time at which it came to us with the shock of a new discovery. And, consequently, though it lays upon us the claim to conform to its truth (if we wish to behave as rational creatures at all) in all those various operations which can be classified under the name of ' putting two and two together,' the claim is one of which we rarely think, and which consequently arouses little feeling. There may indeed have been a time in the life of each individual—there probably was in the life of the race—when ' the multiplication table was exciting ' ; but the wave of excitement it brought with it has shrunk to very small dimensions.

Again, there are judgments of fact so remote from our ordinary affairs that it is hard to associate any emotion with them—except perhaps the joy of discovery when we arrive at them for the first time. We are stirred neither to delight nor to repugnance by the knowledge that the earth goes round the sun. Whatever pleasure or pain the judgment rouses in us would be equally roused if it were reversed, and we learnt that the sun went round the earth. In so far as we are moved or exalted by knowledge of this character, it is not so much the judgment itself that affects us, as its novelty (if it is newly discovered), or the light which it throws upon the whole system of truth of which it is a part.

On the whole, our moral judgments belong to the category of those which are markedly emotional. It is true that a man who has always been a teetotaller will not feel emotion in reminding himself of his motto, ' Never touch intoxicants.' Nor do we always find our feelings stirred when we pass moral judgments on the conduct of others.[1] In spite of these

[1] On this possibility of moral judgments without emotional context see H. Rashdall, *Theory of Good and Evil*, i. p. 168.

exceptions—in spite also of those abnormal cases of men and women of upright lives who seem almost devoid of feeling[1]— the judgments of conscience have usually an emotional context. In so far as they assert claims upon us, they require us either to do something or not to do something. And whenever there is question of doing something other than a purely automatic action, it is unreasonable to expect that emotion will not step in. The thing is either a thing we normally *want* to do or ' like ' doing ; or something we ' dislike ' doing and do not want to do. The perception, therefore, that such-and-such a thing is my duty—specially if it is a duty here and now—may be accompanied by a feeling either of the most intense aversion or of the most intense enthusiasm ; and few such perceptions can be wholly free from some distinct element either of aversion or of enthusiasm.

Often enough, of course, aversion and enthusiasm are mixed in our moral judgments ; we experience the phenomenon of a double consciousness, one side of which welcomes the duty whilst the other repels it. Indeed, the very feeling of aversion which we sometimes have on learning of a duty which claims our obedience is in a sense a good sign ; it implies that we have *some* desire at least to answer the call of duty. If we had none—if we were wholly deaf to the claims of morality—we should be as unmoved on learning or discovering what our duty was, as on learning the exact statistics of the population of India. The young man who had great possessions evoked our Lord's love, for the very reason that he had still retained sufficient idealism to ' go away sorrowful.' His sorrow showed that the pride of possession and the joy of riches had not been strong enough altogether to inhibit or overcome his sense of duty.

2. *Moral Judgments and Moral Taste*

Conflicts of emotions such as these, at times when duty and desire urge in opposite directions, are known to all of

[1] Cp. *Some Principles of Moral Theology*, p. 60.

us. But they must not blind us to the important truth that pleasure and pain, in the ordinary sense of the words,[1] are not the only emotions which accompany our moral judgments. We may, for example, indulge in a forbidden pleasure, but against its pleasurableness is set another emotion, which we call the emotion of shame. The pleasure depends upon some quality in the action which satisfies (let us say) our physical needs or aesthetic tastes, the shame is evoked by its moral quality. Shame is painful no doubt ; but the pain is a moral pain, not an aesthetic or physical pain. Similarly, to endure pain is of course painful ; but if a man endures it bravely we feel approval for his courage. And though this approval is pleasurable, the pleasure is derived not from the fact that pain is suffered (which indeed grieves us), but from the moral quality of courage with which it was suffered. Thus, among the emotions of various kinds

---

[1] Strictly speaking, pleasure and pain are not so much emotions as qualities of all emotions (cp. H. Rashdall, *Theory of Good and Evil*, i. p. 26 ; J. A. Hadfield, *Psychology and Morals*, p. 86 ; T. Ribot, *Psychology of Emotions* (E.T.), p. 16 ; R. H. Thouless, *Psychology of Religion*, p. 94). But in ordinary life we recognise a number of physical sensations producing emotional responses (called by the psychologists 'affects ') of a pleasurable character as to which it is of minor importance that a name should be found for the response ; and we speak generally of these affects as 'pleasures' or 'pleasant sensations,' thus apparently making 'pleasure' itself an affect or emotion. Where the sensation can be referred to a particular sense we define further, and speak of a pleasant 'taste,' 'sight,' 'smell,' 'sound'; commonly we do not speak of a 'pleasant touch,' but retain here the vague word 'feeling' or 'sensation.' Similarly of 'pain' and 'painful.' In these cases the 'affect' may also be referred to— e.g. a '*sweet* and pleasant taste' (i.e. in full, 'a physical sensation producing an affect of sweetness together with the quality of pleasure') ; but as for most of us sweetness always produces pleasure, we are commonly content to leave one of the adjectives out. We do not associate the idea of an 'emotion' with 'sweetness' for the reason that it is an affect produced by one or two classes of physical objects only, and bound up closely with one or two senses only, whereas emotions (e.g. 'hatred,' 'fear,' 'wonder,' etc.) are affects called out by objects of widely varying characters, however sensed. (So Ribot, *op. cit.* p. 50, '*Sensation* is determined and circumscribed by a special organ serving for this purpose only, as in the case of sight, hearing, etc. *Internal sensations* (=emotions), in spite of the nervous apparatus proper to them, have a vaguer character, hence some psychologists call them indifferently sensations or feelings ' ; Rashdall, *op. cit.* i. p. 77.) Similarly the 'feeling of coldness' which is used a little later on as an illustration is an 'affect' akin in many ways to the 'emotion' (say) of fear ; but we do not use the word 'emotion' of it because of its more intimate connection with particular physical sensations.

which surround our actions and invest them with the characteristics of pleasure and pain must be numbered certain specifically 'moral' emotions (the outcome of a 'moral taste,' as it is often called), which, though as a fact pleasurable or painful, often conflict so forcibly with physical, mental or aesthetic pleasure and pain that it is better to use other terms for them, and speak of them as feelings of 'approval' and 'disapproval,' 'praise' and 'blame,' or 'self-respect' and 'shame.'[1]

It was the work of a school of English philosophers of the eighteenth century, among whom Lord Shaftesbury and Francis Hutcheson are the best known, to bring out this fact that the feelings of 'approval' or 'disapproval' aroused by the moral quality of an action are distinct from pleasure and pain as commonly understood. In so doing they undermined the scepticism of Hobbes, who had confidently resolved all moral good and evil into the satisfaction of pleasure and avoidance of pain. At the same time, however, they unconsciously opened the door to scepticism of a similar but more specious kind, which came to its own in the ethics of Hume, and influences a good many people, without their knowing it, even at the present day. This must be our excuse for giving the question a brief consideration.

The problem may be put in various forms. We may ask, What right have we to pass moral judgments? or, On what authority does conscience speak? or, On what evidence are moral judgments based? The last form of the question is the best for our purposes. But its scope must be carefully noticed. It does not mean, On what evidence *do* men base their moral judgments?—for in this as in other matters judgments are often based on less than all the evidence, or on evidence of one out of various kinds which might be adduced. It means, What evidence is available, or *can* be adduced, for judgments of this kind? And the enquiry may be narrowed down further by asking, Are these feelings of approval and disapproval—these verdicts of 'moral

---

[1] Some phrases of this character often applied to *actions* (e.g. a 'praiseworthy' or 'blameworthy' act), really refer to the agent only, as the fact of choice is that which merits approval or the reverse. (We might use 'admirable' or 'repellent' of the action.)

taste '—the only evidence on which our moral judgments are reached, or is there other solid evidence available ?

The point may be illustrated by an analogy. If, instead of formally agreeing when an acquaintance greets us in the street with the words ' Very cold day to-day,' we were to ask how he knows that it is cold, we might get one of several answers. But they could be clearly divided into two classes —the answer which depended wholly on his own feeling of coldness as evidence, and the answers which appealed to other evidence than, or in addition to, this feeling. If he said, ' Of course it is cold ; I cannot get warm anyhow,' he would be judging upon the evidence of the feeling alone. If, on the other hand, he appealed to the thermometer, or to the fact that it was snowing and that icicles were hanging from the roofs, he would be taking other evidence into account—we might say, in effect, that he would be appealing to reason rather than to feeling,[1] even though his own feeling of coldness was part of the evidence on which reason judged. And, if further, it happened that the thermometer registered summer-heat, the sun was blazing down, and water evaporating everywhere, but on having his attention drawn to these facts he still replied, ' It *is* a bitterly cold day—I can't get warm anyhow,' we should be justified in saying to him, ' There is something wrong here. You cannot dismiss the evidence of thermometer and sun and evaporation in such a cavalier fashion. It is clear that you are judging the weather entirely by your own sensation of coldness ; or, in other words, that you are recording your sensations, and then transferring your judgment of them without any justification to the weather.'

It may be that when the perverse individual of whom we are speaking said ' It is a cold day,' he never meant anything more than ' I am very cold ' ; but that he accidentally threw his observation into a conventional form which designated the weather as the cause of his coldness. In that case what was merely a record of sensation would have taken shape, quite accidentally, as a judgment about the

---

[1] Not that reason is independent of sense-impression or feeling, but that it is, in this case, not content with the evidence of *one* such impression alone.

external universe.   The difference between the two is immense.   In the one case ' It is a cold day ' means no more than ' I feel very cold ' ;   in the other case it means what it says—' It is a cold day,' with the additional implication, ' It is a cold day whether you or I feel cold or not.' [1]   Thus the same form of words might conceal either a record of a particular feeling, considered independently of external fact, or an observation of external fact held to be valid independently of any feeling which accompanied it.   And the phrase ' It is a cold day ' can have this two-fold meaning simply because there is other evidence about the temperature besides that of the cold sensation—the evidence of the thermometer, and so forth.

But some of our judgments, however much in form we transfer them to external objects, can never really be more than records of a single sensation, because such a sensation is the only evidence.   If I say ' This is a sweet orange,' or ' This is a pleasant smell,' whilst my friend calls the orange sour and the smell nauseating, there is no further evidence, such as that of the thermometer, to which we can appeal. We may of course summon a third person to share our experience and agree to abide by his decision ;   but, even so, the judgment is still only about how the orange tastes to each of us severally.   ' This flower has a pleasant smell ' can never mean more than ' It smells pleasantly to me,' or ' to a majority of those who experience it ' ;   for though the heat of a day can be attested by other evidence than a single type of sensation, the pleasantness of a smell can only be proved by appeal to the fact that those who experience it find it pleasant.   If anyone challenges my judgment that the smell is pleasant, and declares it to be noxious, there is no instrument for assessing smells which will give an impartial verdict between us, as will the thermometer in the case of

---

[1] This statement of the case may perhaps be allowed to pass for the purpose of the analogy without prejudice to the metaphysical problem of the objective reality of coldness.   Similarly, in the next example, it must not be overlooked that even such subjective perceptions as those of taste may be genuine evidence as to ' objective ' fact—e.g. if to-day's orange tastes differently from yesterday's, it may be evidence either that there is something wrong with the orange, or with me—hypotheses which can be independently examined and verified.

the temperature. Each man's judgment is valid for himself alone, and for him it is final. But it is unverifiable, and therefore wholly invalid as a criterion by which to judge others. We must agree to disagree ; and that is the end of the matter.

In speaking of the temperature and of the sense of smell, we have been dealing not so much with what are commonly called emotions, as with ' sensations ' or ' feelings ' in the narrowest sense of the words. But the same distinctions hold good of emotions as commonly so-called. I may speak of a person as a ' horrible man,' either because his mere presence inspires me with an emotion of loathing and distrust, or because his record, as known to all the world, marks him out as a villain. In the first case I am judging on the evidence of a single emotion only, in the second on wider or ' rational ' grounds. Cases arise in which the only evidence available is that of an emotion. The person in question may merely pass through the room and then vanish for ever from my life, and circumstances may determine that no further information whatever about him is to be procured. If, in such a case, his momentary passing-by inspires me with an emotion of loathing, and my friend (who is also present) with an emotion of liking, the result will be the same as before. Whether we speak of ' sensations ' or of ' emotions,' if there is disagreement between two persons who share the same experience, and no other evidence is available, it is impossible for an impartial verdict to be secured. They must agree to disagree.

The vocabulary employed by the English sentimentalist school of philosophy went far to suggest that moral judgments, despite their apparent assertion of truths external to and independent of our feelings, are no more and can be no more than records of these ' feelings ' or ' emotions ' of approval and disapproval. The suggestion became explicit when Hume wrote, ' An action or sentiment or character is virtuous or vicious because its view causes a pleasure or uneasiness of a particular kind.'[1] In other words, we call

[1] *Treatise on Human Nature*, III. i. 3, cp. *Inquiry concerning the Principles of Morals*, App. 1 :—Virtue is ' whatever mental action or quality gives to a spectator the pleasing sentiment of approbation ; vice

an action 'right,' or a 'duty,' because we have a feeling of approval when we contemplate the idea of its performance. We do not feel approval because we see it to be right ; nor do we feel approval and see it to be right (on other grounds besides that of our feeling of approval) simultaneously. The feeling of approval may be evoked either by a general principle or by a particular action or proposal, but in either case it is the only evidence at our command ; and the moral judgment is simply an automatic record of that feeling.

What, then, on this theory, becomes of the arguments and evidence with which we justify our moral convictions to ourselves ? The answer is clear. They can be no more than what the psychologist calls *rationalisations*—' chains of argument used by the mind to justify itself in the holding of a belief which really owes its origin to something else, to suggestion or to some " affective " root.' [1] The musician is emotionally repelled by the man who has no music in his soul ; it is only as an after-thought that he reasons (if it can be called reasoning), ' Unmusical folk are fit for treasons, stratagems and spoils ; let no such man be trusted.' Caesar is unpleasantly affected in the neighbourhood of persons of ' lean and hungry look ' ; he justifies this aversion by the sweeping and baseless generalisation, ' Such men are dangerous.' Thus the true definition of conscience—that is to say of the psychological factor ultimately responsible and authoritative for our moral judgments—on this theory, would be not ' the mind when it passes moral judgments,' but ' the heart when it experiences moral sensations, or sensations of approval of a particular kind.' And just as the man who insists on saying ' It is a cold day,' without regarding the evidence of the thermometer, is really recording his own

---

is the contrary.' So also Ribot, *Psychology of the Emotions*, p. 291 : ' A judgment (approving or condemnatory) on our own conduct or that of others is the result of a deeper process—not an intellectual one—of an emotional process of which it is only the clear and intelligible manifestation in consciousness '; W. McDougall, *Social Psychology* [12], p. 218 : ' It is notorious that the sentiments determine our moral judgments ' ; Westermarck, quoted *ib.* p. 214 : ' That the moral concepts are ultimately based upon emotions either of indignation or approval is a fact which a certain school of thinkers have in vain attempted to deny.'

[1] R. H. Thouless, *Psychology of Religion*, p. 81. Instances of such alleged ' rationalisations ' are there given.

feelings of coldness, and not making an assertion about the
day at all, so on this theory when we say, 'This action is
right,' we are merely recording our feelings of approval, and
not making any substantive assertion about the quality or
character of the action in itself.

3. *Conscience and Emotion*

In a modified form a great deal of this ' sentimentalist '
theory has passed into modern psychology, though we no
longer speak boldly of ' moral sense ' or ' moral taste ' as a
simple distinct entity. Instead we are supposed to have a
complex sentiment based upon an association of primary
instincts,[1] which finds its satisfaction in action of a moral
character, and grudges if it be not satisfied. The theory
is further reflected in the rhetorical question, ' We do feel—
do we not ? ' to whose pulpit popularity Father Knox has
drawn attention ; and in other popular uses of the word
' sense ' and ' feeling ' (as in the phrase ' a sense of honesty '
or a ' feeling of obligation ') in the meaning of ' conviction.'
Neither these usages, nor the psychological doctrine just
mentioned, involve as an absolute corollary that emotion is the
only evidence on which our moral judgments are based, or
(in other words) that ' morality is merely a matter of feeling ' ;
but there is no doubt that their suggestion tends wholly in
this direction. It is not enough to dismiss the doctrine with
a brusque dictum, ' Propositions cannot be felt.' [2] We have
to consider what it involves, and whether it is really adequate
to the facts.

(1) To begin with, many of our common notions about
morality will have to be altered if we accept it. We can
no longer, for example, speak of the judgments of conscience
as ' unconditional.' The word implies, as we saw, that duty

---

[1] T. Ribot, *Psychology of the Emotions* (E.T.), p. 299 : ' Moral emotion
is a very complex state. Those psychologists in the last century who
maintained the hypothesis of a " moral sense " erroneously considered it
as a special sense with an innate faculty of discriminating good and evil.
It is not a special act, but the sum of a set of tendencies.'

[2] Rashdall, *Theory of Good and Evil*, i. p. 148. Dr. Rashdall of course
discusses the whole problem at length.

is duty regardless of desire, interest or feeling ; or that duty is the same for all in any given set of circumstances, whatever emotions they may have about it. This would have to be changed. A man's duty is now simply that for which he has this feeling of approval ; and if the feeling is absent in respect of any action or class of actions, duty is absent too. Nor would the word ' ought ' any longer have its distinctive meaning. ' You ought ' now means no more than ' I approve ' ; ' You ought to do so-and-so,' is the same as ' If you did so-and-so I should approve you for doing it.' The special quality of obligation, claim or command which we thought inherent in moral judgments would prove to be an entire illusion.[1] On the theory of conscience as a sentiment, therefore, two qualities which we usually think character-istic of our moral judgments prove to be illusory. They are no longer unconditional, nor are they preceptive ; they are merely statements of facts about ourselves and our feelings, not statements of claims upon ourselves. ' I ought to tell the truth ' means simply ' I approve of telling the truth ' and nothing more.

(2) Furthermore, the doctrine limits severely the legiti-mate range of our moral judgments. ' Approval,' in the sense in which we are using it, is strictly speaking only evoked by voluntary and purposive action. The involuntary or automatic may give us ' satisfaction,' but only what is voluntary and purposive can win our ' approval.' We are in a difficulty here, because all the words we use are ambiguous in meaning, and can denote different kinds of pleasurable sensation. But it is clear that we *approve* the gift of the widow's mites to the temple just because it was voluntary ; had someone snatched the coins from her and put them into the box the result might have been equally satisfactory—at all events in the judgment of those whose main interest was in the temple revenues—but we should have had no material or grounds for praising the widow.

Now feelings and emotions are in general involuntary and capricious things, over which their possessor has compara-tively little control. He can indeed by an effort of will

---

[1] So Butler (*Preface to Sermons*) criticises Shaftesbury for ' not taking into account the *authority* of conscience.'

check, stimulate or modify them to some extent ; but he
can rarely induce them if they are not there at birth. ' Feelings ' do change, no doubt ; ' tastes ' can be lost, gained,
improved or modified ; but the control and direction of these
processes is within our power to a very limited degree alone.
Elia tried all his life to like Scotchmen, but was obliged in
the end ' to desist from the experiment in despair.'[1] The
pessimist can rarely force himself to become an optimist, the
optimist usually remains an optimist in spite of all disap-
pointments of life ; and pessimism and optimism are simply
temperamental dispositions dominated by the emotions of
fear and hope respectively. We have it on good authority
that the unreasoned hatred of a gaping pig or harmless
necessary cat is peculiarly difficult to overcome ; and there
are some people who with the best will in the world cannot
bring themselves to like the style of Whitman, let us say, or
Meredith. Love as an emotion cannot be deliberately
induced in anyone. He either loves or does not love—he
cannot force himself to love.[2] So through the whole gamut of
emotions, feelings, sensations we recognise that here are
things which vary with the individual constitution, and which
neither argument nor influence will avail to modify very far.
Violent revulsions of feeling, particularly in the cases of
crowds, can be produced by rhetorical appeal ; but once
the crowd has dispersed, and the orator's personality is
removed to a distance, the currents of emotion tend to revert
to their normal channels. The play of feeling appears to be
in essence involuntary.

It follows, therefore, that it is wholly unreasonable and
unjust to blame a man—that is, on this theory, to feel disapproval of him—for holding different views from our own
in morality. He is recording his own feelings only, and for
them he is not responsible. And yet this is commonly the
most important sphere of moral judgments. We blame a

---

[1] C. Lamb, *Essay on Imperfect Sympathies*.

[2] He can of course behave *as though he loved*, and in this sense ' to
love the brethren ' is a Christian duty. As one form of loving the brethren
is ' thinking the best of them,' and as thoughts undoubtedly influence
emotions, this ' love of the will ' may produce and should produce something
akin to ' love of the affections.' But can it produce that purely emotional
factor in love which we call ' liking ' a person ?

man for stealing, but we blame him far more if he deliberately maintains as a matter of principle that stealing is laudable. Indeed so shocked are we if he persistently stamps the practice of theft with his approval by shamelessly indulging in it, that we force ourselves to regard him as morally irresponsible. We use language to suggest that he is the victim of some strange disease, which in the lower classes of society takes the form of 'moral degeneracy,' and in the higher classes that of 'kleptomania'; and by attributing his insensibility to this cause we manage to lighten the overwhelming weight of blame which would otherwise be his portion. But on the 'moral sense' or 'moral taste' theory of conscience he is probably not blameworthy in the slightest degree. His emotions are most likely involuntary; and in blaming him (even though we try to lighten the weight of blame) we are in fact giving way to an impulse which can only be called illegitimate, irrational, unnatural and inhuman. We may grieve that he does not feel as we do about theft, but we have no real justification for disapproval, any more than we have any right to disapprove of him if he loathes a taste which to us seems pleasant and palatable.

It might be replied that this point of view has, after all, its salutary side. There *are* such persons as genuine kleptomaniacs. There are others who from the moral point of view have 'never had a chance'—brought up from infancy among depraved surroundings, they have never known what it is to respect truth and honesty and purity. Such people, it might be contended, are genuinely blameless; and if the 'moral sense' point of view brings out this truth against the unjust condemnation passed on them by their contemporaries, it is a strong argument in its favour. The contention is valid and important; strict moralists often fail to make sufficient allowance for the overwhelming effect of a bad environment in childhood. Even so, however, the difficulty is not really countered. We ought no doubt to make full allowance for the victim of social disabilities of this kind. But surely common-sense is right in blaming the man who, in spite of every moral advantage in childhood, sinks to evil courses and champions immoral standards in

later life ? Little can be urged for him in the way of extenuating circumstances ; yet on the ' sentimentalist ' view
he also is blameless. He has merely lost a taste which once
he had ; and he is no more *guilty* in the matter than the man
who on reaching maturity loses his delight in infantile
amusements.[1]

(3) It would appear, therefore, that on the theory we are
criticising we have less right than we supposed, and perhaps
no right at all, to blame our neighbour or disapprove of him
for holding moral views which contradict our own—even
though he once championed the same code of ethics as ourselves and has now deserted to a side which we are forced to
regard as not merely different from, but also inferior to, his
first enthusiasms. It follows also that it will usually be
idle of us to attempt to modify our neighbour's views on
moral questions. His approval of theft may be an innate
emotional tendency which is as uncontrollable and unalterable
in him as the approval of honesty is in us. We have no reason
to suppose that God any more intended us to feel alike in
this matter than in many other matters of like and dislike.
The chances of our ever being able to convey to him a taste
for honesty, if he is naturally endowed with a taste for

[1] The only valid answer to this argument would be to surrender the
theory of specific moral emotions of approval and disapproval, and say
that these feelings are merely forms of other emotions, sentiments or
instincts, and that therefore the whole idea of ' praise ' and ' blame '
is illusory and ought to be abandoned. This would be to give up all
that the moral sense theorists were contending for against Hobbes, and
reduce moral judgments to pure fictions without even such shadowy
basis as ' sentimentalism ' provided. There is no doubt a tendency of this
kind in some modern psychological writing, akin to schools of thoughts
which would make all religion a misinterpretation of sex-feeling or herd-
instinct. Its defects in the latter sphere have been well brought out by
Mr. Thouless in his *Psychology of Religion* (cc. 10, 11, 17 ; and also pp. 88 ff.),
and in default of fuller treatment the reader may be referred to that book
for an excellent summary of the arguments against radical scepticism
of this character. All that need be said here is, that if it is difficult to
understand (*infra* p. 23) why an experience, which at best can justify
the judgment ' I feel disapproval at the thought of your doing so-and-so,'
should evoke the precept ' You ought not to do it ' (a form which even
on the moral sense theory is in any case unjustifiable), it is still more
difficult to see why experiences which at best can justify the judgment
' The thought of your doing so-and-so gives me pain ' or ' wounds my
instincts of awe and tender emotions ' should evoke *both* the preceding
judgments, for neither of which can it supply any justification.

theft, are so small as to be negligible ; just as we cannot teach him to find that sweet, which in fact tastes bitter to him. We must not press these points too far, but at least it is true that on the 'moral sense' doctrine of conscience we have less right, less reason and less hope than we commonly imagine to be ours for taking up what to a Christian is the most sacred of duties—the attempt to convert others to live a life according to the mind of Christ. Once again we must agree to disagree.

(4) These consequences, which appear to result from the doctrine that moral judgments depend wholly upon feeling, are serious enough. They involve an almost complete denial of most of the ideas which we attach to the words 'right,' 'ought' and 'duty.' But it does not follow, therefore, that the doctrine is untrue. Its conflict with the normal implications of 'You ought to do so-and-so,' and its corollary that all we mean when we say this is 'I should feel approval if you did so-and-so' (which is certainly very much less than we think we mean), suggest that it does not wholly square with the facts. Nor does it offer any satisfactory explanation of the curious and manifestly illegitimate process by which mankind has transformed its records of emotions into statements of claims ; [1] and this lacuna also redounds to the discredit of the theory. But there is only one kind of evidence that would demonstrate its falsity. To discover whether moral judgments can be more than a record of moral emotions we must enquire whether instances are found in which such judgments and the sentiment of approval are seen to be distinct from one another. If we can find such instances, then it will be clear that our moral judgments, sometimes at all events, employ other evidence in addition, or even in preference, to the feeling of approval ; that—whatever in most cases they *are*, and whatever in all cases they *ought* to be— they *need* not be mere records of feeling ; and that therefore our original ideas about them are not so baseless as the 'moral sense' theory would suggest.

[1] For though it may appeal to 'rationalisation' (*supra* p. 19) or 'association of ideas' to explain the *process* by which the transformation takes place, it cannot explain why the *end* of the process should manifest itself in a statement of claim ; or why any such process should take place at all.

Here may be adduced a curious phrase used by Newman
in the period of mental stress immediately preceding his
secession to Rome.   He is strongly moved to take the final
step, but he writes to a friend, ' It is difficult to know whether
this is a call of reason or of conscience.   I cannot make out
whether I am impelled by what seems *clear*, or by a sense
of *duty*.' [1]   He is of course using the words ' conscience '
and ' sense of duty ' in a meaning of his own, but if we allow
for that his psychological state is both understandable and
interesting.   On the one hand there are clear reasons
which ' impel ' him to go over to Rome.   The word ' impel '
is important ; these reasons, which of course (because they
are reasons) he can state and defend, are more than abstract
statements about the Roman Church.   To ' impel ' him to
take the step they must assert in a form more or less definite
the claim of Rome to his submission.   On the other hand,
something of importance—something which he calls ' conscience '—is apparently lacking ; and he is not prepared to
take the plunge until he is certain that this missing factor
is present.   What, then, is the factor in question ?   It cannot
be ' desire ' or ' pleasure ' ;   Newman would be the last
person in the world to confuse duty with interest.   It is not
reason or any function of reason, for it is definitely contrasted
with reason.   It cannot be anything but just that sentiment
of moral approval for which others also, before Newman,
reserved the title of ' conscience.'   Newman's self-analysis
makes it clear that there is something else (he calls it
' reason ') besides this feeling of approval which ' impels '
us to action, which forces us to recognise claims on which
we can base the judgment ' I ought to do so-and-so.'
It is true that for his own part he is not prepared to
obey this ' impulse ' of ' reason ' until ' conscience,' or
the feeling of approval, chimes in with it. [2]   But this is
not to deny the *validity* of the other evidence, it is
merely to assert (whether rightly or not) that no evidence
can be *conclusive* until the ' moral sense ' also has fallen
into line.

[1] *Apologia*, c. 4.
[2] It is interesting to consider whether he would have obeyed the
' impulse ' of ' conscience ' if ' reason ' disagreed with it.

There are few of us who by analysis of our own consciousness cannot verify Newman's postulates. We have
known times when, for example, on thinking out a problem,
all rational considerations pointed clearly to the conclusion
that duty lay in a particular direction. We were able to
discern the attitude dictated by self-interest or pleasure,
and eliminate that factor from our calculations. But still
something intervened (with or without justification) to
inhibit the action proposed, and we said, ' I cannot bring myself to do it.' What is this inhibiting factor ? People may
call it prejudice, scrupulosity or habit, but these words do
not define it. The first (' prejudice ') merely describes its
results—namely to prevent the arguments of reason from
having their full effect. The second describes its characteristic mode of operation — the guerilla tactics (if we
may call them so) which it adopts. The third, ' habit,'
indicates the process by which it attained its present
power. But *what it is in itself* is not given us by any
of these terms. We are forced to conclude that the
inhibition is imposed by just that feeling of disapproval
of which we have been speaking ; and that we have been
able to reach the judgment ' This is my duty ' on other
evidence.

We conclude then that ' feeling ' is not the only evidence
upon which moral judgments can be based ; and consequently that they need not be a mere automatic record of
feeling, though perhaps they are often little more. The mind,
when it passes its moral judgments, need not derive the whole
of its authority from feeling ; it has, if it cares to use it,
authority of its own to compare the emotions of approval and
disapproval with other evidence, and to draw conclusions
therefrom. We need not amend our original definition of
conscience, nor accept the minimising conclusions of the
' moral sense ' point of view. But several questions arise
at once. For example, what is this ' other evidence ' which
can be employed in framing moral judgments ? And again,
what is the right course of action when, as in Newman's
case, the ' other evidence ' and the sentiment of approval
or disapproval conflict ? The first of these questions we
shall come to in a moment, the second we must postpone

to a later chapter,[1] as it is just one of those ' problems of conscience ' with which we have to deal.

In the meantime, one conclusion at least of practical importance emerges from the discussion. There is an old saying—as old as Aristotle—that ' reason alone never moves to action.' Even if this saying is too sweeping for the facts,[2] it remains true that feeling is a more potent motive force than reason. True enough, as we have said, that feelings cannot be created to order ; they may be manipulated and put into shackles, but no one can tell how soon they will break their bonds. But, within these limits, if a man is to lead the good life he must use all the means in his power to stimulate his moral sensibilities, so that he may not only *know* what is right, but experience also a heartfelt approval of it, and an unquenchable desire to put it into effect. And all who are in any way responsible for his spiritual well-being must co-operate in the process.

How this is to be done is not so much a problem *of* conscience as a problem *about* conscience ; and the discovery and exposition of the appropriate methods is the work of what is known as ascetic theology. It is therefore foreign to the purpose of these chapters ; but that must not blind us to the fact that it is as urgent and important a study as any other in the whole range of Christian thought and life. Indeed it is particularly important in so far as it counter-balances the one-sided interest in actions (as apart from motives and character) which is distinctive of ordinary ethics and moral theology. In so far as they emphasised this truth in an age of rationalism, the sentimentalist philosophers did yeoman service to the cause of Christian morality.

4. *Intuitions*

We turn now to the question postponed a moment ago. What is the ' other evidence ' which the mind can take into

---

[1] *Infra* p. 228.

[2] See the criticism by W. G. Courtney, *Constructive Ethics*, p. 102, and cp. T. B. Strong, *Religion, Philosophy and History*, p. 18 : ' Thought, even in its most abstract forms, has an element of deliberate and purposive activity in it, and there is no point at which these two elements are completely in separation.'

account in arriving at its moral judgments? The answer at first sight seems easy. There is ample material on which the mind can draw. Society presents each one of us from infancy upward with more of this material than we can possibly employ. The example of Christ, the writings of philosophers, the advice of friends, the conventions of contemporary life, the consensus of civilised mankind—here is ample evidence; we do not need to go out into the highways and hedges of thought to find more. In fact, what we need most is to discard as superfluous much of the evidence thus presented to us; to cut it down until it reaches practicable dimensions. This, as a matter of fact, is what we all of us do. Every time we decide, for instance, that Uncle John's advice is usually right, whilst what Aunt Mary says can safely be ignored, we are selecting from the evidence at our disposal and separating the valuable from the worthless.

The problem therefore is not so much, What is the evidence? as, How does the mind manipulate it? What tests does it apply in this process of comparison, selection and rejection? And having put the question in this form we see that 'moral sentiments' can now be included in the evidence. They are not the whole of the available evidence, but they are part of it. Some of us may be inclined (as Newman was) to trust them above the whole weight of the rest of the evidence, some to distrust them even profoundly. But whether we trust or distrust them, reason manipulates them in among the rest of the evidence, and so finally reaches its moral judgments in the form either of general 'principles' or of particular 'precepts.'

The starting-point of reason in reaching judgments of any kind must be some kind of certainty—the 'seeing,' 'admitting' or 'recognising' that a fact subsists or a proposition is true. Such a certainty is commonly called an 'intuition,' though we are in no way tied to the name. No more explanation can be given of this intuitive element in knowledge than of the physical vision or 'perception'[1]

---

[1] Which, of course, in so far as we hold it to be a seeing of *something*, is more than a mere sense-impression; being indeed the result of an infinitely rapid manipulation of various concordant sense-impressions by the mind. *Infra* p. 29.

from which its name is borrowed. It just happens that in every branch of investigation we take certain principles for granted as self-evident—they speak for themselves, they force themselves upon us. We cannot conceive (at all events for the time being) [1] that they could be otherwise. So, too, of facts—we ' see them to be so.' And if our moral judgments are not always based upon records of feeling alone, the only other source to which they can go back, and by which they can test the evidence presented to them in experience, must be rational intuitions of this character.

But at once an obvious criticism meets us. We noticed as a defect of the ' moral sense ' theory of conscience that it relieved us of all right of attempting to convert another to our way of thinking about conduct, and almost of all hope that any such attempt would be permanently successful. But if conscience is at bottom a matter of intuitions, does not the same criticism hold good ? If it be no use disputing about tastes—if indeed we have no right to question the legitimacy of another's taste—is there any use or right in questioning intuitions ? Are they not as primary and irresponsible as feelings ? [2] Are they not indeed (as one contemporary school of psychology would have us believe) no more than the record of ' feelings ' themselves, masquerading as something more reliable ? Admittedly people do differ from us in their moral intuitions ; have we any right to expect them to agree with us, or any hope of persuading them to do so, if the intuitions are genuinely and firmly believed to be true ? If a man cannot ' see ' for himself that stealing is wrong, will any amount of argument convince him of the fact ? It appears almost as if the scholastic tradition we have

---

[1] ' For the time being '—because fresh evidence and experience may lead us to revise and correct them. To say that intuitions are immediate is not to imply that they are infallible. *Infra* pp. 33, 75 f.

[2] Mr. Thouless (*op. cit.* p. 72) seems to hold this depreciatory view of ' intuition,' and regards the appeal to ' intuition ' (which he equates with ' subjective certainty ') as ' suffering from the disadvantages resulting from the rejection of the rational element.' As however his discussion of the rational element in religion (in whose importance he clearly believes) does not contain any statement of the mode in which primary certainties as regards facts and axioms are reached, it is impossible to say how far he would use the word ' intuition ' of such certainties ; or what other word he would substitute for it.

followed, which regards conscience as a function of reason, offers no more right or hope of converting the morally perverted than the theory of the moral sense.

What difference then, if any, is there between a rational intuition and a record of feeling ? Is the former any more reliable than the latter ? How comes it that—in respect at all events of judgments other than the judgments of conscience—we say confidently of these primary certainties, by which we test the evidence of experience, that they are no mere subjective records of feelings, but objective perceptions or intuitions of truth ? The answer surely is that rational intuitions, like rational inferences—from which they differ principally in the fact that they are not the conscious results of a progressive chain of arguments—are themselves capable of being based upon a wide survey of evidence of many different kinds, whilst records of feelings stand upon one piece of evidence only.[1] Intuitions are not in themselves for that reason more trustworthy than records of feeling, but they are capable of giving a more trustworthy account of that which is the occasion, or object, both of the intuition

---

[1] The record of a sense-impression is of course in itself intuitive—we ' see that we see something '—and yet seems not to be capable of a basis in ' a wide survey of evidence.' As a mere record of a sense-impression it is indeed as unverifiable as it is final—the momentary impression occurred, and as to that there can be no doubt ; but it is past and can never be recalled. If however we base upon it, or transform it into a judgment about, an external ' something ' to which we attribute the causing of the impression, this is commonly verifiable by means of additional evidence, gained through other sense impressions and varied by experiment. *Not* to verify it is to frame our judgment upon a single sense-impression, and though in some cases, as we have seen, this may be inevitable, it is always hazardous. The attempt to verify by looking for additional evidence is to treat the matter as a rational intuition ; and as a general rule where a sense-impression can be verified in this way, it has already been verified by the time it has been recorded, so that a statement such as e.g. ' I see a horse ' is both a record of an impression (' I see at this infinitesimal frac-tion of a moment the appearance of a horse ') and a genuine intuition, which if written out in full might be expressed, ' I see at this infinitesimal fraction of a moment the appearance of a horse, and on the basis of a sequence of varying impressions of which this is the last, I affirm intuitively that a horse is there.' Cp. also Rashdall, *Theory of Good and Evil*, i. p. 77 : ' A simple perception of colour must be treated as an intellectual activity when we think of the recognised relation between the person or subject and his object ; as a state of feeling when we think of it merely as a state of the subject and from the point of view of his interest in it.'

and of the feeling. If I analyse consciousness and find that
I have judged it to be a cold day simply and solely on the
ground that I feel cold, I know that I have merely recorded
a sensation of my own which is scarcely adequate to support
my judgment about the day as a whole. If on the other
hand I find that I have already taken note not merely of my
sensation but of the thermometer, the ice on the sponge and
in the bath, and the overcoats and mufflers worn in the street
—even though I recorded no conscious judgment about any
of them, and so cannot be said to have gone through a process
of inference—I may rightly call my judgment ' It is a cold
day ' a rational intuition, and regard it as a more trustworthy
judgment about the temperature than a judgment based on
feeling alone.

The same holds good in all respects of moral judgments.
We can analyse them, even though they appear to have been
reached instantaneously, and discover on what evidence they
were based. It is possible to say, ' Smith is an immoral man,'
and to find on investigation that the only evidence employed
up to the moment of judging was a feeling of disapproval which
his presence inspired. The judgment is then no more than a
record of this feeling, and highly untrustworthy as a statement
about Smith's character. But if analysis shows that, in passing the judgment, I was in possession of other evidence besides
that of feeling—if I had observed his treatment of his wife and
neglect of his children, had known him in a state of intoxication and suffered from his chicanery in money matters—then
my judgment may fairly be called rational. If I consciously argued from these facts to my conclusion, the process was an inference ; if I leapt to the conclusion without any
conscious argument, it is better called an intuition. But in
either case, though it may still be false, it is far more trustworthy, more likely to be true, than a judgment about Smith
which in fact is no more than the record of a feeling about
Smith.

Analysis of our mental states suggests, therefore, both that
reason is an arbiter in moral judgments, as in others, not
wholly dependent upon feeling ; and that it is of the two the
more trustworthy arbiter. It may indeed be said that none
of the evidence upon which intuitions (whether moral or

otherwise) are based is wholly *independent* of feeling ; and this no doubt is true. But, though true, it does not concern us here ; for it affects all kinds of judgment equally. It is enough for us to conclude that there is no distinction between moral judgments and other judgments which warrants our supposing that the former can never be more than records of feeling, or 'wholly subjective,' whilst the latter may be judgments of fact, or genuinely 'objective.' If any judgments are capable of being rational, objective or true to fact, moral judgments are equally capable of being so. Conscience, therefore, has the right, if it see fit, to brand as mere scrupulosity a feeling of approval adverse to its judgment of wrong, or a feeling of disapproval adverse to its judgment of right. It is not necessarily infallible if it thus judges in the teeth of feeling. But it is at least more likely than feeling to reach a true estimate of the facts, provided always that in its survey of evidence it has not ignored the evidence of feeling.

The importance of this conclusion may be shewn by an appeal to popular usage. When all is said that can be said of the failure of argument to convince, and of the possibility of divergences between the intuitions of different people, it yet remains true that we regard reason as that which will unite people, whilst taste or feeling is that which diversifies them. We assume that, if we could rid ourselves of emotional and psychological prejudices, reason would lead us all to a uniform apprehension of truth as true ; we do not for a moment imagine that if we threw aside the shackles of reason we should find ourselves all with complete unanimity of taste. Reason tends always to unity ; feeling or taste to diversity. So whenever we fail to convince a disputant of the truth of some proposition we have been upholding, whether its subject-matter be in the ethical or any other sphere, we appeal again and again to his reason in the hope that he will 'see the point' of our argument. We suspect that the difference between us is no more than apparent ; and that if we can only find the right formula, illustration, analogy or turn of phrase it will at once disappear. And if we have put our case as clearly as it deserves, and exhausted all the resources of logic and illustration, we may indeed admit that we cannot 'see eye

to eye ' in the matter (and that is in words an admission of
an ultimate divergence of intuitions) ; but what we think in
our heart of hearts is that the opponent has allowed his reason
to be perverted by passion or feeling.   We are even prepared
to say that he cannot ' see the point ' because he doesn't
want to see it.   Until his emotional and psychological prejudices are removed, it is no use reasoning with him further ;
when they are removed, reason will convince him of the
truth of what we are saying without further argument.

To classify conscience with reason, and to speak of its
fundamental principles as ' intuitions ' or ' rational certainties,' is to imply, not that *this or that* certainty or intuition
is beyond the power of question, but that (as we may hope)
right and wrong must in the end be the same for all men ;
and that, if the progress of moral education be combined with
discipline of the emotions, all men will come in the end to see
eye to eye in the matter of duty.[1]   To regard conscience, on
the other hand, as an emotion, or taste, or sensibility, is to
imply that in the long run, in all probability, men will no
more agree about duty and sin than they agree about heat and
cold.[2]   We may induce them to try our standards of life
and see whether they approve them or not ; but if they do
not approve them there is nothing more to be said—we have
no right to disapprove.   In Dr. Rashdall's words, ' The
objectivity of the moral judgment ' (which is involved in this
doctrine of conscience as rational) ' does not mean the infallibility of the individual. . . . (It means) that *if I am right*
in my approbation of this conduct, then, if you disapprove
of it, you must be wrong. . . . But if the goodness of an act
means simply that the act occasions a specific emotion in
particular men, then the same act may be at the same time
good and bad '[3]—which is absurd.

[1] Examples of this process of argument and verification, by which
conflicting intuitions on a moral problem might conceivably be unified
are considered in the second part of this book.   In the main they consist in
bringing together cases (real or imaginary) analogous to the one which
happens to be in dispute, in the hope of eliciting, by comparison and differen-
tiation, the true solution of the problem.   Hence the importance of casuistry

[2] So Sidgwick, *Methods of Ethics*, p. 34 : ' The term " sense " suggests a
capacity for feelings which may vary from A to B without either being in
error.'

[3] *Op. cit.* i. p. 145.

We cannot insist too much upon this conclusion that moral judgments are genuinely rational and not mere records of feeling. It is the main bulwark of the Christian position that duty is not something as to which a man has the right to choose or create the claims that he is going to recognise, but that it is something *there*—something outside ourselves—something the same for all—something in the eternal will of God—for us to discover and obey. It is neither an invention nor a convention of society ; though ' invention ' (in its original sense of ' discovery ') is a fit name for the way in which society first came to think of it as duty ; and ' convention ' may be the mode in which it was first presented to us as individuals. But in itself it is something far higher than the human mind or emotions, something eternal of which they can only welcome and reverence transient and partial phases ; something which it is the highest goal of human effort to discover and obey in the fullest measure possible.

The fact that intuitions (whether in the moral or any other sphere) are capable of being based on a wide survey of evidence carries with it the corollary that—though they are never without some basis in fact—they are capable of being progressively revised as new evidence comes into view.[1] This is continually happening in every branch of thought. In the progress of reflection upon experience we become convinced that some of the intuitions with which we started life were mistaken, and these we gradually amend. Others are sub-

---

[1] The classical school of English intuitionists undoubtedly thought of the primary moral intuitions as infallible, and therefore as incapable of revision. In this they were stressing the analogy between intellectual convictions and clear and distinct physical perceptions. Had they recognised, however, that the number of our perceptions which are *so* clear and distinct that we should, when challenged, affirm them without hesitation to be incapable of revision or elaboration of detail, is small compared with the total number of ' awarenesses ' (if the word may be allowed) which we accept and employ as the basis of judgments, they would have agreed that the number of our moral ' awarenesses ' which are even *de facto* infallible must be thought of as extremely limited also. In emphasising the revisability of intuitions in general (though, as is argued below, pp. 76, 90, we do not deny that every individual has *some* convictions, moral as well as intellectual, which are at all events temporarily and *de facto* infallible for him), we are therefore departing from traditional intuitionism on a crucial point ; but on a point as to which 19th century thought has made it clear that 18th century optimism requires a good deal of qualification.

stantiated by each new piece of evidence adduced. Others, again, we discover to depend upon more primary intuitions as corollaries or riders, and these we cease to think of as intuitions or things directly 'perceived,' and regard as conclusions indirectly or discursively 'inferred' as dependent upon more ultimate propositions.

Exactly the same process appears to go on in the matter of moral judgments. Sometimes a principle which we have accepted from childhood is amended or drastically re-stated —we no longer 'see it in the same light,' as we say. At other times an admitted claim upon us is found to be no more than an application of or deduction from a more general claim. We may, for instance, decide that truth and honesty are both particular forms or versions of the more general principle of justice, *Jus suum cuique*, 'to every man his due,' and call them now moral 'inferences.' Again we may discover that the recognition of a minor claim is the only way towards the fulfilment of a major one, as self-discipline in small matters is a necessary condition or means of retaining equanimity in great crises. In all these ways the process goes on. At each stage of life we find ourselves equipped with a certain number of primary intuitions as to the claims we ought to recognise, surrounded by a nebula of lesser ones derivative from them, or necessary to their attainment ; and while these intuitions must be for the moment final and absolute, it is always possible that new experience will throw further light upon them, and lead to their modification or enrichment.

The work may be well or badly done ; we may be right or wrong both in our intuitions and in our inferences ; but well or badly, rightly or wrongly, slowly or quickly, it goes on in the mind of every man who thinks about conduct at all. 'He must expect,' as Browning tells us, [1]

> 'He could not, what he knows now, know at first ;
> What he considers that he knows to-day,
> Come but to-morrow, he will find mis-known ;
> Getting increase of knowledge, since he learns
> Because he lives, which is to be a man
> Set to instruct himself by his past self :—

[1] *A Death in the Desert.*

First like the brutes obliged by facts to learn,
Next, as man may, obliged by his own mind,
Bent, habit, nature, knowledge, turned to law.
God's gift was that man shall conceive of truth
And yearn to gain it, catching at mistake
As midway help, till he reach fact indeed.'

Further, because, as we have already seen, it is the desire
of every reasonable man to subordinate his judgments more
and more to the smallest number of general principles, we
never lose the hope that some day we may be able to reduce
all our moral principles to forms of one all-embracing law.[1]
Hence Christians continually make the attempt to bring all
the teaching of the Church, and indeed all the teaching of
Christ Himself, under one general heading—such as that of
' the fatherhood of God,' ' the brotherhood of man,' or ' the
kingdom of heaven ' ; whilst whole systems of ethics have
grown up round such phrases as ' self-denial,' 'self-realisation,'
or ' the greatest possible happiness of the greatest possible
number.' [2] This attempt at an exhaustive correlation of
duties is commonly and rightly called ' Christian ethics ' ;
and it has a history of its own which goes back beyond
St. Ambrose's ' de Officiis,' the first great western textbook
of ethics, to St. Paul's various catalogues of virtues, and to
the Beatitudes themselves.

A frank and scientific revision of the Christian code of
ethics, in accordance—as far as may be—with the mind

[1] A question often discussed but which does not concern us here is,
Would the ultimate form of this intuition be ' This is right ' or ' This is
good (= worthy of attainment) ' ?

[2] That the ' greatest possible happiness of the greatest possible number '
is the only moral criterion is itself an intuition, as Mill (*Utilitarianism*, c. 3),
Sidgwick (*op. cit.* p. 415) and Rashdall (*op. cit.* i. pp. 48, 148), all
of them utilitarians of one shade of thought or another, agree. Where
utilitarians differ from intuitionists is in their insistence that no principle
can be accepted unless it can be shown, in general or in any particular case,
to be necessary to the greatest possible happiness. So Sidgwick (*op. cit.*
p. 80) says of utilitarianism that it ' demands that the connection between
right action and happiness should be ascertained by a process of reasoning,'
and adds that this demand ignores ' the limitations of human reason which
prevent it from apprehending adequately the connection between the true
principle and the right types of action '— whereas intuitionism commonly
recognises this.

of Christ, is a continual necessity for the Church. Each generation, as indeed each individual also, must decide whether the intuitions by which it has been accustomed to test character, motives and actions are the best and highest available, or whether better and higher intuitions can be discovered. Necessary at all times, this task is no less necessary to-day and under the particular circumstances of the Church of England; but for reasons given in the introduction it scarcely falls within the purpose of the present book. One thing only may be noted about the task. We may be wrong in thinking that any such complete co-ordination of moral laws as that suggested in the last paragraph is possible to any one human mind. Most men go through life with two or three ends in view— professional efficiency, the upkeep and education of a family, the pursuit of a hobby or recreation—which they would find it hard to correlate under a single formula; just as, if Mr. Shaw's picture in 'Androcles' is true to fact, primitive Christianity provided an umbrella under which widely different intuitions found shelter. But there is no reason to suppose that this effort to co-ordinate moral intuitions is anything but laudable. At least it is true that by setting principles in relation to one another, by defining their respective spheres and taking note of their resemblances and differences, we shall learn much more about them and handle them much more surely when we come to apply them to particular cases.

For that is the final work of conscience, to decide what principles from among those commonly accepted should be obeyed in particular cases or groups of circumstances; and similarly to decide what principles should be called into court to enable us to judge the rightness or wrongness of a particular action, and what weight should be attached to the testimony of each. Indeed, if we accept the well-known scholastic distinction between 'synderesis' and 'conscientia,'[1] it is the special work of conscience strictly so-called. Here again there have been moralists who held an unusual position. They have asserted that just as we reach some at least of our general principles by direct intuition (and to this we all

---

[1] *Infra*, Additional Note A: *Definitions of Conscience*, p. 379.

agree), so in every particular conjuncture of circumstances the moral man *sees* at once, without argument or hesitation, what is the right and what is the wrong thing to do.[1] This theory again breaks down, not only on fact but on analogy. On analogy, because though we see intuitively the first principles of geometry—as, for example, that two straight lines cannot, by definition, enclose a space—we do not see intuitively the truth of all the propositions which depend upon them. It has to be proved to us, for instance, that the three angles of a triangle are equal to two right angles. Still less are we able to see the answer to some of the geometrical problems set before us for solution ; that has to be reached by logical methods and the process of experiment and error.

If conscience also is, like geometry, a matter of reason, the same may very well be true there. And as a matter of fact, we find that it is true with conscience. The moral genius may indeed sometimes see the path of duty where it is invisible to others ; and often he will do so where trained philosophers or moral theologians are at fault. But even he knows times when circumstances are too strong for him. Duty lies somewhere in the thicket of possibilities before him ; but thought and prayer are necessary before he can discover it.[2] And he is the first to admit that he needs principles to guide him to discovery—not principles of conduct alone, but also rules of procedure—a knowledge of the rules (if any there are) by which the relevant laws of conduct can be discovered in particular cases and the irrelevant recognised as such and set aside ; as well as a knowledge of the truest definitions of justice, truth and the like, which will exclude invalid determinations of them, but include all valid ones.

It is here that we discover the need for casuistry, as it is called. Every thoughtful Christian is a casuist. Holding

---

[1] This doctrine is sometimes called ' unphilosophical ' or ' empirical,' intuitionism.

[2] As against Bishop Butler's pious conviction that ' almost any fair man in almost any circumstances ' will know what to do (*Sermons*, iii., viii.) we may quote Sir John Seeley's dictum : ' Good men do wrong perpetually because they have not the mental training and skill which may enable them to discern the right course in given circumstances. They misconceive the facts before them and miscalculate the effect of actions,' (*Ecce Homo*, c. ix). Cp. also Sidgwick, *Methods*, 94–97.

C

to his first principles of morality (or intuitions) he finds that often enough there is no question as to which of them he ought to obey in particular circumstances. But often enough also, he finds cases in which he certainly hesitates before deciding whether to act upon a given principle or no. Such cases constitute the problems of conscience ; and systematic casuistry consists in the attempt to classify the different types of problem that may arise, and to discover the right— that is to say the Christian, or truly moral—method of hand-ling each type. It is to this task that we specially propose to direct our attention ; and because our concern is with method, and with the needs of the immediate present, we can for the moment accept as valid the moral intuitions current among Christian people of to-day, without enquiring how far, in their contemporary statement, they fully accord with the ideal Christian standard. Whatever rules we can find for the application of principles to particular cases will hold good whether the principles so applied are the best possible or no, so long as they are the best that we have attained to hitherto. But before we start upon our main enquiry there remain one or two questions about conscience that cannot well be passed over

5. *Indifferent Acts*

We come first to an important problem about the voice of conscience to which moralists have devoted curiously little attention. The judgments of conscience which we have considered so far have all fallen into some such form as ' This is right,' ' That is wrong ' ; ' This is your duty,' ' That would be a sin ' ; ' You ought to do this,' ' You ought not to do that ' These judgments in so far as they regard future actions are in fact *preceptive* ; they enunciate a command. And as every judgment is an answer to an implied question, so here the question asked or answered is—' What ought I to do ? ' ' What is my duty ? ' ' Would this or that action be the right one in the circumstances ? ' But there is a whole class of questions and answers about conduct which appear to belong to the sphere of conscience, but do not express themselves in these forms. What is distinctive of them is that they discard the verb ' ought ' and employ the verbs ' may ' or ' can.' We ask ourselves, ' May I make this promise ? ' ' Can I repeat this joke in the present company ? ' and so forth ; and conscience appears to reply ' You may,' or ' You may not,' as the case may be. Its judgment, in short, if affirmative, is no longer *preceptive* but *permissive* ; it does not now command, but allows.

We say that these judgments appear to belong to the sphere of conscience—that is, that they are moral judgments. This is borne out by the fact that both question and answer imply a moral condition. They are concerned not with what is physically possible but with what is morally permissible. ' May I make this promise ? ' implies ' May I, *as a Christian*, make it ? ' ' Can I tell this story ? ' implies ' Can I *decently* or *honourably* tell it ? ' But still the question is of a different kind from those which prompted the moral judgments with which we began ; it is a question about what we *may* do, not about what we *ought* to do.

Where conscience replies to such a question in the negative —as, for example, ' You may not make the promise '—it at once imposes a duty. ' You may not make the promise ' and ' You ought not to make the promise ' mean one and the same thing. So that in a sense the question is still a question about duty—' May I do so-and-so ? ' implies ' Is it my duty to avoid doing it ? ' But much more is involved than that. If conscience replies in the affirmative it does not *impose* a duty—' You may make this promise ' is quite a different judgment from ' You ought to make this promise '—and yet it guides us to action. We may say, if we like, that in such judgments conscience is declaring our *right* or *liberty* to act in a particular way if we so wish ; but that only puts the problem in a different form. We are not bound to assert all our rights or to use all our liberties ; though if we have a strictly moral right or liberty no one can blame us for insisting upon it at such times as it does not infringe the claims of duty upon us.

Conscience, therefore, appears sometimes to point the way to classes of actions as to which it makes no moral difference whether we perform them or not. We shall not be doing wrong if we use the liberty which conscience gives; but neither shall we be doing wrong if we refrain from using it. Actions of this kind are often called ' harmless,' ' allowable,' ' legitimate ' or ' indifferent ' actions; and the problem at once arises, can anything be *merely allowable* or *altogether indifferent* for the moral man ? Is it not in itself sinful to assume that any deliberate action can be without moral meaning ? Must not every action which we contemplate be either right or wrong *sans phrase*; and are we not bound to ask one question and one question only—not ' Is this legitimate or allowable ? ' but ' Is it right ? '

St. Paul at least seems to contemplate a whole host of actions as to which it does not matter what the Christian chooses. Thus of circumcision he says, ' Circumcision is nothing and uncircumcision is nothing, but the keeping of the commandments of God ';[1] and though he has just enjoined, ' If any man be called in uncircumcision, let him not be circumcised,' the context implies (with a singular ignoring of the great controversy recorded in the Acts of the Apostles) that all he means here is ' There is no need to be circumcised.' Similarly to slaves : ' Wast thou called being a slave ; care not for it ;[2] but if thou canst become free, take advantage of it '—which appears to mean ' It isn't your *duty* to try to be free, though you won't be doing wrong if you hold yourself ready to embrace freedom when it comes.'[3] He does not actually say (on this rendering of the passage) ' There is no need to take the chance of freedom if it offers '; but the tenour of the chapter implies that freedom is at best an indifferent matter to the Christian—the chance of being free, whether he take it or not, will not affect his goodness in the sight of God. If, when the chance of freedom comes, he

---

[1] 1 Cor. vii. 19.

[2] I.e. ' do not fret about it ' (μή σοι μελέτω).

[3] The μᾶλλον χρῆσαι (A.V., R.V.,' use it rather '), translated above ' take advantage of it,' is sometimes interpreted to mean ' choose to remain a slave.' This is possible, both in view of the text and of some aspects of St. Paul's thought, and it is difficult to choose between the two renderings. For our purposes neither makes any difference ; the μᾶλλον makes it clear that no more than a *preference* is expressed between the two. One course may be better than the other, but it does not much matter which is chosen compared with the *duty* of keeping the commandments of God.

prefers to remain a slave, we may call him stupid, but cannot call him a sinner.

The problem becomes even more complex when it seems (as often it does) to involve that so long as a man is doing *well* he is not morally bound to do *better*. In the same chapter from which we have just quoted, St. Paul had to deal with the question of marriage among his converts; and for reasons which do not concern us he delivered himself of the judgment, ' He that marrieth doeth well, but he that marrieth not doeth better.' [1] Yet to those who took advantage of this permission he was able to say, ' There is no sin in it, let them marry.' Similarly of widows, ' If the husband be dead, the widow is free to marry whom she will, only in the Lord; nevertheless she is more blessed if she remain a widow, according to my judgment; and I think that I have the Spirit of God.' So again, ' to the unmarried and widows,' ' It is good for them to remain even as I am; but if they cannot exercise self-control, let them marry.' ' I speak this,' he says ' by permission; and not of commandment.' In other words, no one is morally bound to remain celibate.[2] Liberty of marriage is allowed to the Christian, though the higher life is the unmarried life. To follow up the history of this problem further would take us into a discussion of our Lord's address to the young man who had great possessions, with its distinction between the decalogue as the way of attaining *eternal life* and the complete renunciation of worldly possessions as the path to *perfection*;[3] and thence into the whole puzzling question of the ' double standard ' and the distinction between ' counsels ' and ' precepts,' which Christianity evolved for itself, but reinforced with the parallel Stoic doctrine drawn by Ambrose from Cicero, and by Cicero from Panaetius. Such an historical enquiry need not however detain us; it is concerned more with the problem of official relaxations of the law for Christians than with that of the searchings of conscience.

---

[1] 1 Cor. vii. 38 (see also *infra* p. 168).

[2] But the phrase may mean, ' I have no direct authority for saying this, but give it as a probable opinion.'

[3] This distinction, by which the whole doctrine of ' counsels ' and ' precepts ' was justified in the patristic period and the middle ages, is given only in the Matthean version of the incident, Mat. xix. 21.

We ought, however, to have gathered from the last two
paragraphs that there are as a matter of fact two very different
classes of action to which the names ' allowable ' or ' indifferent ' have been given.   The first are those which (reluctantly
perhaps) moralists have been compelled to call ' allowable,'
because they could not conscientiously regard them as universally forbidden ; the second those which (with equal reluct-
ance) they have not been able to call *more* than allowable,
because they could not conscientiously say that they were
universally enjoined or obligatory.   The first are actions of so
little moral significance—the choice of the material for a suit,
or of a recreation for an afternoon—that the moral genius will
have little interest in them ; the second, actions of so high and
heroic a significance that they can only become duties for
the elect few.   Our interest at present is entirely with
actions of the first class, for it is only in connection with them
that we ask questions of the ' May I ? ' type.   We do not say
' May I as a Christian become a clergyman, or sacrifice my
life for my country's need ? ' (these being allowable actions—
that is, actions not universally commanded—of the second
type) ; we say ' Is it my duty to be ordained, or to make this
sacrifice ? '   But on the other hand we do not say, ' Is it my
duty to wear clothes of this particular pattern of check ? '
or ' Is it my duty to go to the pictures this evening ? '—we say
' May I choose this pattern ? '   ' May I go to the pictures ? '
And the problem before us is simply to decide whether we
have the right to ask questions of this type, and to be satisfied
if conscience returns the answer, ' You may.'

Our natural tendency is to say that for the Christian who
is in earnest about his conduct there can be no question here.
To decide ' I may do so-and-so ' is, as we have seen, simply to
assert a private right or freedom.   But the assertion of a
private right or freedom (so long, that is to say, as it is in no
sense a test case, in which the rights and freedom of others
are equally involved) is surely no more than a form of selfishness ; and selfishness is in itself un-Christian.   And in the
same way, even to enquire as to one's rights and liberties is
selfish, and therefore to be condemned.   The question ' May
I do so-and-so ? ' implies that I *want* to do it, and that I want
to do it for some other reason than that I know it to be right

for me to do it ;[1] and can I ever, as a Christian, have any moral reason for wanting to do something except the reason that it is the right thing to do ?

Again, conscience revolts from the suggestion (which is certainly implied in speaking of ' indifferent ' actions) that there are matters of deliberate choice in which it need not determine the strict question of duty. In every conjuncture of circumstances, it suggests, one course of action must be the right one, and all others wrong ; of two alternatives one must surely be a duty and the other consequently a sin. If therefore a man does not, at every moment of deliberate choice, ask the question, ' What is the right thing for me to do here ? What ought I to do ? ' he is wilfully evading the judgment-seat of conscience ; and if his action is determined by any other decision except that of strict right and wrong, he is voluntarily running the risk of committing sin.

Thus a good case could be made out for the position : ' The Christian will never ask what he *may* do in certain circumstances, but always what he *ought* to do. He will never allow himself or advise others to do even what appears to be harmless, unless he sees clearly that duty points in that direction. He will cultivate the habit of looking for decisions of duty and for them alone, certain that whatsoever springs from anything less than such a decision is, if not a deliberate sin, at least a culpable evasion of the main issues of the moral life.' This would involve the conclusion that just as it is wrong for us to ask the question, ' May I do so-and-so ? ' so also it is wrong to be content with the answer, ' You may . . .'

Against such a position, eminently Christian though it appears to be, we should find ourselves on reflection obliged to urge certain points. It can at least be suggested that the frequency with which questions of the ' May I ? ' type are asked and answered by earnest-minded people is some evidence for their validity. Indeed it would be almost impossible to carry on life without them : the question which we are asking at the moment, for instance, is simply, ' May a Christian ask

---

[1] It might of course imply ' I want to do it, but will not do it unless it clearly appears to be my duty.' But this would be an unusual implication ; it is hard to see why the question in this case should take the ' May I . . . ? ' form, and not simply be ' Ought I to . . . ? '

questions of the " May I ? " type ? ' It is surely inconceivable that a form of speech so recognised and universal
should be wholly invalid in the moral sphere.

As a matter of history, at all events, the most eminent
and earnest of the world's moralists have found it necessary
to admit, in some form or another, the legitimacy of regarding
certain questions as practically indifferent. The Stoics at
first believed that all intercourse in society, all pursuit of
health, comfort and the like, were ' indifferent ' to the ' wise '
or truly moral man—' indifferent,' not indeed in the sense
in which we have been using the word, but as meaning
things which he would not regard if he had them, and not
miss or regret if he had them not, and which he certainly
ought never to pursue. Nothing to him was good or desirable
except the good will ; ' the wise man would not lift a finger
save at the dictates of conscience.' But such a gospel was
too high for the ordinary man ; and the later Stoics were
forced to admit therefore that ' goods ' of this kind were
' preferred,' or allowable to him—that he *might* interest
himself in them, in moderation, without actual sin.[1]

Centuries later St. Thomas, though strenuously defending
the position that—if everything were known, weighed and
considered—no action could be without moral significance,
asserted freely that without this full knowledge (which in
fact is unattainable to men) there must be a degree of ' indifference ' about very many things.[2] This represents the
main Catholic position ; Scotus was far more unguarded on
the whole question.[3] And at least two important bodies of
post-Reformation Protestants pleaded for the recognition
of *adiaphora*, or ' indifferent things '—the first, with a singular
broadmindedness, in relation to religious ceremonies ; the
second, as against the extreme Puritan, in defence of innocent
amusements and recreations.[4] Whatever be the truth in

---

[1] *Infra* p. 139.   [2] *S.T.* i. 2, q. 18, aa. 8, 9.   [3] *in Sent.* iii. q. 41.

[4] On the basis of the Augsburg and Leipzig Interims of 1548, Melancthon
and his friends allowed as ' indifferent ' the Latin Mass, lights, vestments,
confession, unction and episcopacy. Great opposition was aroused by the
theory, and the Formula of Concord (1576) attempted to heal the breach, but
not very successfully. Thus § 1 of Art. X ran :—' Ceremonies or ecclesiastical rites, such as in the Word of God are neither commanded nor forbidden,
are of themselves neither divine worship nor even any part of divine worship ' ;

theory, in practice it seems throughout history to have been necessary to speak of numbers of things as things which one may do or avoid as one likes, without any serious moral issue being involved in the choice.

Finally the theory that the true Christian ought never to assert or enquire about his rights leads to manifest absurdities. For it is his business to respect the rights of others ; and if these others be Christians too the last thing they could wish for would be to have their rights respected, for it is of the essence of Christianity, on this hypothesis, to waive one's rights as much as possible. So that the Christian ideal for society would appear to present a ludicrous picture of individuals all insisting upon respecting each other's rights, and at the same time protesting against having their own rights respected ; as though the inhabitants of the mythical island —so far from earning a precarious livelihood by taking in each other's washing—were to pass their time insisting on doing each other's washing, when no one wished to have any washing done at all.

6. ' I Ought ' and ' I May '

We cannot therefore dismiss the possibility of allowable or indifferent actions out of hand. There is much to be said against the complete condemnation of our ' May I . . . ? ' questions. If we press the enquiry, ' Is the Christian ever justified in asking, " May I do this or that ? " or must he

and § 5, ' One Church ought not to condemn another because it observes more or less external ceremonies which the Lord has not instituted, provided only there be consent between them in doctrine and all the articles thereof, and in the true use of the sacraments. For so runneth the old and true saying, " Dissimilarity of fasting does not destroy the similarity of faith." ' But § 4 limited this permission severely : ' In times of persecution when a clear and stedfast confession is required of us, we ought not to yield to the enemies of the Gospel in things indifferent ; for in such a state of things it is no longer a question of *adiaphora* but of the restoration and maintenance of the truth of the Gospel,' P. Schaff, *Creeds of the Evangelical Protestant Churches* (London, 1887), p. 161. The second controversy arose in the years 1681 and 1687, when a group of Puritan and pietist theologians denounced the opera, card-playing, dancing and even Sunday afternoon walks and children's games as sinful ; and were opposed on the grounds that these were things indifferent. See Hauck-Hertzog, *Realencyclopaedie*, i. 168 ff.

always phrase his moral questions in the form, "Ought I to do this, or ought I not ? " ' instances at once rise to the mind in which important moral judgments are elicited by these ' May I ? ' questions, and better elicited perhaps by them than in any other way.

(1) Something is gained, for example, at times by asking the question, ' May *a Christian* ever . . . ? ' or ' May *any* Christian do such-and-such a thing ? ' and this is often the true meaning of a ' May I ? ' question. If the answer ' No ' be given to such a question, we have at once the statement of a general principle of morality ; and the general principle is more naturally reached in answer to this form of question, and more compendiously expressed in this form of answer, than in any other. It is easier and more natural to say ' No teetotaller may ever drink port ' than to say ' It is the duty of every teetotaller to avoid drinking port '—but the latter sentence (which is the form upon which the strict moralist, who would have us express everything in terms of duty, would insist) tells us neither more nor less than the former. It does not follow from this that an affirmative answer in any sense closes the question, or pronounces the action allowed to be wholly indifferent. To say, for example, 'A teetotaller may drink cider ' (and still more to say, 'A teetotaller may *sometimes* drink cider '), does not give *every* teetotaller the right to drink cider, nor does it give *any* teetotaller the right to drink cider at all times or to excess. It merely states that as far as teetotalism in the abstract is concerned, cider-drinking has nothing to do with it ; it leaves open the question as to whether an individual teetotaller (who, of course, will have other issues to consider besides his teetotalism) is bound or not to abstain from cider at all times, or on this particular occasion. Yet even so the sentence ' A teetotaller may sometimes drink cider ' expresses the truth (if it be a truth) more succinctly than the form which a strict determination of duty would seem to demand—the form, namely, ' It is not the duty of every teetotaller, by virtue of his teetotalism, in all imaginable circumstances to abstain from drinking cider.'

(2) Again, there are times when a scrupulous person magnifies a trivial problem infinitely beyond its real import-

ance, and consequently is deflected by a pedantic legalism from obvious or urgent duties. A priest, for example, who neglected the pressing needs of his parish to wrestle with the problem whether it was his duty to give up reading the evening paper in Lent—who seriously impaired his health, amiability and efficiency by continual reconsideration of the question— would obviously be doing wrong. Conscience ought to say to him, ' It is your duty to stop considering whether your duty is to read the evening paper or no.' But this is a cumbrous form for the judgment to take ; the same result is achieved with far greater succinctness by saying ' Of course you may go on reading the paper.' Here the action in question is pronounced, not indeed indifferent in all cases, but indifferent in this case in relation to more important and urgent claims ; it is the use of the word ' may ' which enables conscience to deflect attention from the trivial to the important issue.

(3) The word ' may ' is therefore appropriate both for the eliciting of general negative principles and where what may be called cases of relative indifference are involved. One other point remains, and that the most important. Strictly speaking the problem of duty can only be settled by a complete consideration both of circumstances and of consequences, for we have already rejected the theory that conscience perceives every individual duty with the directness and immediacy of an intuition or sensation. And in many problems either lack of evidence or lack of time will prevent anything like such a complete enumeration. In such cases conscience could never get so far as saying ' Such-and-such a course is my duty.' It could at best say, ' It is not my duty to refrain from acting thus,' for conscience cannot declare an action to be a duty until it sees it clearly to be a duty.

But if we are justified only in doing such things as are our duty, this decision is not enough to justify us in acting. It only determines what does *not* appear to be our duty ; not what our duty is. The natural result of this would be to encourage us to remain inactive ; and yet unless conscience proclaimed inactivity to be a duty we should have no more right to remain inactive than to act. The truth is that either course may be right, and either wrong, and so far there is nothing to choose between them ; but on the theory that

conscience can only declare duties and that until it does so
we must not act, we are biassed towards inaction, which is no
more a duty than action, and may as a matter of fact be the
worse course of the two.   In refusing to answer our question,
in attempting to leave the matter open, conscience in fact
forecloses the issue in one direction, and so is untrue to itself.
The only phrase that can express the exact truth that all is
uncertain, and that therefore we shall be, if not actually
more to be praised, at all events no more to blame in acting
than in remaining inactive, is the phrase ' You may.'

A single problem of ordinary Christian morality will make
this clear.   We are constantly pestered for subscriptions to
' causes ' or ' movements ' which, though we regard them as
mildly beneficent, do not commend themselves to us as of such
importance that we should contribute to them liberally or
regularly.   What are we to do, then, when the Mrs. Jellybies
of this world besiege us at home or in the office ?   The strict
precisian would say, ' You must not give to this charity
unless you are certain that it is your duty to do so ' ; and
logically he ought to add (though this he might forget to do),
' Nor may you withhold a subscription unless you are conscientiously convinced that to give it would be wrong.'   The
former injunction would definitely deter us from giving ; the
two together would leave things exactly as they were.   But
the normal Christian says to himself, ' The cause is estimable,
the canvasser persistent, and I can spare a trifle.   It isn't
my duty to give, and I have a perfect right to refuse.   But
it will please the lady and relieve me of her presence if I
put my name down for half-a-crown ; it may even do a little
good as well.   Conscience tells me I *may* do it, so that settles
it.'   It is surely wrong-headed to stigmatise this decision as
a flagrant evasion of duty ; yet that it would be, on the theory
that we must always determine duty strictly before acting.

A similar absurdity would result from pressing the theory,
in cases where, for example, it is obviously a duty to give
something to a charity.   Conscience will very rarely be able
to say *exactly how much* ought to be given in any particular
case.   Consideration of the importance of the appeal might
elicit the judgment, ' It is your duty to give not less than five
pounds ' ; calculation of means and prior claims might add,

' It is your duty not to give more than ten pounds.' But months of reflection would still leave us unable to decide whether duty demanded a donation of five guineas, or six guineas, or of seven pounds ten. Nevertheless on our theory we must not fix our subscription at any one of these figures unless we are certain that that amount, and that alone, is the one which we *ought* to give, whilst any of the others would be either more or less than duty, and therefore wrong. Here, therefore, the theory would actually operate in favour of giving nothing, even while conscience proclaimed that we ought to give something between five and ten pounds. We must surely be allowed to say, ' Don't worry about the exact sum. You know you may give anything between these figures; make it seven pounds ten, and write a cheque at once.'

A ' may ' judgment, therefore, such as ' You may make it seven pounds,' seems in certain cases to be not only the simplest but also the only form of judgment which will enable the moral man to do what is obviously the best thing in the circumstances with a clear conscience. Such a judgment, in the case we have just considered, would pronounce the exact determination of the amount to be subscribed to be indifferent in three ways: indifferent in the abstract, as relative to the regulation of expenditure in general, indifferent as relative to the more important duty of giving something at once, and indifferent relative to all the known conditions and circumstances. On the lines of the question ' How much ought I to give ? ' or ' Ought I to give seven pounds ? ' no clear answer might be reached at all. But on the lines of the question ' May I give seven pounds ? ' (with its implication that on this occasion further determination of the exact amount to be given is unnecessary) a practical and immediate answer can be obtained.

We need not deny that in every case, if all the facts were known, one course of action would stand out as the morally right one, and every other as morally wrong. This is to say that there is no such thing as an absolutely indifferent action. But in the imperfect state of human knowledge and foreknowledge many actions must be judged as relatively indifferent. Conscience must at times be allowed to say,

' This is legitimate or permissible ' ; and the individual must
be allowed to take advantage of these permissions. It does
not follow that when he has received such a permission he
can cease to enquire as to his duty. Indeed to do so would
be at once to abuse the permission, and some of the worst
depravities of moral theology may be traced to this cause.
But it *does* follow that he may with a clear conscience avail
himself of the permission until he has ascertained his strict
duty. We need not shrink therefore from recognising permissions as valid judgments of conscience ; or from giving
our opinions in the form ' You *may* do so-and-so.'

Problems of conscience usually present themselves in this
form of ' May I do so-and-so ? ' and are answered ' You may,'
or ' You may not.' Brevity, simplicity and expediency all
uphold the usage. But its exact meaning must always be
kept in mind, and often expressed. ' I may ' does not imply
' I must.' Nor does it answer any question except the exact
question asked ; nor exempt the enquirer from the attempt
ultimately to arrive at a strict determination of duty. Nor,
finally, is it valid except so long as no ' may not ' is uttered.
If we say to an enquirer, ' You may go to the theatre in Lent,'
we do not mean that he *must* go to the theatre ; nor that
he may go on any particular evening or on every evening
in Lent ; nor that he is exempt from enquiring on any
particular occasion whether duty forbids his going that night.
Within these limits, but only within these limits, the answer
' You may ' is valid. It implies that *sometimes* it will not be
a man's duty to avoid a particular course of action, and that
sometimes therefore it may be his duty to embrace it ; that
he must look further to decide when it is his duty to avoid
and when to embrace it ; but that if he cannot come to such
a decision after conscientious enquiry for want either of
time, or of evidence, or of intelligence, no one can blame
him if he uses the permission thus given.

At the same time one general caution requires emphasis.
Permissions must not be sought for where duties are deter-
minable, or until duty, either through lack of time or of
knowledge, is obviously beyond ascertainment. To get into
the habit of asking ' What may I do ? ' rather than ' What
ought I to do ? ' is fatal to the moral life. For this conclusion,

as for others we have reached on this point, we may quote
the eminently wise words of Whewell, who was fully alive to
the problem here involved.[1] ' To enquire,' he writes, ' whether
under special circumstances, violation of moral rules be not
allowable '—or, we may add, habitually to throw one's
moral enquiries into the form ' May I do so-and-so ? '—' is to
show that our thoughts are seeking not the way to conform
to the rule, but the way to evade it.' In other words,
habitual enquiries of this kind suggest that our minds are
set towards the exploitation of our liberties rather than to
the discovery and discharge of our duties. ' To make a
class of *allowable things,*' Whewell goes on, meaning of course
a class of things *allowable or indifferent in all circumstances
and at all times,* ' would be to sanction and confirm this
disposition. We should place an insurmountable impediment
in the way of the moral culture of men if we taught them to
classify actions as good, bad and allowable. For they might
be led to fill their lives with allowable actions, to the neglect

---

[1] Whewell indeed (*loc. cit.*) distinguishes ' allowable ' actions from
' indifferent ' actions ; and the distinction does not run on the same lines
with the difference between the two kinds of ' indifferent ' action which we
noticed on a preceding page. In the former category he places only such
actions as, though generally wrong, might on occasion of extreme necessity
be permitted—' though the general maxims of morality will not authorise
us to pronounce them right, our regard for the condition of human nature
will not permit us (in certain urgent cases) to pronounce them wrong.'
Distinct from these are ' indifferent things '—' those which are neither
good or bad, where a person may take one course or the other without
blame, as for instance, to choose law or medicine for his profession, to spend
more or less upon his dress or table within the limits which his fortune
prescribes, to eat more or less, to study more or less, or to study one branch
of literature or another.' But he at once goes on to show that the difference
is one of degree and not of kind, and that his ' indifferent actions ' are
never wholly or universally indifferent, but only indifferent in relation to
circumstance and the limitations of knowledge. ' Scarcely anything can
be said to be indifferent, when considered with reference to the effect which
it may produce upon our lives . . . for this reason the moralist does not
readily class any action as indifferent.' Thus both ' allowable ' and ' indifferent ' actions are actions which may *sometimes* be permissible, but are
never permissible *at all times* ; the only difference between Whewell's two
classes is that in the former are contained actions which will only rarely be
permissible (as ' to tell a lie ' which may be permitted ' to save one's own
life, or the life of a friend in the like case ' but not otherwise) ; in the latter
those which are commonly, or in most ordinary circumstances, permissible
Both classes, therefore, come under our category of ' indifferent ' actions.

of those which are good ; and it is evident that to do this would be to remove all moral progress and all moral aim.' [1]

Whenever, therefore, we find ourselves faced with questions of the ' May I . . ? ' type, it should be our first endeavour to discover whether, in the particular circumstances of the case, the question ' Ought I . . ? ' could be put with any hope of getting an answer. Only if there is no hope of getting an answer to this second question—the question of duty—within the limits prescribed for us by the time and evidence at our disposal and the pressure of other duties, have we the right to ask the first question—the question of freedom. Where, however, the question of duty appears unanswerable, no objection can be raised to the question of freedom — indeed it becomes a necessary question to put in order that a man may act with a clear conscience. But even when he has ascertained that he *may* do such-and-such a thing, either in general or on a particular occasion, he must still be on the alert for calls of duty which may arise to limit his freedom ; for the freedom conscience has given him is conditional only upon the absence of such calls. It is within these limits, but only within these limits, that in the following chapters we shall allow ourselves to follow the general practice of moral theologians and ask and answer questions of the ' May I ? ' type.

7. *Personification of Conscience*

We have now expanded the judgments of conscience to include permissions as well as precepts—judgments including the verb ' may ' as well as judgments including the verb ' ought.' In so doing we have completed our survey of the types of judgment of which conscience delivers itself. And yet we have to ask whether the whole vocabulary which we have employed is not misleading. In speaking of conscience as ' judging,' ' condemning,' ' answering,' ' permitting ' and so forth we have in fact *personified* or *allegorised* conscience, as though it were an invisible monitor at our elbow, prompting us to what is right and warning us against what is wrong. Language of this kind is common enough ; Lancelot Gobbo

---

[1] *Elements of Morality* [2] (1848), pp. 200 ff.

imagines a discussion between conscience and the 'fiend,' with himself almost in the position of an impartial and disinterested arbiter between them ; the King in 'Henry VIII' speaks of conscience as intervening, with embarrassing results, in the development of his plans and policy. And the frequency with which conscience is called the 'voice of God in the soul'[1] seems to justify this mode of expression. At the same time there is a danger in this personification of conscience which it is at all events wise to recognise.

Conscience is not the only one of our activities, emotions or motives which we treat in this way. Honour, prudence, pleasure, ambition and the like are all personified or allegorised in ordinary speech ; they can all of them 'dictate to,' 'dominate' or 'inspire' us. But in general we are most prone to personify these factors in our conduct when we feel that we are, or wish—if even in a slight degree only—that we might be, dissociated from their influence. The usage hints in each particular case that we do not wholly acquiesce in their 'dictates,' or that we are weighing their 'requirements' against others in the scale. To say that prudence, for example, prescribes a particular course of action, implies that, if we could rid ourselves of the need for prudential action, we should show ourselves fellows of a very different stamp. A man who is normally punctual does not personify his punctuality ; it is only the man who habitually disregards the hour of his appointments who says, 'On this occasion I have recognised the claims of punctuality.' We do not personify our normal desire for food at regular intervals, though we are (in fact) hungry at such intervals ; but at times of famine we speak freely of 'Hunger stalking through the land.'

Thus to personify a passion, emotion or activity is at once to represent it as something abnormal, external, apart from oneself. For this reason we find that moral men do not often personify their own virtues. The moral man does not usually wish to represent his virtue either as abnormal or as something outside himself. He would not call himself the 'victim of loyalty' ; nor would he speak of the 'promptings

[1] So, e.g., Bonaventura, *in Sent.* ii. d. 39, a. 1, q. 3, ad 3 : 'Conscientia est sicut praeco Dei et nuntius ; et quod dicit non mandat ex se, sed mandat quasi ex Deo, sicut praeco cum divulgat edictum regis.'

of honesty' except at such moments as he were seriously tempted to dishonesty—at moments, that is to say, at which his virtuous impulses were only partially identified with himself. ' Love ' perhaps is an exception to this rule ; but even so the exception supports the rule, for it is when and because love comes to a man or woman with all the impetus of an unexpected and irresistible force from outside that we personify it freely, and speak of the power, or the demands, or the sovereignty of love. Only when a virtuous person makes the pursuit of virtue a vice—when in a fanatical effort after self-sacrifice, self-mortification, candour or the like he subordinates and ignores all other motives of good action —do we personify his so-called virtue, and call him ' a martyr to self-sacrifice ' or ' a slave to candour.'

Weak and vicious persons on the other hand—or indeed all persons in their weak and vicious moments—habitually personify their temptations and defects ; and for the same reason. They retain their self-respect in their own eyes, and hope to extenuate their failures in the eyes of others, by representing their lapse as caused by forces extraneous to themselves, whose occasional onset is too sudden to be anticipated, and too severe to be resisted. The tendency is wholly unconscious, no doubt ; nevertheless we need not hesitate to recognise it as the root cause of such common expressions as ' I gave way to evil thoughts,' ' I allowed my temper to get the better of me,' ' I could not resist the temptation,' ' Passion overcame me.' The truth is, in each case, that *the man himself* thought the evil thoughts, or shewed temper, or sinned after temptation, or expressed himself passionately ; and it would have been at once more honest and more hopeful for the future to have faced the truth in this form. But the common trick of personification allows a veil of reticence and self-respect, however thread-bare, to be thrown over the ugly facts ; and there are few of us who do not continually avail ourselves of this method of dissembling our sins, or dissociating ourselves from them, by personification.

It would be tempting to consider how far this artifice of dissociation by personification, deplorable and discreditable though it is in its real nature, has yet played a useful purpose in enriching the vocabulary of psychology, and thereby in enabling the scientific understanding of character to express the niceties and refinements of its discoveries.   The Old Testament writers had a clear apprehension of psychological facts, but they had few terms in which to express them ; and they were forced to assign psychological functions, *faute de mieux*, to physical organs.   It was the man's lips which uttered big swelling words, his feet that were swift to shed blood, his hand—his ' high hand '—that sinned, his reins that mourned, his liver that loved, his heart that thought.   But it is hard to personify these physical organs with any real verisimilitude.   The heart is too regular in its operations, the liver too obviously material, to be the natural subjects of high ideals or overpowering emotions. A man's feet may betray him on a loose stone, but they can hardly *lead* him astray even in the literal, and still less in the metaphorical, sense.   If we are to personify at all, we must have subjects capable of personification ; and if the natural tendency to self-exculpation finds a way of dissociating itself from guilt by fictitious personification of this character, this fact may well have had considerable influence in making men dissatisfied with the theory of physical centres for psychical phenomena.   The popularity of modern psychological developments, with their unprecedented enrichment of the scientific vocabulary, may not unreasonably be traced in part at least to the same cause.   There is a certain refuge for the recurrent sinner in discovering a whole new galaxy of complexes, inhibitions and the like, on which, as upon independent or semi-independent entities, he may throw the responsibility for his sins.

At all events, we may conclude that whenever a person habitually personifies a psychological function, he is more than likely to be expressing a felt or desired dissociation of himself from it.   The man who continually appeals to ' duty ' or ' honour ' or ' conscience ' is a man whom somehow we inevitably regard as a hypocrite.   A robust ' I can't do such a thing,' in reply to a dishonourable proposal, is unexceptionable ; but ' Honesty forbids it ' suggests at once that the speaker is sorry that honesty forbids it ; or is cloaking some discreditable reason for refusal, which he wishes to dissociate

from his own apparent motives, under the name of ' honesty.'
So when young Gobbo appeals to ' conscience,' we are clear
that he is sorry conscience should have intervened at all ;
and when King Henry expounds how his ' conscience first
received a tenderness,' we know that his real motive was
self-interest, but that—to conceal this fact by a double
artifice—he has both personified the motive and given it a
more estimable name.

Sir William Gilbert, whose Savoy Operas and ' Bab
Ballads ' did more to expose the shifts of hypocrisy disguised
as conscientiousness than any satire since the ' Provincial
Letters,' is continually illustrating this fact. Captain Reece,
the worthy commander of the ' Mantelpiece,' disguises ami-
able inefficiency and a chaotic régime under the motto,
' It is my duty and I will.' The man-of-war's man is guilty
of outspoken treachery to his foster-brother at the bidding
of ' this heart of mine ' ; and the bad baronet seconds his
efforts with the plea (tunefully voiced in duet) that ' Duty,
duty must be done.' The pirate's apprentice submits to
force majeure at the same irresistible and convenient call of
duty. ' Etiquette,' ' family pride,' ' early English art '
are all prostituted by personification to cover the hypocritical
ends of the individual—even ' compulsion ' throws a convenient cloak round the peccadilloes of the wayward curate.[1]

The upshot of these apparently irrelevant considerations
is that it is dangerous even for the upright man to think
or speak too much of conscience as an independent agent
' commanding,' ' forbidding,' ' condemning,' ' acquitting,'
' allowing.' Conscience is not something alien and external
to myself ; and the more I think of it as such the more I
am apt to regard it as a tyrant whose rulings I must by hook
or by crook evade. Conscience is just *myself* ; not indeed
my whole self—for (as I know only too well) I am not a
unified personality, but a complex of contesting and only
half-harmonised interests—but my best self, or my higher
self, or my true self, or whatever other name I can employ

---

[1] ' For years I've longed for some
     Excuse for this revulsion,
   Now that excuse has come :
     I do it on compulsion.'—*The Rival Curates.*

to express the required meaning. To make conscience an *other* than myself is to identify myself with those lower motives against which my higher self is in arms ; or at best to treat myself as the resultant and plaything of forces—conscience included—over which I have no control. The danger may not be a great one, but it is there. The exigencies of language force us often enough to speak of conscience as a distinct entity ; but we must continually remind ourselves that it is no such thing. When conscience speaks, it is my own best self that speaks ; when conscience blames, it is I who am feeling justifiable remorse. Conscience is myself in so far as I am a moral man ; and the problems of conscience are simply the problems which the moral man has to solve in a moral way—using the reason which God has given him to discover the path of duty through the obscurities which conceal it from view.

CHAPTER II

LOYALTY

1. *Conscience and the Community*

THE preceding chapter should have made it clear that when we speak of conscience as the mind of man passing moral judgments, we imply that each man has on certain terms—on what terms we must ask later—the right, the capacity and the duty of framing moral judgments for himself. They need not be any the less the voice of God to man on that account. Reason was given to man by God ; and if reason is properly used it will discover the truth of God, as in matters of knowledge, so also in matters of conduct. As to the validity of this doctrine of the supreme authority of conscience there can be little question. We shall see at a later stage how universally it has been endorsed in Christendom ; all we need notice here is its obvious truth. Every man is born into a community, or rather a complex of communities, from which he receives a full code of rules of behaviour. As he arrives at maturity he decides, by default if not by active thought, whether he will remain a member of these various bodies or not. He cannot indeed throw off his membership of the human race ; he may not (so at least we should most of us agree) relinquish his responsibilities to the family into which he was born ; and there will be many national and social characteristics innate or inbred in him, which he could not disown even if he tried. But within these limits we hold him free to consider his allegiances. He is not bound by the accident of birth to remain a British subject, nor by the accident of parental choice a member of the Church of England. The more he owes to Britain or the English Church, the more seriously must he consider their claims upon him. But if after adequate and serious consideration he decides to change his loyalty, and with it, in some degree or another, his code of behaviour, we may think him mistaken or unwise, and may grieve at his defection, but we refuse to condemn him as immoral, unless, indeed, his new allegiance expresses itself in deliberate hostility towards his former compatriots or fellow-churchmen.   And this refusal to condemn is simply an admission of the supremacy of conscience in all human affairs.

It would not be quite true to say that this recognition of the right, capacity and duty of the individual to pass moral judgments for himself—this recognition, in other words, of the fact of conscience—is a wholly Christian thing.   There are traces of it in pre-Christian society, particularly among the later Stoics, from whom the very word 'conscience' itself came into Christian use.   Nevertheless, it is true to say that before Christ the world had little recognition either of the scope or the claim of the individual conscience.   We may see that from an interesting comparison.   One of the greatest types of problem which we are to consider is the conflict between an individual conscience and the expressed will of society—either secular or religious society.   The ancient world was not ignorant of that problem ; and three at least of the greatest masterpieces of its literature are devoted to it—the 'Prometheus' of Æschylus, the 'Antigone' of Sophocles and the 'Apology' of Plato.   But in order to make it appear to the reader or audience that there was any problem at all—that there could be any question of the individual disobeying the law that had been laid down as the will of society—the Greek writer was in each case obliged to present the offender in the most sympathetic, and his or her adversaries in the most unsympathetic, light possible. It was only by emphasising the manifest injustice or cruelty of the judge, and the manifest innocence of the rebel, that the author could for a moment sustain the thesis that rebellion might in some cases after all be right.   For the ancient world as a whole, the law of the community was the conscience of the individual ; he could allege or appeal to no other.

Contrast with these classical examples the treatment of the same problem in Mr. Shaw's 'St. Joan.' Here, if anything, what has to be brought home to a modern audience is the possibility that society may have rights after all against the individual conscience.   In preface and play alike, therefore, Mr. Shaw labours to show every justification which could possibly be urged for the attitude of the ecclesiastical authorities towards the Maid. So greatly has the problem changed in the Christian centuries. In the ancient world the burden of proof lay with those who would assert the claims of conscience against the community ; to-day, notwithstanding the growing tendency of the State to interfere with the lives and habits of its members, it rests upon those who would support the claim of the community against conscience.

We may notice, further, that it is by no ordinary evolution that Christianity has thus come to recognise the rights of conscience. Every influence that has borne upon the Church up to the last two centuries has been in the direction of forcing her to reproduce the dominant note of antiquity— the supremacy of society against the individual. She took over from the Jews a belief in her authority, as the redeemed Israel, to assert unhesitatingly the revealed law of God. She vied with the Greek in her respect for the ' natural law ' manifest (as was believed) in the consensus of civilised moral codes. The pressure of heresy within and persecution without in the early centuries ; the disruption of Roman civilisation by the barbarian invasions ; the struggle of Catholicism first of all against the Empire and then against the national States of the Renaissance ; the dream of national Churches which dazzled post-Reformation Europe—all these were tendencies forcing each religious body concerned, whether Papal or Reformed, to frown severely upon any liberty of conscience that might in the slightest degree foster individualism, indiscipline or disruption. Yet in spite of this, Christianity not merely introduced but maintained throughout as her crowning moral doctrine, the principle, *Conscientia semper sequenda*—' Conscience must always be obeyed '; thereby increasing, as Sir John Seeley says,[1] the ' law-making powers of the individual Christian for himself.' We tend to think of this as the special gift of Protestantism to the world, and perhaps it has been more realised in Protestant than in Catholic lands But it may fairly be asserted, on the one

---

[1] *Ecce Homo*, c. xiii.

hand, that the Reformers had no intention of weakening the claim of organised religion upon individual conformity; and on the other, that even the most autocratic of the popes, Innocent III,[1] asserted with fullest emphasis this primary Christian doctrine. Catholicism has not been the enemy, nor Protestantism the friend *par excellence*, of liberty of conscience. The doctrine is the proud possession of Christendom in all its branches—one of the unique gifts of Christ to the world.

Is it true, then, that antiquity was wholly wrong, and that the community (and let us confine ourselves entirely to the Church, the religious society, to which a man belongs) has no claim upon the individual? Of course it is not true. A scheme of ethics which allowed each man to shape his own course irrespective of the will and teaching and requirements of society would be utterly untrue to the spirit of a religion which thinks of us primarily as members of a body, and that body the Body of Christ. Many arguments combine to show that the Christian cannot ignore the voice of society, but must recognise its claim.

First of all, as Professor Hobhouse has somewhere pointed out, the individual conscience is limited in natural range, whilst the duties which press upon the moral man—the things he ought to be concerned with—are wide as the universe itself. It is society, and society alone, which introduces most of us to the fact that we have duties not merely within the limited scope of our profession, recreations, family and local environment, but also as members of a highly industrialised commercial community in which complex questions of right or wrong have to be decided by the votes of individuals; of an Empire throbbing with inter-racial problems of every kind; and of a Church called to the task of world-wide evangelism. Apart from the voice of society, few of us would hear the call of interests such as these, and yet we all agree that no true citizen or Christian can confine his moral code within any narrower bounds. He has to adjust in his own mind the legitimate claims of society with the legitimate claims of self; the claims of Empire with the claims of the

---

[1] *Infra* p. 227.

village ; the claims of foreign missions with the claims of the parish church. Left to his own untutored conscience he might never hear the distant and wider claims through the din of the nearer and narrower ones ; it is the voice of society that redresses the balance.

Or again, we must remember that the individual conscience is never pure. In theological language, it has been vitiated by original sin. The New Testament speaks of men whose consciences are seared, perverted or defiled. There can be a beam in our own eyes even when we perceive motes in the eyes of others ; and if the eye be evil, how dark is the darkness of the soul ! In the vocabulary of ethics this means that the individual may be mistaken either in his original intuitions, or in his deductions therefrom, or in his estimate of the means necessary to their fulfilment. This possibility is sufficiently established by the obvious facts. If we hold (as surely we must hold) that moral truth is ultimately one and the same for all, and also consistent with itself throughout, it is clear that where two serious-minded men disagree in their moral judgments, or one and the same man recognises as binding two principles which point towards contradictory courses of action in the same case, there must be error somewhere. ' Reason does not contradict itself.' [1] In such cases the voice of society, though not necessarily the only nor the final court of appeal, may be able to point the way to the source of the mistake.

It does not follow of course that where conscience and the judgment of the community come into conflict, the former must always be wrong and the latter right. Athanasius stood against the world, and against a worldly Church for part of the time at least, but history has approved his stand. But it does follow that where conscience and society conflict, conscience need not always be right. Any other conclusion would, in George Meredith's arresting phrase, ' make a cox-comb of conscience.' Even in secular society respectful attention is paid to the considered judgments of the majority ; in a society claiming the assistance of the Holy Spirit, the utterances or decisions of legitimate authority must be allowed

---

[1] H. Rashdall, *Ethics*, p. 57.

full weight against the variations of the individual member. History is too full of iniquities and follies committed in the name of conscience—even those who slew the apostles 'thought to please God thereby,'—to encourage any man light-heartedly to set himself up as an infallible authority and judge of his own conduct. This is a question to which we shall return ; at the moment we may at least conclude that no man can safely oppose his own conscience to the considered judgment of the religious body to which he belongs, except after long and anxious weighing of all the issues involved. So much is obvious on grounds of common-sense alone ; but where membership has been acquired or confirmed by an act of free choice on the part of the individual, not prudence alone, but loyalty as well, dictates the course in question.

2. *Loyalty*

The problem, however, might be put in the following form : ' No doubt a man should weigh all that can be said for a principle of conduct set before him by the authority of society ; and if his own conscience endorses it, should adopt it. This however is merely to say that the mind operates in moral judgments as in other judgments, weighing up whatever is put before it from every source. But just as in other matters we are not required to accept a judgment on authority until our own reason endorses it (though it may be prudent to do so), so also we are surely not required to conform to a principle of conduct set before us by the Church, however authoritatively, until conscience has made it her own ? The authority of the society, therefore, has nothing to do with us. It matters not from what source we hear of a moral principle— from society or from an individual, from an authoritative or from an irresponsible proclamation—until conscience endorses it, it has no claim to our conformity.'

This is a specious argument often put forward at the present day. There is a truth behind it (of which more in a later chapter), the truth namely that where conscience finally and irrevocably rejects as sinful an action suggested to it even by the whole weight of authority, not even that authority can make it the individual's duty in the circumstances to conform. But that is not the point at issue. The question is rather : ' Is it my duty to obey the command of the Church in cases where, though I do not regard that command as sinful, it certainly awakens no responsive echo in conscience ? If I see no value, no reason, no moral obligation upon myself, in (let us say) the precept of communion thrice in the year, am I not free to disregard it, although it has the definite authority of the Church to which I belong ? '

There is a simple answer to this question. A man need not be a Christian to recognise the virtue of loyalty ; and loyalty means nothing whatever unless at the very least it means conforming to the expressed will of society in matters which seem distasteful, harassing, inconvenient or unreasonable to the individual. The implication for a churchman is clear, and could be attested by many citations. Thus Dr. Bevan says [1] :—' In the field of spiritual values a man may reasonably respect the authority of a community on a particular point, even where his own judgment does not confirm it, so long as his judgment does confirm on a large number of other points the judgment of that community.' Similarly Baron von Hügel [2] :—' There can be no Church for us upon earth if we will not put up with faulty Church officials and faulty Church members ' (together, we may add, with their faulty injunctions and enactments) ; ' and we shall never put up with such faultiness unless we possess or acquire so strong a sense of Church membership as to counterbalance the repulsiveness of such faults.' ' It is easy,' writes the present Bishop of Southwark,[3] ' to obey a bishop when you agree with him ; it is not so easy when you believe he is narrow, rigid or mistaken in his views ; but the true test of loyalty is to be found when the individual priest ' (Dr. Garbett was primarily speaking of priests ; but the statement applies to every member of the Church in his respective degree) ' in

[1] E. Bevan, *Hellenism and Christianity*, p. 245.
[2] F. von Hügel, *Essays and Addresses on the Philosophy of Religion*, 1st series, p. 267.
[3] C. Garbett, *Authority and Obedience, and Reservation* (addresses delivered at the Southwark Diocesan Synod, May 12th and 13th, 1925 ; London, 1925), p. 21. Section 5 of this chapter is an attempt to consider some of the important questions raised in this pamphlet.

the spirit of obedience submits against his own inclination or judgment.'

Not, we must observe, ' against his own conscience,' for that the individual may not conform to society if conformity clearly to his mind involves a sin, we have already seen. But where no sin is involved, but only inconvenience or discomfort of greater or less degree, conformity will often be a duty demanded by loyalty. In what cases, if any, apart from that of conscientious objection, it cannot be called definitely a duty, is a matter that must occupy our attention later; for the moment it is enough to notice that the failure of conscience to endorse a principle or precept asserted by society does not in itself exempt us from loyal obedience to that principle or precept.

We must dwell a little longer on this point, however; for it is not one which commends itself at first sight to the modern mind. The Church, it will be said, is an institution which exists to edify, to lead and to teach. As such it has kinship with numerous other societies, with the theatre, for example, with the medical profession, with the staff of a school or college. If I avail myself of the services of any of these institutions, societies or individuals, I have of course certain duties towards them. I am bound to pay for the services they render me. I am bound to treat them with ordinary courtesy and decency. But I have no obligation of loyalty towards them. I may be a fool if I refuse to take the doctor's advice, or allow myself to be bored with the play, or frankly disbelieve what the lecturer tells me; but I am in no way morally bound to do otherwise. I pay my money, and I take my choice as to the use I make of what I pay for. Loyalty does not require me to be either enthusiastic about, or amenable to, these purveyors of edification, instruction or advice. So far as they are concerned, I may act upon that ' complete, disintegrating and shattering philosophy of life' which a modern novelist [1] has embodied in an utterance of her heroine :—' It's such rot doing things we don't like because some one else does them,' or wants us to do them.

It is to be suspected that a great many Christians adopt an attitude very similar to this towards the teaching and

[1] Rose Macaulay, *Crewe Train*, p. 193.

edifying ministry of the Church ; and it is an attitude which is the very denial of that virtue of loyalty which we have just asserted to be an obligation of the Christian as a member of the Church. People listen to what the clergy have to say from the pulpit ; they even assist with some degree of enthusiasm in public worship; but all this is done with an infinity of mental reservations. They hold themselves free to adopt an attitude of aloofness on any point which does not appeal to them, or to disregard any principle of Christian life which strikes them as vexatious and harassing.

It is unnecessary to speak of the lukewarmness and in-efficiency with which this attitude infects the Church, and which is responsible in part at least for the comparatively weak voice which it has to-day in the moulding of public opinion. It is more to the point to enquire whether or no the attitude is justified—whether the analogy with the theatre, the consulting-room and the lecture-hall is a fair one. And at once we notice that while merely casual visits to the doctor or the lecture-hall do not appear to carry with them any obligation of loyalty, the case is entirely changed if we enrol ourselves officially or semi-officially as a patient of the former or a pupil of the latter. To be known as Dr. Jones' patient, but at the same time to be known as a patient who thinks so little of his ministrations as to ignore them at will, is to throw the gravest possible doubt upon his professional capacity. The only honest course is either to obey his instructions or to transfer to another doctor. To attend a course of lectures and at the same time to show oneself wholly inattentive is not merely discourteous; it is also morally inconsistent. Either attendance is a thing worth doing, in which case it should be done *ex animo* ; or it is not worth doing, in which case the sooner it is abandoned the better. The very analogy which seemed to justify Christians sitting loose to the obligations of Church membership fails at the critical point. If they repre-sented themselves as ' enquirers,' or 'interested' or 'occasional' adherents alone, they would retain the right to complete free-dom ; but if they represent themselves, or allow themselves to be known as 'members' or 'regular members' of a body, and claim the privileges of membership, the claims of loyalty at once come into play.

It is not surprising, therefore, that every type of individual or group which in any way attempts to serve the public— even though its services be of the most unessential kind— attempts to form a *clientèle* to which it can give the semblance of a community with common interests or aims. Your doctor, in the friendliest possible way, and with no ulterior motive, is doing just this when he speaks to you confidentially about ' another of my patients.' The newspaper which refers to ' our readers,' the emporium which appeals to its ' kind patrons,' the lecturer who reminds you of ' what we were considering in our last lecture,' are all subconsciously appealing to the instinct of loyalty to a society or body, however fictitious the body actually may be. No tendency is more universal than this one. It points to the inevitable conclusion that every institution, whatever its aims may be, will fail to some degree of its purpose unless it can induce those who have recourse to it to regard themselves in the light of a select and privileged body ; and a body whose members, because privileged, can therefore be appealed to—if only in the most indirect way and to the smallest possible extent—to curb their individual preferences, impatiences, likes and dislikes, in the interest of the corporate life of the community. We may laugh at the tendency when it shows itself in the announcements of shopkeepers or the editorials of a newspaper ; but it has a definite lesson. It implies that the Church, also, to carry out her work effectively, must depend largely on this same instinct of loyalty in her members ; and that everyone therefore who has at heart the well-being, progress and expansion of the Church can do no better work for her than to cultivate loyalty even in little things.

So far, then, the analogy which we have been considering strengthens, rather than weakens, the argument for loyalty as a dominant Christian obligation. But a much more important consideration remains. The Church is, indeed, a body whose purpose is to teach, to heal and to strengthen. But it is a first principle of her life that she performs these functions not through the voice of her hierarchy alone, but through the witness and behaviour of all her members, regarded not merely as individuals, but as a unity of which each atom supplies or supplements the defects of others, and therefore has to be harmonised with those others under a common rule for a common purpose. The distinction between an *ecclesia docens*, or teaching Church, and an *ecclesia discens*, or learning Church, is dangerous enough if it implies a clear-cut division between a clergy whose duty it is to command and a laity whose duty it is to obey without question ; but it is even more dangerous if it takes the form (as it would sometimes appear to do in our communion) of a distinction between a clergy whose duty it is to teach and a laity whose privilege it is to disregard and reject as much as they like. ' The Romish laity,' wrote Bishop Hall some 250 years ago,[1] ' makes either Oracles or Idols of their Ghostly Fathers ; if we make Ciphers of ours I know not whether we be more injurious to them or to ourselves.' The Church is the appointed instrument of divine activity among men, and her efficacy depends infinitely more upon the testimony borne to the character and conditions of the Christian life by each individual member in his respective sphere than upon the official utterances of her leaders. For this testimony to be impressive and successful it must not be discordant or chaotic ; and the duty of loyalty, showing itself in a subordination of individual conveniences and preferences to the expressed will of the whole, becomes of paramount importance.

Much has been written in recent years on the subject of the Church's ' authority,' and very different views are current as to its scope, prerogatives and limitations. All such discussion is at best unilateral, and is bound to lead into a blind alley until the rights of conscience have received equal treatment ; for conscience and the Church have joint authority over conduct. But the only conceptions by which the gap between these two authorities and their respective claims can be bridged are those of ' tolerance ' on the side of the Church, and of ' loyalty ' on the side of conscience. To concentrate attention upon the authority of the Church or the autonomy of conscience is to emphasise the diversity and tension between the two ; to deal with tolerance and loyalty is to mediate for a concordat between them. But the duty of tolerance requires little advocacy at the present day ; in religious

[1] J. Hall, *Cases of Conscience Practically Resolved*, Dec. iii., case 9.

matters at all events the idea has become almost an obsession. Thus the key to the problems surrounding the concept of 'authority,' itself a storm-centre of modern theology, lies in the idea of loyalty; and we are justified in attempting to understand it better by the hope that it will throw new light both upon 'authority' and upon conscience.

Has loyalty then no limits? Does it stand out as exercising a claim upon the individual greater than all other claims? Must he always conform without question? We have already admitted that where conscience declares finally and irrevocably against a demand of authority, not even the obligation of loyalty can make it right to conform. This then is the first limitation to which the plea for loyalty must be subjected; but it is not the only one. We have no right to assume without further enquiry the infallibility on each single point of doctrine or morals of the Church of any one epoch or any one nationality, or indeed of many epochs and many nationalities taken together. To do so would be to substitute for the virtue of loyalty a quality akin to it in name, but very different in nature — the quality of *legality*, in the sense in which Bunyan used the word. The promise that the Holy Spirit shall guide us into all truth stands firm; but it is not at once to be interpreted as meaning either that the Holy Spirit *has* already guided us into all truth, or that He will protect us at all times from every admixture of error.[1] The witness of large bodies of Christians, especially if of many epochs and of many nationalities, is in the highest degree impressive; but it is always possible that its impressiveness is more apparent than real by reason of that natural indolence which often leads men to conform rather than take the trouble of questioning.[2] For this reason, though conformity in matters against which conscience has

---

[1] It is the 'assistance' of the Holy Spirit, rather than plenary inspiration, that is claimed for the Church in systematic theology. I have suggested elsewhere (*Ignorance, etc.*, p. 143) that it might be better to speak of the Church as *indefectible* (i.e. as incapable, under the guidance of the Spirit, of failing in the long run), rather than as *infallible*.

[2] Thus the unanimous acceptance of the Papal claims in the Middle Ages was largely based upon the forged Decretals, and so was more apparent than real.

D

not proclaimed a contrary judgment is often a duty, it may yet be pressed too far ; and when so pressed becomes, instead of a duty, a sin—the sin, in fact, of legality. There is, as we have seen, an interpretation (and it is the common interpretation) of the phrase *ecclesia discens* which involves laity and clergy alike in unquestioning obedience ; and that interpretation, like the other which we have already rejected, is not without its dangers.

If then there is a possibility of error in some at least of the moral judgments of the Church, two questions arise. One is, what is the duty of the individual in the face of this possibility ? Granted that his conscience, while failing to endorse as necessary any particular ruling and law put forward by the Church, is not seriously disturbed thereby, may he be content with conformity until those in authority re-interpret the ' law ' ? Or does loyalty point to a more active attitude than this ? It will be convenient to postpone this question for a moment, in favour of a second, which concerns the degree of error of which we may suppose the Church to be capable. Can we limit the scope within which she may make mistakes as to the will of God for men ? Are there, for example, any fundamental principles as to which the possibility of error—and the consequent possibility of legitimate attempts at amendment—are excluded ? Or, again, are there tests of infallibility—conditions of which we can say that if the Church conforms to them her utterances are incapable of improvement or advantageous restatement ? Did the Councils of the undivided Church of the early centuries realise such conditions ? Does acceptance by the East and West alike at any period, or for any length of time, guarantee infallibility ? And how should such acceptance be reckoned—must it be unanimous, or the result of a majority vote ; and can it be regarded as valid if it was only attained by the persecution and expulsion of possible or actual dissentients ? This is not the place to attempt to answer all these questions ; but we can elicit from the general verdict of the past enough to guide our enquiry in so far as it concerns the problem of loyalty.

3. *The Relativity of Moral Law*

The system of doctrinal or moral principles offered by the Church of any period to the loyal acceptance of its members is made up of several disparate elements. We are not concerned with the doctrinal side of the problem ; but what is true of the moral sphere holds good, with minor adaptations, of the doctrinal. The principles set forward to direct conduct have in all traditional theology been spoken of as ' laws,' and divided into two great classes—the two classes of *divine* and *human* law respectively.[1] Human law presents no difficulty. It includes, of course, civil law ; and in so far as this is endorsed as ' just ' by the approval of the Church of the moment, it must be supposed that it is commended by the Church to the conscience of her members. The powers that be are ordained of God, just as the Church herself is ordained of God. The second division of human law is ecclesiastical law ; which, naturally enough, has both its administrative and its judicial side. As to this human law, in both of its branches, it has always been freely admitted that it may be ' unjust,' and so erroneous ; and that—apart from this— changed conditions themselves may demand changes in the law. The only problems that arise are *how* and *by whom* the law may validly be changed.

With the divine law, however, the case is different. This again has its two branches ; ' natural law,' which is defined as the moral code of which no reasonable man can fairly be held to be ignorant ; and ' revealed law '—the articulation and expansion of this law by the revelation of God Himself in the Scriptures. With a singular realism, St. Thomas Aquinas, whose exposition of this whole subject [2] is the fairest and fullest in the range of systematic Christian theology, admits that it is only the ' first principles ' of natural law, as to which there can be no doubt. The ' secondary ' or ' remote ' principles are left to man to interpret, and are therefore capable of being incorrectly or inadequately interpreted.[3] As regards revealed law, he is less

---

[1] See *Ignorance, etc.*, pp. 137 ff. ; and for the meaning of the word ' law ' in relation to morality, *supra* p. 4.

[2] *S.T.* i. 2, qq. 90–108.   [3] *Ibid.* q. 94, aa. 4, 5.

definite, but it is obvious that Scripture as a whole supplies only the general principles or outline of a moral code, leaving the details to be filled in by the interpretation of posterity. Our enquiry, therefore, branches into two problems; what are the possibilities of inadequacy or error (and so of supplement and amendment) in regard to the 'first principles' of the natural and revealed law, and in regard to the 'remoter principles,' or detailed application, of that same law respectively?

As regards the 'first principles,' certain propositions may at once be granted. We have admitted that morality ultimately assumes the existence of immutable principles of right and wrong which may be called the perfect law of God. We recognise gladly the work of revelation and grace which has set some grasp at least of those principles within the reach of man. We can even tabulate, with every chance of securing agreement, some of the principles of conduct current among men which seem to partake of just that immutable and unalterable character which we regard as distinctive of the divine law; and of these we can for the moment say that a breach of them would be 'wrong in itself' or 'inherently sinful.' In some of these cases we can only rest our conviction of their absolute and compelling character upon an ultimate intuition which we, at all events, find it impossible to question, though the form in which it presents itself may be no more than a particularly noticeable instance of a general principle only imperfectly apprehended. Complete promiscuity in marriage, for example, would seem to be finally wrong for man; and if any group or tribe of persons could be found to deny this principle, we should think ourselves right in regarding them as either too barbaric, or too mentally unbalanced, to be worthy of the name of 'man' at all. In exactly the same way, we cannot contemplate the possibility that it might ever be in accordance with the will of God that a child should be punished by torture, a heretic or witch burnt at the stake, a martyr thrown to the lions, or a human sacrifice offered to appease the divine anger. We may attempt to justify our convictions on these points by argument, but the argument is obviously *post factum*. We argue because we are already convinced, and nothing in the argument adds to the strength of the conviction.

In other instances, though we may not have any clear intuition as to the intrinsic *rightness* of a principle, we may yet hold that its infringement even in a single hard case might be so detrimental to the welfare of society as a whole, or to the attainment of some other ideal (as to which we are intuitively certain that it must be promoted), that no exception to it can be admitted.[1] A Christian might not be clear, for example, as to the inherent 'wrongness in itself' of bigamy, but would without hesitation class it as an act of such grave inexpediency that no permission for it ought ever to be given by any responsible moralist. On the same ground, if on no other, he might support the total prohibition of suicide.

Again, there are principles enunciated by our Lord in the Gospels, as to whose certainty and eternity there can be no reasonable doubt the duties of prayer, fasting and almsgiving, for example ; the principle that uprightness of motive is more important than formal correctness of action in determining moral values ; or that self-sacrifice is the final rule of true social life. Similarly, the Christian community has stood throughout her history for certain duties of religion, such as those of attendance at divine worship on the Lord's Day, and of the due and faithful reception of the sacraments of the Gospel, of which—even if their institution by our Lord Himself were as uncertain as it is sometimes said to be—few Christians of any persuasion would admit that they were other than unchangeable as far as the Church is concerned.[2]

Finally, we may observe that the progress of Christian civilisation has established certain moral positions from which it seems impossible that it should ever recede. Of these also we may predicate the same immutable and ultimate character. Thus to re-establish, with the full encouragement of the Church, the institution of slavery, or to be guilty of wanton cruelty to animals, would be regarded as

[1] On the doubtful legitimacy of this, see *infra* pp. 296-299.
[2] Even here there is of course a notable exception in the case of the Society of Friends.

beyond all question sins against a moral law which admitted no degree of relativity, but was wholly absolute and final.

The principles just stated would appear to stand upon as solid ground as any in the whole realm of human thought. Some of them seem to go back to direct intuitions, others are subordinate to such intuitions either as corollaries or as necessary means of attaining their objects. Yet the territory which they occupy is only partially reduced to order, and they are surrounded by vast and perplexing uncertainties. Some of them, at least, are very general in character, and therefore admit of countless variations in interpretation and application; there is, as Dr. Rashdall said, a general 'consensus as to virtues, but none as to duties.'[1] Others, in the language of technical theology, bind 'semper sed non ad semper.'[2] Many of them tell us what we *ought* to do; few only what we ought *not*—and it is here that the problems of practical morality most commonly begin. Others again express a spirit which we recognise to be integral to the teaching of Christ, but their phrasing brings them into sharp and paradoxical contrast with institutions which no Christian would be likely to disavow. 'We do not write over the Savings Bank, *Take no thought for the morrow*, or over the Bank of England, *How hardly shall a rich man enter the Kingdom of God*, or over the Foreign Office, the Law Courts or the prison, *Resist not evil.*'[3] We recognise of course the authoritative character of these principles; but it is not easy to reconcile our Lord's words with the existence of banks and prisons and diplomats.

To fill in the vast and perplexing gaps thus left in the Christian moral code, other principles of greater or lesser scope have from time to time been elicited from Scripture or reason, and set out as having the same ultimate authority. But sooner or later conscience begins to question the validity of one or other part of this complex scheme, and we are at

---

[1] *Theory of Good and Evil*, ii. p. 443.

[2] 'Eternally but not at every instant'—e.g. prayer is an eternal and immutable Christian duty of the highest order, but it might be wrong in some circumstances to postpone a quite trivial social duty on the plea that the particular moment which called for its performance must be given to prayer.

[3] W. E. H. Lecky, *Map of Life*, p. 230.

once in a quagmire of doubt. We call to mind that many such principles for which in the past men have claimed the same finality have by lapse of time been exposed as fallacious, temporary or misconceived. The legitimacy if not the necessity of the death-penalty for heresy and witchcraft; the sinfulness of lending money at interest; these and many other opinions have for long periods and with the full consent of the Christian people been endowed with the same absoluteness; it is only with the passage of time that they have been modified or altogether annulled.

Thus the Eastern Church prohibited third and fourth marriages as against the natural law.[1] Many of the earlier Western writers forbade even killing in self-defence on the same grounds; it was left to Augustine to define the distinction between justifiable homicide and murder.[2] Clement thought both ear rings and nose-rings equally forbidden by the law of nature.[3] Tertullian could not endure the actor's make-up, or the garland of flowers, because they were unnatural, and ' ours is a God of nature.'[4] Alexander of Hales[5] tabulates the different principles which at various times Cicero, Augustine, Isidore and Hugh of St. Victor included in the content of the natural law, and draws attention to their diversity. The theologians of the middle ages and the post-Reformation period were continually puzzled by the fact that the rule which required Christians to abstain from ' things strangled,' being beyond doubt scriptural and apostolic, had all the characteristics of divine and immutable law and yet had been set aside in the unanimous practice of the Church. If that had happened in one case, might it not also happen in others? Analogies from the history of Christian doctrine will easily suggest themselves. The certainty of damnation of unbaptized infants and heathen, for example, the verbal infallibility of Holy Scripture, and the crude literalism of much popular eschatology, were once universally accepted, but are now so no longer. All of which goes to show that it is not every principle of faith or morals which

---

[1] Origen, *Hom.* xvii. *in Luc.* (cp. Clem. Al., *Strom.* iii. 12) ; Basil, *ad Amphiloch. Ep.* clxxxviii. c. 4 ; cxcix. c. 50 ; *Const. Ap.* iii. 2. Lupus (see *infra* p. 77, n.) deals with the whole question at length.

[2] Aug., *de Lib. Arb.* i. 4 (9). [3] *Paed.* iii. 11.

[4] *de Spect.* 23 ; *de Cor.* 5. [5] *Summa*, iii. q. 27, III. 4, a. 1.

Christian thought has accepted as divine that will survive unchanged the storm and stress of time.[1] The revision of intuitions in the light of fresh evidence is as natural and inevitable a process in the Church as in the individual.

More disconcerting than any of these admissions, however, is the fact that the principles for which we have—rightly as we believe—claimed that they represent the divine mind for humanity as clearly in their own particular sphere as any human phrases can, do not bear in themselves any recognisable guarantee of their infallibility. They are *de facto* unexceptionable; but who shall say that this proves them to be *de jure* divine? That no reasonable Christian appears to question their validity is final evidence for their obligation to-day; but does it forbid the possibility of reasonable Christians legitimately questioning them to-morrow? Acceptance over a long period of time does not imply that the mind of the Church, under the guidance of the Spirit, may not at some future date rightly subject them to revision. Conformity to Scripture has always been regarded as a sure test of divine origin; but every sentence of Scripture is capable of diverse interpretation, and who is to decide between interpretations? The unlikelihood that God would allow the Church to err gravely in matters of fundamental importance may be held as a pious theory (though it is perilously jeopardised by some of the facts), but on what does the doctrine rest except a human and perhaps exaggerated interpretation of a scriptural text?[2] Even the sayings of Jesus have come down to us from the pen of the evangelists; what right have we to assume that they were always correctly reported?

The individual indeed may claim that it is inconceivable that this or that principle should be other than unchangeable. In such a case the principle is without doubt authoritative for him; but its authority is derived not so much from any moral obligation on him not to question it, as from the rational inconceivability of its being open to question which pervades his mind. We may say that he has no 'right' to question it; but the statement comes perilously near to

---

[1] For further discussion of this problem of 'universal laws' or 'things wrong in themselves,' see *infra* pp. 309, 328-331.

[2] St. Jn. xvi. 13, 'He shall guide you into all truth.'

nonsense—for the word ' right ' has no meaning except in relation to the possible. The Church of this century or that may make a similar claim, and once again the principle on whose behalf the claim is made is authoritative for those who make it. But none of these factors guarantee eternal immutability. The best we can say is that the more any principle has commanded and still commands this same unqualified and free adhesion from the Church of many different generations and in many different lands, as also from Christians of every variety of temperament, upbringing and intellectual endowment, the more certain we may be that it approximates as closely as any human formulation can approximate to the truth as it exists in the mind of God ; the more unhesitatingly can we accept it as part of the immutable divine law ; the less right have we to regard it as open to question. Beyond that, however, we may not go. We may make our own the sentiments of a grave Roman Catholic author, Opstraet, of the late seventeenth century.[1] 'A long-standing doctrine or practice in the Church,' he writes, ' cannot be taken *per se* to be the doctrine or practice of the Church. . . . God will never desert His Church, but, as history shows, may for a period allow the truth to be veiled and discipline to be corrupted. For how long and within what limits such a veiling of the truth may continue, neither Scripture nor tradition gives any indication. But the Church will survive, even though for a long period only a few cleave to the true

---

[1] J. Opstraet, *Dissertatio Theol. de Praxi Administrandi S. Poenitentiae* (1692), quoted Döllinger-Reusch, i. pp. 96, 97, as an illustration of the difficulty which anti-probabilist writers found in reconciling the dominance of probabilism with the doctrine of infallibility. But the words might equally have come from a probabilist source—there are passages very like them in Christian Lupus († 1698), *Dissertatio de Antiquitate, Auctoritate et Legitimo usu Sententiae Probabilis (Opera,* vol. xi.),—a well-known collection of examples of ' natural law' set aside by the progress of thought. It is ironical that the only point which probabilists and anti-probabilists had in common was the doctrine that a long-standing and authoritatively endorsed doctrine was not on that account immutable. The probabilist was committed to it, for otherwise he could not justify the use of probable opinions against a long-standing law ; the anti-probabilist was equally committed to it, as probabilism claimed prescription and authoritative recognition for itself. The admission ruined the anti-probabilist case, and left a modified and guarded probabilism as the only valid principle of casuistry in all problems of ' doubt.' (*Infra* pp. 263, 264.)

principles—nay, even though in large parts of the Church no one cleaves to them at all.'

All this is no more than to say of the moral sphere what is commonly admitted in the intellectual, that reason and revelation, or nature and grace—each coming alike from the hand of God—are different aspects of the same process ; and that God uses and has always used the human mind, both in the individual and in the Church, as the channel of revelation. To show that this does not reduce ' revelation ' and ' grace ' to merely pious euphemisms for ' reason ' and ' nature ' (as a devout person might call the habit of washing ' an eternal not-ourselves making for personal cleanliness ' [1]), and that still less does it reduce ' God ' to a synonym for the universe, is the task of apologetic rather than of moral theology. We are concerned here with the practical consequences of what has been said. They are, in brief, that it is impossible to draw a clear line of demarcation between the first principles of the divine law (which are ' immutable ') and its secondary or remote principles (which may vary with human interpretation), unless we are content to limit the first category to those principles only as to which the whole Christian Church has at all times been unanimous, with a unanimity based on freedom and not on constraint, and as to which we ourselves are convinced that it is inconceivable that the Church or any reasonable Christian should ever question or recede from them. Such a limitation indeed retains the full distinction just mentioned, but it reduces our first principles to a comparatively small number of obligations—and those of a very general application—any one of which must be regarded as in fact questionable the moment sane and mature minded Christians begin to question it. It leaves us with the widest possible margin of variable precepts, as to which revision or amendment is always possible.

Nor again can we draw very sharply the line between these secondary principles of the divine law and what we have called ' purely human ' law in the ecclesiastical sphere. In each case we are dealing with something variable, in each case with something in which a divine leading (for there is

---

[1] F. H. Bradley, *Ethical Studies*, p. 283.

such a leading, we must suppose, even in 'purely human' law) is expressed by the lips of men, and so may conceivably be distorted in the very act of expression, and must be capable of legitimate revision. And this, it may be supposed, was in accordance with the purpose of Christ. He enunciated the great outlines of the eternal will of God for man—the duty of loving one's neighbour as oneself, of giving no occasion for stumbling and the like—but He would not violate the conscience of the individual Christian or the Church by laying down a cast-iron code of minutiæ. He 'taught in parables' instead. This should warn us only too clearly to be both modest and tentative in declaring that any detailed principle of conduct is an immutable law of God. That there are such immutable principles we do not doubt ; but the limitations of the human mind, the imperfections of the human vocabulary, and the needs of different ages conspire to introduce a fluctuating element into their temporal promulgation. 'Moral truth,' in Wordsworth's words,

> 'Is no mechanic structure built by rule ;
> And which, once built, retains a stedfast shape
> And undisturbed proportions ; but a thing
> Subject, you deem, to vital accidents ;
> And like the water lily lives and thrives
> Whose root is fixed in stable earth, whose head
> Floats on the tossing waves.' [1]

The conclusion just reached, that the moral law, though absolute in ideal character, is often distressingly relative and fallible in its actual promulgation, lays a grave duty upon the Church of each generation. It is the duty of a constant, painstaking, conservative but brave revison of her moral code. Instances of such revision at work have already been given ; we need do no more than summarise the process. Where the Church finds a principle of which she cannot conceive

---

[1] *The Excursion*, Book V. Cp. also F. von Hügel, *Essays and Addresses* (first series), p. 268 : ' There exists a certain legitimate distinction between, on the one hand, the Realities themselves and the faith of the Faithful concerning them, and on the other hand, the analysis and theory of theologians concerning this faith. . . . The Realities change not ; the faith, the life in them change not ; only our understanding, our articulation of the Facts and of the Faith grow and adapt themselves more and more . . . in and through categories of thought which, more or less, vary across the centuries.'

that it could ever reasonably be called in question by the
mature Christian mind, honestly judging according to the
standards set forth in Scripture as the standards of the Lord,
she may unhesitatingly assert it as having a final claim upon
the adhesion of her members of the moment ; and nothing
will be lost and something gained by adhering to the traditional
phraseology and speaking of it as a first principle of the divine
law.   Where again she finds a principle which (whatever its
past history may have been) appears to her considered and
prayerful judgment to be of imperative obligation upon all her
members by virtue of its importance for the central springs of
their whole moral life, she must in the same way proclaim its
obligation ; and may fitly speak of it, if not as a first principle
of the divine law, at all events as a secondary and derivative one.
Where she finds it necessary to question a principle which
time-honoured acceptance has hallowed as sacred and
endorsed with the title of ' divine ', she must hesitate long
and anxiously before taking any step to dethrone it.   But
if in the end it prove, at all events under contemporary conditions, to be beyond all possibility of question a hindrance and
stumbling-block, she must abandon it as one of those things in
respect of which the guidance of the Spirit is now leading her
into fuller truth.   Where finally a principle, though important,
does not normally affect the mainsprings of the Christian life,
or may be thought of as temporarily desirable only, she need
not fear to regard it simply as a matter of variable human
law ;   claiming adhesion indeed for the moment, but capable of
dispensation at the instance of a higher principle.

4. *Custom and Re-interpretation*

The conclusions we have reached have softened somewhat
those sharp outlines of scholastic theology upon which we have
been working, and which the magnificent building of post-
Tridentine Roman Catholic thought has perhaps tended to
harden even more.   At first sight these conclusions may appear
a flagrant transgression of the limits which should condition
any reverent attempt to re-interpret the legacy of the past.
It is therefore both encouraging and relevant to observe that

our contention as to the legitimacy, and indeed the need, of constant revision of the Church's moral code is wholly endorsed by the great doctrines of moral theology and canon law.

That the Church can revise its code by official action is of course a commonplace of theology. And the almost complete impossibility of setting a limit beyond which lie principles incapable, in theory at least, of such revision means that it can legitimately extend itself to the consideration of all except perhaps the so-called 'first principles' of law whose amendment or abrogation appears to be inconceivable. More important than this however is the recognition of the place of custom[1] in the interpretation and determination of obligations.

Custom, in the words of canon law, can 'introduce, interpret or abrogate' law. To have any or all of these effects it must comply with certain conditions. It must be 'reasonable'—that is to the 'advantage of religion, discipline and salvation.' It must have stood the test of time—this is the meaning of the technical term 'prescription.' A longer period of time is necessary if it is to abrogate existing law than if it is merely to introduce a new obligation. It must be 'general among the multitude' upon whom we think it to have an obligation; and it must have the consent, 'tacit' at all events, of the proper legislative authority,[2]

---

[1] See *Ignorance, etc.*, pp. 146 ff., 155 ff., for detailed references, and for what follows, cp. Lyndwood, i. 2, *verb.* 'injungendo mandamus':—'si liceat [statuto] legem contrariam facere, sic etiam potest per consuetudinem tali statuto derogari, praesertim si introducatur per eum vel ejus auctoritate qui potest dictum statutum prius editum tollere.'

[2] What is the position of a law where there is a conflict between authority and disuse—i.e. where the disuse lacks the approval, tacit or otherwise, of authority? Western theology hesitated and still hesitates upon the question whether 'acceptance' or 'use' by the people is essential to the validity of a law. Gratian's text (*C.J.C.* c. 3, D. iv.)—'Laws are instituted when they are promulgated; they are affirmed when approved by the customary conformity of those who use them'—was ambiguous in itself and underwent widely different interpretations. Sylvester (s.v. 'lex') says that a law to be valid must be 'per inferiores suscepta et approbata.' Others, as Suarez (*de Legg.* i. 11; iii. 19; iv. 16) and Jeremy Taylor (*Duct. Dub.* iii. 1, rule 7), say roundly that acceptance and non-acceptance, use or disuse, have no bearing in themselves on the question of validity. Vasquez (*in Prim. Sec.* disp. 156, c. 5) agrees with them in principle, though he recognises that in some countries ('as, for example,

Custom cannot indeed abrogate or alter the first principles of the natural law, but, as we have seen, we are compelled to regard these first pinciples in the abstract as very few in number ; and custom is universally allowed the right of ' interpreting ' them.[1]

This traditional recognition of the validity of custom, even against positive law, shows how fully the Church allowed for that continual revision, amendment and adaptation of her moral code which we have seen to be of the first necessity for her life. ' Some flexibility of legislation,' writes Canon Lacey, ' is necessary to the well-being of any society. Custom is a delicately flexible organ of legislation, but written law stands rigid unless there is a legislature always ready for action. The statute law of England is in continual flux with the continuous activity of Parliament. But the legislature of the Church is not of this kind. . . . There are parts of the Church where local legislation is fairly vigorous ; but for the most part the written law of the Church is extremely rigid. This having been from very early days the character of the ecclesiastical legislature, the necessary flexibility of law has been secured only by a generous recognition of custom.' [2]

Putting these things together, we conclude that there are practically no limits to the action of custom and desuetude in the introduction and abrogation of claims upon loyalty, provided always that the tacit consent of authority can be assumed. Custom has the same rights and privileges as

Arragon and Poland ') the special conditions of a constitutional monarchy give acceptance after promulgation some part in the validating of civil law. Many authorities quoted by Liguori (i. § 137) hold that non-acceptance or long disuse abrogates a law, not indeed if the ' Prince ' objects, but at all events where, out of sheer ignorance of the nonconformity, he fails to interfere. Lehmkuhl (i. p. 94, § 137), following Liguori (i. § 139, lim. 3), holds further that if the greater part of the community refuse obedience to a law, the remainder are not bound in conscience to observe it ; and quotes with approval the ' opinion of the Doctor ' (Rebellus † 1608) that this holds even in regard to papal enactments—' for although the Pope's legislative power comes from God and not from the people, his clemency is such that he suspends the obligation of a law which is not accepted, to remove occasions of sin.' This, however, he warns us, is true only when there are grave reasons for non-acceptance.

[1] E.g. Suarez, *de Legg.* vii. 17. 6, 7 ; cf. Sylvester Prierias, *Summa Summarum,* s.v. ' consuetudo,' § 14.

[2] *Handbook of Church Law,* pp. 9, 10.

official legislative action.   We need not stop longer to vindi-
cate this doctrine.   It is obviously essential to the conception
of the Church as a living, growing organism, as distinct
from a mechanical organisation.   The analogy of any human
society bears this out.   It must indeed be a genuine ' society '
and not an ' institution,' a ' college ' and not a ' committee ' ;
that is to say, it must exist to live a corporate life, not merely
to administer funds or property in accordance with the terms
of a trust-deed.   Like the institution and committee, it will
have its minute-book, agenda and standing orders ;   but
whereas the work of a committee is bound and ordered
by minutes and resolutions, in the life of a college they are
little more than records of what has already been done and the
manner of doing it.   Customary usage determines all that
happens ;   legislation, if it is anything more than a record of
custom, is designed merely to check the growth of bad customs at the expense of good ones.   The customs of the community are its life-blood ;   laws merely the veins through
which it runs.   A society which is all law and no custom is
to all appearances a uniform whole ;   but its wholeness is
often no more than what Edgar Allen Poe somewhere called
' the specious totality of old woodwork.'   Externally solid
and intact, it may in real truth be rotten to the core.

Even so, however, we are not beyond the range of problems involved in this matter of loyalty.   New custom or
new disuse does not spring into the world like Pallas Athene
fully armed ;   there must be moments, periods, epochs even,
before it is seen as a *fait accompli*, during which no one can
say whether it will or will not in the end so establish itself
as to impose obligations upon the loyalty of Christians, or
again annul them.   It must have its beginnings and its history
—its beginnings in the actions of individuals or groups who
first ignore a law or introduce a practice hitherto unknown ;
its history in the gradually widening recognition and acceptance of this innovation by other groups and individuals,
until the whole lump is leavened.   And this at once preci-
pitates the question—Is not the action of these groups and
individuals in itself wrong ?   Does it not constitute at the
outset an offence against loyalty ?   And if so can any good
thing spring like this from a diseased root—if there is sin

in the beginning must not there be sin in the ending ? Can legitimate custom be developed from an action, or series of actions, one or all of them illegitimate ?

So strongly has this argument been felt by theologians, that Suarez, for example, found himself obliged to admit that new custom and disuse must always spring from ' bad faith,' or sinful beginnings.[1] Even assuming this to be true, however, the bad faith may be either technical or actual, either ' material ' or ' formal,' in the accepted phraseology of moral theology. It is merely technical bad faith when the custom or disuse springs from a conscientious conviction on the part of those who initiate it, that it is *right* in the sight of God ; and that, in so far as it may conflict with existing contrary law, it must be the law which is wrong. In such a case, the action of those who introduce the custom is no doubt a contravention of that standard and obligation of loyalty which we previously spoke of as claiming the Christian's adhesion ; but because it is undertaken at the instance of conscience it must be set down as actually guiltless—the claim of loyalty has been superseded by a higher law. But not every custom which has validly established itself in Christendom can look back to so blameless an infancy. As a ' good ' deed may be done from a bad motive, so a custom of which the conscience of the Church in the end approves may spring originally from tainted beginnings. In a different and better sense than the usual we may say of such a custom, *Fieri non debuit, factum valet.* The approval of the Church does not justify those who first in a spirit of disloyalty went against the existing law of the Church, but it may justify, and that in the fullest degree, the custom itself which their actions initiated.[2]

Sometimes, then, but not always, valid custom originates in actions which cannot be thought of as inculpable.

---

[1] *de Legg.* vii. 7, ' Peccaminosae saltem in principio.'

[2] To avoid this conclusion some of the older theologians said that ' good faith ' was necessary for reasonable custom. In general, however, even if Suarez's extreme position is not accepted, this other extreme is equally set aside ; and the general conclusion is that custom can be induced either in good or bad faith ; e.g. de Lugo, *de Just. et Jur.* vii. 6, 96 ; Lehmkuhl, i. § 177, p. 120 ; G. Bauduin, *de Consuetudine in Jure Canonico* (Louvain, 1888), pp. 62-65.

A custom or mode of thought laudable in itself is some-times championed against authority with an obstinate intransigence savouring only too clearly of disloyalty and self-will. It is not the source of a custom, nor the methods which have fostered it, but its issue in Christian approval, which stamps it as legitimate. That it can be legitimatised by general approval under the conditions pre-viously noticed does not admit of a shadow of question ; and when so legitimatised, it has—or ought to have—for Christian people the force and obligation of fully-promulgated law.

We have to think, then, of the Church's code of obligations as we think of any other living system of thought. It is a corpus made up of many different elements. It can boast of some principles which have obtained from the beginning, and of which it is for practical purposes inconceivable that they should ever alter. It has others which have changed with the changing ages, but still in a new form command the approval of the communal conscience. It looks back in history to other principles, valid and useful enough perhaps in their day, but now pensioned off in the process of Christian thought, and surviving merely as witnesses to the voice and aspirations of earlier days ; victims of that ' silent evanescence of obsolete doctrines ' [1] which is so healthy and necessary a process. But the moral possession of the Church is far richer than this. Ideas, opinions, customs, principles are to be dis-cerned there in every different stage of development. Some are still in the most embryonic form imaginable—mere hints of what the conscience of humanity may proclaim in the future ; dim transitory questions as to the wisdom of enact-ments at present in full force ; intuitive glimpses of obliga-tions yet to be discovered. Others are on the high road to canonical or customary acceptance by the Church. Others, again, after a period of popularity, are declining from their zenith ; they have failed of their ambitions and their rout is within sight. Everywhere there is life, everywhere change, with a Church holding out her hands both to the past and to the future, and growing and developing with every moment of her existence.

W. E. H. Lecky, *Map of Life*, p. 222.

Such is the romantic picture of the inner life of the Church
as envisaged by what at first sight seemed the prosaic canon
law of custom. It reveals what George Eliot calls a ' mixed
condition of things '; but in modern England as in mediæval
Florence such a condition may be ' the sign not of hopeless
confusion, but of struggling order.'[1] If it be a true picture—
and no one who thinks of the Church as a society more living
and creative, by reason of her divine mission, even than a
civil State, a municipality, a university, can fail to recognise
its truth—it confers upon each group and individual new
rights and obligations within the limit of their capacities.
It gives them individually and collectively the right and the
duty of reflecting upon all these incipient customs, ideas and
opinions—some of them destined to failure, others to success—
and of coming to conscientious decisions for or against them.
' Catholic Christendom,' as Newman wrote,[2] ' is no simple
exhibition of religious absolutism, but presents a continuous
picture of authority and private judgment alternately ad-
vancing and retreating as the ebb and flow of the tide. It is
a vast assemblage of human beings with wilful intellects and
wild passions, brought together into one by the beauty and
the majesty of a Superhuman Power . . . for the melting,
refining and moulding, by an incessant noisy process, of the
raw material of human nature—so excellent, so dangerous,
so capable of divine purposes.' In that ' noisy process ' the
moral law of the Church is also ' melted, refined and moulded.'
The issue may be expressed either in canonical enactment
or in unofficial custom ; but whichever form it take, it will
still be brought about by the voice of individual consciences
demanding the abandonment of old principles, or the recognition of new, with a consensus which ultimately proves
irresistible.

5. *The Church of England*

That constant, spontaneous and unofficial revision of the
moral code which the fallibility of its human promulgation
makes necessary for the Church, and which the canon law of
custom endorses as a wholly legitimate process, may be seen

---

[1] G. Eliot, *Romola*, ch. 57.   [2] *Apologia*, ch. 5.

more feverishly at work in the Church of England perhaps than in any other body. This need hardly cause surprise. Circumstances over which that Church has had very little control have made official legislation almost impossible for her for over three hundred years. Her thought about Christian principles has therefore been moulded almost wholly by custom, and that not in the sphere of conduct alone.

Opinions vary, naturally enough, as to the value of the results achieved; indeed, the results themselves vary in different spheres. In the realms of doctrine, biblical criticism, ecclesiastical history, and philosophy, for example, Anglicanism has wholly vindicated its unique form of Christian polity. Without surrendering anything that appertains to the fundamentals of our religion, it has reached a concordat with the best secular thought more satisfactory than any which stands to the credit of other bodies claiming an equal place within the general tradition of Catholic Christendom. In the spheres of public worship and private devotion, on the other hand, the results have been less admirable. In neither of these cases has the liberty of Anglicanism made for vitality, experiment or progress. As regard public worship the reason is of course clear; it is the one field in which authority, so far from tolerating or encouraging liberty and the free development of custom, has defied the true Anglican tradition, and set itself, until very recently, to stamp out all variation and experiment. In the only corner of public worship left unregulated—that of hymnody—the Church of England may certainly be said to have led the way in the last two hundred years. The lack of originality and resource in Anglican private devotions, which may be estimated by comparing the Anglican 'Manuals' of the last fifty years with those of other Christian bodies, is more difficult to explain, for here there has been no official repression. But private devotions derive their inspiration and modes of expression in the main from public worship; and the formalism of the latter in the Church of England until recent years would sufficiently account for the disappointing character of the former.

What, then, are we to say of the ethical achievements of the Church of England under this régime of intellectual and moral liberty combined with general loyalty to the Christian past ? One thing is clear. We have in the main avoided the error of regarding either pietism or docility as the highest virtues of the Christian. In consequence the Church of England, if not the first Christian body in recent times to recognise the moral responsibility of the individual in regard to the wider issues of social life, is certainly not the last to do so.[1] So much stands to our credit. On the debit side it cannot well be denied that there is about formulated Anglican ethics a hesitating and negative atmosphere which the individual often finds intensely disappointing. A tendency to vague generalisation, to pious platitude, to compromise with conventional standards, to the avoidance of pronouncements which may prove unpalatable to public opinion, results in an almost complete absence of any attempt to deal with the immediate detailed problems of the moral life in a healthy and bracing manner. The hungry sheep look up and are not fed—not through any conscious or blameworthy negligence on the part of their pastors, but because Anglicanism has somehow lost the tradition of definite statement and bold decision.

The situation, however, is far from being without hope. Ethical enquiry has undergone a rapid revival in the last generation, and the enquirers are no longer content with vague generalisations. The distinctive temper of Anglicanism produced ethical writing of the highest importance and interest in the seventeenth century, when the pressure of acute problems of conduct forced the intellectual leaders of the Church to grapple with questions both of principle and of detail. There is no reason to suppose that the revived ethical interest of the present century will prove a less effective stimulus ; and if our confidence in this respect is justified Anglican ethics may within the next few generations achieve results comparable with those of Anglican philosophy, biblical criticism and doctrinal exposition.

But it is not enough that the Anglican experiment in Christian constitutionalism should justify itself by results,

---

[1] For a general survey, see *Historical Illustrations of the Social Effects of Christianity* (C.O.P.E.C. Commission Report, vol. xii., London, 1924), sect. 5.

as we hope it may, in the ethical as in other spheres of thought. We must be assured that its single-handed attack upon its problems in all these spheres is justified also in principle. Partly by canonical action, but far more by the free operation of custom, the Church of England has already developed, and may develop far more fully in the near future, a system of Christian thought and life distinctive of itself. That the *Church as a whole* has both the right and the duty of revising her code has been argued in preceding paragraphs. But do that right and duty belong in equal measure to what are sometimes called the 'branches' of the Catholic Church? Are there limits beyond which no 'branch' can legitimately go in re-interpretation? And if so, has the Church of England kept within those limits, or transgressed them? And finally, if they have been transgressed, has the Church of England any claim upon the loyalty of the Anglican in matters in which she herself has been disloyal? The problem is one which embraces all spheres of Christian thought and life—doctrinal and liturgical as well as moral—but we may consider it primarily with reference to the last.

Three separate questions seem to be involved, and in each case traditional theology gives a clear and definite answer.

(1) The most obvious objection to the right of Anglicanism to a free revision of the moral code is based upon its 'particular' or merely national character. The Church of England is at best one communion out of many—two 'provinces,' it is sometimes suggested, 'of the western patriarchate,' but no more. Re-interpretation therefore, whether by law or custom, can only be legitimate for her within the narrow limits of autonomy allowed to a provincial legislature. Similarly, it may be said, and as a consequence, no member of the Anglican body has the right to adopt any attitude except that of implicit obedience to 'Catholic tradition' in matters outside the sphere of provincial authority and enactment.

Here is a problem which requires careful consideration. The English articles claim for a 'particular or national' Church the right to its own specific legislation in matters of purely human ordinance.[1] The claim is expressed with

---

[1] Art. xxxiv. of 1563.

studied moderation, and the argument of preceding paragraphs goes far to enlarge its scope. The line between 'merely human' and 'wholly divine' ordinances cannot be so strictly drawn as has sometimes been thought. No principle of conduct is 'purely human'; none, on the other hand, has fallen from heaven without some measure of human enunciation. None therefore can be regarded as wholly free from the abstract possibility of error and so of re-interpretation. If, then, the individual Christian has the right to express and act upon a conscientious conviction of his own—even though it be opposed to the judgment of his fellow-Christians past and present—in all but the most fundamental of these matters,[1] the same right must belong with even greater propriety to a group of Christians sufficiently self-conscious to claim for themselves a real measure of autonomy and self-government within the full communion of Catholicity.[2] 'Conscience is always to be followed,' and what holds good for the conscience of an individual is even more valid for the conscience of a 'particular or national' Church. Whatever we may think of the policy of Henry VIII in ecclesiastical matters, we may at least echo in this sense the fine words of his statute [3] :— ' When any cause of the Law Divine happened to come into question . . . the body Spiritual < of the Realm of England >

---

[1] And even in the most fundamental questions, the truth is not that he has no *right* to vary from his neighbours, but that such variance is ' impossible ' or ' unthinkable.' It is, for example, ' unthinkable ' that a mature and conscientious Christian could hold it right to burn witches ; but if he *did* do so conscientiously, could we consistently deny his *right* in the matter even though (with equal right) we thought it essential to demand his exclusion from the Christian commonwealth ? (*Supra* p. 76.)

[2] The point is well put by J. N. Figgis in *Our Place in Christendom*, pp. 137 ff.

[3] 28 H. viii., c. 12 (A.D. 1552), Gibson, p. 966. Henry, of course, did not conceive the Church of England as a separate entity from the Body Politic ; it was the same body, administered for spiritual purposes by a set of spiritual officials responsible to the Crown. So also Hooker :—' Church and Commonwealth import things different, but those things are accidents, and such accidents as should always dwell lovingly together in the same subject.' ' If the Commonwealth be Christian, that very thing doth make it the Church.' It was only ' under the dominion of infidels that the Church of Christ and their Commonwealth were two societies independent ' (*Eccles. Pol.* viii. 1, 6). Canon Lacey, quoting these passages from Hooker, adds :—' Even now in England, alone perhaps of all countries in the world, there are men who shut their eyes to facts, and continue a stammering utterance of the categories of Hooker ' (*Marriage in Church and State*, pp. 179, 180.)

now being usually called the English Church . . . always hath been reputed and also found of that sort, that both for knowledge, integrity and sufficiency of number it hath always been thought, and is also at this hour, sufficient and meet of itself, without the intermingling of any exterior person or persons, to declare and determine all such doubts, and to administer such offices and duties as to their rooms spiritual doth appertain.'

We may compare with this the remarkable declaration in the Constitution of the Church of the Province of South Africa, as amended and confirmed by the Provincial Synod of 1876. The Church ' receives and maintains the faith of our Lord Jesus Christ as taught in the Holy Scriptures, held by the primitive Church, summed up in the Creeds and affirmed by the undisputed General Councils; secondly, receives the Doctrine, Sacraments and Discipline of Christ, as the same are contained and commanded in Holy Scripture according as the Church of England has set forth the same in its standards of Faith and Doctrine . . . and further, it disclaims for itself the right of altering any of the aforesaid standards of Faith and Doctrine . . . *Provided that, in the interpretation of the aforesaid Standards and Formularies, the Church of this Province be not held to be bound by decisions in questions of Faith and Doctrine, or in questions of discipline relating to Faith or Doctrine, other than those of its own Ecclesiastical Tribunals, or of such other Tribunal as may be accepted by the Provincial Synod as a Tribunal of Appeal.'* [1]

What the South African Province of our communion claims for itself may surely be claimed, with full loyalty to the whole body of the Christian Church, by the Provinces of Canterbury and York. The limits of the claim deserve careful notice. The right to *alter* those fundamental principles of Christian thought and life which in fact we cannot conceive to be alterable is wholly renounced. But the right to *interpret* them in accordance with the changing needs of the day as conscience demands is fully and openly asserted. So much and no more do we claim for the Church of England,

[1] *Constitution of the Church of South Africa* (Capetown, 1915), Art. 1. The clause had an interesting and noteworthy history, which will be found in H. Lowther Clarke, *Constitutional Church Government*, pp. 329–334.

and the claim is based upon the primary Christian principle that conscience, whether of the individual Christian or of a national and self-conscious group of Christians, must be obeyed; and that nothing can proscribe its right to obedience. To deny the claim is therefore to deny the first principle of all Christian thought about conduct.

So much for theory. In actual fact, Anglicanism has on one point at least definitely and officially contradicted a theological principle (with vast implications for conduct) which the whole of Western Christendom for many generations regarded, and a large part of Christendom throughout the world to-day still regards, as without qualification divine and revealed. In rejecting the claim of the papacy to an administrative supremacy *jure divino*, the Church of England once and for all committed herself to the position that no principle, however fully divine authority has been claimed for it in the past, is in fact exempt from reverent and unprejudiced reconsideration. In adopting that position we can be fully convinced that she was acting within the legitimate sphere allotted to every self-conscious group within the Church by the principles which have found full expression and acceptance in the undisputed canon law of custom; and we can with the greater assurance adopt the same position in regard to other ordinances for which at one time or another divine and plenary authority has been claimed.

(2) A second objection may, however, be raised. For custom to have its full effect, as we have seen, it must be ' reasonable '—that is, must promote the well-being of religion and morality in the Christian community. In the present condition of the Church of England we are becoming aware of the fact that in the past three hundred years, though she has swept away many abuses, she has also allowed many practices of value to fall into disuse. With regard to these practices, it may be said, a custom of non-observance or disuse now obtains, and has obtained for several centuries with the consent of authority. But if we grant the original practices to have been ' reasonable,' in the sense in which we have used the word, their disuse must be to some degree ' unreasonable.' Is it fair therefore to think of them as no longer binding upon the Christian conscience? Have they

been validly abrogated by custom ?   Does not the dominant
' Protestantism ' of the reformed Church of England (in
itself, as many would suggest, ' unreasonable ') mean that
none of its relaxations of ' Catholic ' practice can be regarded
as legitimate ?

This position has been stated with disarming frankness by
Father Wilfred Knox.   ' It might be urged,' he writes,[1] ' that
since the Church of England is part of the Catholic Church, it is
necessary in any attempt to ascertain the implications of the
corporate religious consciousness of Christendom to consider
the weight of the Anglican part of the Church.   Theoretically
this is true ; practically it is not.   For in so far at least as
the official pronouncements of the English Church are concerned, they are vitiated by the fact that they are invariably
the result of an attempt to compromise with that element of
purely Protestant opinion which has since the Reformation
succeeded in maintaining a foothold within the limits of the
English Church.   From the point of view urged above, the
value of religious experience is confined to those who accept
at least the general outlines of the Catholic conception of
religion ; the experience of those who reject it is worthless
precisely to the extent to which they reject it.   Consequently
the weight of the corporate consciousness of Anglicanism as
formulated in its official pronouncements will remain negligible
so long as it is the expression of an attempt at a compromise
with those who entirely reject the general principles of
Catholic devotion.'

The point is difficult, and has a practical bearing upon
contemporary problems.   It involves both Anglican law and
Anglican custom in equal condemnation.   If, for example,
it is held that the rubrics and the Articles of 1563 forbid the
mediæval practice of reservation of the Eucharist for the sick,
the abrogation of the practice is the work of canonical enactment.   If, on the other hand, the rubrics and Articles, when
interpreted properly, are thought not to forbid the practice,
its disuse must be attributed to the operation of custom.
And if, further, the practice itself—as many hold—is to the
advantage of religion, whilst the Anglican atmosphere, as

[1] *Catholic Movement in the Church of England*, pp. 153, 154.

Father Knox suggests, is so vitiated as to make all its pronouncements ' unreasonable,' the abrogation of the practice
is in any case invalid.   It has still a full claim upon conscience;
and loyalty demands of each individual parish priest that he
should revive it unless conscientiously convinced that it is
wrong ; nay more, that he should disobey a bishop who
forbids its revival, for the action of an individual bishop
cannot over-ride a provincial law.

At first sight this conclusion appears formidable.   But
Christian experience is not without knowledge of the problem,
and has supplied a different answer.   The abrogation of a
law is wholly within the power of the competent legislative
authority, and it is universally agreed that for such abrogation
no formal pronouncement is necessary.   Any action or
inaction, from which the authority's intention that the law
should no longer oblige can be definitely inferred, is sufficient
to prove abrogation.   So Suarez quotes as a well-authenti-
cated opinion the sentence : ' The moment the prince's
will that the law should oblige ceases, the law is revoked
without any formal enactment ';[1] all that is needed is that
there should be ' sufficient evidence of the fact ' ('ut de illa
sufficienter constet ').   From this it is perfectly clear that if
the legislative authority, so far from abrogating a law officially,
no more than knowingly tolerates its disuse on the part of
the people, it has even so 'sufficiently expressed ' its will that
the law should be abrogated.   And here no question of 'reasonableness ' arises.   However ' honest or holy or profitable '
the law may be, Jeremy Taylor says, it may yet be validly
abrogated ' provided it be not necessary.' [2]   Suarez similarly
allows the abrogation of laws ' even though they are neither
useless nor unjust,' so long as there is *some* just cause, e.g.
that they are 'somewhat rigorous,' or ' not very useful,' or
because ' greater fruit is expected to result from their abrogation, or because greater dangers or evils will so be avoided.'
Even the mere ' abundance of laws ' may be a good reason
for abrogating some of them.[3]

---

[1] *de Legg.* vi. 27. 15—'Cessante voluntate principis de obligatione
legis, revocabitur lex sine alia promulgatione.' Cp. *Duct. Dub.* iii. 6, 7.

[2] *Duct. Dub.* iii. 6, 7.

[3] *de Legg.* vi. 25. 6, 7. In practice we may say that this doctrine of
'tacit abrogation by connivance at desuetude' amounts to the same

This gives us a perfectly clear principle to apply to our problem. Disuse, if it has even the tacit connivance of authority, abrogates any law that is not strictly 'necessary'—that is, as we may say, any law that is not a matter of absolute first principle. Still more is this true of official abrogation by canonical action. In neither case are we required to weigh up the 'reasonableness' in itself of the disuse or abrogation, nor yet of the general attitude and outlook of authority. Given the competence of authority, no other question can arise either in theory or in practice. We have already argued that the Church of England is competent to interpret and adapt to its supposed needs any traditional principles of which it is not inconceivable that Christendom should demand their alteration, and the official pronouncements to which Father Knox is inclined to take exception are no more than the canonical channels by which this competence is expressed. It follows therefore that the argument from the dominant 'Protestantism' of the Church of England must be abandoned, whether in theory or in practice.

(3) But while this position in general is to be accepted, it may still be held that a tiny factor in the peculiar circumstances of the Church of England makes free interpretation less legitimate within that communion than elsewhere. By the Act for the Submission of the Clergy, which received the canonical assent of Convocation,

---

thing as the doctrine of 'abrogation by reasonable custom,' provided that 'reasonable' be taken in a minimum sense. So it often is ; e.g. Sylvester quotes a long list of 'laws' abrogated by 'custom,' of none of which can it be said that the custom is specially 'reasonable' (s.v. 'Lex,' § 13). Thus though he admits that the old rule of election of prelates by popular acclamation has been validly abrogated, he cannot speak highly of the 'reasonableness' of the abrogation ; it comes from 'the ambition and wantonness which has undermined the whole Church.' In an emotional moment scarcely natural to his encyclopædist mind, he exclaims, 'O quis det illa tempora redire quibus populi sibi eligant et acclament antistites ; qui ideo nunc rari sunt sancti, quia crebro instituuntur iniqui et omnium clericorum pejores.' (Ib.) He is speaking, it is true, of official revocation ; but when we compare with this Suarez's judgment that only such a degree of 'reasonableness' is required in custom as is necessary for valid revocation (op. cit. viii. 6, 16 f.), we see that in practice consent of authority converts almost any desuetude into reasonable contrary custom. Lehmkuhl (i. p. 120, § 177) says definitely that reasonable desuetude need not be 'ex omni parti rationabilis, expers ab omni peccato.'

it was provided that all existing canons, 'not contrary to the laws of the realm or the king's prerogative,' should ' be used and executed as before, until further order were taken .'[1] There is no doubt that this provision is still binding as part of the statute law of England ; it has been cited and acted upon up till quite recent times.[2] Custom, it is true, is not held to operate with the same effect in relation to statute law as in relation to canon law ; and therefore the opinion of ecclesiastical lawyers who are not canonists is irrelevant to the matter. But, even so, is it not at all events possible that where canonical authority definitely declares certain precepts to be binding *in perpetuo*, we have a law which custom cannot abrogate ? If that be so, then we must admit that the whole of the mediæval canon law, except as repealed by the Convocations with royal licence and assent, is still of vigour in the Church of England,[3] and claims loyal obedience from the conscience of every Anglican.

Happily we are not tied down to this conclusion. Where a law expressly names and forbids certain customs, it is true that they can never be validly re-introduced unless circumstances wholly outside the contemplation of the law intervene.[4] But where the law merely ' forbids contrary custom ' without explicitly and in detail denouncing it, desuetude and custom can operate as before. In such a case indeed, a longer ' prescription ' is needed than for a custom not introduced in the face of contrary law. Our authorities state the necessary period to be an im-

---

[1] See *Ignorance, etc.*, p. 149.

[2] Phillimore, *Ecclesiastical Law* (1895), i. pp. 14, 15. Note, however, that Halsbury, *Laws of England* (1910), xi. pp. 375, 376, holds that the old canon law can only be cited in so far as it has ' continued and been uniformly recognised and acted upon since the Reformation,' and quotes precedents for this : ' Unlike the Statute law, the common law of the realm in matters ecclesiastical may become obsolete and abolished by general and long-continued non-use and custom to the contrary.' This modern recognition by the common law of the legitimacy of abrogation by disuse in matters ecclesiastical is of extreme importance, and strengthens the argument in the text.

[3] And is of vigour (subject to the proviso hinted at in the last note) as part of the *statute* law of England until repealed by Act of Parliament.

[4] Suarez, *de Legg.* vii. 19. 24 ; G. Bauduin, *de Consuetudine in Jure Canonico*, p. 95.

memorial time : [1] but the great canonist Prosper Lambertini (Pope Benedict XIV) interpreted this as meaning no more than ' the memory of living man ' ; [2] and his interpretation is commonly followed.

Nothing therefore can shake us in our conviction that the Church of England is as free as any other Christian body to go forward with the task of re-interpreting the legacy of the past. To do this will in no way be disloyal to the Catholic Church which is the whole Body of Christ. This is not to say that she is bound to be right in her re-interpretation. If the Churches of Jerusalem, Alexandria, Antioch and Rome have erred, we cannot exempt the Church of England from the same possibility. To dethrone the infallibility of Rome is not to instal that of Canterbury in its place. Nor is it to say that the Church of England, or any other group of Christians, can lightly, wantonly and unadvisedly begin to revise and overhaul the fundamental principles of Christian thought and conduct. In those rare cases (and history shows how rare they are) where the Vincentian canon of *Quod semper et ubique et ab omnibus* can be applied, nothing but absolute and conscientious conviction after the most devout, exhaustive and heartsearching enquiry would justify even a momentary wavering of allegiance. In other cases the weight and extent of traditional consensus must carry with it the greatest possible hesitation and caution before amendment or restatement be adjudged necessary. Hastiness, impatience, prejudice and opportunism are sins which cannot be too carefully avoided in this task. These, and not the desire to jettison what is corrupt and outworn, are the faults to be deplored in what we often call ' Protestantism ' ; these, and not the desire to restate the truth in terms congenial to contemporary thought, the faults which vitiate much that goes under the name of ' Modernism.' But, with the due observance of these precautions, the work must go on, excrescences be cut away, and principles adapted to changing circumstances ; and a particular or national Church is wholly free to lead the way.

Much work of this kind awaits Anglicanism in this

---

[1] Bauduin, *op. cit.* p. 96; cp. *Cod. Jur. Can.* c. 27.
[2] *Constit.* ' Inter Multa,' 4 April 1749; Bauduin, p. 101.

generation, not least of all in regard to moral theology—indeed it has long been overdue. The Church of England has admittedly left her children far too long without adequate guidance in the many intricacies of morality ; but she cannot repair the damage in a day. A careful sifting of the conscientious judgments of Christians of every generation and every state of life, along the lines just indicated, is urgently necessary before she can set before her members a detailed moral code adequate to their needs. Neither an unthinking acceptance of principles accepted in other branches of the Church, nor a hasty rejection of them, will meet the exigencies of the case.

6. *What Loyalty Involves*

With this work of elaborating the moral code of the Church of England—this work of ' Christian ethics ' to which we alluded in the last chapter—we are not now concerned, though no Anglican ' Summa ' of moral theology is possible till it has advanced much further than the point it has at present reached. We may content ourselves with a brief consideration of our second question—the light that is thrown upon the duty of the individual by our discussion of custom and loyalty. Loyalty, it is agreed, demands that where conscience does not proclaim with any certainty for or against a principle of conduct propounded by the Church, an individual Christian should set aside any temporary or personal inconvenience which may be imposed upon him by observance, and conform to it. ' Less than this,' to use one of Jeremy Taylor's familiar phrases, ' would be less than duty.'

But at once we are faced with a problem of such magnitude that, even at the cost of a slight anticipation, it must be noticed here. ' I agree,' the hesitating Churchman might say, ' that conformity is generally obligatory on any point as to which conscience gives an uncertain voice. You tell me that neither Lambeth nor Rome is infallible : and that statement also I am disposed to accept. If, then, they disagree on a point of importance, and conscience gives me no

help, to which would you have me conform ? If it is right
for an Anglican always to do as they do in England, well
and good.   But, if, as you say, England may be wrong on
some points and Rome right, it seems that I cannot light-
heartedly conform to the Anglican rule and thereby help to
delay the adoption of what may prove to be the truer rule
of Rome.   There are too many kings in your ecclesiastical
Brentford, too many Richmonds in the ethical field.   It
is to the Church *as a whole* that my allegiance is due :
what shall I do in matters where two great branches of it
disagree ? '

Let us grant for the moment that an Anglican *may* conform to the Anglican rule in any matter of this kind so long
as his conscience sees no objection to it : [1] and that it would
be *better* for him so to conform than simply to go his own
individualistic way.   But the objection just raised implies
that—without necessarily wavering in his general allegiance
to Anglicanism as against Rome—he has some doubt as to
the validity of the Anglican principle in question, whatever
it may be.   A concrete case will illustrate this.   A priest in the
Church of England is aware that his formularies expressly give
him the right to marry after ordination : he is equally aware
that any such right would have been unequivocally rejected
by pre-Reformation Christendom, and is still rejected both
by the Roman and by the Eastern Churches.   This is enough
to make him doubt, not so much whether the Church of
England has gone beyond her competence in the matter, as
whether, though competent to deal with it, she has not come
to a wrong decision—a decision prejudicial to the best interests of the Church.   He may be willing enough to conform ;
but to which opinion shall he conform ?

The matter is a pressing one, even if no question of
immediate matrimony is involved.   The attitude and outlook
of a man definitely engaged to a celibate life cannot but be
wholly different from that of one for whom marriage is
legitimate.   And the former attitude and outlook may have to
be deliberately adopted if Anglican infallibility on the point
cannot be assumed.   The perplexed priest is bound by his
ordination vows not to preach against the permission given

[1] Authority for this assumption is quoted below p. 227.

by the Church of England to her clergy to marry.[1] But that is quite different from holding himself free, without further enquiry, to take advantage of it in his own case. To do the latter with a clear conscience he would have to be certain that Anglicanism was right in this particular matter; and it is just on this point that we have assumed him to be doubtful.

Principles of such importance are involved in this question that we must defer further consideration of it till a later chapter, where other problems of a similar character will throw further light upon it.[2] Even at this stage, however, it demonstrates the unsatisfactory and difficult position in which a serious Christian is bound from time to time to find himself, if conscience fails to return a clear answer to his questions. In so far as enquiry, reflection and prayer can help him to reach moral judgments on points of practical importance, it is obviously his duty, on these grounds alone, to summon them to his assistance. Other reasons of no less importance point to the same imperative duty. A conscience which hangs between two alternatives, and makes no effort to decide between them, is a conscience in a state of suspended animation. To allow authority to provide a cloak for moral indolence is only one form of cowardice. 'The appeal to authority, whether by saying, "What was good enough for our fathers is good enough for us" (a thing nobody ever does say), or by saying, "What is good enough for us is good enough for our children" (a thing which numbers of people say), is no more than an appeal to stagnation.'[3] And stagnation is equally involved if the appeal to authority takes the form, 'What is good enough for the group of Christians among whom I happen to have been born, and whose general outlook on life I have accepted without criticism or reflection, is good enough for me.'

Stagnation of conscience—the unthinking acceptance of whatever principles of conduct happen by accident to be nearest—is the next stage to complete moral indifference.

---

[1] Unless of course he found himself, even after full consideration of his ordination promises, conscientiously obliged to do so. *Infra* p. 283.

[2] Chapter VI., 'Doubt,' p. 255 ff.

[3] W. Temple, *Church and Nation*, p. 176.

It leads almost inevitably to a life which may by accident remain superficially respectable, but is bound to collapse in any serious moral crisis. For his own moral well-being and usefulness the individual must do his best to bring this unhappy state of things to an end. If it is right for him to conform to the authority of the Church so long as his own conscience gives no decided utterance, it is equally right, equally his duty, to take such steps as will bring his conscience to a final decision of its own. He is not bound to do so in a moment, still less is he bound to divert his efforts from immediate and necessary moral activity in the discharge of his daily duties to the detailed consideration of abstract problems. But wherever he finds himself with a judgment in the form, ' Here is a mode of behaviour enjoined upon me by the Church in which—though I cannot call it immoral—I see neither right nor reason,' he must recognise that he is in the presence of a problem to which, sooner or later as occasion offers or necessity demands, he must attempt to find a more decided answer.

If this be his duty to himself it is his duty also to the Church at large. If he has her welfare at heart, he must play his part in the process of selecting from among a vast number of competing practices and opinions the dominant laws and customs of the future. He will play a part in that process anyhow, if in no other way than by an indolent and prejudiced adherence to tradition, or an unregulated and unreflective acceptance of each new idea. His attitude will influence others, and help to determine what customs or disuses shall prevail. If this be so, it is right that it should be adopted on reasonable and conscientious grounds, and not by virtue of a merely temperamental conservatism or liberalism. Only as members of the Church set themselves to play their part in the framing of custom in an intelligent and responsible fashion, have we any right to suppose that they are fully co-operating with the Holy Spirit in the task of keeping the Church's ethical system aligned with the self-revealing will of God for man.

E

7. *Loyalty and Casuistry*

The beginner in moral theology is often at a loss to define the difference between his subject and that commonly called Christian ethics. Several points of divergence are of course obvious. Christian ethics is the statement and vindication of the main principles of the moral life, and as such is a study with which the Church cannot dispense. Moral theology concerns itself not merely with the statement of those principles, but also with their application to specific and particular problems (and this is what is known as casuistry) ; as also with the means by which their realisation in actual conduct can be secured—a branch of study commonly called ascetic theology. In both these respects it is wider in scope than Christian ethics in the ordinary sense of the term.

But a further difference between moral theology and the Christain ethics to which we are nowadays accustomed lies in the weight which the former attaches to the duty of loyalty It may be a mere accident of philosophy, but it is nevertheless true, that few books on Christian ethics lay much stress upon this paramount duty of loyalty to society (including that divine society the Church) in the sense in which we have conceived it. They do not indeed ignore the fact that the Christian has duties to society as well as to individuals. They insist that among those duties must be reckoned that of thinking out the true principles of morality, and putting the result before the conscience of society both by word and deed. But what they often fail to realise is that this process of thinking things out is slow, fragmentary and—for the individual—unending ; and that while it is taking place it will often be his duty in loyalty to conform to social principles which his own conscience, though it may not condemn them outright, does not spontaneously endorse.

This failure of common thought to recognise the full implications of loyalty springs from a failure to face the facts of life. It ignores St. Paul's great question, ' What hast thou that thou did'st not receive ' ? [1] Emerson wrote a well-known essay in praise of non-conformity, under the

---

[1] I Cor. iv. 7.

title of ' Self-Reliance.' Its main purport was that conscience should throw overboard all the traditions and customs which it had inherited, and legislate for itself with a clean slate. The original ' intuitions ' of the human mind had been over-laid by the debased ' tuitions ' of society ; man was ' mendi-cant ' in all his judgments. The doctrine may have been medicinal for the America of his day ; but it is founded on a false view of life. The ' tuitions ' of society, its unconscious moulding of character, precede all intuitions of the individual. He can only see as society has taught him to see, though he may see things in other shapes than those in which society sees them. Conscience is not a discoverer of the unknown, but a craftsman working upon the known ; and it is folly in a craftsman to jettison the tools or the materials with which he has been provided merely because he has not yet been able to find a use for them. Prudence alone suggests that until they have been tested and finally found wanting they should be kept in store in case they may be required for an unexpected purpose. If prudence suggests this course, loyalty endorses it. We receive from society not merely the traditions we criticise, but the canons of criticism which we apply to them ; and it is ungrateful and unfair to accept the one gift and spurn the other before we have used every effort to find out whether both—as they come from the same source—cannot be held together in the same system.

For the same reason, though perhaps more rarely, con-science as a craftsman should be content to work with tools admittedly faulty, or even gravely defective, until it is absolutely certain that it has found better ones. The tenacity with which Erasmus clung to a papacy whose corruptions he had been one of the first to recognise and denounce, is a magnificent example of this exercise of loyalty ; and the possibility that he was to some extent influenced by un-worthy motives, while it may reflect upon himself, does not destroy the significance of his attitude. Still more remarkable is the conclusion of the anonymous playlet, ' Julius Exclusus,' commonly attributed to him, and certainly emanating from the same circle of thought. The infamous Pope is applying at Heaven's gate for admission to the society of the blessed, and expounds and vindicates to a scandalised St. Peter the full tale of his enormities. As the dialogue ends, St. Peter exclaims, ' There must be good in the world too, if such a sink of iniquity can be honoured merely because he bears the name of Pope ' ; and the attendant spirit replies, ' That is the real truth.' [1] Whatever we think of the Reformation, its necessity and its causes, this certainly is the real truth about the spirit of loyalty which animated some of the noblest natures of the age. They recognised the fact expressed by Frederick Denison Maurice in the fine words : ' Law carries with it for the conscience a witness of divinity, even when those who administer it have become devilish.' [2]

How much this question of loyalty should dominate Christian thought may be seen from a single instance. The great recurring problem of traditional moral theology is the question of the ' unjust command.' Again and again the mediævalists come back to it ; and it is significant by contrast how little attention is given to it by the moralist of to-day. Taken in its widest sense it comprises most of the problems which the ordinary man has to face. Let ' command ' mean not merely a direct injunction laid upon him by an immediate superior, but any precept or custom of the thousands which permeate the social atmosphere in which he moves. Let it be thought ' unjust,' not merely if it flagrantly defies the dictates of conscience ; but also if it be (as so many customs are) of doubtful authority ; or if its applicability in a given case be questionable ; or if, whilst its authority and applicability are above suspicion, it cannot be obeyed unless some other precept or custom of apparently equal weight be violated. There are the poles between which conscience fluctuates in many of the cases where its judgments are hard to come by. On the one hand stands loyalty, with the demand for obedience ; on the other is found—not mere self-seeking and individualism ; these present no problems to conscience, but only to will—but some circumstance which makes conscience itself hesitate to agree.

To these questions we are to come. They are presented always by ' hard cases,' either real or imaginary. For conscience to solve them rightly it must be in possession of

---

[1] J. A. Froude, *Life and Letters of Erasmus*, p. 174.
[2] F. D. Maurice, *The Conscience*, p. 158.

such principles—if any there be—as are of proved value in the matter. To the science which enables conscience to deal with ' cases ' the name of ' casuistry ' has naturally enough been given ; and neglected though it is to-day it has had a history so strange and changing that it would repay careful study, even if it held out no promise of real usefulness for the problems of life.

CHAPTER III

1. *Cases of Conscience*

ABOUT the year 1672,[1] the ingenious Dr. Barlow, who by a judicious practical casuistry of his own had achieved in that chequered period successive distinction as Bodley's Librarian, Margaret Professor of Divinity, Provost of Queens', and finally Bishop of Lincoln (non-resident), committed to paper his 'Directions for the choice of Books in the Study of Divinity.' Among the more normal subjects of the curriculum he assumes that it is 'necessary for a Divine to have some Casuistry, and to know more, that upon occasion he may consult them.' 'For Protestants,' he writes, 'there is no part of Divinity which has been (I know not the reason) more neglected, very few having writ a just and comprehensive Tract of Cases of Conscience.' He commends, however, Sanderson (with whom he himself, as a matter of fact, had frequently corresponded on the subject); Amesius ('a nonconformist, and therefore *caute legendus* as to that particular; but otherwise he writes very rationally, and what he resolves is short, and the Texts he urges very pertinent; so that when he is out (which is not usual) you lose not much; and when he is right, you have it in little time'); and Bauduinus (Baldwin). Of 'Popish Casuists,' he mentions Azpilcueta, Toletus and Filliuccius as of 'greatest note and authority'; whilst from the Jesuits—'of which sort of Casuists,' he says parenthetically, 'amongst those who do not (as some do) with ambiguous words and soft expressions disguise and mollify their harsh and horrid opinions, I shall name a few who write plain Popery, and openly endeavour to prove their most desperate opinions,'—he selects for special

---

[1] So *Dict. Nat. Biog.*, s.v. The pamphlet was first published after his death in 1692.

opprobrium Escobar, Tamburini, Laymann, Bordonus, and Guimenius (Moya).[1] He also recommends a study of the Summists, of whom ' the more ancient before Luther, when they writ more secure, speak plain Popery, the latter are more cunning and cautious, yet sufficiently erroneous '; his final opinion of them all being adequately expressed by the epithets of ' Roman Janizaries,' ' the Pope's Pretorian band,' ' *Capitolii Custodes, et Pontificiae omnipotentiae jurati Vindices.*'

We may take the good Bishop at his word, and enter upon the study of casuistry, or (as he would have said) of ' casuistical divinity.' The Church of any epoch, as we have seen, finds itself equipped by inheritance with a body of moral principles of widely varying provenance, directing its members as to what they ought to do and to avoid. The same is true of each of those members severally. Every such principle is partially illuminated by the known instances in which it holds good ; without such known instances it would remain a mere unmeaning formula endowed with all the terrors of the unintelligible. Instances of this occur commonly enough when children have unwisely been taught to use ' Manuals of Self-Examination ' intended wholly for adults. They imagine themselves guilty of sins which they have never committed, and never could commit, merely because the formulæ set before them are wholly meaningless. The ' sin against the Holy Ghost ' has proved a similar pitfall even to fully-grown Christians. Thus every principle, to be morally operative, must be accompanied by illustrations and examples—or at all events by an intelligible definition, which is no more than a generalisation from known examples.

Illustrations and definitions, however—even the most appropriate—are apt to mislead when brought face to face with new circumstances. Comparison of the new and the old suggests that an analogy holds good between the two in every respect, but there may be just one significant difference which renders it wholly invalid ; and the difference is not always apparent at the first glance. Because Elisha allowed

---

[1] Of whom the best that can be said is (with Prümmer) ' non est auctor commendandus.'

Naaman to compromise with idolatry in the house of Rimmon, it cannot be inferred that a new convert to Christianity may always or ever avail himself of a similar compromise. There are points of resemblance between the two cases, but there are points of difference too ; the all-important problem is to discover whether the resemblances so outweigh the differences as to make the compromise allowable in the new case as in the old.

The process of continuous revision, amendment and extension of the Christian code, which in the last chapter we suggested to be not merely a desirable but also an inevitable feature of the Church's life, is a process consisting in the main of applying the old illustrations to new problems, to discover whether the new so corresponds with the old in all essential features that the same principle will cover both. The more we collect valid illustrations of each particular principle, the less room for doubt as to its applicability in normal circumstances there will be ; the more hope there will be also of reaching a definition at once so precise and so inclusive as to make further examination of instances superfluous. If that hope is realised, the law will be defined in relation to the hitherto unforeseen and an unexplored area charted in the map of conduct ; a new judgment—new, though based on an infinite number of precedent judgments and examples—will be reached where all was uncertainty before. Mr. Chadband does not rank high among the world's moralists, but the method he employed in seeking a definition of ' truth ' was unexceptionable. He selected, indeed, illustrations of an unusual character, but he tested them one by one to eliminate erroneous conceptions : ' If the master of this house was to go forth into the city and see an eel, and was to come back, and was to call unto him the mistress of this house and was to say, " Sarah, rejoice with me, for I have seen an elephant ! " would that be Terewth ? Or put it that he saw an elephant, and returning, said, " Lo, the city is barren, I have seen but an eel," would *that* be Terewth ? . . . No, my friends, no ! ' [1]

Every such conquest of the hitherto undefined is in fact

[1] *Bleak House*, c. 25.

an effort and achievement of casuistry.[1] For casuistry is, by derivation, the science of dealing with ' cases ' of conscience ; and a ' case,' whether in conscience or in law, is a collection of unforeseen circumstances—a new instance —in regard to which the principles of conduct or law have not hitherto been defined. It may be easy enough to define them ; there may be hosts of analogies and precedents which are decisive ; and in such an event the effort involved will be so slight that we shall scarcely regard the problem as a ' case,' or its solution as a piece of ' casuistry ' at all. It is natural enough to confine the words ' case ' and ' casuistry ' to problems in which the circumstances make the determination of principle sufficiently difficult to cause at least a moment's check and reflection—to what we often call ' *hard* cases,' in fact. But even if we defer to this common usage, we must still remember that *every* new collection of circumstances in which our actions can be the subject of a moral judgment, however much it may resemble the experience of the past, is in respect of that in it which is new a genuine and unforeseen ' case ' ; and every determination of what is right in such cases is in strict language an effort of casuistry.

This work of determining the limits of principles in regard to new and varied circumstances is particularly difficult in matters relating to social intercourse—matters such as truth, for example, and justice. ' You are not bound by a contract extracted from you by fear ' is a sound enough principle, but what is the ' fear ' which relieves you of the obligation ? ' Fear of immediate and certain violence ' is obviously a valid excuse, and so far we have a clear example of the meaning of our principle ; but what about the other cases which may arise ? Will any ' fear ' excuse us—a wholly imaginary or hypothetical ' fear,' the ' fear ' of some altogether trivial injury, the ' fear ' of an injury in the remote future ? And, on the other hand, does the principle imply that you may voluntarily propose a contract or make a promise to save yourself from some ' feared ' injury, without

---

[1] 'La science des devoirs qui se cachent, mais qui veulent être cherchés et trouvés.'—R. Thamin, *Un Problème Moral dans l'Antiquité* (Paris, 1888), p. 316.

ever intending to perform its terms ? May you use fraud against force ? And if so, on all occasions, or on certain occasions only ? These questions and others like them had to be handled fully by the founders of Roman jurisprudence before a working system of contractual law could be established ;[1] and moralists are as much implicated in the problems as lawyers.

And yet the interpretation of a known principle is not the most difficult type of case that can be imagined. We have already recognised that one of the most important of claims is that of loyalty to society, and that its limits and demands are singularly difficult to determine when it appears to claim conformity to rules that are irksome, distasteful, meaningless or even obnoxious to the individual. So, too, the individual is surrounded by innumerable customary claims of varying degrees of authority, as to each of which it seems necessary that he should define his moral attitude. What, then, is to happen in ' cases ' where two obligations of the same loyalty appear to conflict with one another (as they may very well do under the imperfect conditions of human legislation) ; or, worse still, where the conflict lies between the demands of two different loyalties ? How are we to decide when the two principles in conflict, whether dependent upon the same loyalty or not, have either or both of them a partial or customary authority alone ? Or, again, since conscience itself is, as we have seen, but an imperfect instrument, it sometimes happens that we have so defined our principles of morality and accepted them as binding that in certain circumstances—regardless of any question of loyalty—two of them will appear to prescribe directly contrary actions. How are such problems to be resolved ?

It is easy enough to say, ' Deal with each case as it arises.' But this only means, ' Apply your principles according to the merits of the case, and not with a cast-iron and unswerving rigidity ; be prepared to find that each case will give you new and better knowledge of your principle.' ' The gladiator does not make his plans until he reaches the arena,'[2] no doubt ; but when he comes at length to his plans, he forms them, however rapidly, on experience and

[1] *Pandect.* iv. 2, 3. [2] Seneca, *Ep.* 22.

principle. Granted that we have the laws 'Be just,' 'Be truthful' and so forth, and have even defined them to some extent by past experience and examples, by what methods are they to be further defined in relation to the hitherto unexperienced? How are we to recognise whether a new 'case' so resembles the old ones that the same principle applies to both? By what procedure shall I determine whether the inviolability of a secret binds me as absolutely if the secret menaces the well-being of society, as it does if the secret is harmless? Or how am I to decide when accidental knowledge about others must be kept secret, and when it need not? Here what is needed is not merely a further definition of the term 'secret' in relation to the new problem—anyone can say, 'This is a case in which you *must* (or must *not*) observe secrecy.' What is needed even more urgently is a method or rule of procedure by which the *right* further definition can be secured, and the moral identity between the new case and the old be established, so that any decision which is reached can be defended, on principle, as right and equitable.

The purpose of a sound casuistry, that is to say, will be directed first of all not so much to the definition, interpretation and application of principles of conduct, but to the discovery of sound methods along which these principles can truly be interpreted and applied as need arises, or along which conflict of principle can be solved; and in virtue of which the solutions proposed can be vindicated. Not a multitude of rulings, but soundness of method is what is first required; for a morality which is made up solely of precepts and examples arrived at haphazard, and without methodical inter-relation, is no more a satisfactory system of ethics than a collection of haphazard facts is a genuine system of knowledge. If the process of knowledge consists in the discovery, modification and application of principles, the process of moral knowledge consists in the same; and in each case the possession of a sound method of going about the work is an absolutely indispensable preliminary.

2. *The Equipment of the Casuist*

It will scarcely be supposed that any system of casuistry, however scientific and methodical it might be, could ever be fool-proof; that is, could ever reach such a pitch of perfection that it would render up satisfactory results to any enquirer who applied it automatically to his problems. Even a sound grasp of scientific method does not ensure success. It will not indeed betray anyone who possesses it, but the value and scope of his results will depend in addition upon the degree to which he is endowed with the necessary genius or temperament for scientific enquiry. That genius or temperament is made up of many separate elements. It includes the power to see which problems are important and which are relatively unimportant ; the power to visualise new combinations of *data* which will offer a field for fruitful experiment ; the power to discern between relevant and irrelevant pieces of evidence. ' You know my methods, Watson ; apply them,' is at first sight as fair a piece of encouragement as any amateur detective could hope for from his professional colleague. But the difficulty with Watson lay wholly in the fact that he had not got the type of mind which could apply the methods. He never saw all the facts ; he was incapable of selecting those which had primary significance for his purpose ; he was always being led aside into by-ways and blind alleys of investigation in which he lost the main thread of the enquiry. A grasp of scientific method will not make up for the lack of a scientific mind.

And if the right type of mind is necessary in scientific enquiry, it is equally necessary for successful casuistry. The subject matter with which casuistry has to deal comprises the various claims which in each particular set of circumstances appear to affect the problem of what action is to be taken. Here, too, relevant claims must be distinguished from irrelevant ; side-issues must be recognised as such and firmly kept in their places ; accidental resemblances and misleading analogies must be ruled out of court ; and no secure judgment can be reached (however wise and proper the method employed) until we are certain that every appropriate claim has been taken into account, and all the different possibilities of action fully enumerated. A casuist of less ingenious outlook than the Vicar of Wakefield might have failed to discern his naïve but effective solution of the problem of preventing the return of an unwelcome visitor; and so have been at a loss in dealing with the situation. 'When any one of our relations was found to be a person of bad character, a troublesome guest'—so that guileless clergyman writes—'or one we desired to get rid of, upon his leaving my house I ever took care to lend him a riding-coat or a pair of boots, or sometimes a horse of small value, and I always had the satisfaction of finding he never came back to return them. By this the house was cleared of such as we did not like.' Intelligence, insight, fertility of imagination, are all of them necessary to the casuist; without them the decision appropriate to the full demands of each particular case may all too easily be missed.

But something else is needed too; and it is here that casuistry seems to differ, in degree if not in kind, from other forms of scientific enquiry. My judgment whether a statement is true or not is sometimes affected by the extent to which the admission of its truth will have palatable or unpalatable consequences. 'Even with the most honest and careful scientific workers the usual attitude towards a fact which seems to conflict with their theories is irritation, and either a refusal to accept it or else an elaborate rationalisation to account for it, which seems ridiculous to other people.'[1] I demand more evidence before I accept as true a statement which gives me pain, than I do in the case of one which gives me pleasure. But I recognise that to allow distaste to blind me to truth is the complete contradiction of anything that can be called impartial scientific enquiry; and that to set out to prove something to be true, regardless of the real facts of the case, because I want it to be true, is the worst possible attitude to adopt in regard to truth. The danger therefore that likes and dislikes will blind us to truth in our ordinary judgments and enquiries is not a very great one, though even here we must be on our guard against it.

[1] R. H. Thouless, *Psychology of Religion*, p. 86. For the word 'rationalisation,' see *supra* p. 17.

But as regards the judgments and enquiries of conscience the danger is very real indeed. These judgments and enquiries are concerned not so much with 'truths' as with 'claims' or 'obligations' expressed by precept and custom; and (as we have seen) every claim or obligation upon ourselves is apt to meet with an emotional response of considerable strength. If then even an unpalatable truth must knock rather loudly at the door before it gains admittance, an unpalatable obligation has a far more difficult task. The whole weight of dislike may be thrown into the breach against it, and it will have a hard struggle to make its footing good. Its only real hope of establishing itself is in those hearts which make it welcome.

It follows, therefore, that we cannot expect conscience— even when equipped with a sound casuistical system and the necessary insight and imagination—to reach the truest results in its enquiries, unless those passions which commonly assert themselves against the claims of morality have to some degree been quelled. There is only one way of quelling them, and that is to make all recognised claims of conscience at home in the heart by conforming to them in practice. We can discipline ourselves to obey the dictates of conscience; and in so doing we stifle the opposition put forward by self-love and self-interest, and are the more able to recognise new obligations when they present themselves either spontaneously or as the result of enquiry. The exact estimate of claims in particular cases (which is the goal of casuistry) depends upon the recognition of claims; and the full recognition of claims is only possible to those who in practice defer to them.

This is true even where the claims about which we are deciding are purely hypothetical (as to what a man *ought* to do in such-and-such imaginary circumstances), or refer to events long since past (as, for example, whether Brutus *ought* to have refused to join the conspiracy against Caesar). For in dealing with these imaginary or historical problems, as equally in dealing with any problems of to-day on which we are asked to advise, only one method is possible. We ' put ourselves in the place ' of the person whose problem it really is, and attempt to see the claims which beset him with just that additional clearness which is possible to us because no personal interest of our own is involved. But even though we have thus the advantage of position of Adam Smith's impartial spectator, we have still to *recognise* the claims involved. Though impartial, we must not be indifferent ; and even disinterestedness will not help us much to recognise in another's case claims which we have habitually disregarded in our own.[1]

None, therefore, but the morally earnest are safe guides in casuistry ; nor can it be a profitable subject of study for any but the morally earnest. Only a man who is genuinely trying to be honest is properly equipped to decide upon the claims of honesty, whether in unforeseen circumstances or in conflict with other claims. Gregory the Great was right in warning against casuists who ' penetrate duties with their understanding, but trample them underfoot in their lives ; who teach things which they have learnt not by practice but by study only.' [2] Not everyone indeed among those who are seriously trying to live Christian lives will make a good casuist ; experience, intelligence, reflection, imagination, as we have seen, are all necessary as well. But it can be safely affirmed that no one who is *not* trying to live the Christian life has any right to attempt to weigh up its moral niceties, or any hope of solving its problems. Moral theology in general, and casuistry in particular, can safely be erected only on the basis of a genuine moral earnestness.

It is for this reason that an uninstructed Christian is sometimes able to reach a morally satisfying solution of a case of conscience, where philosophers and divines are at fault. It is not that he has a special ' moral sense ' or power of intuition that has been denied to them ; not that he is better equipped intellectually ; simply that the long-continued habit of deferring to the different claims of conscience as they present themselves in ordinary life has given him an estimate of their relative importance which no one—apart from such

---

[1] M. Thamin (*op. cit.* p. 349) mentions as a personal experience that in putting a series of imaginary problems before a class composed mainly of the children of small property-owners, he found them to be rigorist in matters which did not touch them personally, but lax in matters concerning the duties of landlords.

[2] *de Reg. Past.* i. 2.

a habit—can hope to attain. By being truthful he has acquired a just apprehension of the importance of truthfulness; by being unselfish he has learnt to give unselfishness its true weight and value; and he walks with certainty in consequence, where mere theorists wander at a loss.

To this phenomenon of the uninstructed Christian soul acting as a spiritual and moral guide to men far more versed in knowledge and affairs, we may perhaps attribute the popularity of those doctrines of conscience as a direct 'feeling'[1] or intuition of right and wrong in particular circumstances which were mentioned in the first chapter. Where such doctrines are held, casuistry of course—even of the highest kind—is regarded as wholly superfluous. Conscience is thought of not only, in Rousseau's words, as the 'best of casuists,' but as the only casuist there can be. But it is not enough in this life to walk by simple faith; we must also be able to give a reason for the faith that is in us. The same holds good in relation to conduct. It is one thing to see what is the right course of action, another to be able to defend it as such, and make its rightness obvious to others. The man who strives earnestly after goodness will no doubt most easily see what is right in particular circumstances; but if in addition he reflects upon each problem and solution as they occur to him, he will be able to elicit the principles which underlie them, and so to help the innumerable troubled souls which *cannot* see what is right. This reflection upon things and actions seen to be right, with its achievement of principles which will help to discover, by analogy and precedent, what is right where the right cannot easily be seen, is what we mean by casuistry; and it is surely absurd to say that such reflection is either idle or foredoomed to failure.

3. *The Misuse of Casuistry*

The function we have claimed for casuistry in the moral life is very different from the odious achievements with which

---

[1] For the moral sense doctrine (like the intuitionist) can be stated either as involving a sense of approval and disapproval of general propositions, or of particular actions and proposals; or, indeed, of both.

the art has usually been credited. 'I am anxious to shew you,' says the bland old Jesuit in the 'Provincial Letters,'[1] 'how we have smoothed the use of the sacraments, and particularly of penance.' But his words have a wider meaning, and 'the practice of virtue as a whole' might be substituted for the 'sacraments' or 'penance' without overstating Pascal's condemnation of the system. 'It is here,' the Jesuit goes on, 'that the benignity of our Fathers shines in its truest splendour; and you will be really astonished to find that devotion'—(and here, for our purposes, we may again read 'virtue as a whole')—'a thing which the world is so apt to boggle at, should have been treated by our doctors with such consummate skill, that, to use the words of Father le Moyne in his 'Devotion made Easy,' "demolishing the bugbear which the devil has placed at its threshold, they have rendered it easier than vice, and more agreeable than pleasure; so that, in fact, simply to live is incomparably more irksome than to live well." Is not that a marvellous change now? '

This is moderately gentle satire; when Pascal speaks in his own person his bitterness of denunciation is unmitigated. ' Your doctors,' he says,[2] 'violate the great commandment on which hang all the law and the prophets; they strike at the very heart of piety; they rob it of the spirit that giveth life; they hold that to love God is not necessary to salvation, and go the length of maintaining that this dispensation from loving God is the privilege which Jesus Christ has introduced into the world. This is the very climax of impiety. The price of the blood of Jesus Christ paid to purchase us a dispensation from loving Him! Before the Incarnation, it seems, men were obliged to love God; but since "God so loved the world as to give His only-begotten Son," the world, redeemed by Him, is released from loving Him! Strange divinity of our days—to dare . . . thus to render those worthy of enjoying God through eternity who never loved God all their life! Behold the Mystery of Iniquity fulfilled!'

---

[1] Letter ix.—M'Crie's translation.

[2] Letter x.—In defence of Le Moyne should be read H. Bremond, *Histoire Litteraire du Sentiment Religieux*, i. (' L'Humanisme Dévot '), pp. 358–377.

No doubt Pascal—and still more the crowd of lesser names who for two centuries at least followed in his steps [1]—took sentences out of their context, misunderstood the issues involved, generalised from particularly scandalous instances. No doubt, also, the ' Provincial Letters ' reflect a period when casuistry, newly possessed of the new weapon of probabilism, was wounding itself even more than its enemies thereby. But the propositions condemned by the reforming popes are full of evidence for the general truth of Pascal's accusations; and the attempts to evade the condemnation by equivocation are even more illuminating.[2] Among the many immoral propositions condemned by Alexander VII[3] were these :—(No. 2) A nobleman may accept a challenge to a duel to avoid the imputation of cowardice; (Nos. 17, 18) calumniators, witnesses and unjust judges may be murdered if there is no other way of avoiding their attacks ; (No. 19) a husband may murder his unfaithful wife ; (No. 26) a judge may accept a bribe in an inconclusive case. Innocent XI[4] condemned the following :—(No. 8) Gluttony is no sin if it does not injure health ; (No. 12) as practically no one (not even a monarch) has an income in excess of his needs, practically no one is called upon to give alms ; (Nos. 13, 14) we may desire the deaths of others, even our parents, for the sake of any good that may accrue to us thereby ; (No. 15) a son who has killed his father in a drunken brawl may rejoice at the fact without sin if he has come into a large inheritance thereby ; (Nos. 26, 27) mental restriction, equivocation and perjury of all kinds are legitimate whenever the welfare of person,

---

[1] Out of an infinity of books and pamphlets may be mentioned a series of articles by F. Meyrick (Fellow of Trinity College, Oxford) on *Moral Theology of the Church of Rome* in the *Christian Remembrancer*, 1854, reprinted with additional matter (correspondence between Meyrick and Manning), 1855 ; and a long article on the ' Doctrine of the Jesuits ' in the *Quarterly Review* for 1875.

[2] See, e.g., Döllinger-Reusch, i. p. 39 ff.

[3] Decrees of 24th Sept., 1665 and 18th March, 1666. Denz.-Bann., Nos. 1102, 1117, 1118, 1119, 1126. A reviewer of the first edition of this book kindly drew my attention to the fact that my paraphrase of Denz.-Bann.,1106, was misleading. For the purpose of this chapter it does not seem necessary or desirable to reproduce the proposition literally, either in Latin or English ; I have therefore deleted it altogether.

[4] *Propp. damn.*, 2 Mart., 1679. Denz.-Bann., Nos. 1158, 1162, 1163, 1156, 1164, 1176, 1177, 1180, 1181, 1194, 1198.

honour or possessions is at stake ; (No. 30) a man of position
may kill anyone who slaps him or hits him with a club and
runs away ; (No. 31) a thief may be killed even if he is only
taking a single gold piece ; (No. 44) you may without mortal
sin slander a neighbour to defend your own honour ; (No. 48)
fornication is innocent in itself, and only wrong because
forbidden ; and many others of the same kind.

The doctrine of ' philosophic sin,' condemned in 1690,
which maintained that no action was mortally sinful unless
the agent was actually thinking of God at the moment
of committing it,[1] allowed almost any enormity to be perpetrated with impunity, and deserved Pascal's fullest strictures. ' What a blessing this will be,' he cried, on learning
of the doctrine, ' to some persons of my acquaintance. I
must positively introduce them to you ! You have never,
perhaps, in all your life met with people who had fewer
sins to account for ! They never think of God at all . . . and
therefore according to you they have never committed sin.
Their life is spent in a perpetual round of all sorts of pleasures,
in the course of which they have not been interrupted by
the slightest remorse. These excuses had led me to imagine
that their perdition was inevitable ; but you, Father, assure
me that these same excuses secure their salvation. . . . I
had always supposed that the less a man thought of God,
the more he sinned ; but from what I see now, if one could
only succeed in bringing himself not to think upon God at
all, everything would be pure with him. Away with your
half-and-half sinners who retain some sneaking affection
for virtue ! They will be damned, every soul of them. Commend me to your arrant sinners—hardened, unalloyed,
out-and-out thoroughbred sinners. Hell is no place for them ;
they have cheated the devil by sheer devotion to his service ! '[2]

In their proper context, as will be suggested later on,
some at least of the Jesuit maxims were not as scandalous as
they appear at first sight. But it is impossible to white-wash
them to more than a limited extent. How then can it be
maintained that casuistry is anything but a detestable
degradation of all that is good in Christian morality — a

[1] See *Ignorance, etc.,* p. 86.
[2] *Lettres Provinciales,* iv.

' series of rules for the evasion of rules ? ' [1] We may indeed
set these abominations on one side as excesses due to a
diseased passion for abstract theorising (a not uncommon
source of monstrosities, intellectual as well as moral), or to
the crude realism of the Jesuit *Welt-politik*. We may even
maintain that their authors were without exception men of
no moral standard at all. But none of these explanations
hold good for a moment. They are completely exploded
when once it is realised (as since the appearance of M. Ray-
mond Thamin's epoch-making study of casuistry in general,
and of Stoic casuistry in particular, it cannot but be realised)
that every one of the Jesuit devices for making morality
easy was known to the Stoics fifteen centuries before. Equivocation, mental restriction, direction of intention and the
rest :—in all these things ' the Jansenists of antiquity,'
as M. Thamin rightly observes, ' were the precursors of
Escobar and Caramuel.' [2] Nor are the Middle Ages or the
patristic period innocent of devices of the same character.
Only probabilism would appear to be the peculiar possession
of the Jesuits ; and even this, as Concina pointed out in the
eighteenth century,[3] had its roots in the principles of the

---

[1] C. F. d'Arcy, *Christian Ethics and Modern Thought*, p. 103.
[2] R. Thamin, *Un Problème Moral dans l'Antiquité*, preface.
[3] *Apparatus ad Theologiam*, iii. diss. 1, c. 1 ; cp. R. Thamin, *op. cit.*
pp. 36, 71, on Cicero. The observation is on the whole acute and just ;
though both Academics and Sceptics reached a pitch of uncertainty beyond
anything admitted by the Jesuits. Christian probabilism is erected on a
background of certainty ; it says ' When in doubt take a probable opinion,'
but adds in effect, ' but often you will be certain as to your course of action,
and then you must act on the certainty.' The Academic or Pyrrhonist,
on the contrary, held that certainty was unattainable ; the former insisted
upon the ' more probable ' course in every case, the latter—holding that
as much could be said for any opinion as against it—allowed any ' probable ' opinion (i.e. in effect, any opinion whatever) to be followed. Concina
tweaks the probabilist's tail by saying that not even Pyrrho would have
allowed the ' less probable ' opinion to be followed. But this is unfair ;
to Pyrrho all opinions were equally probable—even, we may suppose,
those which the least puritanical of Jesuits would still shrink from with
horror as *minime probabiles*, and therefore forbidden.—Cicero, as a professed
Academic, reminds his readers at regular intervals of the value of probabiliorism in a somewhat perfunctory manner (cf. *de Off.* iii. 4 (20), iii. 7 (33) ;
also ii. 2 (7)—where he denounces the probabilism of Pyrrho), but in spite
of this ' all systems which seemed to secure to moral principles a sound
basis had for Cicero a great fascination. He was in his later days fas-
cinated by the Stoics almost beyond the power of resistance. . . . He begs

Academics, and still more of the Pyrrhonists and Sceptics of antiquity. We are compelled to enquire whether there is not something in the nature of casuistry itself which forces it into the service of a hypocrisy whose only interest is to find some religious cloak for the pursuit of a lax and immoral existence.

The answer appears to be that not conscious hypocrisy, but moral rigorism—its very antithesis—is the real begetter of the worst excesses of casuistry. Not men of low passions, but men of high principles, first made its abuse a necessity. Where a man imposes upon himself, or a society imposes upon its members, principles of too sweeping, too academic a character, and does so moreover with the determination to enforce them on all occasions and at all costs—(as who would not, if they are principles of vital importance?)—a crisis will arise at which the principles involved must either be defied or evaded ; and the fewer and wider they are the greater the danger becomes. The fault lies in the misuse of the original examples employed to illustrate the principle. The moralist has failed to grasp the essential point in them which justifies the application of the principle, and has associated its obligations with purely accidental features which do not really call for its observance. Thus the law is made to bind in whole categories of cases in which it has really only partial relevance, even if it is relevant at all.

We can imagine, for example, an immature legislator taking the principle, ' Thou shalt not lie,' and basing his exposition of it upon the case of George Washington. He might notice that the heroic child not only (as it happened) stated the actual facts, but also the facts as he conceived them to be ; and this would save him from the mistake of thinking that anyone who, however unwittingly, misrepresented the real state of things was morally guilty.[1] But if he failed to observe that Washington was only a little

the Academic School to refrain from giving an uncertain sound (' balbutire,' *Disp. Tusc.* v. 75) '—(J. S. Reid, *Academica of Cicero*, p. 17).—Augustine's views on the Academics in general and Cicero in particular, in the treatise *contra Academicos* written at Cassiacum immediately after his conversion, are particularly interesting and important.

[1] I.e., as Alexander of Hales puts it, what is to blame is ' falsitas dicentis ' not ' falsitas dicti.' *Summa*, iii. q. 37, m. 3.

boy caught *flagrante delicto* in a heinous offence, and went
on to apply his principle, 'We must always state the facts
as we believe them to be,' to all men in every combination
of circumstances—however widely different from the child
Washington's—the resultant confusion would be appalling.
Under such a regime we should be bound down to avoid the
slightest deviation from the truth not merely in the great
cases where the salvation of life and country was at stake,
but in all sorts of trivial matters.   The courteous conceal-
ments, reticences and compliments by fiction which are a
commonplace of life would at once become things forbidden.
You could no longer say that you were 'rather busy,' or
'unable to accept' an invitation; nor could you 'regret
that you were otherwise engaged,' or be 'pleased to have
seen' an importunate friend, or 'be doing nothing in particular' in answer to a tactless enquiry, unless these things
were strictly true—as they rarely are.

What is to happen then?   The pressure of 'hard cases,'
of common courtesy, of crises where the lie must be told to
avoid irretrievable disaster, is too great to be resisted.   Wise
legislation will set to work to re-examine the principle with
the help of fresh examples, and thus to discover *why* it is
that conscience approves of George Washington's veracity,
and yet does not condemn a patriot's lie.   The result may be
to add some limiting clause to the original definition, or even
to abandon it and start again with a new and more promising
one.   We may find ourselves content to say that the principle, 'Thou shalt not lie,' has a claim upon us which is
among the most important of the claims we are bound to recognise, and which must only be waived, either in types of cases
or in particular instances, with open eyes after careful consideration.   Or we may, in addition to contracting the scope
of the obligation in this way, content ourselves also with a
less sweeping definition, or even with a simple enumeration
of the occasions on which there can be no doubt that a lie
will always be illegitimate—for the gratification of malice,
for example, or pure self-interest, or pure self-exculpation.

But such a course is not always free from danger.   Once
we are forced to eat our words and say, 'I see now that I
asked too much, or stated my principle too rigidly,' we have

brought the whole authority of the law into question, and shaken it to the foundation. A few shocks of this kind can be survived, but many would be fatal. And even if it were harmless in this respect, the course is not one which invariably commends itself to the high principled. With them it is often a matter of conscience to maintain the rigour of the law at all costs ; they adhere obstinately to the parrot-cry (—the ' slogan,' in the pet phrase of modern journalism—) of the original definition. Like Austin Feverel, every rigorist is ' morally superstitious ' ; he makes of his ' system of aphorisms ' a fetish whose cult he dare not mitigate. ' Disputing, excusing, cavilling upon mandates and directions ' are the immediate and inevitable sequel ; and these things, as Bacon wisely says,[1] ' are a kind of shaking-off of the yoke, and assay of disobedience.' If disobedience is to be avoided and yet the law apparently maintained in all its integrity, one of two courses must be adopted ; and it is hard to say which of the two is the more demoralising.

The law-giver himself (whether he legislates for his own soul or for a community) may tabulate a list of exceptions to his principles ; and invent whole categories of ' innocent,' ' white,' ' jocose ' or ' useful ' (' officious ')[2] lies which are not to be considered lies within the meaning of the Act. So Jeremy Taylor says bluntly that ' we may lie to children and idiots,' and tells how one Hercules de Saxonia, a medical man, saved the life of a madman who, imagining himself to be Elijah, refused to take food, by sending in to him a ' fellow dressed like an angel ' with the command to rise and eat.[3] ' To lie like a physician ' was intended as a compliment to both sides, adds Taylor, in his day. Bishop Webb enumerates unhesitatingly the types of falsehood which ' are not lies.'[4] ' Terminological inexactitudes ' would appear to be exempt from blame on the authority of a living statesman ; ' corroborative details intended to give verisimilitude to a

---

[1] *Essay* xv.

[2] Dr. Johnson would have added ' *formular* lies,' see Boswell's *Life*, an. 1773, ' It has always been formular to flatter Kings and Queens ; so much so that even in our church service we have " our most religious King " used indiscriminately, whoever is King.'

[3] *Duct. Dub.* iii. 2, 5 ; i. 5, 8, § 28.

[4] *Cure of Souls*, p. 200.

bald and unconvincing narrative' are vouched for by an
imaginary courtier. At first sight harmless enough, this
practice (as everyone knows who has ever been guilty of
making exceptions to his own rule of life) is the first step in
a moral descent which may easily and rapidly become pre-
cipitous. For where is our list of exceptions to stop? If
we have once begun to make exceptions, why should we
hesitate to add one or two more to the catalogue? Yet
this is one method by which the law is ' adapted ' to fit hard
cases. In addition to being dangerous it is morally illegitimate, because—if the hard cases genuinely deserve exception
—the law should so have been stated as never to include them.
The only proper procedure is to labour towards the understanding of the law until we are able to state it in a form which
will exclude whatever merits exclusion, without employing
the device of official exception. Anything else is not an
' adaptation,' but only an emasculation of the law.

The second method by which lip-service can be rendered
to the law as originally stated, whilst hard cases are allowed
for, is at once more subtle and more obviously illegitimate.
It consists in the exact scrutiny of the formula in which the
law is expressed in order to find some means of escape from
its severity. Once again the problem of lying gives us an
example. To lie is forbidden, we agree; and to speak contrary to what is believed to be true, or ' contrary to one's
mind,' [1] is a lie. Well and good; but the definition does not
exclude ambiguity and equivocation, and therefore nothing
prevents our using words which *we* shall be able (perhaps with
a slight stretch of imagination) to interpret correctly of the
facts as we believe them to be, but which the listener will most
certainly interpret in the contrary sense. We have ' spoken
according to our mind ' and honour is satisfied; the interpretation he puts upon our words is his affair, not ours. Or
again, our principle says ' to speak,' but not ' to speak
aloud '; if then we supplement a spoken lie with mental

---

[1] The classical definition—e.g. Petr. Lomb., *Sent.* iii., d. 35, ' Cum quis
significando enuntiat contra id quod animo sentit, ut aliud sit clausum in
pectore, aliud linguâ promptum.' Cf. Aug., *de Mend.* 3, ' Aliud in anima,
aliud in verbo vel aliquibus significationibus.' Portia's ' This bond doth
give thee here no drop of blood ' (*Merchant of Venice*, iv. 1) is an admirable
example of the type of casuistry indicated in this paragraph.

words which will convert it into the truth for us—even if what is silently added is the negative particle itself—we have fulfilled the obligation of truthfulness. It is incredible perhaps at the present day that sophisms of this kind should have held the field for centuries. But the facts are so; and they illustrate the truth, not that the attempt to allow for hard cases is illegitimate, but that it is bound to show itself in discreditable forms if laws too sweepingly and rashly stated are treated as sacrosanct at all costs.[1]

Casuistry, as we have defined it, is no more than the attempt to extend the principles of morality to unforeseen cases and new problems. As such its operations are at once necessary and laudable. But each extension of a law must involve some modification of it, and each new example of its application must be allowed, though perhaps in no more than the slightest degree, to throw new light upon its essential character, and reveal such accretions of the unnecessary and accidental as still cling to it. Where this is realised, and the consequent adjustments and reformulations of the law are wisely made, casuistry is the friend and servant of morality. Where, on the contrary, the law, down to the last jot and tittle of its contemporary formula, is treated as immutable, casuistry becomes its enemy. It resorts to shifts and sophistries which, however generous in their original intentions, are bound to weaken the fibre of morality and bring the study of hard cases into disrepute. The lean kine in Pharaoh's dream devoured their well-favoured brothers; by a similar unfortunate process the abuse of casuistry has monopolised the name, and excluded from its scope that true use of casuistry which is no more to be despised or to be avoided than is equity—which is indeed simply equity operating on a large scale.[2]

---

[1] Instances of the condemnation of casuistry through failure to recognise this fact are given in *Additional Note B*, 'Two Modern Views of Casuistry, p. 381 f. For further discussion of the problem of lying, see below, pp. 191 ff., 337 ff., and *Note G*, p. 399.

[2] Aristotle's account of equity (ἐπιείκεια—*Eth. Nic.* v. 10) is the first systematic investigation of the nature of casuistry. 'Equity is a correction (ἐπανόρθωμα) of the law. Every law is expressed in general terms, and there are some matters which cannot be accurately dealt with in general terms. . . . In such cases the law lays down what is right for the majority of cases, without losing sight of the consequent inaccuracy

The bad odour into which 'casuistry' has fallen belongs, therefore, to its abuse rather than to its real nature ; and that abuse itself has its rise not so much in hypocrisy or lax immoralism as in the aberrations of a high-minded moral rigidity. To what depths it can sink we have already seen ; there is no more terrible picture than that of the rigorist turned casuist in self-despite. He proclaims his moral solvency to all the world, but refuses to pay a penny of his just debts ; he 'resembles the man who carries on his person nothing but bank-notes of large denominations, and so excuses himself from payment on the grounds that he has no small change.' [1]

< in the remainder >—an inaccuracy which springs neither from the law nor the legislator, but from the nature of the case, as an inevitable condition of human action. When, therefore, a law is laid down generally, but manifest ground for exception appears in a particular case, it is right that this failure of the legislator (due to his expressing himself in general terms) should be made good exactly as he would make it good if he were present, or would amend his law if he took the case into account.' This gives the double purpose of casuistry—to adjust the law *ad hoc* for a particular case, and at the same time to work for an amendment of the law so that cases which ought to be excluded should be excluded. With a singular appreciation of the moral possibilities of good casuistry, Aristotle goes on to speak of the equitable man (i.e. the casuist) as one who commonly 'adjusts the law,' not in his own favour, but, if necessary, in favour of others *against himself*—' he does not insist on his rights to the damage of others, but is willing to take less than his due, even where the law is on his side' (ὁ μὴ ἀκριβοδίκαιος ἐπὶ τὸ χεῖρον ἀλλ' ἐλαττωτικός, καίπερ ἔχων τὸν νόμον βοηθόν, ἐπιεικής ἐστι). He is aware of the rigorist objections to casuistry :— ' How can equity be praiseworthy, if it is different from what is just ? Either justice or equity' (as we should say, ' either the law or the casuist ') ' must be wrong' (οὐ σπουδαῖον), and deals with them effectively. St. Thomas repeats the greater part of this without addition in *S.T.* ii. 2, q. 120.

One or two other Aristotelian terms show how close the question of casuistry lay to the surface of his mind. Φρόνησις (*ib.* vi. 5) is the power of taking a general survey of moral law and selecting all that is applicable to the needs of a particular case ; it is only possible to the man who habitually defers to the moral law (σώφρων—the man who ' guards his φρόνησις' by this means), and needs experience of life before it can be perfected (vi. 7, 8, ' a young man may become a good mathematician, but not a good casuist, because he lacks experience '). Εὐβουλία (good deliberation) is the process by which the φρόνιμος reaches his moral judgments (τῶν φρονίμων τὸ εὖ βεβουλεῦσθαι—vi. 9) ; and, as reasoned and disciplined, differs from εὐστοχία (instinctive moral tact) and ἀγχίνοια (sagacity)— though neither of these natural endowments is to be despised.

[1] Gustave Droz, *Tristesses et Sourires*, p. 31, quoted Thamin, p. 69 ; cp. Thamin's own revision of Montesquieu's epigram, ' Les hommes honnêtes en gros deviennent fripons en détail.' (*Ibid.* 325.)

Casuistry then, to use the word for once in its accepted evil sense, is a weed which grows most readily in the soil of rigorism. Not the casuist who tends the plant, so much as the rigorist who prepares the soil, is to blame for the resultant horror. No doubt also hypocrisy, theorising and ambition have helped the process. But in the main it is bigotry of the Puritan type which produces a pliant sophistry by reaction. Bunyan could grow satirical about Mr. By-Ends of Fair Speech (whose ' grandfather was a waterman, looking one way and rowing another '), Mr. Hold-the-World, Mr. Money-Love and Mr. Save-All, and the ' two small points ' in which they ' differed somewhat from those of the stricter sort.' [1]   He could hold up to scorn their cases of the Minister and the Tradesman whom they allowed to increase their incomes by a sacrifice of principle. Mr. Self-Will, who ' held that a man might follow the vices as well as the virtues of the pilgrims,' is pictured as a casuist of the most degraded type. But a more impartial critic might have seen in By-Ends, Self-Will and the like no more than men puzzled by the difficulty of accommodating the rigid Puritan principles to the complexity of ordinary life, and recognised that it was the self-centred high-mindedness of Bunyan and his friends which drove them to their unworthy expedients and evasions. By-Ends and Christian are both products of the same system, and Bunyan unconsciously condemned his own narrow rigorism when he wrote : ' There is a way to Hell even from the gates of Heaven.' [2]

Or, if a lighter argument for our contention be allowed, we may turn once more to the inimitable Savoy Operas. Each of the series centres on a situation which, in their author's honour, we call Gilbertian. But a Gilbertian situation intrigues us merely because it shows a principle (usually but not always a trivial one) pressed to rigorist extremes

[1] ' First, we never strive against wind and tide ; secondly, we are always most zealous when Religion goes in his Silver Slippers.'—*Pilgrim's Progress*, part i.

[2] Cp. also Pascal, *Pensées*, vii. 13 : ' Man is neither angel nor beast ; the pity is that when he would make himself an angel he makes himself a beast '; Montaigne, *Essays*, iii. 13 : ' They try to get outside themselves and escape from the limitations of humanity. Fools that they are ; they become beasts, not angels ; they sink instead of rising ' (quoted Thamin, *op. cit.* p. 62).

without exception, and impinging with a clash of unmitigated absurdity against the facts of life. That flirting is punishable with execution; that the death of the heir-apparent, however accidentally compassed, must be visited by the lingering and humorous penalty of boiling oil; that no fairy may marry with a mortal; that all shall be equal at the Court of Barataria; that the bad baronet shall commit one crime a day throughout life—'principles' such as these are held up to ridicule in a dream-world where everyone flirts, and the heir-apparent (himself incognito) is only alleged to be dead, and peers and peris intermarry *en masse*, and liberty is carried to the pitch of anarchy, and the baronet is brought up as a blameless peasant. Sometimes, indeed, Gilbert took more serious subjects as his theme; once even he put upon the stage the oldest and most-discussed casuistical problem in the world. The rollicking band of pirates who advance upon the ruined chapel, 'to seek a penalty fifty-fold for General Stanley's story,' are the lineal descendants of St. Augustine and Immanuel Kant; and the plea that the lie, which

> 'in popular diction
> Is known as an innocent fiction,
> Is not in the same category
> With a regular terrible story,'

echoes the protest of sane moralists of all ages against the demand for veracity at all costs. But whether his thesis was serious or bizarre, Gilbert never failed to press home the same conclusion—that unswerving rigidity in morality is bound to shipwreck upon the rocks of common-sense.

Nor did he fail to draw our second conclusion, that the only escape from an intransigent and unworkable morality lies in 'casuistry' of the baser sort. Sometimes indeed the knot of absurdity is so tightly tied that not even casuistry can loosen it, and the time-honoured stage-expedient of an exchange of children at birth has to be introduced to save the situation. But generally a dialectical evasion is evolved comparable in its ingenuity to the most successful flights of the Jesuits, and running on the same lines as theirs; and the triumphant sophistries of the 'Mikado,' 'Iolanthe,' 'Pirates' and 'Ruddigore' are worthy of Escobar and Diana.

The lesson which is concealed in the pages of the ' Pilgrim's Progress,' and publicly proclaimed by the Savoy Operas, is written large in history. The impossible demands made upon the Stoic ' wise man,' the dead hand of a decayed scholasticism upon the Church, the menace to ' serene good sense ' emanating from the ' moral intoxication '[1] of Puritanism, the uncritical worship of an inspired book which made of the Scriptures an unalterable corpus of law—while the slow progress of thought was substituting for these morality of a more practical and flexible kind, impatience and short-sightedness found a quicker way of escape by means of unjustified exceptions and unconscientious evasions. We must examine both processes at work—the good and the bad, casuistry wisely used and casuistry horribly abused—in the development of moral thought, before we can be sure that our own methods of handling detailed problems of conduct are vindicated by the experience of Christianity. But Christianity was born of Judaism and put out to nurse with Hellenistic thought ; and in ethics, as in doctrine, a full understanding of its growth is only possible if something is known of the forces which moulded its infancy.

4. Judaism

Whether casuistry, then, becomes the friend or the enemy of true morality—whether its activities will be legitimate and beneficent, or illegitimate and vicious—depends in the main upon the presuppositions from which it is forced to start. Where law is treated as the servant of life, and therefore capable of adaptation and development, casuistry will do nothing but good in the hands of wise and experienced persons. Where, on the other hand, law is regarded as the master of life, as something sacrosant and unbending even in its most trivial details, the study of hard cases will produce nothing but that system of evasions to which the name ' casuistry,' with all its odious implications, is in ordinary usage reserved. The true attitude towards law, as we have

[1] H. Bremond, *Histoire du Sentiment Religieux*, i. p. 404. The phrase ' ivresse morale ' is borrowed direct from Bonal, a broad-minded Franciscan of the period.

suggested, is the former of these two. The eternal law of
God is, indeed, unchanging and perfect. In part at least,
as we believe, it has been revealed to men, so that not every
moral principle current among men may be adjudged wholly
relative and transient. But the revelation comes to man
through the minds and lips of men, and so at best is a very
imperfect approximation to the eternal will of God as God
Himself understands it. It is the privilege of man to attempt
to formulate the law progressively in terms nearer to the mind
of God, and in this attempt the more he considers the variety of
problems to which the moral law must in the end provide an
answer—the more, that is, he studies ' cases '—the better will
he be equipped for the task.

Judaism took the exactly opposite view. The law had
been revealed once and for all in its plenitude, and St. Matthew records as from his Master's lips a characteristically
Jewish saying about it, that not a jot or a tittle of it should
be changed. Not, indeed, that the whole law was here and
now accessible to the faithful. No less than three thousand
precepts had been forgotten during the tragic period of mourn-
ing for Moses.[1] It was the business of the Rabbis and the
Sanhedrin not merely to recover these lost Halakoth, but
to ' fence ' the law still further with new precautionary
prohibitions, or by introducing such bye-laws and interpretations as were necessary. These ' fences ' and bye-laws
once promulgated remained binding for ever.[2] Temporary
abrogation of specific commands was occasionally allowed,
within strict limits; but no part of the law could be abrogated permanently[3]—for God had said : ' Thou shalt not add
thereto nor diminish from it ' (Deut. iv. 2). In general, hard
cases must suffer—' the law does not take account of circumstances ; it is not based on conditions which rarely occur.' [4]
The law, moreover, is not amenable to trial by reason. Many
of its precepts are laid on us for discipline alone ; and the
belief that ' everyone of them has a ground in the nature

---

[1] F. Weber, *Jüdische Theologie*[2] (1897) (new edition of *System der Alt-
synagogalen Theologie*), p. 94.
[2] Maimonides, *Guide for the Perplexed*, iii. 41 (ed. Friedländer, London,
1904), p. 347.
[3] *Ibid.*   [4] *Ibid.* iii. 24. (Friedländer, p. 308.)

of things, and Solomon knew what it was,' is wholly false.[1]

Here was a field in which the worst form of casuistry might easily flourish. A system so tradition-bound must surely admit no compromise with ordinary life—wholesale evasion by fiction would seem the only alternative. Such evasion there undoubtedly was. It is true that our Lord accused the Pharisees rather of externalism than of evasion ; but the casuistry of the Corban is obviously an expedient to evade two conflicting duties by playing one off against the other—for the money withdrawn from the support of parents for the service of God was not as a matter of fact devoted to that purpose.[2]   The ' straining-out of the gnat and swallowing of the camel' suggests that the Pharisees, like the casuists of a later age, had discovered some means of compounding for sins they were inclined to by damning those they had no mind to. Some ignoble purpose obviously lies behind the quibble that to swear by the temple ' is nought,' though ' whosoever shall swear by the gold that is in the temple is a debtor.'[3]   But for all the fact that the word ' casuistry,' in its most invidious sense, is commonly used of the Pharisaic system, few of the recognised authorities on rabbinism produce anything which resembles evasion of the law on any large scale. It is significant that in one passage at least our Lord seems almost to accuse the Pharisees because of their lack of casuistry—they ' lade men with burdens grievous to

---

[1] Maimonides, *Guide for the Perplexed*, iii. 26 (p. 312) ; cp. iii. 31 (p. 321).

[2] Mark vii. 11, Matt. xv. 5. See the relevant notes in (e.g.) Hasting's *Dictionary of the Bible*, i. p. 479 ; Edersheim, *Life and Times of Jesus the Messiah*, ii. pp. 19 ff. Probably *qorban* was in our Lord's time merely a highly emphatic and somewhat profane form of asseveration, and the phrase in the Gospels would be equivalent to, ' You shall get nothing out of me, by God.' But the Rabbis, perhaps to restrain the habit of profanity, treated this as a solemn oath which could not be broken without perjury against God ; and if a son, after saying *qorban*, changed his mind and wished to help his parents, he could only evade the guilt of perjury by making a present to a friend who could then make a present of it to the parents. If this is so, what our Lord was attacking was rigorism rather than casuistry. Origen, *in Matt.* xi. 9, mentions a similar practice in regard to debts, in which the oath played the part of the fraudulent bankruptcies of later days, and this suggests that evasion was the real object in view. There is a useful note on the interpretation of Mark vii. 11, in A. E. J. Rawlinson, *St Mark*, ad loc.

[3] I.e. ' bound by his oath,' as R.V. marg., Matt. xxiii. 16.

be borne, and they themselves touch not the burdens with
one of their fingers.' [1]

Such instances of Pharisaic casuistry as come most commonly into view are concerned with mitigating the rigours of
Sabbath observance without whittling away the absoluteness
of the command. It is a commonplace in this connection to
refer to that fictitious conversion of two adjoining houses
into one by opening doorways between them, or joining
them with beams, so that the precept forbidding the carrying
of food from house to house on the Sabbath might be disregarded in the spirit though kept in the letter.[2] Equally
well-known is the equivocation by which, though it was not
allowed to go more than 2000 yards from the Sabbath ' place ' [3]
on the Sabbath day, ' the place ' in question could be selected
2000 yards from the actual point of departure, so that double
the distance might be covered if desired.[4] So too a
sheaf of corn might not be moved on the Sabbath, but a
spoon, as required for the necessities of life, might ; if then
the spoon were put upon the sheaf the two might be moved
together without breach of the commandment.[5] These
evasions, trifling enough in themselves, were no doubt serious
breaches of the true spirit of morality, and they were all the
more surprising because in other directions the Rabbis showed
an ethical sanity in dealing with the Sabbath—and indeed
with other principles equally authoritative—which redounds
to their credit.

Thus it was universally accepted that any precept of the
law could be set aside where danger to life was concerned.
Rabbi Israel stood alone, perhaps, in holding that prayer
might be offered to idols if life could be saved thereby ;
though even he restricted the permission to cases in which
publicity could be avoided.[6] In general, however, the salvation of life superseded all other commands. A heathen
doctor could be called in for this purpose, although intercourse
with the heathen was in general strictly prohibited.[7] So

---

[1] Lk. xi. 46.
[2] E. Stapfer, *Palestine in the Time of Christ*, p. 354 ; E. Schürer, *Jewish
People in the Time of Jesus Christ*, II. ii. p. 120. (E.T., 1888.)
[3] Exod. xvi. 29.   [4] Schürer, *op. cit.* II. ii. p. 122.
[5] Edersheim, *op. cit.* ii. p. 56.   [6] Weber, *op. cit.* p. 33.
[7] Weber, *ut sup.*

obviously necessary is some relaxation of the law of this kind that it is surprising to find it supported by a perversely ingenious exposition of Scripture ; but the Rabbis found their justification in the exact turn of phrase of Leviticus xviii. 5.—'Ye shall therefore keep my statutes and my judgments, which if a man do he shall live therein.' It was pointed out that *live* and not *die* was the expression used, and therefore that ' statutes ' and ' judgments ' alike were subordinate to the primary requirement of life-saving.[1]

The Sabbath law at all events was freely set aside in the interests of life. ' You may desecrate one Sabbath to keep many Sabbaths ' was a phrase employed ; another, strikingly akin to a saying of our Lord's, ran in the form : ' The Sabbath is delivered into your hands, and not you into the hands of the Sabbath.'[2] Naturally enough this led to considerable quibbling about the exact moment when life became endangered[3] : and there must have been some Rabbis at least who sympathised with our Lord's extension of the principle to cover all cases of humanitarianism. Lighting and putting out a fire on the Sabbath was prohibited by the law itself ; but this injunction could be disregarded not only where life was at stake, but where the operative cause was fear of burglars or of evil spirits, or an invalid's need of sleep.[4] Necessary work was allowed on the Sabbath, as the Gospels show, and although tying and untying a knot was one of the thirty-nine forms of work forbidden, where the knot retained a garment, hat or shoe the prohibition was relaxed.[5]

In this respect, therefore, it would appear that the Rabbis adopted an eminently sane outlook towards the law. Nor were they rigorists as regards veracity. How far liberalism went in this matter does not appear—at all events a ' necessary lie ' might be told to cheat a robber or a tax-gatherer. The evasion of taxation, indeed, seems to have been regarded—as at other epochs—with equanimity ; it is significantly noted that the Scriptural prohibition against wearing a mixture of linen and wool might not be waived ' even in

[1] *Jewish Encyclopedia*, i. p. 162 ; cp. I. Abrahams, *Studies in Pharisaism and the Gospels*, i. p. 129.

[2] *Jewish Encyclopedia, ut supra.*   [3] Stapfer, pp. 355, 356.
[4] Exod. xxxv. 3 ; Stapfer, p. 352.   [5] *Ibid.* p. 350.

F

order to defraud the revenue.'[1] Hasty vows which made too great a demand upon the devotee could be commuted or evaded if an appropriate method of doing so presented itself, and the technical name of 'a door' was in common use for such a method.[2] It cannot be asserted that these mitigations of the law are wholly free from the taint of casuistry, in the lower sense of the word; but if they went no further than this, and were publicly recognised as valid, they would scarcely undermine the moral foundations of society. At all events there appears to be little evidence of any such widespread evasion of moral obligations as distinguished some of the Stoics and the Jesuits.

The moral deficiencies of Judaism lay elsewhere. This is not the place to consider that externalism for which our Lord principally arraigned the Pharisees. One other feature in the system however deserves mention, because it illustrates the true use of casuistry misapplied by the peculiar temperament of the nation. Gamaliel is often regarded with approval for the tolerance of Christianity he exhibited in the Sanhedrin, and his epigram : ' If this counsel or work be of men it will come to nought, but if it be of God ye cannot overthrow it, lest haply ye be found even to fight against God,'[3] is one of the famous phrases of the New Testament. But what influenced Gamaliel was not so much tolerance as timidity. A new and unexpected light is thrown upon his attitude by another sentence attributed to him in the 'Sayings of the Fathers' : ' Get thee an authority and be far from doubt, and do not give the tithe by guesswork.'[4] He refused to act upon his own initiative. In this he showed himself a typical Jew. ' Why even of yourselves judge ye not what is right ? ' is our Lord's comment upon this aspect of their character.[5] ' Jewish piety consisted,' as Sir John Seeley says,[6] 'in a certain

---

[1] Schürer, I. ii. p. 71 ; see Lev. xix. 19 ; Deut. xxii. 11.
[2] Weber, p. 33. [3] Acts v. 38, 39.
[4] *Pirke Aboth* i. 16. It is to be noticed that Oesterley (in R. H. Charles' *Apocrypha and Pseudepigrapha*, ii. *ad. loc.*) takes 'be far from doubt' as a warning against scrupulosity. But the context clearly determines the sense in the opposite direction, and it is so interpreted by Herford and Taylor. [5] Luke xii. 57.
[6] *Ecce Homo*, ch. xvi. The reference is presumably to the N.T. usage of εὐλαβής, etc., 'expressing Jewish, and, as one might say, Old Testament piety '—'leaving nothing willingly undone which pertained to the circle

timid caution or wary walking in the old paths ; and when they became Christians it is remarkable that they gave to those who continued to be what they had originally been the title of "cautious men." ' The desire to interpret, articulate and apply the law which gives rise to the wisest efforts of casuistry can go too far ; you cannot plot out the map of life beforehand with the full detail of an Ordnance Survey.

Yet this was what the Rabbis attempted to do—to have an authoritative ruling in readiness for every contingency which might arise. It is casuistry of the sounder kind, for if your general principles are correctly stated they ought to be capable of the most detailed application, given a true knowledge of the circumstances of each several case. But it is impossible to anticipate these circumstances in all their manifold and rich variety, especially when among them are included the hidden motions of the individual heart ; and the assumption that all possible contingencies have been provided for, and that every case which arises must therefore come under one ruling or another, is in practice as fruitful of moral error as any other fallacy. Again, detailed legislation is bound, in fact, to produce that externalism to which we have just alluded. The intricacies of the heart defy exhaustive classification, but types of action can be pigeon-holed ; and moral rulings therefore tend to concentrate upon the outward action and to ignore the inward motive, till in the end the importance of purity of motive is all too easily forgotten.

Yet even if the attempt to legislate beforehand for every emergency could be successful—whether in the case of the Rabbis or of any other school of morality—so that no possible contingency to the end of time remained unprovided for, the result would still be disappointing. No place would be left for conscience in the guidance of the individual life, and without such a place, man, though he might be moral— though he might indeed achieve acts of the greatest heroism in

of prescribed duties '—' accurately and scrupulously performing that which is prescribed, with the consciousness of the danger of slipping into a careless and negligent performance of God's service, and of the need therefore of anxiously watching against the adding to or diminishing from, or in any other way altering that which has been by Him commanded '—' making a conscience of changing anything, of omitting anything, being above all things fearful to offend '—Trench, *Synonyms of N.T.*, pp. 174, 175.

obedience to this infinitely-detailed law—would still miss something of his inheritance. He would lack just that factor in life which changes him from the obedient servant of an absent deity to the autonomous soul in immediate communion with God. He would be passively tractable instead of actively creative, always among the herd and never among its leaders; his interest centred in the legally safe rather than in the morally praiseworthy. Nor is this all. Let us assume that externalism could be avoided by such meticulous enumeration of cases, though in the last paragraph we were forced to the conclusion that it could not. Even so, we should be left face to face with a moral perversion every bit as dangerous—the perversion technically known as ' scrupulosity '—the perversion, in fact, from which Gamaliel suffered. Knowledge that somewhere or other in the encyclopædic archives of the law your particular case has been provided for must, if you are conscientious, create in you an intense anxiety not to ' do the wrong thing,' and often enough will result in that exaggerated interest in little sins, to the exclusion of greater and more immediate issues, to which reference was made in an earlier chapter. Hooker stated the case with characteristic moderation when he wrote : ' In every action of common life to find out some sentence clearly and infallibly setting before our eyes what we ought to do (seem we in Scripture ever so expert), would trouble us more than we are aware.' [1]

The wise moralist, therefore, though he recognises that the law is flexible, developing and adaptable, and so has no need of that casuistry which is in effect no more than equivocal evasion, will recognise also that he must restrain the instinct to legislate for all the minutiæ of life, and so avoid the three dangers of externalism, scrupulosity and passive tractability. The Rabbis, so far from restraining this instinct, indulged it to the top of its bent. Dr. Montefiore, indeed, has made out a case for the type of morality expressed by the 119th Psalm and the detailed legalism of the Rabbis.[2] The trivialities of law, he suggests, were loved

---

[1] R. Hooker, *Laws of Eccles. Pol.* ii. 8, § 7.
[2] Foakes Jackson and Kirsopp Lake, *Beginnings of Christianity*, i. pp. 59, 60.

by the Jews in the same way as the members of a family
delight in all the tiny household conventions which have
grown up among them, and are punctiliously observed as
giving a flavour and piquancy to the routine of domesticity.
The law ' partook of the nature of a delightful secret between
the Jew and his heavenly Father.' There is real truth in
this observation ; but when brought into comparison with
the interminable controversies of the rabbinic schools it
cannot escape the criticism that it is an unreal idealisation of
the facts. The well-known problems of the egg laid upon the
Sabbath day ; of the exact moment when the Sabbath began
(the gloaming ? the appearance of one, two or three stars ?) ;
of the various kinds of writing which were or were not allowed
upon the Sabbath ; of the degree in which vessels of different
shape respectively contracted defilement ; of the legitimacy
of using ditch, tank or spring water for ritual purification ;
of the amount of food necessary to constitute a meal before
and after which grace must be said, and the like—these
' airy and impertinent observations of the Jews,' as Jeremy
Taylor calls them,[1] need not be recapitulated here ; but they
do not seem to fit Dr. Montefiore's formula. If they added
piquancy to anything at all, it can only have been to academic
discussion, not to vital religion and the worship of a divine
Father. And close behind them loomed the three dangers
of which we have spoken.

The eighteenth century saw a similar outcrop of moral
pedantry in Roman Catholic casuistry. Attempts were made
to tabulate the exact sums of money which in each state of life
would constitute a grave theft, the exact distance in yards from
the open Church door within which the faithful might satisfy
the precept of ' hearing mass,' the exact degree of inebriation
which converted drunkenness from a venial into a mortal
sin. This trifling with matters which deserve more robust and
responsible treatment survives in some manuals of moral
theology to the present day ; it may be confidently believed
that it is no more than a traditional survival. But it represents a danger against which casuistry must always be on its
guard, and from which the Christian Church did not wholly
emancipate itself when it threw off the yoke of the Mosaic

---

[1] *Duct. Dub.* II. iii. 1, § 2.

law. There are still people whose ' only fault it is,' in the words of the Professor at the Breakfast Table, ' that nature wrote out the list of their virtues on ruled paper and forgot to rub out the lines.' ' The accidents and circumstances which make sins great and small,' wrote Richard Baxter,[1] ' are oft-times so numerous and various that no rules can be laid down to serve all times, no more than in Law and Physick any Law-works or Physick-books will serve all cases without a present experienced judicious counsellor.' In such cases, he says, ' present Prudence and Sincerity must do most.'

5. *Stoicism*

The temper of primitive Christianity reacted too strongly from Judaism for the rabbinic spirit to penetrate it very deeply. Such legalism and casuistry as it exhibited came in the main from another source. The moral system of western Christendom, though in essence of a very different character, was forced by circumstances into the mould of Roman Stoicism ; Ambrose, Lactantius, Augustine were all profoundly influenced by Cicero. And Cicero himself, though he professed the Academic rather than the Stoic philosophy, inherited his moral outlook from a long Stoic tradition which had already passed through several phases, and in its course exhibits just that depravation of too rigid ideals by means of a too pliant casuistry which on general grounds we have already learnt to expect.

The first Stoics reveal something of the characteristics of the great Hebrew prophets. Like them they transfer the centre of ethical interest from society to the individual ; like them they find goodness to consist wholly in correspondence with the ethical law, and not in conventional observances. Like them (though for a very different reason and in a very different spirit) they insist upon social service as a first principle of morality. But prophecy died before its tenets were accepted as regulative of the intercourse of a whole society, and that function—in whose discharge is the sole test of an ethical system—passed to the law. Stoicism, on

[1] *Christian Directory*, i. 3, 6.

the other hand, though it had many imitators and plagiarists in the Roman Empire, had no real competitor until Christianity matured ; and the Stoic philosopher realised that if anyone were to guide the struggling masses on the road to virtue, it would have to be himself. Casuistry therefore was an inevitable development ; the only question was, Would it be casuistry of the legitimate kind ? Would it steadily and wisely apply the general principles of morality to new problems; or would it evade their incidence by ingenious sophistries ?

The answer was soon apparent, and the surviving fragments of ancient Stoicism show how complacently it often treated the problems and frailties of everyday life. Two reasons contributed to the result ; the first, the nobility of its demands; the second, their perverseness. The Stoics' ideal was that of a life according to reason,[1] and reason to them was the complete antithesis of emotion. Thus not merely emotion, but all the things to which emotion usually attaches itself—health, sickness, wealth, poverty, family and social ties—must be written off if not as hindrances, at all events as matters of complete indifference to the moral life. The wise man would adopt an attitude of complete 'apathy' towards them ; even ' hatred ' of them would be too emotional, and therefore the mark of a fool.

Between such a philosophy and the affairs of normal citizenship there could be no legitimate alliance. Two forms of union, however, were attempted. In the former, of which on the whole Panaetius and Cicero, his disciple and admirer, are representatives, the system itself was modified to admit a relative degree of moral value in the pursuit of health, wealth and the amenities of life [2]; the ideal of apathy—the ignoring of the emotions—was exchanged for that of 'eupathy' —their regulation by reason.[3] It is in this form that Stoicism

[1] See E. Zeller, *Stoics, Epicureans and Sceptics* (E.T.), p. 215 ff., for a full account. More recent discussions in R. D. Hicks, *Stoic and Epicurean*, p. 90 ff. ; E. V. Arnold, *Roman Stoicism*, pp. 276 ff., 346 ff. ; W. L. Davidson, *Stoic Creed* (note, however, that Davidson, p. 51, says somewhat oddly, ' Stoic Ethics did not find casuistry very congenial ').

[2] From being treated as purely indifferent (ἀδιάφορὰ) they came to be regarded as 'preferable.' (προηγμενὰ).

[3] Diog. Lært. vii. 115 ; cp. Cic., *Tusc. Disp.* iv. 6, 12—the εὐπαθείαι, or disciplined emotions, which were admitted as legitimate were rational joy, rational aversion and rational desire.

chiefly affected Christianity, but it was a form wholly different in essence and conception from the original system. In so far as it evolved out of that system, however, it shows casuistry doing its rightful work of re-interpreting general principles in accordance with the needs of new experience.

The second form of alliance between Stoicism and common life was far more questionable, and shows casuistry at its worst, whittling away the demands of a rigid system by means of unworthy evasions and chicanery. It is doubtful at what point it began ; Zeno and Chrysippus themselves are credited with *obiter dicta* which seem to illustrate it. It took its rise in one of the fundamental doctrines of the system—that since no external ' goods ' are of any value, the motive of an action, and not the action itself, is the only thing that need be considered ; the end will justify the means.[1] Thus the wise man could, in the pursuit of virtue, dissemble, lie, deceive and engage in activities which not merely the high-minded but even the ordinary man would condemn. This was the famous doctrine of the ' economy '[2] of truth and morality, which Christian writers adopted because of its usefulness in justifying the less edifying episodes of the Old Testament. Seneca, as quoted by Lactantius,[3] said openly : ' The wise man will commit actions of which he does not approve, using them as stepping-stones to higher things. Without abandoning his virtue he will adapt himself to circumstances, and for his own purposes will employ means which others utilise in the pursuit of glory or pleasure. He will vie with the worldling in luxury, with the fool in folly, but his method and his purpose will be different from theirs.' He may employ mental restriction and equivocation when it suits his ends [4]; and ' depart from the narrow path '[5] of virtue to help a friend. He may say that

---

[1] Seneca, *de Ben.* vi. 11. 3 : ' Voluntas est quæ nobis ponit officium'—illustrated by Chrysippus' story of the two boys who were sent to fetch Plato. The one who looked for him diligently is rewarded, though he failed to find him ; the other who took no trouble in the search is punished, though as a matter of fact he chanced on Plato by accident whilst loitering at a puppet show.

[2] Also called συμπεριφορά, *Anbequemung,* ' diplomacy,' Epict., *Diss.* iii. 14.

[3] *Div. Inst.* iii. 15.

[4] Sen., *de Ben.* iv. 39. Cicero, *de Off.* iii. 29 (107)—the time-honoured case of the lie to a pirate.

[5] ' Declinandum de via est,' Cic., *de Am.* 17.

wealth, health and reputation are desirable when he knows them to be worthless ;[1] he may wear a manner wholly contradictory to his real feelings.[2] Drunkenness is forbidden to him ; but he may be ' in wine '—a nice distinction—if it will drive dull care away.[3] He may purchase the friendship of tyrants by pandering to their lowest passions.[4] Even the worst types of sexual perversion,[5] and cannibalism itself,[6] were in theory at least legitimate if occasion demanded them.

This doctrine is no more than that which the Jesuits were later to republish under the name of ' directing the intention ' ; and the Stoics robbed the Society of Jesus of the credit they would fain have taken from the discovery. ' By this means,' Pascal is informed, ' our doctors discharge all their duty towards God and towards man. By permitting the action, they satisfy the world ; by purifying the intention, they satisfy the Gospel. This is a secret, sir, which was entirely unknown to the ancients ; the world is indebted for the discovery entirely to our doctors. You understand it now, I hope ? '[7] The amazing consequences deduced from the maxim were often due, as we noted previously, to idle theorising and a love of abstract paradox ; in the case of the Stoics they sometimes reveal nothing more than a contempt for conventional moral standards which has of course its good side. What is clear, however, is that the Stoics made a real attempt to find solutions for every-day moral problems ;[8] and that some of them at least—Diogenes of Babylon seems to have been a principal offender—were regrettably lax in their decisions.

---

[1] Chrysippus *ap.* Plut., *de Stoic. Repugn.* 5.

[2] Sen., *Ep.* 5 : ' Intus omnia dissimilia sint ; frons nostra populo conveniat.'

[3] Diog. Laert vii. 118 ; Seneca, *Dial.* ix. 17. 4.

[4] Seneca, *de Ben.* vii. 20. 3 ; cp. Tac., *Ann.* xiv. 2.

[5] Diog. Laert. vii. 129, 188 ; Stob., *Ecl.* ii. 118 ; Plut., *de Stoic. Repugn.* 22.

[6] Chrysippus, see Zeller, p. 289. Cannibalism as possibly legitimate in case of extreme hunger is also discussed by Osiander, *Theol. Cas.* ii. 7, n. 198.

[7] *Lettres Prov.* vii.

[8] In spite of the protest of Aristo of Chios, a pupil of Zeno, who ' limited ethics to the most fundamental notions,' and thought the application of these notions to particular problems ' to be useless and futile '—' fit only for nursemaids and pedagogues but not becoming for philosophers,' Zeller, pp. 60, 61 ; Thamin, p. 41 ff.

The cause of this laxity should·by now be clear. The Stoic who remained true to his high principles had no message for the ordinary man ; his code admitted of no compromise with the world. The braver spirits adapted the code honestly until it became a new philosophy capable of ultimate incorporation into Christianity. The more timid or more obstinate refused to do so ; and were forced, while still paying lip-service to their creed, to evade all its main requirements by dishonourable shifts and quibblings. In Stoicism, as much as anywhere else in history, there can be traced both the legitimate and the illegitimate activities of casuistry.

Few witnesses to the content of the Stoic ethical discussions are more important than Cicero, though he did not call himself a Stoic. He gives us a clear insight into the range of the problems discussed ; he records some of the lax decisions arrived at, and shows how Panaetius and his school took the bolder line of adapting principles, rather than of evading them, at the demand of practice. But Cicero himself was no casuist, and gives little help in the problems to which he introduces us. He held firmly to the belief that there could never be any genuine problems of conduct, because duty and interest must always point the same way. Consequently he only discusses such cases as bring out this principle ; and by interpreting ' interest ' in a somewhat limited sense he manages to produce a fairly watertight exposition of his thesis. Occasionally, indeed, as in his praise of Regulus,[1] the Roman tradition of keeping good faith with the enemy at all costs leads him to flights of altruism in spite of himself. But in general he is prosaically conventional.

Panaetius had contemplated a work on morals in three volumes, the first dealing with duty, the second with expediency, the third with the apparent conflict between the two.[2] But the third part was for some reason left incomplete, though the treatise was composed thirty years before its author's death. To the suggestion that there is no such conflict, and that therefore Panaetius deliberately left it untouched, Cicero gives an impatient negative, for the suggestion

---

[1] Cicero, de Off. iii. 30 (109) ; 31 (111).   [2] Ib. iii. 2 (7–9).

flies in the face of all known facts. The conflict involved, however, is only a conflict between the apparently expedient and the truly expedient or wholly moral.[1] It was this that Panaetius intended to discuss ; some unforeseen accident prevented the completion of the design, but Cicero is prepared to step into the gap.[2] He therefore sets himself to show that, on the level of conventional morality at all events, honesty is always the best policy,[3] and that the only rule in such cases is the old Stoic saying, 'Whatever is right is expedient ; and nothing which is wrong can be expedient.'[4] So in the second part of his book he explains at almost unnecessary length how virtue will always secure its possessor popular favour and esteem, while vice and self-seeking lead to public ruin. Expediency can never really conflict with duty ; it need never, therefore, enter into the moralist's calculations at all.

In spite of this, however, Cicero does allow the strict letter of the law to be set aside by calculations of expediency, and thus his practice is more flexible than his theory ; or rather (for this is the truth) his theory breaks down in practice, and he is left not with an abstract and inviolable code of ' Lie not,' ' Steal not ' and the like, but with calculations of a more elastic order. ' May I,' he asks, ' if I am starving steal food from a wholly worthless fellow ? '[5] As the text stands Cicero appears to answer this question with an emphatic negative ; but modern editors[6] ascribe this decision to a rigorist interpolator. At all events his next case—which is no more than a variant of the last—is treated in a different manner. ' May not an honourable man steal a blanket from a cruel and inhuman tyrant, to prevent himself from freezing ? ' Easily answered :—if mere consideration of yourself is your motive, it would be a sin ; but if the preservation of your life is of real importance to the State, the theft (for which, with Ancient Pistol, he now merely uses the word " convey "[7]) is blameless. Especially is this

---

[1] Cicero, *de Off.* iii. 7 (34) ; cp. ii. 3 (10).

[2] *Ib.* iii. 7 (33).   [3] *Ib.* 3 (17).

[4] *Ib.* 4 (20). 'Quicquid honestum est idem utile, nec utile quicquam quod non honestum.'

[5] *Ib.* iii. 6 (29).   [6] E.g. Holden, *ad loc.*, and others quoted by him.

[7] *de Off.* iii. 6 (31), ' transferre.'

true when the blanket belongs to a tyrant, for the right thing
to do with a tyrant is to put him to death out-of-hand ; and
the mere pilfering of his goods is consequently quite unobjectionable.

In the relations of commerce Cicero insists upon a high
standard. We owe to him some of the classical problems
which casuistry has discussed in all ages. He gives us the
case of the Alexandrian merchant [1] who brought a large
cargo of corn to Rhodes in time of famine, knowing (what the
Rhodians were ignorant of) that his monopoly would be
broken in a few hours' time by the arrival of a whole corn-
fleet. May he honestly conceal this knowledge, and so sell
at famine-prices ? By rights Cicero should have attacked
this problem from the standpoint of the ' just price ' ; but the
doctrine of the ' just price ' is scarcely glanced at. Diogenes
of Babylon and his pupil, Antipater, had long disputed the
point ; Antipater decided for complete candour, Diogenes
allowed the merchant to get the best price he could without
falling foul of the law. Diogenes' arguments are disingenuous ; but neither of the disputants, nor even Cicero himself
(who sides with Antipater), has touched the root-question of
principle—the conditions which must determine legitimate
gain. Whewell's discussion is better than either ; and because
it shows the progress made by sane casuistry throughout the
centuries may fairly be quoted here.

The obligation to disclose relevant facts is, ' in great
measure,' according to Whewell, ' defined by the general
understanding existing among buyers and sellers. . . . The
buyer does not depend upon the seller, nor the seller upon
the buyer for (his) information. He who has, or thinks
he has, superior information . . . takes advantage of it and
is understood to do so ; and prices are settled by the general
play of such opinions, proceeding from all sides. But if
a seller possess information which he is not understood to
have,[2] and takes advantage of it, he violates the general

---

[1] Cicero, *de Off.* iii. 12 (50). See also Grotius, *de Jure Pacis*, etc., ii. 12. 9 ;
Whewell, *Elements of Morality*, Bk. II. ch. xv. p. 306. The problems of
monopoly are a commonplace of all casuists. For further discussion of the
problem of the ' just price,' see below, p. 198 ff.

[2] This would have been clearer if Whewell had added, ' because it is
of a type wholly abnormal in matters of the kind.'

understanding, and thus is guilty of deceit. If the merchant in question asks such an exorbitant price for his corn as to imply that no further supply is probable, he falls under this blame. On the other hand, he is not bound to sell his corn to-day for the price to which it may fall to-morrow when the other vessels arrive ; for as a trader, he may take advantage of the greater skill and foresight which has brought him first to the post. . . . But if the buyer asks questions on this subject, the seller may not tell a lie. And if the seller is silent as to this circumstance, he takes upon himself the responsibility, as a moral agent, of making an equitable estimate of the gain to which his unsuspected superiority of knowledge entitles him.' Thus the matter becomes in the end a problem of the determination of the ' just price ' ; but even Whewell does not continue it beyond this point, in spite of the advances made by the schoolmen in dealing with the question.

Cicero next introduces the cognate problem of the concealment of defects in an article offered for sale. The problem is of course one which every casuist has handled ; horses and houses are the usual vendibles instanced. Cicero [1] chooses the house—a poor house indeed, for it is ' dangerous to health ; [2] serpents are to be seen in every bedroom ; the timbers are rotten, and the whole place tumbling down.' But, strangely enough, no one knows of these defects except the vendor. There would seem to be no case at all here, and indeed Cicero, following Antipater, says as much without hesitation. A similar case was that of Centumalus, who sold his house, but concealed the fact that a demolition-order had been issued against it by the municipal authorities ; [3] and here indeed Cato as official arbitrator declared the sale void. But it is interesting to notice Diogenes' arguments in defence of such reticences. ' No one is compelled to buy the place ; and every intending purchaser has the right to inspect and enquire. You can advertise a jerry-built tenement as a " Fine Well-built Mansion for Sale " without coming on the windy side of the law ; surely therefore mere

---

[1] Cicero, de Off. iii. 13 (54) ; cp. similar cases mentioned in iii. 23 (91).
[2] Or possibly ' haunted,' see Holden, ad loc.
[3] de Off. iii. 16 (66).

concealment of facts is less blameworthy than such open mendacity ? And what a fool a man would look if on your principle he were forced to word his advertisement "For Sale : a Thoroughly Unhealthy House."' There is obviously something to be said on Diogenes' side, though he has not proved his case ; and the real point at issue—when is a defect relevant to the price, and when not ?—is scarcely touched.

Here, again, later discussion clarified the matter, as may be seen, for example, from the cases discussed by Aquinas, Baxter and Hall.[1] But, even so, exact discrimination is impossible unless all the circumstances of each case are considered. Pontas, a famous and upright French moralist of the early eighteenth century, held that you might sell a shying horse [2] (provided that the price took account of the defect) without mentioning his idiosyncrasy to the purchaser, as the latter could not suffer thereby. Collet, one of his editors, and apparently an indifferent horseman, was of a different opinion. 'If M. Pontas,' he writes plaintively, 'had run the risks which I ran on the Saumur road through the vice of a shying horse, he would not have regarded this defect as of no importance to the purchaser.' [3]

Cicero has obviously chosen extreme cases of dishonesty for discussion in order rather to prove his thesis than to aid the genuinely troubled conscience by examining really difficult and dubious cases. That he knew of such problems is sufficiently clear. The sixth book of Hecato's ' de Officiis,' he mentions,[4] was full of them. Must a man sacrifice his own life for the life of his slaves, for example, in a time of famine ? If something has to be thrown overboard in a storm at sea, which must go first, a worthless slave or a valuable racehorse ? We may shudder at the low estimate set on the life of a slave, but granted that that was a commonplace of the time, here is a real problem. Hecato knows of many others. If one plank only survives from a shipwreck, may the wise man (that is, the man of real moral value to the community) tear it away from the ' fool ' (who to the Stoic, as to the Jewish moralist, was always a moral degenerate) ?

---

[1] *Infra* pp. 198-202.   [2] ' Cheval ombrageux.'
[3] Migne-Pontas, *Dictionnaire de Cas de Conscience* (Paris 1863), s.v. 'Vente,' case 27.   [4] *de Off.* iii. 23 (89).

If he be owner of the ship, as well as a wise man, does that not give him unqualified right to the plank ? If two men both reach the plank, ought each to try to make the other take it ? And if they do what is to happen then—are both to drown ? When, if at all, ought a son to inform against a sacrilegious father, or one engaged in treasonable conspiracy against the State ? If a vendor in ignorance offer you a rarity at less than its market price, need you inform him of its true value ? May I pass on to another as genuine a counterfeit coin which I have myself received in good faith ? Am I bound by a promise extracted from me by force or fraud ? [1] All these problems are genuine problems of conscience— some more, no doubt, some less—but Cicero merely glances at them in passing. The reason is obvious. He is no casuist at heart ; he selects his instances merely to prove that knavery is impolitic—if for no other reason, at all events because of the infamy it brings.

That this is so is clear from the famous story of the Syracusan banker, which he tells at great length, and in which no problem of conscience is in the smallest degree concerned. Canius, a Roman knight, was on holiday at Syracuse, and thought of buying an estate there. The banker Pythias, hearing of this, allowed Canius to use his own gardens, which he alleged not to be for sale, and invited him to a dinner-party there. But he used the influence, which (as Cicero says) bankers have, to perpetrate a gross fraud on the unsuspecting Roman. During the course of the dinner innumerable anglers appeared with boat-loads of fish, all of them alleged to be caught in the grounds. Pythias even went to the extent of saying that his was the best piece of fishing in all Syracuse. The sequel is obvious. Canius insisted on buying the place at a ruinous price, and at once emulated Pythias's ostentation by arranging another banquet. It was only when no anglers appeared that he began to have his doubts ; and even then he had to ask his next-door neighbour whether they were taking a day off, learning to his horror that no one ever fished those waters, and that the apparent catch of the day before was wholly unprecedented.

[1] The pirate, iii. 29 (107).

Cicero, therefore, is more a witness to the prevailing interest of the Stoics in detailed moral problems, and of their tendency at times to a laxity of outlook, than a casuist himself. The problems he recorded, however, passed wholesale into Christianity, and provided a storehouse of questions, some of which at least were pressing in every age. Others —such as that of the plank in the shipwreck—are of less normal occurrence ; but academic casuists throughout the centuries enjoyed them every bit as much. Another repertory of abstract problems, even more remote from ordinary life, was provided by the tasks set as exercises or declamations for budding law-students in the schools of rhetoric. These, indeed, do not reappear so frequently in Christian thought, though the 'Gesta Romanorum' is full of them ; but they illustrate the growing passion of the Western world for ethico-legal discussion, and its growing tendency to substitute equity ' for excessive absoluteness in paternal power and excessive strictness in justice.'[1] Little survives of them except the statement of the problems, and some shorthand notes of their treatment by famous exponents. They are often highly imaginative in conception and unsavoury in character ; they betray the hand of the novelist rather than of the lawyer. Pirate chiefs and their beautiful daughters, stern parents, romantic youths, treacherous friends, betrayed maidens, quixotic patrons and all the figures of the cheaper melodrama appear in them for perhaps the first time in history. But sometimes, at least, problems of real moral importance emerge.

Should a slave, for example, administer poison to his master dying of a horrible disease, at the latter's express request ? How far may the consecrated accessories of worship be put to secular purposes in case of need ? When, if ever, is suicide legitimate ? May the execution of a criminal be made a public exhibition ? What sacrifices may art demand of its votaries ? May a criminal's house be burgled to secure evidence against him ? What are the limits of filial duty ? What restitution should be made to those who have suffered for the common good ? These and many similar problems

---

[1] H. Bornecque, *Sénèque le Rhéteur : Controverses et Suasoires* (Paris, n.d.).

underlie the exaggerated theses of Seneca's 'Controversies.'[1] In them are enshrined the final pagan examples of that interest in the eternal problems of practical morality to which the Stoics pointed the way, and which the Christian Church was to attempt to satisfy. With Stoics of both schools, as with the Roman lawyers, she shared this interest; it was providential for her history that she took as her guide in morals the sane principles of Panaetius as handed on by Cicero, and not the combination of rigid theory with lax practice which marked the degeneracy of Stoicism, nor the readiness to make the worse appear the better cause which characterised the rhetorical exercises of the Imperial lawyers.

[1] E.g. Seneca Rhet., *Controv.* i. 7; iii. 6; iii. 9; iv. 4; ix. 2; x. 5, 6, etc.

CHAPTER IV

1. *Casuistry and the Gospels*

CASUISTRY, in the popular sense of the word, is so degraded a thing that the mere mention of it in connection with our Lord savours of the worst profanity. And yet if we are right in giving the word a wider meaning than the usual, and interpreting it of all attempts, legitimate as much as illegitimate, to extend and adapt the moral law to fit new cases, Christ was the greatest of casuists. More than this, it is clear that ' plain men ' and rigorists alike held Him to be a casuist in the worst sense of the word. The demand that He should ' speak plainly ' comes indeed in the Fourth Gospel ; but it echoes incidents in the Synoptic record. Peter, who wanted a definite and unequivocal ruling as to the number of times he should forgive his brother ; Martha, who was clear that Satan finds some mischief still for idle hands to do ; the Pharisees, who saw their divorce problem as one to which a simple ' Yes ' or ' No ' answer could be given—these and other enquirers must have been surprised when that which was so obvious to them seemed not at all obvious to Him. It is the plain man's quarrel with casuistry, that it never gives simple answers to simple questions ; that it is always obscuring the straightforward precepts of common-sense morality with qualifications, and cautions and reservations.[1]

Our Lord was straightforward enough on occasion, as countless passages in the Gospels show. The difficulty lay in the fact that no one could be certain of getting a straight forward answer to his question. ' Who is the neighbour whom I am to love ? ' is a straightforward question ; but the

---

[1] Compare the criticisms so commonly directed against Browning's later ' casuistical' poems : *Prince Hohenstiel-Schwangau, Fifine, The Inn Album, Red-Cotton-Night-Cap Country.*

Lord answers it with a description of the neighbour who shows love for you. ' Here is a woman taken in adultery,' presents a clear-cut issue ; ' Let him that is without sin among you cast the first stone ' confounds the issue at once. ' Who is the greatest in the kingdom of heaven ? ' involves no difficulty ; but the paradox of the little child makes both question and questioner look foolish. ' By what authority doest Thou these things ? ' could be answered in one word ; why drag in irrelevances about the Baptist ? Even the answer to the tribute-money question is not without its ambiguity ; a coin is not necessarily ' Caesar's ' because it bears his image and superscription. In every case our Lord's epigram seems to draw aside a curtain, revealing behind the original simple question a medley of confused principles and problems. It is as though He would show His listeners the complexity of factors which have to be taken into account—which the good casuist must take into account—before even the simplest of simple cases can be solved.

The plain man must have found all this perplexing ; but it was invigorating too. Morality, we are forced to conclude, is not a trim museum of neatly-parcelled duties, as the Scribes and Pharisees would have it, but a garden stocked with flowers of every kind, whose growth must be ordered indeed, but not reduced to a cramped and unnatural simplicity. No question is as simple as it looks , or rather, if a question looks simple it is only because we have not seen all that it really involves. This characteristic of revealing moral issues to be more complicated than they appear at first sight is distinctive of very many of the parables. The four comments on the parable of the Unjust Steward—' The children of this world are wiser in their generation than the children of light,' ' Make to yourselves friends of the mammon of unrighteousness,' ' If ye have been unfaithful in that which is another's, who will give you that which is your own ? ' ' Ye cannot serve God and mammon '—appear to be hints of so many separate ways of interpreting it. But what is certain is that Christian thought has never been satisfied to regard them as exhausting its meaning ; it has come back to the central theme again and again, in the belief that under that strange paradox lies hidden some ethical truth of quite

new and startling importance. Nor does the Unjust Steward
stand alone. Parable after parable conspires to shock the
plain man out of his pathetic faith that moral judgments are
easily come by. Even to this day he finds the sermons he
has heard about the Labourers in the Vineyard and the
Wedding Garment as unsatisfying as those on the Unjust
Steward. For the sermons over-simplify the problems,
and though the plain man is the apostle of simplification,
he has yet the grace to see that there are some occasions
when simplification is only a parody of truth. ' A platitude,'
in Lord Morley's words, ' is not turned into a profundity
by being dressed up as a riddle ; ' but a riddle may teach us
that there are profundities which our platitudes ignore.

It is well known that St. Matthew, on the one hand,
and St. Mark and St. Luke on the other (if we may still use
the traditional nomenclature for the first three Gospels),
held different theories as to our Lord's reason for speaking
in parables.[1] The former ascribed to Him the purpose of
revealing truth, of bringing it to the surface ; the latter,
that of concealing it, of hiding it from the plain man's view.
As far as His ethical teaching is concerned we may reconcile
the two points of view by saying that the parables were designed to reveal that truth is a thing concealed, to bring to
the surface the fact that it is deeply hidden below the outward
appearances of life. Not the three parables we have mentioned alone, but almost all the parables disclose apparent
miscarriages of divine justice—divergences between God's
judgments and man's. For what offence is the rich man so

---

[1] Mt. xiii. 13 : διὰ τοῦτο ἐν παραβολαῖς αὐτοῖς λαλῶ, ὅτι βλέποντες οὐ βλέπουσι,
καὶ ἀκούοντες οὐκ ἀκούουσιν οὐδὲ συνιοῦσι. καὶ ἀναπληροῦται αὐτοῖς ἡ προφητεία
Ἡσαΐου ἡ λέγουσα, ᾽Ακοῇ ἀκούσετε καὶ οὐ μὴ συνῆτε· καὶ βλέποντες βλέψετε, καὶ οὐ
μὴ ἴδητε κ.τ.λ. (A.V. ' Therefore speak I to them in parables, because they
seeing see not ; and hearing they hear not, neither do they understand.
And in them is fulfilled the prophecy of Esaias, which saith, By hearing
ye shall hear and shall not understand ; and seeing ye shall see and not
perceive ' etc.) Contrast Mk. iv. 11 : ἐκείνοις δὲ τοῖς ἔξω ἐν παραβολαῖς τὰ
πάντα γίνεται· ἵνα βλέποντες βλέπωσι, καὶ μὴ ἴδωσι, καὶ ἀκούοντες ἀκούωσι, καὶ μὴ
συνιῶσι κ.τ.λ. (A.V. ' But unto them that are without, all [these] things are
done in parables, that seeing they may see and not perceive and hearing
they may hear and not understand ' etc.) Lk. viii. 10 : τοῖς δὲ λοιποῖς ἐν
παραβολαῖς, ἵνα βλέποντες μὴ βλέπωσι, καὶ ἀκούοντες μὴ συνιῶσιν. (A.V. ' But to
others in parables, that seeing they might not see, and hearing they
might not understand.')

grievously tormented ? Why is not the mercy of a fuller revelation to be granted to his brothers ? Why are the last to be first and the first last ? Why are only a few chosen of the many called, and on what principle ? What made the sin of wrapping the talent in a napkin so grievous ? Was there not an element of justice in the elder brother's complaint ? Did the foolish virgins deserve so severe a condemnation ? Is there no cause for joy in the ninety and nine just men ' who need no repentance ' ? We can find answers to these questions, no doubt ; but it is significant that the answer has to be looked for before it is found. It does not lie on the surface, and that is where the plain man would have it lie.

That the judgments of conscience are not easily reached ; —that the application of general principles to specific cases is a task demanding expert handling ;—that there are more things in the human heart than are dreamt of in academic ethics ;—that the casuist is right in suspending judgment and weighing conditions and circumstances ;—all this is an invigorating and much-needed lesson for the plain man, be he moralist, confessor, preacher or laymen. We may call it Christ's first lesson to the world in ethics. He achieved it by a vivid realism—a refusal to consider any question in the abstract. Everything had to be discussed in the concrete, in relation to a particular example. Often enough the example is given by His actual environment. Would you argue about Sabbath observance ? You must do it within sight and hearing of the palsied man or crippled woman whose relief you would dare to postpone for twenty-four hours. Shall we discuss the legitimacy of the death-penalty for adultery ?—Then do it in the Master's presence, and let us see whether you will cast your stone at the unhappy woman crouching at His feet. Is it the problem of the right use of money that vexes you ?—Then look at the sinner who has wasted her savings on the jar of ointment, and be bold to tax her with vain expense. Do you hanker to combine comfort with the service of God ?—Then spend a night with Christ by the open roadside, with no place in which to lay His head, and ask yourself if you can endure. Do you hesitate to call riches a danger ?—Then watch the young man going

back sorrowfully to his great possessions before you draw
your final conclusion.

When circumstances failed to produce the test-case
to which our Lord submitted every principle, the need was
supplied by a parable ; but of the parables we have said
enough for the moment. Sometimes, however, He took
another course, and forced the questioner to apply his question to his own case. ' *De te fabula* ; how do you stand
in relation to that of which we are speaking ? ' In a lesser
teacher this might seem a mere trick to escape from com-
promising situations ; but, apart from anything else, in the
case of our Lord it is all of a piece with His invariable method.
' Whether is it easier to say, Thy sins are forgiven thee, or,
Take up thy bed and walk ? ' is a question to which there
is no answer ; except that, as the cavillers cannot answer it,
they have no right to criticise One Who dared to say both.
' Let him that is without sin among you cast the first stone,'—
' If I by Beelzebub cast out devils, by whom do your sons
cast them out ? '—' The baptism of John, was it of heaven
or of men ? '—' Whom say *ye* that I am ? '—in every instance
He forces men to realise that they themselves are implicated
in the things they talk about ; that their own lives and
surroundings present enough data to enable them to test
their principles or solve their doubts, without wandering
into the realms of abstract enquiry. ' Never mind what it
sounds like in theory, but see how it works out in practice,'
is the casuist's invariable reply to the facile generalisations
and paper systems both of plain men and of rigorists ; and it
is beyond all doubt the test which our Lord applied Himself,
and would have everyone apply to all their attempted
solutions of the problems of life.

If the plain man found Christ perplexing, as we suggest
must have been the case, it is beyond doubt that the rigorist
found Him deplorably lax. On every point of importance
He seemed to compromise with the world ; and compromise
and laxity are the first accusations brought against casuistry
by the Puritan. He ate with publicans and sinners ; His
disciples did not fast, nor wash their hands before meat ;
His behaviour could with some measure of verisimilitude
be stigmatised as that of a ' gluttonous man and a wine-

bibber.' Nor is it always noticed how our Lord fed the flame of this accusation. Compromise is written all over the parable of the Wheat and the Tares, despite its uncompromising ending with the harvest ; for compromise is essentially of this world, and it is in this world that no step is to be taken to sever the good from the bad. The story of David and the shewbread is a classical instance of compromise designed to meet a hard case ; our Lord quotes it to support a compromise in a case which could not conceivably be called hard. Indeed He goes out of His way to declare compromise and complacence to be of the essence of God's nature—' He sendeth rain upon the just and unjust ' alike. To a Christian—to St. Paul for instance—this is a sign of mercy, long-suffering, forbearance ; and the Christian scheme tries throughout to reach a compromise between mercy and justice. But this in itself is of the essence of casuistry ; to labour at a ' case ' until each of the divergent laws which seem to bear upon it gets such measure of satisfaction as the circumstances allow.

For it is clear that our Lord, for all His transcendant interest in the individual, did not relax His hold upon principles. He was no Delphic oracle, giving isolated replies to individual questions, without a unity of thought to combine them in a consistent whole. Every answer and utterance recorded of Him can be traced back to an underlying law ; we can even see the technique or scientific method by which He applied the law to the particular case. Both these points deserve attention. As to the law itself, He had little sympathy with the violence of revolution. It is often said of Him that ' He came not to found a new Church, but to redeem a Church which was already there ' ; it is equally true that He came not to promulgate a new law,[1] but to purify and adapt a law already in existence. ' Have ye not read in the Scriptures . . . ? '—' How is it written . . . ? '—' They have Moses and the prophets . . .'—these are all direct appeals to the law as it is. Loyalty to society means, as we have already seen, a reverent acceptance of current law, in principle if not in detail, as the starting-point for ethical

---

[1] The essence of the ' new commandment ' (Jn. xiii. 34) lies in the new *example* :—' As I have loved you*, that ye also love one another.'

enquiry; and if this is so, then Christ is the world's outstanding example of true loyalty.

Thus Sir John Seeley is right in noting,[1] as the primary characteristic of the Gospel ethics, that it would have been easy for Christ to 'pronounce the old law entirely true or entirely false'; but that instead He held it to be 'true and divine, yet no longer true for Him, no longer His authoritative guide'—a divine deposit to be worked-over by conscience in accordance with new light and new needs. 'At first sight,' Seeley continues, 'this must appear both unnatural and paradoxical'; but it is the only possible attitude for a conscience which would be true to itself and yet loyal to what it has received and the source from which it has received it. This 'working-over' of the law was to be done in the concrete, not in the abstract; it had to be brought to the test of hard cases and there put on its trial. But on what rules of procedure was the trial to be conducted? By what methods are we to decide when a hard case warrants, or indeed demands, a permanent re-statement of the law, and when it is in fact an irrelevance? We are apt to suppose that the Gospels give us no evidence on this matter; that Christ saw as in a flash the truth about cases, as about principles, by virtue of the intensity of union between Him and His Father. Nothing could be more dangerous than this opinion, implicit though it is in much of our teaching about the Lord. Nothing could be more derogatory to His real humanity than to suggest that He had no need, as we say, to 'think things out'; to argue from facts to principles, and from principles to conclusions; to wrestle with problems until by constant adjustment and re-adjustment of the data the solution was found. Nothing could be more fatal than to suggest that Christ enunciated a few laws, and dealt with a handful of cases, but left us no guidance as to method. If that were true, the Christian moralist could draw from his Master's example no incentive to *think* about his problems, and no hope that reason, though a gift of God, held in itself some of the means by which conscience might reach its conclusions. And so we should reach that divorce between 'reason' and 'conscience' with which Newman was so unnecessarily

---

[1] *Ecce Homo*, ch. 16.

oppressed,[1] which makes of ' conscience ' little more than a transient unregulable emotion, and leaves thought and common-sense wholly on one side in all matters which affect morality.

Happily we are not condemned to this. Nothing can be more untrue to the facts than to suggest that our Lord did not think, and think methodically and progressively, about the problems which faced Him. It may savour almost of irreverence to attempt to trace the processes of thought of the Incarnate Son of God ; and yet no consideration of His teaching, however superficial, would be anything more than a caricature if it failed to take account of this factor. The truth is, that our Lord was severely technical and scientific in His interpretation of the old law, which was to be the new law too, in the light of particular instances. He had two invariable rules of procedure which He applied with unswerving strictness in every case ; and it was the relentless logic of this method which drove Him to what the plain man found paradox and the rigorist laxity. Without this key, the Gospel ethics are little more than a series of aphorisms and *obiter dicta* ; priceless in value even so, yet episodic and fragmentary. With the key, we can trace our Lord's method of reasoning from premises to conclusions, and so test by His example the methods we ourselves adopt in our own reasonings upon conduct.

The first of the two principles by which our Lord regulated His re-interpretation and application of the law was that of internal consistency. The law must not be allowed to contradict itself. What is true of the gold in the temple, cannot be untrue of the temple itself ; what is true of the altar is true also of that which is upon the altar. Where faith is found, whether in Israel or outside of Israel, the covenant to faith must hold good. ' Thou shalt not tempt the Lord thy God ' may not be forgotten when we appeal to the prophecy, ' He shall give His angels charge concerning thee ' ; ' Thou shalt worship the Lord thy God ' is universal in scope. He that made the outside of the cup and the platter made also the inside ; there cannot be one rule for one and the contrary for the other. It is inconsistent and therefore wrong to

[1] *Supra* p. 24.

treasure salt which has lost its savour ; to be mysterious about a city set on a hill ; to hide a candle under a bushel ; to fidget with the mote while ignoring the beam ; to strain out the gnat and swallow the camel ; to put the new patch on the old garment ; to bear leaves without fruit. Behind His attacks on the formalism and hard-heartedness of the Pharisees there is clearly audible in our Lord's language His deep-rooted resentment of their inconsistency. Their lives were a moral disunity—what else can be said of men whose veneration for the law is at once so complete that they will tithe the meanest garden-produce, and so lacking that they wholly ignore its weightiest precepts ? This hatred of inconsistency, this quest of the seamless robe in morals, sank deep into Christian imagination, and the ' double-minded ' man—the man whose conduct is incoherent—is the recipient of as much scorn as any other type of character.[1]

His second principle is that of analogy. What applies in one case must apply in all similar cases, especially in those of greater urgency. What is true of the lilies of the field and the birds of the air, must be even more true of the children of God. What is legitimate in the case of an ox or an ass, is even more legitimate in the case of a daughter of Abraham. The rejoicing when a lost coin or lost sheep is found vindicates our rejoicing over a lost son come home at last. Wisdom is justified of all her children, and the dictates of worldly wisdom have their parallels in the heavenly sphere. The king who plans the campaign, the builder who estimates for his tower, the weather-prophet who studies the clouds— if we admire their qualities of foresight or attention, we must emulate them in spiritual as in temporal things. Faithfulness in small things is a sure indication of faithfulness in great. If we being evil give good gifts to our children, much more will the Father send His Holy Spirit upon those who ask for Him. The *a fortiori* argument has never been used more constantly or more impressively than by Jesus ; ' How much more . . .' is one of His favourite phrases. His use of the parable, like Æsop's use of the fable, as the chief vehicle of His teaching, is to be put down to the same cause ; that

---

[1] δίψυχος, Jas. i. 8; Hermas, *Pastor*, Vis. ii. 2, 7 *et pass.;* cp. E. von Dobschütz, *Christian Life in the Primitive Church*, pp. 316 ff.

He preferred the parable to the fable, seeking His analogies from the actual doings of men rather than from the imagined doings of beasts and birds, is due to His primary and absorbing interest in the human subject in ethics.

These two rules which our Lord employed so constantly must be regulative of all casuistry. That casuistry works by choosing incontrovertible examples of the operation of a law, and then applying them by analogy to parallel cases, we have already seen; and this is no more than Christ's second rule in operation. His first rule is no less fundamental. Where two principles of the same authority give conflicting answers in the same case, one or both must be re-stated; conscience cannot tolerate a final inconsistency between its dictates. But here we are brought face to face with a new consideration of primary interest. The re-statement of laws to fit all circumstances is a matter of superhuman difficulty; if achieved at all, it is achieved only as the result of slow reflection and constant discussion. In the meantime the world's work has to be carried on, and carried on, on the old imperfect principles, as equitably as may be. So the casuist, though he does not abandon his interest in the exact formulation of principles, finds it his first duty to decide what is to be done in this or that case; both because the need is more urgent, and because it is by the discussion of cases that new light is thrown upon the principle.

In the matter of truthfulness, for example, the casuist is interested in reaching such a definition of veracity as will allow what (on the old imperfect definition) must still perforce be called a ' lie ' to be told in circumstances when conscience obviously regards it as legitimate or laudable. But we may question whether so exact a definition is to be found within measurable time, and in the meantime we are asked continually : ' Is this " lie "—which perhaps, when the final definition is found, will prove to be no " lie "—permissible ' ? So too with murder. Here some degree of accuracy has been attained in definition—the taking of life, we say, in self-defence, or in lawful punishment, or in war, is not ' murder.' But many questions about life-taking still remain ; the definition, even when limited in these respects, is still vague enough, whilst men's consciences are troubled

as to this particular act of slaying or that. The two processes
—definition of the law and decision of cases—have to go on
pari passu.

Here, too, our Lord's example is warrant enough. He
did not hesitate to re-define; He would take a precept ('Ye
have heard that it was said . . .') and give it a new interpretation with His own ' But I say unto you . . .' Yet He does
not go all the way in re-statement. He lays down no new
code; and His own precepts (as history shows) are capable
of diverse interpretations. He is too occupied with cases to
spend His time in codification alone ; indeed we may suppose
that He would not have us review the code at all except by
constant reference to cases.

But at this point the comparison appears to fail us. The
casuist, as we know him in experience, is constantly engaged
in discussions to which our Lord's words afford no parallel ;
discussions, too, which verge on the morbid and unsavoury.
He is continually asking or being asked : ' When may I lie ? '
' When may I steal ? ' And though the implication of this
is that the lie or the theft, if allowed, will prove (when ' lying '
and ' stealing ' have been properly defined) to be neither lie
nor theft at all, he is touching pitch all the time, and we
cannot believe but that his hands will be defiled. He is
making exceptions and setting laws on one side ; and exceptions, as we have seen, are only a step removed from equivocation and evasion.

Our Lord's hands are never defiled. He does not lie ;
He does not discuss the propriety of lying on occasion. We
cannot imagine that He would ever do so. And we naturally
ask, ' Does not casuistry at this point fall below the standard
set by Jesus ? Is it not therefore to be adjudged something
less than Christian ? ' We must draw a distinction before
we attempt to answer this question. It is one thing to
determine when a claim made upon conscience in any given
circumstances is invalid ; it is another thing to discover
the best way of rejecting the claim in those circumstances
without weakening its general validity. An analogy from
ordinary life may help us here. Occasions often arise when an
unpleasant truth has to be told, and many of us may recognise
them ; but only a few have the invaluable capacity—we call

it ' tact '—of so telling the truth as to produce the maximum effect with the minimum of harm.

Now there is such a thing as *moral tact*, the discovery of the *best* way of doing the right or allowable thing. It comes partly from experience, partly from genius ; it can be trained, but cannot be implanted where it does not exist. And it is arguable, for example, that in cases where to deny the truth is the only way that we can see of satisfying the claim of truth to be concealed, a better way, which did not deny the truth, might be found by one possessed of moral tact in a higher measure. There is an awkward way and a deft way ; a blank denial of the truth or perversion of the facts—though it may be the only moral solution of a problem within sight— is certainly lacking in deftness. There must be a form of words no less adequate to ‚the case, yet neater and more appropriate, if only we could find it. But often we have no time to spend in finding it ; and then the blunt and awkward lie is our only resource.

Contrast with this the astonishing deftness of Christ in His moral solutions. It is one of the standing wonders of the Gospel record. He is constantly required to find words in which to satisfy the needs of a delicate situation—when the charge of blasphemy is aroused by His claim to forgive sins, for example ; or in the incident of the woman taken in adultery, or the rebuke to Martha, or the various exchanges of the day of contradictions—and in no case could we by any stretch of imagination conceive of any turn of phrase more fitted to the situation than that which He actually uses. It is this unparalleled power of putting the deepest thoughts in the simplest words, with an unerring choice of exact propriety for each occasion, which gives the Gospel dialogues their unending vivacity and charm. It would (if we may say so reverently) make the fortune of any writer of fiction ; and it is therefore the strongest possible testimony to the authenticity of the Gospels, for no moral genius whom the world has ever known has possessed it to a like degree.

But apart altogether from its apologetic value, it shows in what respect even the best human capacity must always fall short of the divine example. We cannot hope to acquire in more than the most elementary degree this extraordinary aptitude of finding the right solution appropriate to each problem. We may see in general what claims have to be satisfied, but our methods of satisfying them will at best be blundering and heavy-handed. No nicety of thought and word and action can be too exact in the more delicate problems of morals ; and the genius for the appropriate which alone can command such nicety is a rare gift, never bestowed in a measure equal to the tasks which confront it. We may meet the claims which demand satisfaction, but in every case we are in danger of ignoring others to which some deférence at least should be shown. Sometimes we can see no further than to select the most urgent claim and meet that at the deliberate expense of others which we know to be valid, though in a lesser degree. We may satisfy most of the needs of a situation, but we can hardly hope to satisfy all. And to leave a need unsatisfied is the same as to ignore a duty.

So far as human criticism can go in such a matter, it cannot even breathe the suspicion that our Lord blundered in His solutions. Their delicacy and complete appropriateness stands above criticism. And this is the point at which even the best casuistry falls short of the Christian ideal and must confess its failure. The casuist, like his critics, is of the earth earthy, and though he attempts to show men the best way of discharging their obligations in the complications of life, the earth still clings to his decisions. They may help to save from the absolutely wrong, but for sheer frailty of vision they cannot envisage the absolutely right. Hence, only too often, they remain tainted with the mire of the problems which they attempt to solve. The honest casuist does not consciously ' sell cheap what is most dear ' ; but with that one reservation what is true of another student of human nature and its fortunes, the dramatist, holds good of him :

> Alas ! 'tis true, I have gone here and there,
>   And made myself a motley to the view,
> Gored mine own thoughts, sold cheap what is most dear,
>   Made old offences of affections new ;
> Most true it is that I have looked on truth
>   Askance and strangely . . .

O for my sake do you with fortune chide,
  The guilty goddess of my harmful deeds,
That did not better for my life provide
  Than public means which public manners breeds.
Thence comes it that my name receives a brand,
  And almost thence my nature is subdued
To what it works in, like the dyer's hand ;
  Pity me then, and wish I were renewed.

Jesus solved His own problems and those of others without falling back on ' public means which public manners breeds.' In that respect the best Christian casuistry falls infinitely short of His example. But so also does the best Christian thought and life in every respect ; and we have no cause to blame the one aspiration for a failure in which all share alike.

2. *St. Paul*

There is nothing therefore in the practice of our Lord which stamps casuistry as illegitimate ; indeed, were it not for the odium into which the word has fallen we could with complete propriety speak of a ' casuistry of the gospels.' The apostolic age, in its turn, provides important witness. St. Paul plumed himself upon his ability and success as a casuist. If we were not certain from many incidents in his career that his concessions were confined within strict limits, his statement of method would be alarming in its frank opportunism : ' Unto the Jews I became as a Jew, that I might gain the Jews ; to them that are under the law as under the law, that I might gain them that are under the law ; to them that are without law as without law . . . that I might gain them that are without law. To the weak became I as weak, that I might gain the weak ; I have become all things to all men, that I might by all means save some.' [1] This is Aristotle's Lesbian rule [2] with a vengeance.

Certainly both friends and enemies took advantage of

[1] 1 Cor. ix. 20–22.

[2] *Eth. Nic.* v. 10, 7, on ' equity ' : ' The rule of what is indeterminate is itself indeterminate also, like the leaden rule in Lesbian building ; for the rule is altered to suit the shape of the stone, and does not remain the same ; so do decrees (of equity, to correct the law) differ according to different circumstances.

this boasted facility of adapting conduct to occasion. His enemies openly accused him of barefaced lack of principle (' Let us do evil that good may come ' [1]) ; and suggested that this depravity was rooted in doctrine (' Let us sin that grace may abound ' [2]) as well as manifested in conduct. They accused him of holding his promises in small respect,[3] and of being ready to interject, ' Yea, yea,' and ' Nay, nay,' [4] light-heartedly as occasion demanded it. As for his friends, an incident on his last journey to Jerusalem is in the highest degree instructive. It shows that not St. Paul alone, but St. James as well, had a sense of the adaptation of principles to circumstances which must have stood them in good stead. The occasion is well-known. A rumour had gained currency which credited St. Paul with a hitherto unheard-of laxity towards the Jewish law. He was, so men alleged, no longer merely teaching the Gentiles to ignore it, but also encouraging the Jews among the Gentiles to do the same.[5] There is no reason to suppose that he had ever adopted this position either in his own case or in that of others—the evidence, in fact, is all the other way. Indeed it supplies another instance of that attempt to ' please all men in all things ' [6] of which he was so proud ; for there can be no doubt that the strict logic of St. Paul's position would free the Jewish convert from the yoke of the law as effectively as the Gentile.

However this may be, St. James does not hesitate as to the right course of action. The apostle of the Gentiles must disarm suspicion and show himself a loyal Jew by taking four men ' who had a vow' into the Temple, and there defraying the expenses of their ' purification.' We have no means of deciding whether, to Paul the Christian, this episode was anything more than meaningless. His attitude towards Jewish vows is unknown, and the incident at Cenchreæ,[7] which seems at first sight to determine it, may equally well (as the text stands) be interpreted of Aquila. But the significant point in the Jerusalem episode is that neither James nor Paul considers the question as to the religious value of the

---

[1] Rom. iii. 8.   [2] Rom. vi. 1, 15.   [3] ἐν 'ε λαφρίᾳ, 2 Cor. i. 17.
[4] 2 Cor. i. 18. The reduplication is apparently meant to suggest the eagerness with which he would signify assent or dissent as the occasion required.
[5] Acts xxii. 21.   [6] 1 Cor. x. 33.   [7] Acts xviii. 18.

rite involved. Meaningless or otherwise, so long as Paul's conscience is not revolted by the suggestion, the general standing of Christianity will be bettered by his taking part in the occasion. Besides affording an example of intelligent adaptation of principles to circumstances, the incident therefore is also of importance as illustrating that rule of conformity which we have seen to be part and parcel of loyalty unless conscience determines outspokenly against it.

The intricacies of St. Paul's general attitude towards the Jewish law do not here concern us. But as regards the Christian code it is evident that he was no mere traditionalist. Like all good casuists he brought any precept which was doubtful or disputed to the bar of reason, and forced it to give an account of itself there. In this, however, he was either acting against his natural temperament, or unhappy in his method. By nature he preferred a dogmatic to a reasoned statement of the truth ; twice at least he bases his teaching on ' what he has received,' and on one occasion, after a singularly maladroit excursion into dialectic, he breaks out with a barefaced appeal to the belief that what ought to be must be identical with what is : ' If any man seem to be contentious, we have no such custom, neither the Churches of God.' [1] The arguments by which he supports his teachings are rarely clear, sometimes fallacious, and occasionally perfunctory—witness his defence of the bodily resurrection by the introduction of a new and almost unheard-of type of ' spiritual body,'[2] his singular argument against the unveiling of women in the assembly,[3] his difficulties with the problem of antinomianism,[4] and his hasty adoption of the Antichrist myth to prevent the Thessalonians drawing the logical conclusion from his eschatology.[5]

The kindest course is to assume that the laborious processes of discursive argument were too slow and uncongenial for St. Paul's enthusiastic and practical mind. If we dismiss this explanation of the facts, which certainly seems the best, we shall be forced to place him among those of whom Emerson[6] wrote that ' if we know their sect we know their argument.'

[1] 1 Cor. xi. 16.   [2] 1 Cor. xv. 44.   [3] 1 Cor. xi. 3–15.
[4] Rom. vi., *pass.*   [5] 2 Thess. ii. 1–12.
[6] R. W. Emerson, *Essay on Self-Reliance.*

G

' I hear a preacher announce for his text and topic the expediency of one of the institutions of his Church. Do I not know beforehand that not possibly can he say a new and spontaneous word ? Do I not know that with all this ostentation of examining the grounds of the institution he will do no such thing ? Do I not know that he is pledged to himself not to look but at one side, the permitted side, not as a man, but as a parish minister ? He is a retained attorney, and these airs of the bench are the emptiest affectation ! ' The essayist's embittered comments on this type of character are wholly wide of the mark. Preachers and apologists of this category—and there are few of us, Emerson himself included, who do not fall into it at one time or another—are not necessarily hypocrites, sophists or sycophants ; most commonly they are men whose convictions are stronger than their power of criticism. They do not deserve the wholesale condemnation meted out to them ; but even so it is hard to imagine St. Paul as belonging to their type.

Still, it is true that he found himself more at ease either in expounding the uncontroverted doctrines and principles of Christianity, or in exploring the wide field of morality left undecided by the liberty of the Gospel. Neither of these tasks, however, was free from its casuistical problems ; and St. Paul embraces them with avidity. In exposition he continually found himself faced with the desirablility of ' economising ' truth—adapting its order and presentation, that is to say, to the spiritual condition of his hearers. Here again was something on which he prided himself ; he knew when to speak to people as ' spiritual ' and when as ' carnal,' when to feed them with ' meat ' and when with ' milk.' [1] If we may judge by the results, however, his method was not so successful as he thought. St Luke in the 'Acts ' obviously intended to illustrate the dexterity of his practice in this respect ; but all we find is a certain ingenuity of approach to the subjects handled. To the Lycaonians he dwells on the goodness of God in nature ; to the Athenians he ministers a popular pantheism of the kind he supposed congenial ; on the Temple steps he attempts to appease the popular clamour by a straightforward account of his early life, upbringing

---

[1] 1 Cor. iii. 2.

and conversion ; and he knows the appropriate compliments with which to address Felix and Agrippa. But the exordium finished, he is as a rule singularly unfortunate in the introduction of his main topic. He comes to it bluntly, without ' economy,' and in a manner which invariably secures for it the worst possible reception. The Lystran speech is a fragment only, and we cannot judge from it. But the speech at Pisidian Antioch failed to conciliate the Jews to whom it was primarily addressed ; and when the ambitious effort at Athens culminated in nothing more than the old discredited doctrine of the resurrection of the dead, the meeting broke up with a ' mockery ' of the speaker only half-concealed by the polite phrase, ' We will hear thee again of this matter.' [1] At Jerusalem, he fails to prepare in any way for his account of the divine commission to go to the Gentiles,[2] and the result is a renewed attack upon him which Lysias with difficulty foils ; at Cæsarea he wins no more than Festus' undisguised doubt as to his sanity, and Agrippa's cold contempt for his enthusiasm

Here again, we conclude, St. Paul's temperament came into conflict with his theories. He wanted to be a casuist, to ' economise ' the truth and present it in palatable form and graduated quantities. But zeal got the better of prudence every time ; and the whole truth is blurted out long before it has been properly prepared for. It is small wonder therefore that he made so many enemies ; small wonder, also, that he was so constantly misunderstood. He set out ' to please everyone,' but many were not pleased. He tried to bring peace, but his enthusiasm for the Gospel turned it into a sword in his hands. He was a casuist in mind but a zealot at heart, and he never managed to double the two rôles successfully. It is beyond all question providential that—if he was to fail—he failed in casuistry rather than in zeal. Christianity had not yet won its spurs ; and in the heat of battle there is little room for those nice problems which a statesman is bound to consider in the tranquillity of peace. The Church, as it passed from Asia into Europe, needed a general rather

---

[1] Acts xvii. 32. This aspect of the incident is well brought out by E. Meyer, *Ursprung und Anfänge des Christentums*, iii. pp. 104, 105.

[2] Acts xxii. 21, 22.

than a diplomat ; it is to St. Paul's credit that he tried to be diplomat as well as general, and scarcely to his discredit that he sometimes fell short of this complex ideal.

The same is true of that other field of argument in which he allows the needs of individuals to affect the incidence of principles. Circumstances made him the apostle of indifference. He had rejected the law, and with it the principle of legalism as a whole ; and the Christian code which he inherited was unusually simple and free from specific determinations of duties. At some times, therefore, he insists that all things are lawful to the Christian, at others (with perhaps less theoretical consistency though greater validity in fact) that a great many things are. Among ' indifferent things ' he classes celibacy and marriage, slavery and freedom, an honorary and a stipendiary ministry, the eating of or abstention from meats sacrificed to idols. These then, in theory, are matters about which the individual conscience is wholly free to legislate for itself. But the legislative power thus allowed to it is somewhat honorific. In practice, St. Paul lays down for the Christian in these matters not ' precepts,' perhaps, but at all events ' counsels ' which are little more than precepts decently veiled. Here again, zeal outruns discretion, and the desire for unity all but culminates in a demand for uniformity. The individual is free to choose for himself, but he receives the strongest possible hint of the alternative St. Paul wishes and indeed expects him to choose.

Thus in the seventh chapter of 1 Corinthians he lays it down that the Christian is free to live a married or a celibate life ; but the scales are heavily weighted on the side of celibacy. The concession of marriage is grudgingly made : ' It is better to marry than to burn ;'—' Such shall have trouble in the flesh ;'—' He that is married careth for the things of the world. . . . I speak this for your profit.' Celibacy, on the other hand, receives the highest commendation :—' It is good for a man not to touch a woman ;'—' I would that all men were even as I myself ;'—' It is good for a man so to be ;'—' He that is unmarried careth for the things of the Lord ;'—' He that giveth not in marriage doeth better.' [1] The oblique discouragement of a practice is often more effective psychologi-

---

[1] Or ' marrieth not.' See K. Lake, *Earlier Epistles of St. Paul*, pp. 185 ff.

cally than a direct prohibition ; and a Christian man and maid seeking matrimony could scarcely be more effectively deterred from it even by being told that it was sinful in itself. St. Paul is too honest to command every Christian to be celibate, but we cannot think that, at this period of his life at all events, he would have grieved much if Christians had forsworn marriage altogether.

Much the same applies to the less vital question of the stipendiary ministry. The ninth chapter of the letter from which we have been quoting is an impassioned defence of the right of the minister to a salary and to the domestic life which a salary makes possible. Nothing could be more vigorous or emphatic than this defence. It is reinforced by quotations from the Old Testament, by a series of analogies from ordinary life, by appeal to the example of Cephas and the brethren of the Lord, and by an allusion to our Lord's saying, ' The labourer is worthy of his hire.' Everything points to a situation in which the apostle is vindicating his right to demand payment, or meeting the accusation of professional evangelism. The vehemence of the argument is consistent with nothing else. Suddenly the letter takes a surprising turn ; we find that St. Paul is vindicating his right to *refuse* payment. ' I have used none of these things . . . (but) when I preach the gospel I make the gospel of Christ without charge, that I abuse not my power in the gospel.' Those who ' examined him ' must have called in question his ministry for the very reason that he served in an honorary capacity This in itself is not surprising ; what does surprise is that the apostle should combine an entirely unnecessary and very forcible plea for apostolic salaries with a justification of his own refusal to receive a salary.

Only one suggestion really meets the case, and that is that, though in logic he admitted the validity of a stipendiary ministry, in heart he was strongly opposed to it. He ' glories ' in his own honorary services, and to make his ' glorying ' the more effective he parades all the reasons which might have induced him to take payment. Both types of ministry are in theory legitimate, but in practice (St. Paul hints) the honorary type is infinitely more noble than the other. Cephas and the brethren of the Lord might read the first fourteen

verses of the chapter with equanimity; but the fifteenth
verse, with its proud ' But I have used none of these things,'
would come as a severe blow to their self-respect—all the more
because St. Paul has not hesitated to point out [1] that it is not
by the possession of private means, but by doing two men's
work, that he is able to preach the Gospel without expense to
his hearers.   In effect, while defending the mere legitimacy
of the honorary ministry, he has glorified it to such an extent
as to represent is as the only ministry worthy of the name.

Thus his own strong prejudices prevent him in practice
from leaving the choice in things indifferent as open to the
Christian conscience as in theory he admitted it to be.   Nor
is this the only barrier he puts in the path of that Christian
freedom which in the abstract he preaches so strenuously.
The problem of the ' weaker brother, ' of ' scandal,' in technical terms, has always been a test of sound casuistry.
Insistence upon our spiritual duty to the weaker brother is
perhaps wholly distinctive of Christianity.   ' Scandal ' is the
assertion of Christian liberty to a degree which shocks the
more tender (though not necessarily the more Christian)
consciences in the Church.   It may be caused in one of two
ways, either by leading the tender consciences to doubt
whether the majority, and with them as a rule the hierarchy,
still retain enough of the grace of God to make it a duty to
remain in communion with them; or by suggesting to them
that a course of action is allowable which they themselves
condemn, and tempting them, though still uneasy, to conform
to it out of deference to the example of others.   It is ' scandal '
of this latter type which St. Paul considers, and once again
casuistry and rigorism come to grips in his mind.

On the one hand, he is clearly impatient of the ' weaker
brother ' and his peevish censoriousness.   ' Who art thou
that judgest another man's servant ? '[2] he writes to him; and
again, ' Let us not therefore judge one another any more.'[3]
Elsewhere he says : ' With me it is a very small thing that
I should be judged of you or any man's judgment '[4]; and
a little later, ' Why is my liberty judged of another man's
conscience ? '[5]   This clears the stage for a rational treatment

---

[1] Cor. i. iv. 12   [2] Rom. xiv. 4.   [3] *Ib.* verse 13.
[4] i Cor. iv. 3.   [5] i Cor. x. 29.

of each problem on its merits. There are times when the critic is too perverse, too narrow-minded, for a sane Christian to bother about his scruples any further. The assertion of liberty is sometimes at least an obligation, even if the avoidance of scandal is as well ; the former need not be subordinated to the latter if the weaker brother pushes his demands to wholly unreasonable and un-Christian limits. Even the rigorist Sanderson [1] allows that, if the weaker brethren ' take offence where we give none, it is a thing we cannot help, and therefore the whole blame must lie upon them ; ' we expect St. Paul after his strong vindication of Christian liberty to be at least as liberal-minded.

But when he comes to the details of his problem, casuistry deserts him, and he shows himself a rigorist once more. The question involved is that of feasts in idol-temples, with the cognate problem of all meats—for ' whatsoever is sold in the shambles ' has presumably been sacrificed to an idol first. The extreme rigorist position would be to say, ' In any case to partake of such meat is, if not wrong in itself, so entirely inexpedient as to make it unlawful for the Christian.' St. Paul is very far from taking up this position. On the contrary he writes, ' He that eateth eateth to the Lord ' ; [2] ' I know and am persuaded by the Lord Jesus that there is nothing unclean of itself ' ; [3] 'All things indeed are pure ' ; [4] 'As concerning the eating of those things that are offered in sacrifice unto idols, we know that an idol is nothing in the world ' ; [5] 'Whatsoever is set before you eat, asking no question for conscience' sake.' [6]

But in practice his views on the danger of ' scandal ' are so strong that the theoretical permission amounts to little or nothing. A word, a glance of disapproval from the weaker brother must annul it ; and St. Paul does not even hint that any unreasonableness on the critic's part can alter this ruling. ' If thy brother be grieved with thy meat, now walkest thou not charitably. Destroy not him with thy meat, for whom Christ died. Let not your good be evil spoken of . . . Let us therefore follow after the things which make for peace, and

---

[1] *Cases of Conscience* : No. 2, ' Of the Liturgy ' ; No. 7, ' Of Scandal.'
[2] Rom. xiv. 6.　　　　[3] *Ib.* verse 14.　　　　[4] *Ib.* verse 20.
[5] 1 Cor. viii. 4.　　　　[6] *Ib.* x. 27.

things wherewith we may edify another. For meat destroy not the work of God '[1]—and so forth in the Epistle to the Romans. Similarly, in 1 Corinthians : ' Take heed lest this liberty of yours become a stumbling block to them that are weak . . . If meat make my brother to offend, I will eat no flesh while the world standeth, lest I make my brother to offend ' ; [2] ' If any man say unto you, This is offered in sacrifice unto idols, eat not for his sake that showed it, and for conscience' sake . . .—conscience, I say, not thine own, but of the other.' [3]

We may say, of course, that St. Paul is here choosing the nobler path, and surrendering his liberty to the higher law of charity. We may remind ourselves of Christ's precept not to cause offence to any of His little ones. But this ought not to blind us to the fact that there are weaker brothers and weaker brothers, and that St. Paul appears to draw no distinction between them. We have only to remember some of the things for which the ' weaker brother ' has stood in history—the funereal Sunday, the prohibition of games and literature and the drama, the ostracism of the artist and the actor, the condemnation of biblical criticism and theological re-interpretation—to see that St. Paul's advice in the matter of ' idol-meats ' would have been disastrous if the Church had followed it on the larger scale. Discrimination between the weaker brother who is genuinely charitable and anxious to see all that is good in an opponent's position, and the weaker brother who is merely pig-headed and immovable, is of fundamental importance if Christianity is to remain Christianity. But of the need for such discrimination St. Paul, for all his theoretical casuistry, gives us no hint in this discussion. It would appear to be all one to him whether the person who takes offence is a child groping earnestly after truth, or a prig refusing to contemplate the possibility of its existence elsewhere than in his own narrow and bigoted mind.

It is only fair to the apostle to point out that, in some of the matters at least in which he was concerned, he was not so tender about the weaker brethren. Indeed he allows himself to call them ' false brethren unawares brought in, who came in privily to spy out our liberty which we have in Christ

---

[1] Rom. xiv. 15 ff.　　[2] 1 Cor. viii. 9–13.　　[3] *Ib.* x. 28, 29.

Jesus that they might bring us into bondage.' [1] There is no reason to suppose that these persons,—converts from the Pharisees, the ' Acts ' calls them, [2]—were less conscientious or high-minded than the weaker brothers who objected to the eating of idol-meats ; but St. Paul treats them very differently. The Council of Jerusalem, as is well known, is surrounded by a mist of uncertainty, but the one clear fact which emerges is that no consideration of offence deterred St. Paul from vindicating the doctrine of Christian liberty. If he made concessions at all, and it is hard to believe that he did, they were of the most temporary character imaginable. Here, then, he solves the problem of scandal in a sense opposite to his conclusions in the matter of meats sacrificed to idols ; casuistry, we may say—the determination of the principle in relation to the circumstances of the particular case—comes to its own again.

These vacillations of St. Paul are extraordinarily instructive. In theory he was obviously a convinced casuist ; in practice he sometimes put his casuistry into effect, though not always, and neither so often nor so consistently as he supposed. But in so far as he practised what he preached in this matter, it was wholly to the good ; indeed, it would appear to be the one factor which prevented the Church from relapsing into a rigid little Jewish sect. If we are to quarrel with him on any point, it must be in respect of the occasions when rigorism got the better of liberalism. Even here a good deal can be said on his side. It might be urged, for example, that his general prohibition (as in effect it is) of idol-meats is in itself a legitimate exercise of casuistry ; he has weighed up the requirements of charity against those of liberty, and found that in this case—in contrast to that of circumcision—charity takes precedence of liberty.

The facts indeed are somewhat against this conclusion ; for it to be true we should have expected some kind of argument to show that if the whole Church perforce became vegetarian, [3] nothing much would be lost, whereas if circumcision were made universally compulsory the fundamental

---

[1] Gal. ii. 4.   [2] Acts xv. 5.

[3] As in fact it would, as practically everything ' sold in the shambles ' had been slain in sacrifice.

principles of the Gospel would be denied. Despite this, however, the theory is not altogether untenable. And in any case, a too sudden access of liberty is a heady and intoxicating thing ; there was good reason, as the Gnostics were soon to show, why the bonds of discipline should not be relaxed too rashly. On the smaller matters St. Paul's casuistry may from time to time have failed him,[1] but wider survey shows him one of the world's greatest casuists. Few have succeeded in holding the balance between rigorism and liberalism, between conservatism and progress, more evenly than he ; and to his success in this respect the Church is indebted even more than she is aware.

3. The First Experiments

We may pass rapidly over the centuries immediately following the apostolic age. At a comparatively early date bishops and councils began to codify the discipline of the Church, and to determine the penalty for offences. In most cases these offences were sufficiently outstanding and obvious to require no casuistical determination. But sometimes a canon is found which bears traces of the adaptation of the

---

[1] We may instance another failure in addition to those given above. It will appear in Ch. VI. that some determination by which the Christian may be allowed to take the benefit of the doubt in genuinely doubtful cases is an essential postulate of rational morality. St. Paul will have none of this. The doubtful conscience is bound down to take the safer course : ' he that doubteth is condemned if he eat, because he eateth not of faith (i.e. with a free conscience), for whatsoever is not of faith is sin ' (Rom. xiv. 23—the text continually quoted by tutiorist controversialists). That this was no mere *obiter dictum* but a formed conviction with the apostle is shown by his employment of it in the whole Corinthian problem. What the Church at Corinth needed was obviously a strong organisation with authoritative officials and discipline. St. Paul had never hesitated to introduce such a system elsewhere ; at Corinth he deliberately avoids doing so. The reason is clear. The Church at Corinth was dominated by the conviction that every member of it was inspired by the Spirit and needed no other control ; and St. Paul, though he had obvious doubts about the contention in this case and never acted upon it elsewhere, will not take the benefit of the doubt and make Corinth conform to the ordinary régime. The result incidentally was fatal ; forty years later, though they have now a ministry, the Epistle of Clement shows that they habitually disregard it. St. Paul allows an experiment in mob-rule of which he strongly disapproves, merely because he cannot be *absolutely* certain that it is wrong.

law to the circumstances of the particular case, and often it can be inferred from the relative severity of the penances imposed that the attempt to arrange moral precepts in a hierarchy according to their gravity (an attempt whose importance will come before us at a later stage) is already in progress. Thus St. Peter of Alexandria, St. Basil of Neo-Caesarea and others deal with the problems of Christians who have lapsed into paganism during the persecutions, and they are careful to recognise that mitigating circumstances—severe torture, painful imprisonment, the threats of masters to slaves,[1] and so forth—reduce the heinousness of the offence ; and that a lapse can be wholly forgiven if cancelled, on repentance, by a brave confession of faith.[2]

Persecution in fact brought up a whole host of problems of exactly the kind which later casuists loved. What is to be said of those who, though pretending to go up to the altars to sacrifice or to make written renunciation of the faith, did not do so in actual fact, but deceived their oppressors by some kind of artifice ?[3] Might the rich Christian morally buy his escape from the prison to which he has been committed for his faith ? What of those who committed the sin (for it is a sin, says Peter) of voluntarily and unnecessarily throwing themselves in the way of torture, exasperating the government both against themselves and their friends ; but who did so in ignorance and good faith ? A more elaborate problem had to be settled ; there were clergy who, like the last type of confessor, ' voluntarily and temerariously ' exposed themselves to torture, and then broke under the strain and lapsed into Emperor-worship ; but who rehabilitated themselves by a second and more enduring confession of the faith. What was to be thought of their moral state ? Could they take up their priestly office again, or must they be cut off from the Church altogether, or may they (and this is Peter's solution) be readmitted to lay membership ? All of these problems the Bishop handles and solves ; not indeed giving his

---

[1] Pet. Alex., *Cann.* 1, 2, 6 (Routh, *Reliquiae Sacrae*, iv. 23 ff.) ; contrast *Cann.* 3, 4, the heavy penalties upon those who gave way through mere fear of persecution, or who failed to show penitence after their lapse. Peter became Bishop of Alexandria in 300, and died a martyr's death in 311.

[2] Pet. Alex., *Can.* 8.

[3] E.g. by getting a pagan friend to impersonate them, *Can.* 5.

reasons, but evincing a sound moral judgment throughout.

Similar problems are handled in the canonical letter of Gregory Thaumaturgus, the first Bishop of Neo-Caesarea, who died some forty years before Peter. A Gothic invasion had devastated Pontus in or about the year 255, and there were Christians who had not hesitated to loot the ravaged area, appropriating to their own use such unconsidered trifles as the invaders had left among the ruins. Their excuse was that these were ownerless goods which they had picked up, and that finding is keeping; at all events, some added, what we have found merely counterbalances the loss we have suffered at barbarian hands. Not even if the alien property had been transported from elsewhere and left by the invader in the house of its ultimate finder, does Gregory allow the latter to retain it. Other Christians, again, had been impressed into the barbarian army, and there under *force majeure* had rivalled their captors in savagery, or had guided their line of march. Much could be said in their defence, but rightly or wrongly Gregory will have none of their excuses; they are to be permanently debarred from the Christian body.

We need not delay longer over these authoritative decisions. Rash oaths, usury, marriage questions, the legitimacy of the military profession, a full discussion of unintentional injuries,[1] the grounds which justify separation between man and wife (as also the question of what water creatures are to be accounted fish and what are not), are all dealt with officially by St. Basil of Caesarea in the first of three canonical letters to Amphilochius, Bishop of Iconium.[2] The problems raised by the case of girls whose parents have dedicated them in infancy to virginity, and who on coming to years of discretion find themselves without a vocation for that life; of women who professed themselves to virginity under the influence of heresy, and later became Christians;

---

[1] *Ep.* clxxxviii., *Can.* 8. This is as interesting a discussion as those of Abailard and Aquinas, and I should certainly have mentioned it in the appropriate place in *Ignorance, etc.*, if it had come to my notice earlier. The immediate problem before Basil is that of the man who ' takes up a hatchet to his wife.'

[2] *Ep.* clxxxviii., perhaps 374 A.D.

of foolish vows and promises ; [1] of women who marry on insufficient presumption of their first husband's death ; and of condonation of sin, are treated in a second letter. [2] A third [3] enacts penances for offences in these and similar connections. And in these letters, in contrast to those of Peter of Alexandria, there is more of argument and evidence, though we are still far from the full casuistical discussions of later ages.

There is one instance in the first letter to Amphilochius, however, which appears to reveal Basil as a casuist of the less reputable kind. The facts are uncertain, but the Benedictine editors give them as follows. The priest of a district of Mestia had been deposed for some offence ; and the parish was therefore without a minister. The bishop Severus transferred to Mestia another priest, Cyriacus, whom he had ordained to a cure of souls at Mindana, and who (at his instigation) had taken a vow to remain at Mindana. No other priest seemed to be available, and the problem arose, was the parish of Mestia to remain without the sacraments, or was Cyriacus to be forsworn ? Basil's solution is ingenious enough. The Mestian parish is (apparently by a stroke of the pen) to be transferred to the ecclesiastical district of Voroda, and there by a legal fiction incorporated with Mindana ; so that Cyriacus, though geographically in Mestia, is ecclesiastically still at Mindana. Basil has some hard things to say about the bishop Severus, who by a succession of rash, if not unworthy, actions was the original cause of the whole trouble ; but he is convinced that all the necessary moral conditions are satisfied by his solution. [4] We cannot however regard the conclusion with the same complacency. Episcopal decisions of this character would very quickly bring the sanctity of vows and promises into serious doubt. Some kind of *ad hoc* adjustment of the particular case was necessary, of course ; but far more necessary was an investigation into the obligation of rash promises, or of promises which never contemplate

---

[1] The problem of rash vows is a hardy annual in casuistry. Centuries later Baldwin draws attention to the folly of those who, in pious memory of the death of John the Baptist, vow never to eat sheep's head ; and of others who, through similar respect to St. Lawrence, forswear the eating of toast.

[2] *Ep.* cxcix. [3] *Ep.* ccxvii. [4] Can. x.

the ultimate turn of events, to prevent such a situation—and, it may be added, such a solution—ever happening again.

Other cases discussed and decided in the early ages need only be mentioned. Clerical vegetarianism created some trouble ; the Council of Ancyra (A.D. 314) decided that such faddists must at least show that their vegetarianism was not a matter of Christian principle by tasting meat, or at all events vegetables dipped in gravy, after which they might be allowed to indulge their own prejudices.[1] The Pauline preference for long hair was held by the Council of Gangra (Can. 17) to prohibit women from cutting their hair short as a pious exercise ; whilst no pious intention was held to justify a child in refusing support to his parents (Can. 16). The whole council, in fact, was occupied with cases of conscience in which exaggerated asceticism and normal Christian loyalty were in acute conflict. The Roman bishops, similarly, were continually called upon to decide upon difficult cases of every kind—from the complicated questions involved in the condition of Christian slaves under Jewish masters to the problem of pagan temples in mission districts, which might either be destroyed, or merely (as Gregory the Great preferred) be deprived of their idols, and then converted into Christian churches.[2]

Alongside this official travail of the Church with the detailed exposition of her claims upon loyalty, went an unofficial activity of theologians in the same sphere. Of the two divergent forms which casuistry can assume—the wholly justifiable extension of wise general principles to fit new problems and circumstances ; and the dangerous though inevitable whittling-away of laws too sweepingly laid down, in the interests of particular exigencies—it is the former which meets us most of all in the early centuries. Clement of Alexandria in his ' Paedagogus ' goes through the whole routine of daily life, showing how the Christian should behave himself at each moment of the toilet, the banquet or the conversazione. He is writing, obviously enough, for the Mayfair of his time, and his object is to restrict to decent proportions the laxities of society girls and youths. But he has a curious interest in mere table

[1] Can. 14.   [2] Greg. Magn., *Epp.* xi. 66, 76.

manners, which suggests that luxury did not altogether go hand in hand with refinement among his contemporaries; and his aversion to hiccoughing amounts almost to a disease. So far, however, from attempting to exempt his readers from the severity of law, his aim is to induce them to adopt some of its severity and discipline for themselves. So eating, drinking, the spending of money, laughter, loose jokes, crowns and ointments, beds and bedding, clothes, shoes, ear-rings, jewels are all passed under review;[1] and we cannot complain that the standard he sets is in any way other than sane and Christian.

He makes reasonable concessions to popular frailty; pleasantry is allowed, though buffoonery is not; cut flowers may be enjoyed at table, but it is luxurious to wear them on the person.[2] He has occasional dicta that surprise the modern mind—as, for example, on the subject of baths, which, he says, women may take for cleanliness and health, but men for health alone.[3] Every now and then cases arise where a discussion in the later vein must have taken place. The 'kiss of peace,' though an apostolic ordinance, had given rise to scandal;—should it be abolished in the altered conditions of society?[4] Wigs also had caused some searchings of heart. They were undesirable in themselves, of course; but did they invalidate the sacrament of confirmation as well? Had the bishop genuinely 'laid hands' on the head of a candidate wearing a wig? Clement thinks not, and this strengthens his general objection to the practice.[5] Or, again, though luxury in dress was strictly forbidden, might the rule be relaxed in the case of a Christian woman who desired thereby to retain an erring husband's affection?[6] Already we begin to see that pressure of rigorism which was to lead to the worst excesses of casuistry.

This rigorism is found at its height in Tertullian, Clement's North African contemporary. Tertullian was a rigorist by temperament, and circumstances gave him an opportunity of indulging his eccentricity to the top of its bent. With a gloomier outlook on life than Pascal, and an even more mordant and scathing power of epigram, he rivalled Pascal

---

[1] Clem. Alex., *Paed.* ii., iii.   [2] *Paed.* ii. 5, 8.   [3] *Ib.* iii. 9.
[4] *Paed.* iii. 11.   [5] *Ib.*   [6] *Ib.*

in his opposition to compromise of every sort and kind. He deals, among other things, with the eternal problem of the behaviour of the Christian in persecution ; and the casuists who attempted to argue that it might occasionally be justifiable not to court certain martyrdom meet with cavalier treatment at his hands. There is only one text in the Gospel, he says, that they have the wit to remember, and that is, ' When they persecute you in this city, flee to the next ' ; only one action of our Lord's that appeals to them—His retirement from the violence offered Him at Nazareth ; only one proverb on their lips—' He who fights and runs away will live to fight another day.' [1] The principles he alleges are startling in their evangelical severity. We must not flee from persecution, for—with all other happenings—it proceeds from God [2] (what a principle to apply to disease and suffering !) ; whatever is not expressly allowed in the Gospel is forbidden [3]—a wholly impossible rule on which to act ; we must not attempt to supersede sheer faith in the divine assistance by any kind of human intervention. Those who attempted to buy immunity for their Church-services by bribing the Roman soldiers are sternly rebuked on these grounds—' Faith,' he says, ' can remove mountains ; it can certainly make short work of the military.' [4]

The conditions of entry to the Church are made as rigorous as the conditions of communion. No person connected even in the remotest degree with idol-worship—even though no more than a mason or painter engaged in the building of the temple—may be allowed into the Church.[5] To those who disingenuously quoted St. Paul's words, ' Let every man abide in the calling wherein he is called,' [6] he replies curtly that this principle would justify the unconditional baptism of professional thieves, forgers and actors. Craftsmen engaged in making the accessories to pagan worship must apply their craft in other directions. Instead of making statues they should make sideboards ; instead of idols, tallboys ; and after all, he adds, with a touch of worldly wisdom which

---

[1] *de Fuga*, 6, 8, 10.　　　[2] *Ib.* 4.　　　[3] *de Cor. Mil.* 2.
[4] *de Fuga*, 14 : ' Fides si montem transferre potest, multo magis militem.'
[5] *de Idol.* 4, 5.　　　　　　[6] 1 Cor. vii. 20.

sorts oddly with his militant other-worldliness, though their new jobs will not be so remunerative they will find the employment more regular.[1] Schoolmasters, whose professional holidays are regulated by pagan festivals, and who are engaged with a curriculum consisting largely of pagan myths, must retire from their occupation before they join the Church.[2] Soldiers converted to Christianity are under the same obligation,[3] and no consideration of wife or family may hold a man back from abandoning any of these proscribed occupations. 'Faith fears not famine,' and that should be enough.[4]

But even in Tertullian there are traces of a more accommodating casuistry; he finds ways to mitigate the spirit of his rigorism without violating the letter. 'The end justifies the means' is almost achieved in his dictum that a man may attend a heathen betrothal, marriage or name-giving, in spite of its association with a sacrifice :—'If I attend on account of the sacrifice indeed, I shall be guilty of idolatry ; but if for any other reason, I shall merely be a spectator of the sacrifice.'[5] Similarly, though the schoolmaster may no longer teach the pagan classics, he is not debarred from reading them if he wishes to, for that involves no co-operation in the sin of others.[6] Most remarkable of all, he finds a compromise even for the craftsman who cannot leave his work to become a Christian without ruin :—'You ought to count the cost before baptism, like the prudent builder in the gospel.'[7] This dictum can only have one meaning— that the unfortunate catechumen should remain in association with the Church, though unbaptized, until circumstances make it more possible for him to change his trade or retire. Among such circumstances the possibility of subsisting upon the charity of the Church was always to be reckoned with ; Cyprian is prepared to give financial assistance to enable a professor of the dramatic art to retire 'on a frugal

[1] de Idol. 8.   [2] Ib. 10.
[3] de Cor. Mil. 11. The Council of Arles, 314, forbade soldiers to abandon their profession even in peace-time, so that, in striking contrast to Tertullian, the 'first formal ecclesiastical decision relating to the matter is a decisive recognition of the lawfulness of military service' (F. E. Brightman in H. B. Swete, Early History of Church and Ministry, p. 326).
[4] de Idol. 12.   [5] Ib. 16.
[6] Ib. 10.   [7] Ib. 12.

allowance ' from the Church, and so qualify for full membership.[1] The popularity of death-bed baptisms in the early
Church was probably due in the main to this recognised
principle of ' counting the cost '—you remained in your
forbidden profession until your last illness, and then, when
no further problems could arise, called for baptism, which, it
would appear, was readily given.

A second African lawyer, Lactantius, whom Constantine
chose as tutor to his son Crispus, was another rigorist. He
had a full classical education, and he inveighs in no measured
terms against the lax casuistry of Carneades, the Academics
and the later Stoics. Cicero, he says [2] (referring to the
' de Republica ') had failed to refute Carneades on those
classical problems of the insanitary house and the plank in
the shipwreck to which we have already alluded ; he proposes
himself to fill the gap.[3] His method is surprising. He
denies that the ' just ' man will ever find himself in circumstances in which a deviation from the strict letter of the law
need even be considered. Why should he snatch a horse
from a wounded man in battle, or a plank from a shipwrecked
mariner ? Battle and shipwreck are out of the purview of
his life, ' for he is not at enmity with any human being, nor
does he desire what belongs to others. Why, then, should he
undertake a voyage or seek aught from another land, when
his own is sufficient ? Or why engage in war when his mind
is at peace with all men ? ' But in the improbable event of
his finding himself in such circumstances he will remain true
to himself and the immutable principles of his morality.[4]
Not even a falsehood is allowed him in any circumstances ;
' in the path of justice and virtue there is no place for
lying.' [5]

4. The Abbot Joseph and St. Augustine

It was round this problem of lying, with its kindred
questions of rash or inconvenient promises and vows, that

---

[1] Cyprian, *Ep.* ii. The man was actually a baptized Christian about
the legitimacy of whose profession Cyprian's correspondent had doubts.
[2] *Div. Inst.* v., cc. 15–18. [3] *Ib.* 17.
[4] *Ib.* 18. [5] *Ib.* vi. 18.

the first Christian casuistical discussions of any note gathered. Not only were the old Stoic questions still in the air ; new problems created by persecution and the threat of martyrdom, as also by the duty of protecting the sacred books and vessels from sacrilegious hands, all pointed towards the exemption of 'necessary,' 'useful,'[1] 'harmless' or 'legitimate' falsehoods from the general condemnation of lying—a condemnation which countless scriptural texts (especially a favourite verse in Psalm v.[2]) endorsed with unequivocal emphasis. There was however a further reason why Christianity in particular was forced to face the problem of lies. The Bible, it is true, unhesitatingly condemned all lying ; but the Bible also recorded, with complacency if not with outspoken approval, instances of unblushing mendacity on the part of the patriarchs, their allies and descendants. Unless Scripture was to contradict itself, some way must be found of showing either that these lies were not lies, or that they were legitimate in the circumstances. And so the Fathers, especially in their Commentaries on the Scriptures, abound in discussions of Rahab's lie, and that of the midwives in Egypt ; of Jehu's feigned adoption of Baal-worship as a means of exterminating the Baal-cult ; of David's dissimulations ; of Abraham's lie about Sarah, and Sarah's lie to the angel ; and above all of Jacob's unblushing deception of Isaac.

Jerome quite recklessly precipitated a controversy of this kind with Augustine about a New Testament incident. He refused to believe that St. Paul would ever have dared to rebuke St. Peter openly. Yet the text of the Epistle to the Galatians asserts clearly that Paul 'withstood Peter to the face.' There was a way out of the difficulty which Origen had previously suggested, and Jerome boldly adopted it ; it was to assume no less than three successive 'useful' deceptions. St. Peter merely *feigned* to withdraw from the society of Gentiles, in order to keep the adhesion of the Jews ; St. Paul then *feigned* to rebuke him publicly, to keep the Gentiles in countenance. And finally—though this indeed Jerome did not assert, but Augustine rightly saw that

---

[1] 'Officiosum,'—the word is commonly used of those lies which 'do a service' to someone.

[2] Ps. v. 6. 'Thou shalt destroy them that speak leasing.'

it was implied [1]—Paul gave a false account of the whole matter to the Galatians, in order to keep up the original fiction.[2] To support his contention that the whole affair redounded to the credit of both parties concerned, Jerome goes so far as to speak of Jehu's ' useful and timely dissimulation ' [3] in inviting the Baal-worshippers to their own slaughter, and argues that if *this* was blameless the other must needs be too.

Jerome's ' Commentary ' was published about 386 A.D. Within ten years of that date occurred a conversation in which, with the unblushing approval of all concerned, there was manifested a laxity about the whole question of promises and lies which is unsurpassed even in the worst period of Jesuit excesses. This piece of Christian immoralism springs from a most unexpected quarter—one indeed to which the whole Church looked as to the home of saintliness and purity. Two young monks of Bethlehem, John Cassian and his friend Germanus, set out to visit the hermits and solitaries of the Egyptian desert under promise to return within a given period. So impressed were they with the superior sanctity of the life and character of those they met in Egypt, that the thought of returning to Bethlehem grew more and more distasteful to them ; and they sought counsel with the Abbot Joseph, the holiest of their new friends. Cassian gives an account of the interview in his 17th ' Conference,' and reveals Abbot Joseph as one of the few personages in Christian literature worthy to be compared, for his bland and confident disregard of the moral law, to the kindly old Jesuit of the ' Provincial Letters.' So much do the utterances of the two resemble one another that it is difficult to bear in mind that, while Pascal was writing in scathing satire, Cassian is recording in sober earnest a discourse for which he felt nothing but the most wholehearted approval and enthusiasm.

For the Abbot Joseph has no hesitations on the point which has been put to him. He bids them break their promise with impunity. ' We ought always to seek,' he says, ' that which exposes us to the smallest loss ' ; and so if (as they

[1] Aug., *Ep*. lxxxii. 2 (4) (ed. Ben.).   [2] Hier., *in Ep. ad Gal*. ii.
[3] ' Utilis simulatio et assumenda in tempore.'

allege) Germanus and Cassian will ' suffer a daily increase of coldness ' in their spiritual life by leaving Egypt, it is better for them to incur the smaller ' loss ' of a falsehood and broken promise, ' which is done once for all and need not be repeated.' [1]   The end justifies the means, and a good intention is all that matters ; ' therefore we must consider this and not what is actually done.'   ' Some men have arrived at the height of righteousness by means of acts altogether reprehensible. . . . They put up with the necessity of a blameworthy start, not out of disregard for God, nor with the purpose of doing wrong, but with an eye to a needful end.' [2]   Jacob's lie to Isaac is a case in point.   We must assume that it was the only way to achieve the blessing in question (otherwise it would have been ' unfair, treacherous and sacrilegious ') ; but on this assumption we need not hesitate to conclude that God ' regarded the falsehood as excusable and worthy of praise, because without it Jacob could not achieve the blessing of the first-born ; and that should not be regarded as a sin which arose from the desire for blessing.' [3]   So Jacob ' to his credit acquiesced in the lie to which his mother instigated him. . . . He did not doubt that the guilt of the lie would at once be washed away by the stream of his father's blessing ; that the breath of the Holy Spirit would dissolve it like a little cloud; and that richer rewards of merit would be bestowed on him by means of this dissimulation than by means of the truth which was natural to him.' [4]   Cassian and Germanus therefore, for their part, need not hesitate—not to break their promise, for that Joseph will not say; but—to ' correct the short-sighted arrangement' [5] they had made in undertaking to return to Bethlehem.

Despite their respect for the good Abbot, the young men found his doctrine stronger meat than any to which they were accustomed.   Germanus suggests that, excellent though Joseph's attitude may be, it is in danger of giving the weaker brethren an excuse to sin.   This argument the Abbot brushes impatiently on one side ; he has little sympathy for weaker brethren.   ' If they are on the road to ruin,' he says, ' they will find plenty of other examples to lure them on ; you need

[1] Cassian, *Coll.* xvii. 8.   [2] *Ib.* c. 11.   [3] *Ib.* c. 12.
[4] *Ib.* c. 17.   [5] *Ib.* c. 14 : ' Emendatio dispositionis improvidae.'

not reject an "economy" useful to yourselves out of consideration for their weakness.'[1]   Still Germanus is not
satisfied, and urges that Jacob's lie may have been allowable
under the Old Covenant, but that all lies are forbidden
under the New.   Joseph is at once aroused to defend the
credit of his hero, impugned by the suggestion that he was
only doing what was normally allowable in his day.   Lies,
he says emphatically, and with appropriate citations, were
as much condemned in the Old Testament as in the New;
there is no difference on that point.   But in spite of the condemnation 'they were properly employed as a last resort
when some need or plan of salvation was bound up with them.
We cannot refuse to employ these artifices which we hear that
holy men adopted, when need arises.'   He proceeds to give
further instances from the lives of approved hermits, showing
that lies may profitably and excusably be employed in the
pursuit of Christian humility,[2] or 'to save one's life, or to
procure a blessing, or to conceal a mystery, or in zeal for God, or
to enquire the truth.'[3]   We are scarcely surprised in the end
to hear Germanus confess that 'in many cases a lie is meritori-
ous,'[4] or to learn that the two young men 'corrected their
short-sighted arrangement' by postponing their return to
Bethlehem for seven years, to the great annoyance of their
superiors.[5]

The frankness and *naiveté* of Abbot Joseph is such as
to exempt him from all suspicion of bad faith.   He revels in
his freedom from the shackles of truth and fidelity, and his
reservations are few and slight.   'A lie,' he says, 'is like
hellebore, which is useful if taken when deadly disease is
threatening, but if taken when not required by great danger
brings immediate death.'   'When any grave danger is bound
up with admitting the truth, we must take refuge in lies,
though we ought to feel it a humiliation of conscience.'
'God looks at the inner desire of the heart, not at the word
spoken.'   'One man may be justified by a lie while another
is guilty of eternal sin by the truth.'[6]   The strait-laced
precisian who will never lie or break his promise is guilty,
in Joseph's eyes, not merely of a selfish concern with his own

---

[1] Cassian, *Coll.* xvii., cc. 15, 16.   [2] *Ib.* cc. 21 ff.   [3] *Ib.* 25.
[4] *Ib.* c. 22.   [5] *Ib.* c. 30.   [6] *Ib.* c. 17.

salvation, but also of spiritual red-tape and obstinacy. 'If we seek our own good only, and want obstinately to retain what is best for ourselves, we must speak the truth even in urgent cases, although by so doing we may be guilty of another's death. But if we prefer the advantage of others to our own and satisfy the demands of the apostles we shall certainly have to put up with lying. We cannot keep a perfect heart of love unless we relax a little in things which concern strictness and perfection in our own lives, and so like St. Paul become weak to the weak that we may gain the weak.' [1]

So also with promises :—'I cannot call to mind,' he concludes, 'any reasonable or experienced Fathers who have been rigorous or immovable in the matter of their promises. As wax melts before the sun, so has their resolution melted before reason ; and they have without hesitation embraced the better part when it presented itself. Whenever I come across a man who pertinaciously keeps his promises, I always find that he is unreasonable and inexperienced.' [2] The Abbot mitigates this opinion slightly in the conclusion of his discourse ; but nothing can alter its general tenour, or impugn his main position that truth and falsehood are matters of expediency only, though it may be of spiritual expediency.

Abbot Joseph, no doubt, is an extreme case. But language and opinions of this kind were in the air ; and it only needed an appropriate occasion to produce an outburst of laxity on the one hand, and a rigorist rejoinder on the other. The occasion came about twenty years later. One of the first heretics to suffer the death penalty, nominally at least for heresy, at the hands of the secular power, was the Spaniard Priscillian, executed by the usurping Emperor Maximus in the year 385. The Priscillianist movement had been distinguished in its infancy by a rigorous ethical code ; but possibly the stress of persecution, possibly a moral eccentricity based upon their curious theological views, allowed them to practise a widespread dissimulation of the truth. Like the Abbot Joseph they held that falsehood was allow-

---

[1] Cassian, *Coll.* xvii., c. 19.
[2] *Ib.* c. 26.   Cassian also discusses lying in *Inst.* v. 37, 39.

able for a holy end. ' Swear or forswear, but do not betray
the secret '[1] was their motto. They were prepared to go to
extremes in agreeing with the multitude, to conceal from
them truths which they would only misunderstand. They
are accused of falsifying the Scriptures and forging apocryphal
documents to commend their doctrines.[2] There is nothing
in these allegations which goes very far beyond the casuistry
of the period ; even the saintly Gregory of Nyssa had not
hesitated to forge letters—and that unskilfully—to his
brother Basil for spiritual ends.[3] Basil indeed was unlucky
in this matter ; Chrysostom had tricked him into becoming
a bishop by a similar fraud, and had the temerity to defend
his lie at great length—' for a well-timed deception, with a
good end in view, is often so advantageous that people are
sometimes punished for neglecting to employ it.'[4] But
the profession of lax opinions of this character by a
whole sect, and one moreover guilty of a dangerous and
subversive heresy, was a different and more serious matter ;
and it brought into the field on the rigorist side no less a person
than Augustine.

Augustine had long since had his attention caught by
the problem of the lie. In a series of letters [5] he had taken
up Jerome's challenge about the incident at Antioch, and
had defended Paul from the charge of lying as strenuously
as his opponent defended Peter from that of vacillation.
The controversy lasted nine years or so, owing to delay in
the transmission of letters. In the course of it Augustine
rejected all the different theories of ' officious,' ' expedient '
and ' useful ' lies, and of ' honourable economies ' or ' dispensations ' from the truth, which were in circulation ; and
challenges Jerome, if he insists upon his point, ' to supply
us with rules by which we may know when a falsehood may

---

[1] ' Jura, perjura, secretum prodere noli,' quoted by Aug., *Ep.* ccxxxvii.
(ed. Ben.) ; cp. Leo, *Ep.* xv. ; Ambrose, *Ep.* xxiv. ; Sulp. Sev., *Hist.
Sacr.* ii. 46 ff.

[2] Leo, *Ep.* xv. 16.

[3] Basil, *Ep.* lviii.

[4] Chrysost., *de Sac.* i. 5 (59). Probably, however, this was a different
Basil ; see J. A. Nairn's edition of the *de Sacerdotio* (Cambridge, 1906), p.
xxxiv. Other early examples of the defence of lying on occasion are to be
found in Clem. Alex., *Strom.* viii. 9 ; Origen, *Fragm. ap.* Hieron. *c. Ruf.* i. 18.

[5] Aug., *Epp.* xxviii., xl., lxxv., lxxxii. ; cp. *Ep.* clxxx.

or may not become a duty.'[1] He alleges that Jerome
was in the end converted to his view,[2] though the evidence
does not altogether bear him out. But letters would not
carry the weight of what he had to say, and with a covert
allusion to Jerome he published, about the year 397, his
book, 'About Lies.'[3] Priscillianism roused him to greater
efforts still, and a second book, 'Against Lies,'[4] was the
result. It was high time that something authoritative should
be said ; for the orthodox were already deeply infected with
this particular error of the Priscillianists, and were pretending
to be converts to the heresy in order to learn its secrets and
betray them to the authorities.[5] Augustine was even more
shocked by this duplicity on the Catholic side than by the
Priscillianists themselves ; and perhaps this accounts to some
extent for the alarming rigidity of his views.

The outlook of both pamphlets is identical. Augustine
divides lies into eight grades, from the most harmful (lies
in ' religious matters,' or lies ' which hurt someone and
benefit no one ') to the most innocuous (those which ' hurt
no one and benefit someone,'—above all when this ' benefit '
is of a spiritual character—to save him from sin, for example) ;[6] and root and branch he condemns them all. Not
indeed that they are all equally sinful. Some are far more
pardonable than others ;[7] but all are to be avoided. His
principal argument is that a lie is one of those things which
are evil in themselves, hence no degree of excellence in the
motive can atone for it.[8] In two confused passages[9] he
attempts to show that veracity is the highest of virtues,
higher indeed than chastity—not even then in defence of
bodily purity may one lie. And this extreme position is
adopted with full recognition of the catastrophes it will
involve. May you lie to defend a man who is hard-pressed
by a murderer or an agent of justice ? No ; you must say,
' I will neither lie nor betray him,' or ' I know where he is,
but will never tell you ' ; if these expedients fail, you must

[1] *Ep.* xxviii. 5.   [2] *Ep.* clxxx.   [3] *de Mendacio.*
[4] *contra Mendacium* (c. 420 A.D.).
[5] *Retract.* ii. 40 ; *contra Mend.* 2 (2)–7 (17).   [6] *de Mend.* 14 (25).
[7] *Ib.* 18 (42) ; *c. Mend.* 8 (19), 9 (20) ; cp. *Enchir.* 18 (6).
[8] *c. Mend.* 7 (18).
[9] *de Mend.* 18 (41) ; *c. Mend.* 18 (38).

acquiesce in his death rather than deny the truth.[1] If a parent, himself dangerously ill, asks whether his dead son still lives, you must tell ' the truth which will kill ' (*homicida veritas*) rather than the ' lie which will cure ' (*salubre mendacium*)—tragic though Augustine admits the alternative to be.[2] Even where a man's eternal salvation is at stake— as, for example, if an unbaptized person can only be rescued from death and baptized by means of a falsehood—you must condemn him to hell rather than lie.[3] When we remember Augustine's views on the eternal torment which awaits the unbaptized, nothing could be more illustrative of his rigorism than this decision. A modern defender of Augustine has said of these two books that they are ' sparing in the solution of practical problems.'[4] The statement wholly misrepresents the facts. Augustine considers the principal ' practical problems ' in detail, and has one invariable and final solution—' Never lie.'

It is not only the ' practical problems ' he considers ; he has taken account of the objections to his theory. Of the Old Testament instances, indeed, he makes short work. Many of them he dismisses as ' figurative ' of spiritual truth ; Jacob's lie, for example, is not ' mendacity ' but ' mystery.'[5] Abraham in Egypt did not lie; Sarah *was* his half-sister,[6] and besides (as he explains elsewhere)[7] something had to be done. It would have been trusting too much in God's providence to leave to Him entirely the defence both of the husband's life and the wife's honour ; for it is ' a point of sound doctrine that when a man has any means in his power he should not tempt the Lord his God.' In a curiously modern way he abandons the attempt to justify in full some of the Old Testament lies. The midwives were charitably disposed, but they would have done better to tell the truth ; in that case they would have been killed by Pharaoh and have gone to heaven at once.[8] Rahab's lie, though equally

---

[1] *de Mend.* 13 (22–24).   [2] *c. Mend.* 18 (36).   [3] *Ib*: 20 (40).
[4] A. Vermeersch in *Gregorianum* (1920), p. 430. Augustine is ' multus in excusandis sanctis Veteris Testamenti, sat jejunus autem in solvendis practicis difficultatibus.'
[5] *c. Mend.* 10 (24).   [6] *Ib.* 10 (23).
[7] *In Quaest. Gen.* c. 26 ; *c. Faust. Man.* xxii. 33 and 36.
[8] *c. Mend.* 17 (34).

kind-hearted, was wholly unnecessary, and therefore blameworthy. She was a ' most cautious woman,' and had hidden
the spies so carefully that in any case they would not have
been discovered ; or, if they had been, God could have
saved them had He so wished.[1] As for Jehu, he was a bad
man anyhow ; his lie, so far from meriting Jerome's commendation, was ' impious,' and the sacrifice that followed it
a ' sacrilege.' [2]

He is less felicitous in dealing with other objections.
His doctrine that truth is the highest of virtues, and must
be preserved at all costs, was a mere piece of dogmatism ;
and he is forced at last to defend it on grounds of utility—
once admit the legitimacy of lying in an urgent case, and
when will the process stop ? [3] He has to admit the principle
that of two evils we should choose the least,[4] and it is only
by a moral individualism of quite shocking crudity that he
saves the resultant situation. The integrity of my own soul
(he suggests) outweighs not only any other welfare of my
own, but even the spiritual welfare of others—which indeed
is no concern of mine.[5] To those who defended the ' compen-
sative lie ' (i.e. the lie which is told with no selfish purpose,
but in a spirit of altruism) by saying that just as a millionaire
does not feel the loss of a single bushel of corn, so the genuinely godly man cannot be harmed by a trifling and merely
technical ' sin ' of this kind, he can only reply that that does
not justify you in stealing the bushel—which merely evades
the point of the argument.[6] The whole episode is a distressing example of rigorist intransigence attempting to stem
the attack of casuistry, and forcing casuistry on to illegitimate lines through sheer unwillingness to admit it even in its
legitimate form.

We have dwelt at some length upon this problem of mendacity and its treatment, because it furnishes a test-case
by which all casuistry may be judged. The problem is to
find a method by which the verdict of common-sense—that
a 'lie' is sometimes the lesser of two evils, and so in the circumstances blameless and even laudable—may so be combined

---

[1] *c. Mend.* 17 (34).   [2] *Ib.* 2 (3).
[3] *Ib.* 18 (37) ; *de Mend.* 18 (38, 39).
[4] *de Mend.* 18 (38).   [5] *Ib.* 9 (12).   [6] *Ib.* 12 (19).

with the Christian condemnation of lying in general as to offer a principle upon which perplexities of this kind may be solved without on the one hand opening the door to widespread laxity, or on the other inflicting intolerable hardship upon innocent individuals in abnormal circumstances. We shall have occasion later to consider whether such a solution can be found. Here we need only notice very briefly the subsequent history of the problem.

Augustine's position became the dominant one for the western Church, with one modification :—since some lies are of lesser gravity than others, all lies whose motive is not malicious came to be regarded as venial. Gregory the Great admitted the seriousness of the problem—' Either by a lie you must slay your own soul, or by speaking the truth bear hard upon the life of your neighbour.' [1] But he repeats Augustine's lesson. ' All lying is to be seriously guarded against, though some kind of lying is of a lighter complexion, as if a man lie in rendering good.[2] . . . But even this kind of lying the perfect avoid with the greatest care, and will not even save another's life by deceit, lest they hurt their own souls in busying themselves to defend another's flesh. No doubt this kind of sin, as we believe, is easily forgiven ; for if any sin is to be written off by virtue of godly results accruing therefrom, surely this is of such a kind, which pity herself, the mother of all good works, accomplishes.' [3] Gregory regards the New Testament as setting a higher standard in this matter, as in others, than the Old ; and though he recognises the altruism of the Egyptian midwives, he does not excuse their lie from the guilt of self-interest :— ' By the act of sparing they protected the lives of the children ; but by lying, their own lives.' Similarly, Isidore of Seville refuses to allow the Christian to defend anyone's life by fraud.[4]

Gratian, in the twelfth century, reproduces Augustine's position in full, including his exculpation of Abraham and Jacob. ' Jacob,' he says, ' no more lied in calling himself Esau than our Lord did in calling John the Baptist Elijah

---

[1] *Moral. in Hiob.* viii. 6 (9).
[2] ' Praestando ' ; *aliter* ' vitam praestando '—' in saving life.'
[3] *Mor.* xviii. 3 (5). [4] *Syn.* ii. 10.

—he had *become* Esau by the purchase of the birthright.' [1]
At the same time he dallies with the other solutions of
the problem. He thinks there are some lies which need
not be called lies ; [2] and after quoting with approval Jerome's
exculpation of Jehu, says complacently, ' So now we see what
lies are venial and what are to be condemned.' [3] Alexander of
Hales maintains that what is forbidden is any lie, whether
' pernicious, useful or jocose,' which comes from a mortally
sinful motive ; 'lies whose motive is venial are quite different.' [4]
Some authorities hold that all useful or jocose lies are venial
only. Alexander does not agree with them, but gives a definition of mortal and venial motives which in practice would
allow almost any lie of these categories to pass as venial.[5]
St. Thomas's discussion is singularly uninspired, and amounts
to no more than saying that all lies are wrong, but some are
only venial.[6] Antoninus of Florence, the master-confessor,
carries on the tradition down to the period of the Reformation.[7]

This solution of the problem is not wholly valueless in
practice. It enables well-intentioned lies to be condoned
where necessary, and yet maintains the formal condemnation
of all lying. But it suffers from two obvious defects. The
weak-willed are only too apt to think that what is merely
' venial ' may be indulged in with impunity ; and there is
no reason to suppose that this tendency would be less operative in the matter of falsehood than elsewhere. Further,
the theory is, strictly speaking, irrelevant to the issue.
A venial sin is still a sin, whereas some of the 'lies' for which
we are pleading are clearly not sins at all, but either wholly
excusable or even morally obligatory. The best we can say
of any venial sin is, ' We recognise that there were extenuating
circumstances, but still you ought not to have done it ; '
whereas there are some lies of which we feel bound to say,
' You were quite right in the circumstances in lying as you

---

[1] *C.J.C.* c. 22, C. xxii. q. 2.   [2] *Ib.* c. 7.   [3] *Ib.* c. 21.

[4] *Summa*, iii. q. 37, m. 6: ' Generaliter hic prohibetur omne mendacium
ex mortali libidine proveniens, quodcumque illud fuerit, sive videlicet
perniciosum sive officiosum sive jocosum. Secus autem est de iis quae
ex veniali libidine proveniunt.'

[5] ' Mortal ' is a ' love of temporal good in preference to eternal ' (' amor
supra Deum ') ; ' venial,' a ' love of temporal good in subordination to
eternal ' (' amor sub Deo '), *ib.*

[6] *S.T.* i. 2, q. 110, aa. 3, 4.   [7] *Summ. Conf.* ii. tit. 10, c. i. 91.

did—it was the only course open to you.' There are, no doubt,
lies which *are* venial sins, but they are not the ones which
cause the difficulty.

In spite of these very obvious criticisms, the Augustinian
theory held its ground.   Indeed, the criticisms do not seem to
have been raised, for the simple reason that the illegitimate
casuistry of equivocation and mental restriction was already
in the field.   As early as Raymund of Pennafort,[1] the
accepted answer to the murderer's enquiry as to his intended
victim's whereabouts was *Non est domi*, or *Non est hic* ;   which
the murderer (not being a casuist, presumably) took to mean,
' He is not here,' though the speaker interpreted it as, ' He
is not taking a meal here.'   Lyndwood merely gives the ordinary mediaeval ruling when he allows a confessor, questioned
as to something he has heard in the confessional, to say,
' I know nothing about it,' with the mental addition of ' as
a man,' or ' that I can tell you.' [2]   It is curious that this
' confusion between moral truth and verbal truth,' as it
has been called,[3] came in for so little criticism, but as long
as it went unchallenged the problem of lying, naturally
enough, was in abeyance.   It was as easy to equivocate
as to lie, and whereas the latter might be held a venial sin,
the former was deemed wholly unobjectionable.

Francis Bacon indeed had a poor opinion of the practical
value of ' equivocations and oraculous speeches,' but held
that ' no man could be secret except he give himself a little
scope ' for them ;   they are merely the ' skirts and train of
secrecy.' [4]   Even Jeremy Taylor was inclined to think
equivocation ' something less than a plain lie.'   ' It is,' he
says, ' like a dark lantern ;   if I have just reason to hold the
dark side to you, you are to look to it ! . . . *I use that way
to save my conscience and to escape a lie.* . . . Equivocation
may upon less necessity and upon more causes be permitted
than lying.' [5]   Of mental restriction he thinks less favourably
—' the whole affair is infinitely unreasonable ; ' but he agrees

---

[1] *Summ. Pen.* i. 10. 4.   Raymund died in 1275.
[2] *Prov.* v. tit. 16, *verb.* ' Confessionem.'
[3] [F. Meyrick] *Moral Theology of Church of Rome* (London, 1855).
[4] *Essay* vi.
[5] *Duct. Dub.* III. 2, rule 5, q. 3.   The instances he gives of successful
equivocations are less hackneyed than those usually advanced.

with Gregory the Great that ' a pious cozenage ' (apparently much the same thing) must sometimes be used to ' obstruct the mischief of tyrants,' and that this also avoids the ' guilt of a lie.' [1] In the Roman Church the reforming popes made a brave but unsuccessful effort to combat the evil, and it persisted in a modified form as late as Alphonso Liguori. Where so easy a method of avoiding not merely lying but even the problem of lying was current, it is small wonder that the latter was rarely discussed.

5. *The Middle Ages*

We must get back, however, to the middle ages. The barbarian invasions, and the mass-conversions of the invaders, brought Christianity back to a realisation of fundamentals. It was no longer a question of instrumenting the moral law and adjusting its incidence to abnormal problems; it was a question as to whether there should be any moral law at all. So the ethical literature of the seventh to the tenth centuries— the so-called ' Penitential Books '—deals scarcely at all with problems of conscience. The ' Penitentials ' are occupied with maintaining the bare essentials of Christian conduct; and a glance at any one of them, such as that of Archbishop Theodore, will show how gross were the sins which they had to repress. But the establishment of the Empire brought better times with it, and for five centuries casuistry performs its true function of steadily developing the moral principles of the Church from wise beginnings to wise conclusions in particular cases or types of case. The result, though in the end it tends towards too great an elaboration of detail after the fashion of the Pharisees, is in the main impressive and remarkable.

Three great movements combined to produce this result : the codification of the canon law culminating (for our purpose) in the ' Decretum ' of Gratian (c. 1140) ; the unhurried and conscientious progress of ethical enquiry begun by Abailard, and reaching its greatest height in St. Thomas Aquinas ; and the extension of the practice of private confession, which

[1] *Duct. Dub.* III. 2, rule 5, q. 2.

the fourth Lateran Council made virtually obligatory, and which at once called for a supply of manuals for confessors dealing with problems of detail. In the fourteenth and fifteenth centuries these three streams coalesced in the ' Summæ Confessionales,' of which the ' Summa Summarum ' of Sylvester Prierias († 1523) is at once the latest and the fullest example. They provide the confessor both with the canon law, the ethical principles and the casuistical applications demanded by each of the problems he has to consider. To understand the painstaking, honest and on the whole salutary work done by the middle ages in this ambitious attempt to educate the Christian conscience through an entire curriculum from first principles to particular conclusions, we have only to wander at large through the pages of St. Thomas's ' Secunda Secundæ ' ; but fine examples of the method and its success can be found even earlier. We may take two for our purposes from Gratian.

A problem is first stated as follows :—' A bishop has made a statement on oath which turns out to be false, though he thought it true. When the apparent perjury becomes known, his archdeacon swears that he will never obey the bishop again. The bishop compels him to obedience, and is then accused of perjury on two counts : (a) as a principal, for his original false statement on oath ; (b) as an accessory, for causing the archdeacon to break his oath.' How far is the bishop guilty on either or both of these counts ?

Gratian is of course more interested in the legal than in the ethical side of his problems. But he recognises that the business of canon law is to approximate as far as possible to true morality, and it is in the main as a moral problem that he treats the matter. Allowing for the sanctity with which oaths and vows were regarded, we cannot but admire the fullness and fairness of the discussion. The canonist divides the problem into five stages : (1) Are oaths ever allowable in view of Matt. v. 37, ' Whatsoever is more than this is sin,' and James v. 12, ' Swear not ' ?—With this our English Article xxxix. may be compared. (2) Is it perjury to swear to a falsehood thinking it to be true ? (3) Was the archdeacon's oath in any case immoral and unlawful ? (4) If so, was it his duty to keep the oath or not ? (5) Granted that it was the archdeacon's duty to keep the oath, was the bishop an accessory to perjury in forcing him to break it ? But this summary does Gratian less than justice. In the course of his treatment he diverges into the problems of lying, of ignorance as an excuse for sin, of the interpretation of oaths and promises, and of the validity of oaths taken by children ; whilst he glances at such questions as whether it is a sin to swear by the devil, and whether such an oath is binding. With immense diligence he quotes authorities on all these points ; but, true to his principle of resolving discords between authoritative utterances,[1] he earnestly looks for the principles involved, and attempts to bring them to light.[2]

In the next ' Causa ' he attacks the problems of war, punishment and toleration. Certain dioceses have lapsed into heresy and are forcing the inhabitants of adjoining dioceses, by threats and torture, to accept their tenets. The Pope orders the catholic bishops of the province, who have received civil jurisdiction from the Emperor, to defend the orthodox from the heretics, and to use all means in their power to bring the latter back to the faith. The catholics raise an army and carry on war both openly and by stratagem against the heretics ; some of the latter are executed, some degraded or dispossessed, some imprisoned with hard labour. The remainder revert to the faith on compulsion. Gratian sees no less than eight main problems here, and discusses them one by one :— (1) Is fighting a sin ? (2) What is a just war ? (3) May we fight to defend our allies ? (4) Is punishment lawful ? (5) Is capital punishment allowed ? (6) May evil-doers be compelled by force ' to live honestly ' ? (7) May the goods of heretics be confiscated, or are their new possessors to be held guilty of theft ? (8) May spiritual persons engage in war, either on their own authority, or on that of the Pope and Emperor ? But here, as before, other issues are seen to be involved ; and Gratian presents his readers with carefully documented opinions upon such various subjects as the duty of non-resistance, the use of stratagems in war, the difference between force and persuasion in moral education,

---

[1] Gratian's own title for the *Decretum* was *Concordia Discordantium Canonum*.

[2] *C.J.C.* C. xxii.

H

suicide, the legitimacy of fighting during Lent, the taxation of the clergy, arson and brawling.[1]

But while these high subjects are under discussion, the needs of ordinary consciences are not forgotten. We may take, for example, St. Thomas's classical consideration of buying, selling and restitution. All the old Stoic problems and arguments meet us once again. May I sell a thing for more than it is worth ? Does a defect in the thing sold invalidate the sale ? Ought the vendor to declare the defects of what he sells ? All the old illustrations recur as well—the one-eyed horse, the jerry-built house, the Alexandrian corn-merchant. But St. Thomas has a principle, based upon Aristotle's doctrine of ' commutative ' justice as an ' equality of exchange,' [2] which enables him to avoid desultory discussion. It is the theory of the ' just price '—the price, namely, at which the sale will normally result in approximately equal benefit to both parties. This price cannot be fixed by abstract theory, but depends upon a nice appreciation of the circumstances.[3] For practical purposes it may be fixed by the State, or determined less formally by the general consensus of merchants and purchasers. In less technical language, the just price is that which would enable an impartial observer to say, when the bargain was completed, that both sides ought to be satisfied. This principle of ' mutual satisfaction,' ' equal advantage ' or ' common benefit ' [4] determines the whole discussion ; for in the particular circumstances of each transaction the price has to be adjusted so as to secure equality of justice.[5]

Thus if the vendor has a particular wish to retain his goods, whilst the purchaser is set on acquiring them, the price may have to be raised considerably, in order that the

---

[1] *C.J.C.* C. xxiii. Cp. also C. xxvi. on divination, magic and the reconciliation of excommunicates ; C. xxviii. on the ' Pauline privilege ' ; and the very complicated case in C. xv. There is a good example of casuistry of the lower order in C. ii. q. 7, where the old (and unworkable) rule ' laymen may not accuse clerics ' is interpreted by Gratian in the sense : ' laymen *of infamous life* may not accuse clerics.'

[2] *Eth. Nic.* v. 5. 8 ff.

[3] 'Non est punctualiter determinatum, sed magis in quâdam aestimatione consistit,' *S.T.* ii. 2, q. 77, a. 1, ad 1.

[4] ' Communis utilitas.' *Ib.* corp.

[5] ' Ita quod modica additio vel minutio non videtur tollere aequalitatem justitae,' ad 1.

former may be adequately compensated for his loss. On the other hand if the buyer has great need of the commodity and the seller none, the price should not be raised, though the buyer may of his own free will pay more. Again, if the vendor, not knowing the value of his goods, offers them for sale at less than the just price, the purchaser should not take advantage of his ignorance, but must make him a fair return for the satisfaction the acquisition of the commodity will bring to himself.

Similarly, every defect must be taken into account before the transaction can be considered complete ; even if the vendor was ignorant of the defect he must make proportionate restitution when it is discovered. Nor may artificial products be sold as the real article at the same price, for they can never give exactly the same satisfaction as the real article. Thus even if ' synthetic gold and silver ' were as ' durable, medicinal and capable of giving pleasure ' as the natural product (and as a matter of fact, St. Thomas says, they are not), their price would still have to be fixed with reference to their artificial character. They have neither the ' dignity ' nor the ' purity ' of the natural metal ; and therefore, other things being equal, the price must be lower to fit the purchaser's lessened satisfaction.[1]

It follows, of course, that all substantial defects must be declared by the vendor. But his interests also must be guarded. He is not bound to placard the defectiveness of his wares in public ; only where there is a genuine enquiry [2] by a *bona-fide* purchaser need he volunteer the relevant information in confidence. This will do him no harm, for the purchaser, being in earnest, will estimate the good and bad qualities of the article, ' since a thing defective in some particular may nevertheless have many real uses.' [3] There is of course the danger that the purchaser, on the strength of the defect, may attempt to beat the price down ; and in the case in question the vendor has no remedy against this. Where, however, it can be guarded against without injustice, it is legitimate for him to consult his own interests.[4]

[1] *S.T.* ii. 2, q. 77, a. 2.
[2] ' Qui ad emendum accedit,' q. 77, a. 3, ad 2.   [3] *Ib.*
[4] ' Potest licite indemnitati suae consulere vitium rei celando,' *ib.* corp.

Thus if the defect is obvious and not dangerous to life
or limb (the one-eyed horse reappears at this point), the vendor
may lower the price proportionately without mentioning the
defect.   It is not at first clear how this would help him,
but there is perhaps a real piece of business sagacity involved.
If you say, ' I have a horse for sale, but it has only one eye,'
you appear to be apologising for your goods, and consequently
lend a handle to any instinct the buyer may have for driving
a hard bargain.   If on the other hand you merely parade the
one-eyed horse without comment, and leave the purchaser to
say, ' Why, it has only one eye ! ' you can at once reply,
' Of course it has, you surely don't think I should let it go
at this price if it had two ? '—and 'he would have to be a very
barefaced bargainer to try to beat you down further.   It is
at all events arguable that St. Thomas combined with his
religious and theological genius a certain commercial shrewd-
ness which at this point stood him in good stead.

Not that the Angelic Doctor was wholly without qualms
about commerce.   With Aristotle [1] he felt that there was
something wrong in the conception of profit and bank balances.
He was still under the influence of the idea of barter, and
thought that ' considered in itself' commerce, as distinct
from the exchange of produce for the necessities of life, ' had
something wrong about it.' [2]   And is it not true that in this
also he was showing a genuinely Christian spirit ?   He
believed, of course, that a man should live up to the reasonable
requirements of his station.   But the accumulation of wealth
beyond this point by taking advantage (even in a moderate
degree) of the needs or follies of others seemed to him ' rather
shameful.'   It did not square with that ideal of ' mutual
benefit ' which dominated his theory of the just price.   If
the producer does not need what he produces nor the whole
of the profits he derives therefrom, it is surely his business
to adjust prices and wages until his income is adequate to
his reasonable needs, but no more.   This would bring money
back to its true place as a medium for the exchange of necessities, and free it from the stigma of being something which

[1] *Pol.* i. 9.
[2] ' Negotiatio secundum se considerata quamdam turpitudinem habet.'
S.T. ii. 2, q. 77, a. 4.

people continue to pursue for the sake of luxury and ostentation long after their legitimate needs are satisfied.

Whatever we may think about St. Thomas's economic theory, it is certain that his doctrine of the ' just price ' dominated ethical thought about commerce far into the modern period. Mediæval and Roman Catholic writers followed him loyally; others made no less use of him. Richard Baxter's important discussions of the same questions have recently been made accessible to the modern reader; [1] Bishop Hall's quaint and pithy treatment is less well known. The just price, the Bishop says, is that which ' cuts equally between buyer and seller ; so as the seller may receive a moderate gain, and the buyer a just peny-worth.' If demand exceeds supply and prices rise, the seller ' must be so affected as that wee grudge to ourselves our own gaine, that wee bee not in the first file of enhancers ; that wee strive to be the lowest in our valuation, and labour whatever wee may to bring down the market.' In all transactions, even the sale of luxuries, ' conscience must be the Clarke of the Market.' [2]

On the defective commodity he agrees entirely with St. Thomas. If the defect is dangerous (' the horse bee subject

---

[1] *Chapters from Baxter's Christian Directory*, edited by Jeannette Tawney, with a Preface by Bishop Gore (London, 1925). The selections are admirably made, and the book is remarkably inexpensive.

[2] Joseph Hall, *Cases of Conscience Practically Considered* (3rd ed., 1654), dec. i., case 2. Other ' commercial ' problems discussed by Hall are: (1) ' Whether it be lawful for me to raise any profit by the loane of money ? ' (He is doubtful about this, but allows it under strict limitations.) (4) ' Whether I may sell my commodities the dearer for giving days of payment ? ' (5) ' Whether and how farre monopolies are or may be lawfull ? ' (Not at all ; but copyright and patents are allowed.) (6) ' Whether and how farre doth a fraudulent bargaine bind me to performance ? ' (7) ' How farre and when am I bound to make restitution of another man's goods remaining in my hands ? ' (In all cases unless absolute poverty prohibits it ; but this does not mean that fraudulent bankruptcy is allowable, for ' many a one, like to leud cripples that pretend false soares, counterfeit a need that is not, and shelter themselves in a willing Jaile, there living merrily upon their defrauded creditor whom they might honestly satisfie by a well-improved libertie—this case is damnably unjust.') (9) ' Whether those moneys or goods which I have found may be safely taken and kept by me to my own use ? ' (leading to a vehement attack on the practice of ' God's grace,' or ' wrecking,' in Cornwall). (10) ' Whether I may lawfully buy those goods which I shall strongly suspect or know to be stolen or plundered ? '

to a perilous start or stumbling ; the house sold have a secret crack that may threaten ruin ; or the landlord be liable to a litigious claim which may be timely avoyded '), the fact must not be concealed. If on the other hand the defect is not dangerous and ' the buyer will peremptorily rely upon his own judgment and as presuming to make a gaine of the bargain,' he must not be charged as much as for a sound article, but you may be silent about the defect ; ' for if apparent (obvious) defects bee not discerned by the buyer, hee may thanke himselfe '—the seller is not to blame. The Bishop does not give reasons for his conclusions, but they are clearly the same as St. Thomas's ; and although Baxter is in general slightly more rigorist, on this point [1] he is in complete agreement.

6. *Post-Reformation Casuistry*

Joseph Hall and Richard Baxter bring us to the modern period and the Reformed Churches. It is one of the most striking testimonies to the high moral level of mediæval casuistry as a whole that the Reformed Churches at once set themselves to produce a casuistry of their own based on mediæval models, and largely indebted to mediæval authorities. At a time when every ground of contention that could be alleged against Rome was eagerly sought out, in this regard the Reformers found something to imitate rather than to attack. That the mediævalists wrote ' plain Popery ' (as Bishop Barlow said) is not to be wondered at ; and anti-Roman writers make the most of this fact, as also of individual lax decisions and eccentricities of argument. But little else of a definite kind is urged against the Papists. The Reformed casuists all give them more or less grudging mention, quote them continually, and admit that, like the children of Israel, they are forced to go down to the Philistines to have their shares and coulters sharpened.[2] On one point there is unanimous agreement, the immediate necessity for the public

---

[1] I.e. ' when you deal with one who maketh a far greater matter of that fault than there is cause, and would wrong you in the price if it were known,' *Christian Directory*, iv. 19, 3.

[2] So Ames, *de Conscientia*, Preface (1630) ; *Duct. Dub.*, Preface (1659).

provision of books of casuistical divinity ; [1] and such delay as occurred in the process is due merely, as Taylor and Ames both tell us, to the more pressing demands of the anti-Roman controversy.

Still, the output of Reformed casuistry in the seventeenth century is very considerable. For the Calvinists the leading authority was William Perkins (of whom Fuller said that he ' first humbled the towering speculations of philosophers into practice and morality '), of Christ's College, Cambridge, who died in 1602 ; and his restless and unhappy disciple, William Ames (Amesius, † 1633). The Lutherans looked back to Frederick Baldwin (Bauduinus), professor of theology at Wittenburg, who died at the early age of fifty-two in 1627. Anglicanism can boast of three episcopal moralists—Robert Sanderson, Bishop of Lincoln († 1663), of whom Charles I said (with a reminiscence of Henry VIII's praise of Colet), ' I take my ears to hear other preachers, but my conscience to Dr. Sanderson ' ; Jeremy Taylor, Bishop of Down and Connor († 1667) ; and Joseph Hall, successively Bishop of Exeter and Norwich († 1656)—all three of them men whose lives and characters are as deserving of study as their books. To them should perhaps be added, besides Bishop Barlow, John Sharp, Archbishop of York († 1714), whose two short *Discourses on Conscience* are masterpieces of compression and sound argument. Independency is represented by Richard Baxter († 1691), whose indefatigable spirit drew him into this sphere of controversy as enthusiastically as into many others. These, however, are only the greater names ; a long bibliography of lesser writers could easily be put together.[2]

It is a singular fact that at the end of the seventeenth century this Reformed casuistry died as sudden a death as any in history.[3] No one cause can be assigned for it ; but

---

[1] Taylor, *ut sup.*

[2] So, for example, in Döllinger-Reusch, i. p. 28 ; Hauck-Hertzog, X, p. 120 ; and for older lists, J. F. Buddeus, *Institutiones Theologiae Moralis*, Part I., Int., §§ 23, 24 ; *Duct. Dub.*, Preface.

[3] Cp. *Historical Illustrations of the Social Effects of Christianity* (C.O. P.E.C. Commission Report, vol. xii., London, 1924), p. 108, with special reference to the casuistry of commercial honesty : ' What meets us in the sixteenth, and still more in the seventeenth century, is the decline of the whole body of ideas of which the attempt to create a Christian casuistry of economic conduct had been the practical expression. . . . By the beginning

we may suspect that in Holland and Germany at least the phenomenon of pietism, dating from the publication of Spener's ' Pia Desideria ' in 1676, and striking at the roots of ecclesiastical organisation and discipline, had much to do with it.[1] Buddeus, the greatest Protestant theologian and scholar of his age, composing his ' Moral Theology ' in 1711, speaks kindly enough of his casuistical co-religionists, but quite obviously regards their labours as wasted. To him morality is so clear that a mere statement of general principles is all that is needed. In England, on the other hand, it may be supposed that the emergence of naturalism under the ægis of Hobbes, culminating in the simple philosophy of deism, monopolised the attention of theologians and at the same time infected their theology ; nothing else can account for the fact that the ingenious mind of Bishop Butler so completely ignored the complexities of the moral problem. But whatever the cause may be, from the beginning of the eighteenth century to the present day systematic casuistry has had its representatives only in the Roman communion.

How are we to judge of this century of Reformation casuistry ? It is difficult to give an answer. It has none of the consistency and system of its counter-Reformation sister. Each writer goes his own way and blazes his own path. Of the Anglicans, Sanderson's ' Praelections on Law and Conscience,' and on the ' Obligations of an Oath,' are models of

---

of the eighteenth century the view that trade is one thing and religion another, if not explicitly asserted, is tacitly accepted.' This is scarcely fair to Roman Catholic moral theology ; it may have failed to 'work out a social theory applicable to the condition of a society where economic development was entering on seas uncharted by the mediæval moralist' (*ib.* p. 109), but it did not abandon the earlier and healthier view that trade was a matter with which religion was directly concerned. As regards commercial ethics in particular, the Report puts down the failure of [Protestant] casuistry to the 'naturalistic social philosophy' with which the name of Grotius is as closely associated as that of Hobbes. It quotes from J. Meyer, *Das Soziale Naturrecht in der Christlichen Kirche* (pp. 33 ff.) : ' The Puritans developed their sociological ideas directly out of their religion, they determined their attitude towards society and industry in the name of God. Grotius led the way to a complete severance of the two realms. Religion stands by itself, it has nothing to do with natural law ; and natural law stands by itself, it has nothing to do with religion. The two realms of human life are entirely neutral in relation to one another.' The Report itself is less favourable to the Puritans (*Historical Illustrations*, pp. 111–114).

[1] So also Hauck-Hertzog, *ut sup.*

serious and thoughtful treatment, but they deal with general principles rather than particular cases ; whilst his thirteen ' Cases of Conscience,' though of profound interest and revealing a sound grasp of true casuistical method, are too few to give us much help for the present day.   Hall's thirty-seven ' Cases of Conscience Practically Resolved' deal with all the old test problems—promises, lies, rate of purchase, restitution, homicide and the like—and are full of quaint aphorisms and sound common-sense decisions.   But he has no discussion of method, nor is it clear on what principles he is reaching his conclusions.   ' Ductor Dubitantium ' is erudite, tortuous and garrulous, and its author's promise to ' avoid all questions that are curious and unprofitable,' and to give rules ' whereby a wise guide of souls will be enabled to answer most cases that shall occur,' is altogether forgotten in a maze of discussion, illustration and digression.   Perkins and Ames produced what can at best be called mere sketches of the subject , and even Baldwin, though his work is much lengthier, has a habit of evading uncomfortable questions which makes him an unsatisfactory guide.

On our test question of lying for example, Ames unhesitatingly attacks and condemns the whole Jesuit doctrine of mental reservation, but his own positive contribution to the problem is confined to the sentence, ' It is sometimes lawful, so long as truth is not violated, to utter words from which in all probability the hearers will draw a false inference.   This is not lying, nor false witness, but merely giving others an opportunity of making a mistake, with a view not to their committing sin, but rather to their avoiding it.'[1]   Baldwin is even more surprising.   After nine hundred and fifty pages (nearly 300 of which are given to cases of conscience arising from intercourse with angels good and bad, devils, madmen, melancholics, wizards and spectres) he comes to the problem of mendacity, and the leisureliness of his progress hitherto leads us to expect a full and interesting treatment.   He denies that any lie is allowable in ' religious affairs,' but as to ' civil affairs '[2]—which is the crux of the matter—all he says is : ' For a lie strictly so-called the intention of deceiving alone is not sufficient ;   there must be also a private desire to lie,

---

[1] Ames, *de Conscientia*, v. 53.   [2] ' In rebus politicis.'

arising out of laxity of disposition or Satanic instigation, with the result that the lie is directed to the contempt of God, the personal gain of the liar, or the detriment of his neighbour. . . . And so those holy men, who for an honourable end have used some honourable deception (or rather artifice), are guiltless of this sin; such were the midwives of Egypt, Rebecca ' (this of course is a veiled allusion to Jacob's lie), ' Jehu and others whose honourable deception not only does not prove them guilty, but even commends them.' And then, as though perfectly content with his conclusion, he hurriedly brings his entire book to an immediate close with the words : ' But here I break off, as I think I have said enough of cases of conscience.' [1]

Not all our authorities are so disappointing. John Adam Osiander's great ' Theologia Casualis,' in four volumes averaging a thousand pages each, is packed with decisions on the mediæval model for almost every problem that can arise ; though he shows an unnecessary interest in such trivialities as the detection of character from physiognomy.[2] Baxter's ' Christian Directory ' (as Mrs. Tawney's recently-published selection shows) is practical, clear and to the point. But in general it may be said that the lack of a continuous and authoritative tradition, the pressure of other interests, the growth of philosophic individualism, with the consequent decline of the sense of loyalty as distinct from the habits of passive obedience or of open nonconformity, and the rarity of that wide experience of human nature which only the most sympathetic and highly-gifted can have where the confession is not a regular institution, all combined to sterilise the Reformed casuistry. From the beginning of the eighteenth century you may look in vain for anything

---

[1] ' Verum hic abrumpo, et de casibus conscientiae satis dictum judico ' —Baldwin, *de Cas. Consc.* iv. 17, 18.

[2] *Theologia Casualis*, Intd. (de Conscientia), c. 1, n. 39. The good man may be known by (among other things) his large square ears ; the bad man by his long and narrow ears, bushy eyebrows, protruding teeth, thin lips (' labia exilia '), nasal voice, curved back, lean shanks (' tibiae valde graciles') and arched instep. The taciturn man is shorter in the upper limbs than the lower ; the garrulous man, in addition to reversing this characteristic, has a ' honeyed ' face (' mellinus ') and prominent ears. Untrustworthiness is shown by a ridged and furrowed face. Some 35 types of character are classified in this way.

approaching a systematic grasp of the particular problems of morality. It is for the historian of modern Christianity to say how far this fact has been the cause of that impotence of the Churches which is so often deplored.

Rome laboured under no such difficulties. The Reformation made it necessary for her to go back once more to first principles, and Suarez, Vasquez, Soto and Melchior Cano—to name no others—were indefatigable pioneers in the field of ethics. But their vast and discursive treatment could not meet the practical needs of the new age, and the ' casuists ' strictly so-called—not Jesuits alone—arose as a body of experts to do for them what the Summists did for the Schoolmen. Confessors' manuals poured from the press to help Jesuits and Dominicans in their work of recapturing the conscience of Europe. The enormous array of new problems demanded, however, a new method. Authority could not lay down exact rulings for every case in such a multitude, so it contented itself with expressing the limits beyond which variation could not be countenanced, leaving the confessor a free hand within those limits, subject to certain minimum requirements as to ' necessity,' ' just cause ' and so forth. Rulings are no longer expressed, as in the older and simpler days, in the form ' must ' and ' must not,' but in the form ' may ' and ' may not '; and where the pre-Reformation confessor found that a rigid determination of the former kind made it impossible for him to adjust the ' law ' to the needs of the particular case, the new system made such variation legitimate and easy, at all events within the prescribed limits. Where the limit was undefined, some lax casuist sooner or later went beyond anything which the Christian conscience would allow ; and the condemnation with greater or less promptitude of his proposition by the Pope filled in the gap of which the Church was thus made aware.

The technique of probabilism will come before us in a later chapter. All that need be said here is that the ' probable opinions ' which have often excited so much vituperation were no more than determinations of deviation from the normal which might *sometimes* be allowable within the general limits of Christian morality. No ' probable opinion ' was *always* allowable. There must always be some doubt as to the applicability of the normal rule in the particular case in question, some valid ground of urgency, necessity or justice to suggest the legitimacy of divergence. It is this fact which is commonly overlooked by controversialists from Pascal onwards. 'You may do so-and-so' did not mean, 'You may *always* do it'; it meant, 'You may do it if on serious consideration the unusual character of your circumstances makes it necessary for the attainment of some more important end.' No doubt lax casuists and immoral Christians appropriated permissions of this kind to themselves on illegitimate occasions. But duly safeguarded by definition of the 'circumstances' in question or by carefully selected 'cases' as precedents, this new method gave an elasticity to Catholic morality which was urgently needed, and yet did not foster disruptive and individualist tendencies. It steered a middle course between the rigours of Puritanism and Jansenism, and the laxity of irresponsible private chaplains.

Protestantism misjudged the Jesuits because it assumed that their apparently 'lax sentences' represented an attempt to annihilate the moral law for all, whilst in reality they were no more than the justifiable and necessary adaptation of that law to extreme cases. It suspected them of what we have ventured to call the illegitimate form of casuistry, whereas what they were engaged upon was in the main legitimate; and it harboured this suspicion for the very reason that its own unbending morality was incapable of adaptation, and could only be evaded by illegitimate means if it was to survive in a work-a-day world. A much fairer estimate of the true state of things than that usually found in non-Roman books may be quoted from a writer whose general sympathies are anything but traditionalist.[1] 'The Jesuits,' he says, 'did exactly what the Puritan State also did—they took their authority seriously, and tried to apply it to actual human life.' (Here we suspect the writer is more than kind to Puritanism. It 'took its authority seriously enough'; but the short-lived Reformation casuistry shows

---

[1] T. C. Hall, *History of Ethics within Organised Christianity*, pp. 557-561. Contrast H. Rashdall, *Theory of Good and Evil*, ii. p. 432 : ' The business of the Jesuit moral theology was not to help people to be as good as possible, but to show how they could be as bad as possible without suffering for it.' This is a singularly *ex parte* statement from a scholar of the first rank.

that it soon gave up the attempt to 'apply it to actual life.') 'It seems almost absurd,' Professor Hall continues, ' to accuse the Jesuits of " lowering the ethical standards of the confessional " by their lax casuistry. They found every man of power and prominence with a " pocket chaplain," and, in the real interests of morality, supplanted them by trained and experienced casuists. The sympathy of Protestantism for Jansenism is really greatly misplaced. . . . From the Roman Catholic point of view ' (i.e. the point of view which refuses to leave everything in morals to the untutored conscience of the individual) ' Jesuitism was right and Jansenism not only wrong, but dangerously wrong. . . . The Jesuits were not the only father-confessors to abuse their trust ; but Jesuitism taught in season and out of season that it *was* a trust. . . . When we turn to Jansenism' (and, we may add, to Puritanism too), 'all that is found is a stricter legalism, an unflinching application of external morality.'

We may illustrate further the contention that, properly understood, the Jesuit casuistry was not as lax as would appear, by considering two examples whose apparent insensibility to all true moral considerations made them favourite points of Protestant attack. The older morality had said, ' A monk may never lay aside his religious habit ; ' the new casuistry gave it as a probable opinion that he might do so if he were setting out to engage in an immoral adventure.[1] The matter is unsavoury enough ; but the new casuistry was right after all. It did not enjoin the monk to lay aside his habit, nor give him a general permission to do so ; still less did it set its approval upon the forbidden pursuit to which this act was accessory. But whereas the old morality would have been forced to say that the monk who perpetrated immorality in disguise must inevitably be a greater sinner than the monk who went about it unblushingly, the new casuistry admitted that in some cases the disguise might be wholly indifferent as compared with the enormity perpetrated by its assistance, and in other cases that it might even be a sign of grace. It was left to the confessor, with that intimate knowledge of the circum-

---

[1] E.g. Escobar, *Theol. Mor.* Tr. vi. ex. 7, § 3 ; and cp. Pascal, *Lettres Prov.* vi.

stances to which he alone could attain, to decide between
these alternatives. And clearly the new casuistry was right.
It enabled the confessor to ignore the sin of disguise in cases
where it seemed right to do so. And it recognised that the
disguise might even be indicative of a spark of decent feeling
still left in the sinner's heart, a sign that even in his lapse he
had some thought, however perverted, for the credit of
his order ; and therefore might be a matter for commendation,
and not for additional blame.

So, too, with the other case—that of the unfaithful wife
taxed by her husband with her infidelity. The old morality
with its rigid, ' Thou shalt not lie,' would condemn her for
a double sin if she denied the offence ; the new casuistry
saw that the matter was more complicated than this.[1] The
husband might already be so beside himself with anger and
suspicion that an immediate confession would lead to blood-
shed, whilst postponement to a calmer moment would evade
these consequences. The husband might have been equally
or even more unfaithful, and only anxious to wring out his
wife's admission in order to be free of her with the maximum
of advantage to himself. Confession might bring irretrievable
ruin to the children. It is wrong to say that in no conceivable
case may the wife dissemble ; we must allow that at least
on rare occasions concealment may be the legitimate or even
the right attitude to adopt. This is the meaning of the
apparently scandalous maxim, ' A wife may for a just cause
conceal her infidelity by equivocation or mental reservation ; ' [2] and it means no more than this. No more than in
the former instance does it imply a condonation of infidelity.
No more than in that instance does it give permission except
in the rarest of abnormal cases. But it recognises that such
cases may arise in a semi-Christianised society, and that if
the confessor is to deal with them wisely and appropriately
there must be some admitted method by which he can dis-
dispense from the rigours of the law.[3]

[1] Alph. Lig. iii. §§ 162, 170. The maxim is found as early as Angelus
de Clavasio († 1495), *Summa Aurea*, s.v., ' Juramentum,' iii.

[2] For reasons already given the ' opinion ' always gave permission for
an equivocation or reservation rather than for a direct lie.

[3] For a spirited defence of the general Jesuit outlook as against Jansenism, see H. Bremond, *Histoire du Sentiment Religieux*, vol. 1 (' L'Humanisme
Dévot '), especially pp. 386 ff.

If the Jesuit books had been intended for, or accessible to, the general reader, rulings of this kind would of course have caused the utmost moral danger. Perhaps as it was they were misused to an alarming extent. If so, however, their misuse must be put down not so much to their contents as to the character, training and outlook of those who used them. But the books themselves were right in principle, for they recognised a fact which is meeting us over and over again in our enquiry, that there are very few moral principles which human language can express at once so absolutely and exactly that no possible exception to them can be imagined. We may think that they went too far in the attempt to allow for such exceptions, and even to define the circumstances in which they were likely to arise. But even so we must admit that they faced the intricacies of human conduct squarely, and did not evade the issue as so many abstract and high-principled moralities have done.

The phase of history to which these lax rulings belong is over. There are questionable principles in Liguori; his defence of equivocation, for example, is one which gave both Manning and Newman difficult moments.[1] But in many respects his 'Moral Theology' is still adaptable to every-day needs; and its modern successors, rightly interpreted, contain little to give offence and much that is admirable, though they must always be read with a full consciousness of their exact purpose. They are books of casuistry rather than of ethics or of pastoral theology; and casuistry deals explicitly with hard cases and hard cases only. Further, they are intended for the use of the trained confessor, not of the penitent. For this reason they cannot be translated word for word for the use of the English Church, in which the discussion of moral problems is public to all; in which the layman is as often called upon to advise as the priest; and in which the deference paid to a ruling is determined more

---

[1] For Manning, see [F. Meyrick] *Moral Theology of the Church of Rome*, 1855 (correspondence between Meyrick and Manning); for Newman, *Apologia pro Vita Sua*, c. 5: 'I avow at once that in this department of morality, much as I admire the high points of the Italian character, I like the English rule of conduct better. . . . I plainly and positively state, and without any reserve, that I do not at all follow the holy and charitable man [Liguori] in this portion of his teaching,' and cp. *ib.*, Note G.

by the sincerity and gravity of its author than by his position or office in the Church.

Because of these characteristics of Anglicanism, the chapters which follow discuss their problems not so much from the point of view of the confessor or director as from that of the troubled conscience itself; though it will be easy enough for the reader—should he wish to do so—to transpose them for the use of a confessor. Difficulties arise, indeed, where a penitent is engaged, in all good faith, in a course of action which the Church condemns; and to the problem of whether in such circumstances absolution may be given a section of the next chapter must be devoted.[1] But apart from this it is clear that the penitent of whom it can be said that he is doing what he 'ought' to do, or 'may do,' has a final claim to absolution; whilst the penitent who is consciously doing what he agrees with the Church to be wrong is not entitled to it. Our business is to investigate hard cases in the hope of finding what 'ought' to be or 'may' be done, and in so doing we can call the casuistry of the past to our assistance. In so far as any answers can be reached that commend themselves to the reader, they will be valid for him whether he is regulating his own life, or is attempting, formally in the confessional or informally by advice, exhortation or reproof, to regulate the lives of others.

[1] Pp. 246-254.

PART II

PROBLEMS OF CONSCIENCE

PART II.—PROBLEMS OF CONSCIENCE

CHAPTER V

ERROR

1. *Conscientious Nonconformity*

OUR review of the history of casuistry should suffice to show that the most difficult cases of conscience never wander far from the problem of loyalty—the problem, that is, of adjusting the conflicting claims of the conscience of society and of the conscience of the individual to one another. Much of this adjustment can be made by the official action of the society. We have watched the process at work, in the history of organised Christendom, in the successive definitions of councils, bishops, canonists and recognised theologians—all defining, in relation to new types of problem, the incidence of general claims in more specific terms. It is matter for discussion how far it is wise or Christian for the Church to go in such definition, and how much, on the other hand, ought to be left to the individual to decide for himself with or without assistance, but that is not our present problem. Many of us would be inclined to agree that the Church of England has not gone far enough in this matter, whereas the Church of Rome has, perhaps, gone too far—though it is often forgotten that there are problems as to which even the Church of Rome through her official channels has merely returned the answer, 'Nihil est respondendum.'[1] But whatever the character of the organisation may be, the same types of problems are bound to emerge, and it is reasonable to suppose that Christian experience has discovered, in part at least, the true method of dealing with them.

[1] As in the problem of the legitimacy of giving absolution by telephone (S. Pen., 1st July 1884—Gury-Ferreres, ii. pp. 278, 279). Most Roman Catholic theologians infer from this that the practice would be illegitimate except in cases of extreme urgency ; some of them (e.g. T. Slater, *Moral Theology* (1908), ii. p. 64) hold it to be entirely invalid. Cp. also Prümmer, iii. p. 230, and references there.

Three such main types of problem may be discerned, not indeed wholly dissociated from one another, but sufficiently distinct to merit separate consideration. (1) There may, in the first place, be direct and apparently final conflict between the conscience of the individual and the will of his Church. Where such a conflict arises it is commonly called one of ' error '; and though traditionally this title implies that it is the individual who is in the wrong, it is sufficiently justified by the obvious truth that if society and the individual differ as to what it is right for the latter to do, one of them *must* be ' in error.'

(2) There are cases again of which we saw something in the chapter on ' Loyalty '—cases in which conscience gives no certain utterance, but is more or less hesitant between two alternatives. Here, if society expressed a strong and unanimous view on one side or the other, it would obviously be the individual's duty for the time at least to defer to it. If, on the other hand, society expressed no view at all, we should have a clear illustration of an ' indifferent ' action, and the individual would be free to choose either alternative without blame. But where to the hesitation or indifference of the individual conscience is added a suspicion or proba- bility that society prefers one course rather than the other, though certainty cannot be reached on this point, we have a problem of the kind known as ' doubt.' At such a time con- venience suggests liberty of choice and freedom from re- striction ; loyalty pleads for the safe course until it is certain that society imposes no obligation ; and conscience is un- decided between the two.

(3) A third type of problem is that of a conflict between two duties, each of them exercising a considerable claim or demand upon the individual. The type is one with which everyone is familiar, and which produces only too often the most agonising distress of mind. For problems of this kind traditional theology reserves the name of ' perplexity.' They are not indeed so closely bound up with loyalty as the other two ; or rather, loyalty is often engaged in them upon both sides. Each of the two contesting claims may be asserted by conscience not merely *proprio motu*, but also by virtue of loyalty, either to a society which

seems to demand obedience to both, or two societies—
Church and State, trades-union and the constitution, home
and profession—each of them exerting its claim in opposite
directions.

Our first undertaking must be to consider the problem
of ' error,' or ' conscientious nonconformity,' as it might
better be called. This problem, indeed, to a sensitive conscience, can be as poignant and thorny as any. Mr. Shaw
has recently focussed attention upon it once again by his
fascinating treatment of the story of Joan of Arc. Yet we
must not allow that classical instance to blind our eyes to
the innumerable minor problems of the same kind that
surround us every day. In ' St. Joan ' the heroine is called
upon by the Church to regard as hallucinations of the devil
the visions which to her are manifestly of Divine origin.
Conscience forbids her to do so ; and the inevitable tragedy
follows. In our time there are those who would not hesitate
to allow (whether rightly or wrongly we need not at this
point consider) that the law of the Church, as in force at the
moment, insists upon—let us say—the fast before communion,
or complete abstention from the use of contraceptives in
marriage, or certain regulations designed to prevent devotions before the reserved sacrament ; who, nevertheless,
after full consideration of all the circumstances involved,
find themselves conscientiously obliged to disobey and disown the ruling in question. A similar case is that of the
priest or layman who cannot conscientiously accept what he
recognises to be the official interpretation of some article in
the Church's creed.

The problem at once takes the form, What is to happen
now ? Ought the dissident in all cases to resign his membership of the body ? Or are there some cases in which he may
still remain a member ? Must he publicly avow his conscientious nonconformity and ask the Church for her ruling ?
Or may he remain a secret dissentient, ' passively obedient '
in so far as he takes no step publicly to disown the doctrine
or practice which he reprobates, but ' passively resistant ' in
so far as in private he disregards and disbelieves it ? For
worldly people these questions have no importance ; but
those who are in earnest about their religion and their Church

loyalty must know of many cases where the matter is both tragic and urgent.

2. *Discipline, Suasion and Force*

It is easy to cut the problem of error short in one of two ways, either by the curt affirmation that the Church has no right to interfere in any way with the conscience or behaviour of any serious-minded Christian ; or, on the other hand, by insisting that the individual is bound either to submit, and to submit whole-heartedly, or to resign his membership. But even at the outset it would seem doubtful whether either of these simple solutions is the true one, or could establish its validity by an appeal to the teaching of Christ, the practice of the apostles or the verdict of Christendom as a whole. The first suggestion implies that the voice of God speaking through the individual conscience is so final and absolute as to annul in its entirety the voice of God speaking through the conscience of the community ; its inevitable corollary must be that the Church has no right either to impose tests upon would-be members, or to discipline those on whom it has conferred membership. The second suggestion implies that any kind of tolerance, exception, compromise or adjustment to meet the needs of the individual case is wholly illegitimate ; in practice it has had the inevitable result of driving good Christians wholesale into schism. It is worth while, therefore, to dwell upon the principles involved at rather greater length.

No society on earth could exist for more than a few days without a constitution, a code of rules and an element of discipline. The Christian Church is no exception to this rule. Indeed no branch of it has ever attempted to exist wholly without these accessories. Many communions, no doubt, have set themselves to reduce their demands to the smallest possible limits, and to exercise their discipline on the rarest possible occasions ; but so long as they recognise even theoretically their right to demands and discipline they are not in principle different from the most cast-iron system imaginable. But in the case of all human societies except the State, discipline is, in theory at least, exerted by methods of suasion and not by methods of physical force ; and is based upon the consent of all the persons concerned, even though—as in the case of the offender against whom disciplinary machinery is set in force—that consent is of a very unwilling kind

When a man is expelled from a club, for example, it is of course possible for the club to reinforce its action by appealing to the State to restrain him from entering its premises ; but such a course is rarely necessary. What makes the discipline effective is, in some cases, the offender's conviction that he has forfeited his moral right to membership; in others, his consciousness that if he intrudes once more his reception will at best be cold. This is the discipline of suasion, and it can only be effective if it is backed by the consent of the vast majority of the members. The appeal to legal sanctions, which is in the end an appeal to physical force, is an appeal to an alien sphere. In that sphere, indeed, both the club and its member have rights moral as well as legal. These rights, however, are not created by or dependent upon their relation to one another as club and member, but upon their common membership in a wider body corporate which alone among societies is by general consent allowed the exercise of force.

This problem of appeal to the State by a voluntary society is, however, more difficult in two other cases. On the one hand, the member against whom discipline is to be enforced may—especially if he is an official of the society —be in possession of documents or property belonging to the society which he refuses to give up. It then becomes a question for the society whether, on grounds either of expediency or of principle, it will passively suffer this violation of its rights by the recalcitrant member, or will resort to legal action. On the other hand, an aggrieved member may attempt to assert some real or fancied claim against the society by similar measures ; and the society on the same grounds will have to decide whether it will fight the case or come to terms out of court. Nor does this exhaust the possibilities of State action in connection with such minor corporate bodies. It is always possible for the State to take official cognizance of them, and of their aims and methods, and enforce its will against them, either individually or collectively, where it conceives that the public interest requires it.

The Church in any country stands in exactly the same practical relation to the State and the force at its command as these lesser secular corporations—universities, trades-unions, clubs, societies or whatever else they may be. The discipline natural and appropriate to a ' Church ' is, even more than in other cases, a discipline of moral suasion. It depends upon the consent of the members, and may be called, in technical language, purely ' spiritual.' But a ' Church ' may, if it so decides, appeal to the secular courts to enforce its disciplinary action. It may, again, be liable to legal procedure from aggrieved members, or to statutory enact-ments affecting it on the part of the legislature. Modern opinion, on the whole, admits the right of the individual to appeal to the State for justice against the Church, and of the State to interfere, within limits, with the freedom of the Church, if the public interest demands it.[1] We should most of us agree for example with Bentham, that if complete celibacy were preached in the name of religion as the only moral life for a Christian, the State would have the right to interfere on the grounds of general expediency.

In some cases, however, the Church is associated with the State by a ' concordat ' or ' establishment ' recognised by both parties as binding. Here the State sometimes pro-vides special machinery by means of which to reinforce the action of the Church; and the Church in return may, will-ingly or perforce, cede to the State certain permanent visitatorial or other powers in relation to itself, additional to those which the State naturally possesses over all other corporations.[2] This would appear to be the position in which

[1] See, e.g., J. N. Figgis, *Churches in the Modern State*, pp. 102, 103 ; T. A. Lacey, *Handbook of Church Law*, p. 143 ; O. Reichel, *Manual of Canon Law*, ii. pp. 204, 205 ; *Report of Ecclesiastical Courts Commission* (C.A. 200, London, 1926), p. 7—but note Lord Phillimore's ' observations,' P 37.

[2] ' The process of *establishment* means that the State has accepted the Church as the religious body in its opinion truly teaching the Christian faith and given to it a certain legal position, and to its decrees if given under certain legal conditions certain legal sanctions ' (Marshall *v.* Graham,

the Church of England stands. It can appeal to the common law against a recalcitrant member, and its officers are liable to legal action on the part of the aggrieved ; nor has the State abrogated its natural claim to legislate for and about the Church without its consent. But the Church has also in reserve, if it cares to use it, special legal machinery devised for the reinforcement of its discipline by the State. On the other hand it has conceded to the State, or allowed the State to assume, such important powers in respect of itself as the nomination to many of its highest offices, the adminis-tration of many of its endowments, and the promulgation by royal assent of its synodical decisions.

The last point is one of peculiar interest, importance and difficulty. If the convocations of the Church of England should frame a new canon without royal licence and confirma-tion, it is doubtful how far, if at all, such a canon would bind the consciences of her members. Licence and confirmation have for some centuries been recognised as necessary condi-tions for valid promulgation,[1] and without due promulgation no synodical decision has any claim upon loyalty *per se.* It would of course be within the competence of the convoca-tions to decide upon some other method of promulgation, even without the concurrence of the State. Once this decision had been published, royal licence and confirmation would be no longer necessary for synodical decisions to have an immediate claim upon loyalty ; but the step would involve a violent disturbance of the equilibrium of the establishment, and it is scarcely to be supposed that the State would at present regard it with equanimity.

There is nothing in itself un-catholic in this ' establish-

1907). ' The " establishment " principle is the principle that there is a duty ' (i.e. a legal duty) ' on the civil power to give support and assistance to the Church ' (Free Church of Scotland *v.* Overtown, 1904)—Halsbury, *Laws of England* (1910), xi. p. 364. ' When the State has by legislative act established . . . a Church identified by certain doctrines, such Church cannot while retaining the benefit of such establishment [legally] exercise any power of altering these doctrines without the legislative sanction of the State '—*Ibid.* The last quotation is an extreme form of the civil lawyer's view of establishment. The word ' legally ' has been inserted to make its meaning clear. For ' Concordats ' see A. Tardif, *Histoire des Sources du Droit Canonique*, p. 261 ; Maitland-Gierke, *Political Theories of the Middle Ages*, pp. 124, 192 f.

[1] Halsbury, *Laws of England*, xi. pp. 379, 380.

ment ' or ' concordat ' which binds the Church of England to the State, even though many suppose it, not altogether without reason, to be cumbrous, inexpedient, one-sided or undignified. ' Concordats ' of this kind have marked Christian history in all countries and all centuries ; the specific variations in the English example make no difference in principle.[1] But whether the system be satisfactory or not, it has had several important effects which deserve passing notice. Taken together, these effects have gone far to weaken the bonds of discipline in the Church of England ; the ' establishment,' devised in the interests of uniformity, has issued in an excess of individualism.

(1) Thus, first of all, the difficulty of securing royal licence and confirmation has resulted in an almost complete legislative inertia on the part of the convocations. Our earlier consideration of the position of ' custom ' in the life of the Church should have convinced us that the conscience of Anglicanism has not been silent during this period ; it has spoken, however, by custom and not by law. That this has made of Anglicanism a phenomenon almost unique in Christendom is not to be denied. It is all the more interesting because unique ; and the experiment—which we may surely call providential—has obviously not as yet reached its end. In the meantime, however, it has resulted in the general opinion that the Church is impotent to order her own affairs and that individuals are free to take the law into their own hands when and as they please.

(2) More important for our immediate purpose is the

[1] Dean Church has well pointed out, in connection with St. Anselm and the Investiture controversy, that interference of the secular power in Church matters (e.g. elections) is of little moment as compared with the claim of the secular power to confer authority (e.g. investiture). So long as the Catholic principle of the independence of the Church of all human *authority* stands established, a very large degree of *interference* by the secular arm can be admitted in practice. ' The old recognised policy of the Church against the world had been to try to check *directly* the interference of the secular power in *elections* of the higher clergy. . . . But ' what the times required was ' to restore the lost feeling of the sanctity and heavenly mission of the episcopate. . . . What mattered who elected, if they were merely to elect an ecclesiastical baron ? Distinctly, and unequivocally, before it was too late . . . popular and kingly notions about bishops must be broken. . . . They could not keep kings from meddling in elections : but they might keep bishops from receiving their offices on terms which fettered and lowered them ' (R. W. Church, *St. Anselm and Henry I*).

fact that this close and peculiar association of Church and State under which we live has blinded many of us to the truth previously noticed, that the Church's jurisdiction is by nature purely spiritual, and her special discipline a discipline of suasion alone.   This is not the place to consider whether she ought in any circumstances to have recourse to legal sanctions to reinforce her discipline, or use the machinery of law to counter aggression in the same sphere.   'It is far more difficult,' as Dr. Figgis said,[1] ' to condemn persecution absolutely and in theory than the popular axiom would suggest.'   The present Bishop of Manchester goes a long way towards insisting upon a duty of the Church at times to use methods of legal compulsion.   'It may be objected,' he writes,[2] 'that the Church should never in any circumstance employ force—at any rate physical force.   But I believe the objection is due partly to a latent Manichaeism which holds that matter is always evil or at least " unspiritual," and partly to a very just fear that force may be wrongly used if its use is permitted at all.   Yet there are some cases where the Church would plainly be not only at liberty, but morally bound to use force.   Suppose a clergyman begins to give teaching that is absolutely at variance with the doctrine of the Church, the Church may appeal to his better feelings and ask him to resign ; but if he will not, the Church must assuredly have the right to turn him out, and that if necessary by force.'   Whether the Church adopts this course or not, it ought not to have any bearing upon the conscience of her members or their problems.   A canonical decision, whether upon a general or a particular question, should in any case have so full a claim upon loyalty that legal action could in no way enhance it.   But this truth also has been forgotten ; and men tend to speak and behave as though a Church which reserves to itself the right to command obedience by force has lost the right to invite it by suasion, and can be disregarded until it has recourse to force.

(3) A third result of this inter-relation of Church and State in England has been to obscure a vital principle of canon law, and at the same time to reduce ecclesiastical

---

[1] *Churches in the Modern State*, p. 115. Cp. F. von Hügel, *Essays and Addresses*, ii. pp. 192, 273.

[2] W. Temple, *Church and Nation*, p. 167.

discipline to a shadow. The Church may rightly be anxious to dissociate herself from one of her members for many other reasons besides offences which would be appropriately handled in a secular court. But the confusion between the secular 'and the ecclesiastical judge, which resulted from the 'establishment,' has led to the feeling that no cases ought to come before either authority except offences of this latter character. Thus it would be virtually impossible at the present day to cite a layman before an ecclesiastical court for heresy, however dangerous and persistent ; and although nineteenth-century legislation gave to courts of a curiously mixed description wide powers of discipline over clergy in matters both of heresy and of ritual irregularity, the same feeling has prevented their being put into operation in more than a minimum of cases. The reason is simple. Heresy and indiscipline in the conduct of public worship appear—and rightly—to the ordinary mind to be offences of a wholly different kind from violence or open immorality ; and therefore any court which falls under the slightest suspicion of being secular, and enforcing its decisions by secular methods—and every Church court of the present day incurs this suspicion—is regarded as an inappropriate tribunal for dealing with them. For this reason, as much as for any other, discipline is wholly at a discount in the Church of England.

(4) But, further, because of this view that the Church is competent only to exclude from its membership persons guilty of what the State also would regard as crimes, the great principle that ' censure,' even to the degree of excommunication, does not carry with it any necessary moral stigma has been wholly forgotten. As the canonists were quite clear that the Church might be mistaken in her commands,[1] so they were equally clear that she might make mistakes in her discipline. The inevitable corollary was that a Christian whom the Church decided to sever from herself could not by that fact alone be held guilty in the sight of God.[2] Mr. Shaw has justly estimated this principle

---

[1] See note *infra* p. 227.

[2] The ' sententia injusta ' is a commonplace of canon law. See, e.g., *C.J.C.* cc. 1, 27, 44, 46, 48-51, C. xi. q.3 (from Gelasius, Jerome, Augustine, Gregory, etc.), c. 28, X. v. 39 (Innocent III) ; and references in *Ignorance, etc.*, p. 152.

in that dramatic moment of ' St. Joan,' when the inquisitor, after handing the Maid over to the secular authorities for execution, refers to her as ' this poor innocent girl.' Once restore this principle to common knowledge, and allow it to be recognised that the Christian and his Church may part company, even by the official action of the Church, without stigma on either side, and discipline and order can be re-established without that latent fear of injustice which at present inhibits ecclesiastical action.

The Church, then, in spite of all appearances and arguments to the contrary, has a right to discipline its members, and to decide upon the occasions which call for discipline and the methods to be employed. The Church of England, though it has from time to time availed itself of the adventitious means of legal compulsion set at its disposal by the State, has never wavered in its acceptance of the traditional ecclesiastical methods of censure and penance. ' Censures,' with which we may deal first, and of which excommunication is the simplest example, are penalties duly promulgated by canonical authority, after orderly cognizance of a case, which put the offender under ecclesiastical disabilities. These disabilities, in the case of the lesser excommunication, consist of deprivation of the sacraments ; in the case of the greater excommunication, of deprivation of intercourse with the faithful as well. Their execution depends solely upon the loyalty of the officers and members of the community. If the former refuse to withhold the sacraments from an excommunicated person, or the latter to avoid his society, authority—to keep within the bounds of purely canonical action—can only proceed against these new recalcitrants as against the first offender. A situation may therefore arise in which authority finds itself set over against a majority of the faithful who refuse to obey its decisions ; and to avoid such a situation, which would verge upon open schism, it must hold itself bound in its proceedings to take careful cognizance of the temper of the whole community.

There is in this matter a continual interaction between the consciences of those in authority and of the remainder of the body, and from this interaction comes the ultimate decision as to what offences shall be visited with penalties, and on what occasions those penalties shall be imposed. The authorities may, of course, have recourse to the secular arm ; but even here the conscience of the community will have something to say as to their action, though it may not say it at once. If, however, it ends by disapproving, one of two things will happen. Either appeals of this kind to State interference will gradually lapse into complete disuse ; or—if they are persisted in—the community will shipwreck upon the rock of schism. In either case the communal conscience will have asserted itself against the individualistic action of a clique or hierarchy. For authority, as Dr. Figgis wrote,[1] ' arises in a more natural and subtle manner [than is usually supposed]. It is more often instinctive and inarticulate, what we call tone and atmosphere, than categorical and legislative. It arises from that total complex of influences, personal, historical, spiritual, moral, aesthetic, which are greater than the individual, which mould men's minds and wills even when they are unaware of it—to which even the most rebellious anarchist pays toll, even by talking the same language '—and equally (as we may surely add) the most intransigent conservative, by submitting, however grudgingly, to innovations.

3. *The Liberty of the Christian*

The Church's jurisdiction, then, is in a sense purely spiritual, and expresses itself both in demands and in discipline. With the exercise of that discipline, within the sphere of the confessional at all events, we must concern ourselves at a later stage of this chapter. We turn now to the question of the Church's demands, and the position of the individual who conscientiously dissents from them. For our purpose it matters little whether those demands are expressed by long-standing and explicit custom, by synodical enactment, by episcopal mandate, or by the injunctions of a confessor. Such difference as there is is a difference of detail; in principle the problem is the same.

What, then, are the rights or duties of the individual

[1] *Op cit.* p. 158.

dissentient in face of the expressed demands of his confessor, his bishop or his Church ?   The charter of Christian liberty and the summary of Christian morality, as we have seen, are alike embodied in the phrase *Conscientia semper sequenda*, to which theologians and canonists of every age have given adhesion.[1]   The late Master of Balliol quoted in his Ford lectures [2] an early mediæval penitentiary book which laid down the rule that if conscience and the Church disagree, ' we must let conscience go ' ; but apart from isolated and irresponsible utterances of this kind the principle has never been questioned.   It applies, moreover, not merely to commands, but also to permissions.   If conscience commands a certain course of action, the individual is bound to follow it, whatever the Church may say.   If conscience declares him free to act in a manner of which the Church frankly disapproves, he is free nevertheless so to act—though not of course bound to do so—and no one has the right to blame him.

Technically, no doubt, such a conscientious dissentient is in ' error,' but that does not affect the question.   If he finds himself bound in conscience to deny an article of the faith, to disobey a recognised practice of the Church, to defy his bishop, to disregard his confessor, to introduce unauthorised forms of service, his duty lies that way, and he cannot be blamed for doing it.   ' Woe be to that man,'

---

[1] *Supra* p. 61 ;   *Ignorance, etc.*, p. 140 ;   Maitland-Gierke, *Political Theories of the Middle Ages*, pp. 35, 85, 86.   The two classical passages in Innocent III are *C.J.C.* c. 13, X. ii. 13 : ' You may not obey a judge against God, but should rather be prepared humbly to be excommunicated ' ; c. 44, X. v. 39 : ' You ought rather to suffer excommunication than commit mortal sin, even though you cannot prove to the Church that the sin would be mortal.'   Gratian collected an enormous number of patristic and papal authorities on the same point ;   see C. xi. q. 3, *pass.*, esp. c. 52 (from Gregory I, *Epist.* vii. 14) : ' Ad cor proprium semper recurrendum, ut nullius nos ibi lingua implicat ubi conscientia non accusat ;   quem enim conscientia defendit et inter accusationes liber est ' ;   or cc. 91-101, various versions of the dictum ' we must not obey an unjust command.'   In many of the cases the command referred to is one of the civil power, but the principle is applied equally to the ecclesiastical authority (e.g. c. 91, a bishop or abbot) ;   and Gratian concludes with a remark which obviously envisages conscientious nonconformity from the Church : ' Cum ergo subditi excommunicantur ideo quia ad malum cogi non possunt, tum sententiae non est obediendum.'   Cp. also *S.T.* i. 2, q. 19, a.5.

[2] A. L. Smith, *Church and State in the Middle Ages*, pp. 54, 55.

exclaims Bishop Hall,[1] with a metaphor no less forcible than mixed, ' who shall tye himself so close to the letter of the law as to make shipwrecke of conscience, that bird in his bosome.'

At first sight nothing could appear more anarchical than this doctrine, and it comes as a shock to find even the most autocratic of the Popes subscribing to it whole-heartedly. But a considerable restriction is introduced by the consideration that conscience, to confer such rights or duties, must be ' invincible '—which is only another way of saying that the judgment involved must be a judgment of *conscience*, and not of fancy, prejudice, obstinacy or obscurantism. I have dealt with this question at length elsewhere,[2] and need only summarise in a few sentences the considered verdict of Christian theology ; but it must not be overlooked that the matter is one of crucial importance. From the end of the middle ages it has not been required for ' invincibility ' that the dissentient should be actually ignorant of the will of the Church. What is required is that his position should not have resulted from any culpable neglect of duty, whether moral or intellectual ; that he should have taken full account of all considerations bearing upon the question at issue, in so far as he is capable of it, and that in spite of this he should be perfectly clear as to the rightness of his proposed course of action, and should feel no trace of shame or uneasiness in contemplating it.[3] These are severe tests, and it is obvious that they limit the disruptive tendencies of our principle very drastically ; for unless, on examining his conscience, a dissentient finds that it satisfies these tests, he is bound to defer to the will of the Church. Even so, however, the case of the ' conscientious nonconformist ' has been common in all periods of history, and, at all events in matters affecting the creeds and the services of the Church, is common enough to-day.

A Christian, therefore, who finds himself at issue with his Church on a matter of first importance, is bound—or at all

---

[1] *Cases of Conscience*, dec. ii., case 6.

[2] *Ignorance, etc.*, pp. 34, etc. Throughout the rest of this book the word ' conscientious ' is commonly used as an equivalent for the technical term ' invincible.'

[3] I.e. it is required that both his ' moral judgment ' and his ' moral sense ' (or as Newman would have said (*supra* p. 24), both ' reason ' and ' conscience ') should point unhesitatingly in the same direction.

events free—to follow his conscience if its dictates are genuinely 'invincible.' But does loyalty at the same time demand
of him that he should resign his membership ? Still more,
if he is himself a minister of the body, should he at least
withdraw into lay communion rather than preach doctrines,
or conduct services, manifestly inconsistent with the dominant
principles of the body ? Or may he dissemble his real feelings,
and thereby connive at teaching which he believes to be false,
or practices which he regards as superstitious ? [1] The hero
of one of Miss Macaulay's novels is a minister of the Gospel
who is constantly 'losing his faith,' and resigning his living
or pastoral charge. Is his action to be approved of as mani-
festing a true spirit of loyalty, or laughed out of court as a
piece of superfluous quixotism ?

One answer to this question is obvious from the outset
Cases arise where the dissentient, while recognising to the
full the gulf which separates his convictions from the contemporary or traditional doctrines and practices of the
Church, is with equal sincerity convinced that it is his right
and his duty to remain a member or minister within its
ranks. Thus his conscience is 'invincible' on two points—
the first, that he is blameless in the matter in which he dissents from the Church; the second, that he is equally blameless, in spite of this dissent, in retaining his existing position.
Of such dissentients some hold that the spread of
knowledge, the change of thought and the growth of tolerance, which are so marked a feature of modern religion, will
within a comparatively short period bring the majority of
their fellow-Churchmen to see eye to eye with them on the
matter in dispute. 'What Lancashire says to-day England
will say to-morrow ; ' and the suspected minority may in a
few years' time be acquitted as wholly orthodox. Others
regard the struggle before them as longer and sterner, but
feel bound to remain at their posts to protest against what
appears to them some gross abuse, or to supply some urgent
need within the Church, whatever the consequences may
be. With consciences of this temper there is no doubt that
the individual has a perfect right to retain such privileges

---

[1] This last problem, which is one of honesty rather than loyalty, is dealt
with in Ch. VII., Sect. 6, 'Compromise.'

I

of membership and position as he values, so long as he is allowed to do so : and that at all events if his sincerity and earnestness are obvious—as they usually are—no one has the right to blame or criticise him.

To this it will at once be demurred : ' Do you really mean to imply that a priest of the Church of England has the right to ignore his ordination vows, and preach doctrines or introduce rites and ceremonies forbidden by the Prayer Book, the Articles or the direct injunction of his bishop ? ' We must grant at once that he has no right whatever to ' ignore ' the solemn undertakings made at his ordination. If he ' ignored ' them in coming to his decision, his conscience would not as yet have reached that state of ' invincibility ' which alone gives him the right and duty of obeying it ; his decision, in fact, would not be fully conscientious. For such ' invincibility ' to be admitted, all relevant considerations must have been taken into account and fairly faced—and no consideration could be more relevant than the obligation of the ordination vow. Only, therefore, if a priest had seriously and fully weighed that obligation, and come to the absolutely unhesitating conclusion that it did not preclude his adoption of teaching or practices contrary to the formularies he had promised to respect, could his right to public conscientious nonconformity be established.[1] But if he had done so, however incredible his reconciliation of his conduct with his promises might appear to us, we should be obliged to admit the ' invincibility ' of his ' error,' and to respect his right to follow his own conscience wherever it led him.

Recognition of this truth would eliminate from Church life at least one undoubted evil. We often hear it said of ' modernist ' dignitaries, ' They ought to resign their preferment ' ; or of ' catholic ' clergy, ' Why don't they go over to Rome ? ' There may of course be here and there ' modernists ' or ' catholics ' who cling to their position from low or selfish motives, and who would gladly seek some other spiritual home if they could do so without loss of position, income or prestige : men like those 17th-century dignitaries

[1] In the present circumstances of the Church of England he would also have to consider whether the obvious difficulty of putting disciplinary machinery into motion did not make it incumbent upon him to ease the situation for the Church by voluntarily resigning. See further pp. 282 f.

who were so ' absolutely, directly and cordially Papists that it was all that £1500 a year could do to keep them from confessing it.' [1]   But there is not the slightest doubt that cases of this kind are of the utmost rarity.   The vast majority of such ' dissentients '—if we may so call them—are men of transparent honesty, whose decision to remain in the Church has been reached only after constant prayer and earnest thought, and is held in absolute clearness of conscience. We may wonder how it is that a position, which to us seems frankly ambiguous, commends itself to them as so manifestly legitimate or obligatory.   But we have no right whatever to accuse them of dishonesty or disloyalty, except on evidence of hyprocisy of quite conclusive character.

Frequently, however, the solution is not so obvious. The position of the ' nonconformist ' is not, ' I am conscientiously convinced that I may remain in enjoyment of my ecclesiastical privileges ; ' but rather, ' I do not want to surrender them, but I wonder whether I ought to ? '   Conscience is clear on the first question—that in respect of which the member dissents from the community.   It is not clear on the second, as to whether he ought not, in consequence, to sever himself from it.   Every experienced priest is called upon from time to time, and it may be frequently, to advise in cases of this kind.   He is consulted by clergy or laymen who have ' lost their faith,' or have ' intellectual difficulties,' or feel themselves bound to introduce unauthorised service books into their churches, or unauthorised preachers into their pulpits.   They are in open and conscious revolt ; yet they value the spiritual privileges which membership in the Church confers, and the problem presents itself — ' May I still remain in the Church as layman or as priest ? '

It is all-important here, as in other matters of conscience, that the advice should be given, or the problem solved, on Christian principles, if any are available, and not on expediency alone.   Fortunately, however, a well-tried and universally accepted principle is available.   It may be expressed in the dictum, ' No one is bound in conscience to put into force penalties against himself which have not been definitely

---

[1] Lord Falkland, 9th Feb. 1640, quoted W. E. H. Lecky, *Map of Life*, p. 209.

promulgated against him.'[1] The criminal cannot be called upon to act as his own executioner if he is still uncondemned. Exclusion from Church membership is identical with the penalty of excommunication ; and if a man believes in and values the privilege of membership and is clear that he is acting upon the sheer dictates of conscience in the matter in which he dissents, he is under no obligation whatever to excommunicate himself. Though his course of action be contrary to established law and custom, though it appears to him even that ultimate reconciliation of the divergent views is impossible, he may still retain such privileges and comforts as his membership gives him, as long as the Church allows him to retain them. Furthermore, if he holds that he could not surrender his privileges without spiritual loss to himself and perhaps to others as well, it is his *duty* not to put them aside until he is officially and canonically called upon to do so ; and no unauthorised person has the right to throw a stone. Responsibility for the severance of relations or the termination of the individual's public ministry rests with the Church and with the Church alone.[2]

---

[1] So *C.J.C.* c. 5, C. xv. q. 8 ; c. 10, X. iii. 2 ; cp. *S.T.* iii. q. 64, a. 6, ad 2 ; Alph. Lig. vii. § 67 ; *Duct. Dub.* iii. 2, rule 2. An exception, *in foro interno* only, is admitted in the rare case of *ipso facto* excommunications —see *Ignorance, etc.,* p. 154 n.

[2] This conclusion appears at first sight to run counter to the very important opinion of the Bishop of Southwark (reinforced by a trenchant sentence quoted from Bishop Gore) in his synodical address, *Authority and Obedience,* previously mentioned. He says (p. 26) : ' If, therefore, a priest reaches the position in which he finds he cannot teach the doctrine or con- form to the rites and discipline of the Church of which he is a minister when he is deliberately, constitutionally and solemnly called upon by the bishop so to do, there is no alternative left to an honest man but to resign his commission and thus regain freedom to follow his personal convictions unhampered by the promises he had previously made.' The position of the words ' when he is called upon by the bishop so to do ' is very awkward. They cannot possibly imply—as they might at first sight seem to do—that a man who conscientiously and after full deliberation dissents from the doctrine of the Church either *ought* to, or indeed *could*, go back on his con- science at the bishop's monition. Nor can they imply, as again they might seem to do, that fidelity to one's ordination promises need only become an operative moral force when the bishop calls directly for obedience. For if the refusal to teach the doctrine of the Church were genuinely and invincibly conscientious, it could only have been reached in the first instance after honest consideration of what the ordination promise implied, and a definite decision (whether logically justifiable or not, in the particular case, we need not enquire) that it did not imply the necessity of conformity in the matter

4. *Limitations of Liberty*

No principle of canon law is more firmly established than the one just mentioned. Yet it seems to carry with it an obvious corollary, and one which many perhaps will find unpalatable. If it be the case, as it seems to be, that no one need resign his position or membership in the Church until the Church by orderly canonical discipline has deprived him

concerned. That is to say, the moral weight of the promise would have been considered and allowed for long before the bishop's monition came into question; if it had not been so considered and allowed for, the priest could not *conscientiously* (on any serious interpretation of the word) have 'reached the position' of being unable to conform. (*Supra* p. 230; *infra* pp. 282 ff.)

There remain only two ways in which the phrase 'when called upon by the bishop' can be taken. (a) It may be purely redundant, in which case the meaning of the whole paragraph is :—' As soon as a priest finds himself in the position of conscientious nonconformity as regards any part of his public teaching or ministry, it is his duty to resign, even though his own conscience fails entirely to endorse this duty.' This interpretation we have definitely rejected in the text; though in a footnote (p. 230) it was suggested that conscience, before declaring against resignation, would have to consider *both* the force of the ordination vow *and* the peculiar situation produced by the laborious processes of Anglican discipline. (b) If it is *not* merely redundant (and surely it cannot be) it must refer to the moment at which resignation becomes a duty. In that case the Bishop of Southwark's meaning is so close to our own as to be virtually identical with it. The position reached in the text is ' Resignation is not an invariable duty until canonical censure has been imposed,' the Bishop's is ' Resignation is not an invariable duty until the bishop's monition has been canonically issued.' The difference is merely that Dr. Garbett puts the moment of severance a stage slightly earlier in the process. Canonical monition, whether as a necessary preliminary to a censure (see refs., *Ignorance*, p. 152, and add refs. in Gibson, pp. 1094, 1095 ; O. Reichel, *Manual of Canon Law*, ii. pp. 5, 147) or as itself a ' penal remedy ' (*Cod. Jur. Can.* c. 2307) to be supplemented by more severe action if obedience is refused (Noldin, *de poen. eccl.* p. 8 ; Lacey, *Handbook of Church Law*, p. 22 ; Migne-André, *Dictionnaire du Droit Canon* (Paris, 1862), ii. p. 553 ; Halsbury, *Laws of England*, xi. p. 534), is ' of a preparatory nature' (Halsbury, *ut sup.*) ; but even so it cannot be issued until the case has been canonically tried (*Cod. Jur. Can.* cc. 1946, § 2, n. 2 ; 2307 ; Lacey, Halsbury, *ut sup.*). The difference between the two positions is no more than technical, but it seems unnatural to treat monition as a final stage in a process which has always been regarded hitherto as closed only by more severe measures.

The Bishop might of course hear the evidence and give his judgment informally, and without observance of due canonical procedure, but a judgment or monition thus arrived at could scarcely carry with it such grave consequences as Dr. Garbett suggests, unless the offender had agreed to of it, it would nevertheless seem to be less than loyal to presume upon this fact. Common fairness alone suggest that where there is a final difference of opinion upon a point of fundamental importance, the individual should provide the Church with the material and opportunity for a decision as to whether she wishes to retain his services or adherence any longer.

If the divergence is open and notorious, there is indeed no need for the dissentient to take any further action. The Church has all the material she needs, and it is for her to decide whether she will exercise discipline or not. Thus the recalcitrant ' modernist ' or ' catholic ' is not only absolutely blameless (as we have seen) in retaining his position as long as he is allowed to do so when he earnestly believes that he still has a place in the Church ; it is no less legitimate, as far as loyalty is concerned, for him to do so although he is actuated by unworthy or hypocritical motives. He is wrong of course, and deeply wrong, in giving way to such motives. But he is not adding sin to sin by remaining in his position and privileges. His ' nonconformity ' is notorious, and loyalty does not demand that in such circumstances he should resign before disciplinary action has been taken against him. Nor would this conclusion appear to be affected even though his immunity from censure is due to inertia of the proper disciplinary officials ; for, as we have seen, the authorities of the Church are ultimately influenced to action or inaction by the conscience of the whole body. If, then, such a dissentient finds himself immune, the basic reason must be that the Church as a whole is (rightly or wrongly) sufficiently indifferent to his nonconformity to leave him in peace ; and this would imply that the Church itself assents to his retention of his privileges.

accept this procedure and abide by the result as final. Such a procedure is suggested in the *Report of the Ecclesiastical Courts Commission* (C.A. 200, London, 1926), § 21, p. 13 ; Appendix i. pp. 33-35, with the explicit proviso just mentioned.

Of course conscience *may* call for resignation at a far earlier stage, whether on the general basis of loyalty, or the particular basis of fidelity to the ordination vow, or the universal ground of moral consistency. This, however, is not the question at issue ; both the address *Authority and Obedience* and the discussion in the text are only concerned with the problem, At what point does resignation become a *sine quâ non* of loyalty ?

But where the offence or divergence is ' occult '—known that is to say, to one or two at most, and in all probability never likely to be known to more—it would still seem to be the duty of the ' offender ' to put his case before someone with authority to speak for the Church, and to abide by the result. This can be done by consulting a priest, either informally under the seal of secrecy or formally under the seal of the confessional ; and the priest can in either case of course refer the matter to higher authority for decision, provided always that he does and says nothing to betray the identity.

Every now and then, for example, there are to be found in a parish a couple living together as husband and wife, who, unknown to any of their neighbours, have never been married. They have sometimes carried on this existence for many years in complete accord and fidelity to one another, and may be surrounded by a growing and happy family of sons and daughters. Imagine, further, that one of them at least before contracting this irregular alliance has separated from a lawful partner, whether by divorce or otherwise, so that they cannot in either case contract a new marriage by ecclesiastical law, or (in the second case) by ecclesiastical and civil law alike. And suppose—as sometimes happens—that they are absolutely and sincerely convinced that their present union is wholly in accordance with the will of God, and regard the blessings which have attended it as incontrovertible evidence to that effect. There is no doubt that their alliance is an offence against the Church's moral code ; there are many who, without recognising the validity of that code, would still regard the case as involving a transgression of all natural or civilised morality. It is a clear example of ' error,' but of ' invincible error.' Would the couple in question be doing right in receiving Holy Communion, in taking their part in Church life and work, even in holding parochial office, secure in the conscientious conviction that there was nothing wrong in their mutual relations, and in the firm belief (warranted perhaps by circumstances special to the case) that the facts would never be discovered, and that therefore no danger of scandal to the Church would arise ?

If the line of argument we have been pursuing is a true one, they would have a further duty. It would be the duty of consulting the Church officially, though privately, through one of her accredited representatives, and abiding by the official decision thus reached. It is here that one important aspect of the confessional comes into view—an aspect, moreover, which in the voluntary use of confession specially characteristic of the Church of England is often overlooked. The confessional is an official though secret tribunal of the Church. Its decisions may be deferred, but they cannot be deferred indefinitely. Sooner or later someone—the priest or his canonical superior—must decide whether he is to absolve or to refuse absolution, and refusal of absolution is tantamount to secret excommunication. It implies that the Church does not desire to consider the 'penitent' as one of her communicant members so long as he persists in his present course of action. Technically he is in mortal sin,[1] and as such his position is too ambiguous—if nothing more—for him to be regarded as a fit recipient of the Holy Communion ; and loyalty demands that if he has been refused absolution he should abstain from presenting himself for communion.

This may seem a hard doctrine. It is mitigated by one or two considerations which will be adduced in a later section of this chapter. To that section also we will relegate discussion of the very grave responsibility which this aspect of the confessional involves for the individual confessor ; of the means by which that responsibility may be alleviated ; and of the answer which he should give, or be instructed to give, in cases such as the one under discussion. But we have still to consider whether our general conclusion is satisfactory— that persons in invincible error of conscience are bound in loyalty, unless they are equally conscientious in holding that there is no need to do so, to submit their 'error' to the Church for her official decision thereupon, and to abide by that decision, even though it be given in the secrecy of the confessional. And it must frankly be admitted that this conclusion, though it can quote the authority of Origen,[2] is sup-

---

[1] I.e. 'material' (or technical) mortal sin ; for God alone knows whether he is in 'formal' (actual) mortal sin.

[2] If there is any doubt whether a person deserves to remain a member of the Church or not, 'he should make a private confession and receive direction whether *exomologesis* is required or no.' Origen, *Hom.* 2 *in Ps.* xxxvii. 1, 2, 6, cited Brightman, in H. B. Swete, *Essays on Church and Ministry*, p. 357.

ported neither by traditional canon law and moral theology, nor by the general principles which seem to inspire the customary life of the Church of England.

' That no one is bound to incriminate himself,' as Jeremy Taylor pointed out,[1] is a universally accepted rule. The modern Roman codex lays down that the parties to a suit are bound to answer the judge and acknowledge the truth, *unless their own guilt is in question.*[2] The older rule was that an accused person, if questioned, was bound in conscience to acknowledge his guilt when the judge enquired legitimately, and legitimate enquiry could begin if the offence was matter of common knowledge or was already half proved.[3] Refusal to answer in such a case was, according to St. Thomas, a mortal sin.[4] With lapse of time the principle was modified. Liguori is still in two minds about it ;[5] but modern writers agree that even when ' legitimately interrogated ' an accused person is under no obligation, or at all events under the very slightest obligation only, to confess the truth of the charges made against him.[6] If, then, canonists agree that no one can be called upon, or is under any moral obligation, to become a witness against himself, it is obvious that he is still less bound to constitute himself his own accuser.

Furthermore, those whose cases we are considering are in ' invincible ' or conscientious error. They are convinced, that is to say, that though the Church may condemn their action or condition, it is as a matter of fact blameless in the sight of God. They cannot, therefore, be in actual mortal sin ; such a state is only possible where the offender is fully conscious that he is doing wrong. And as actual mortal sin is the only kind of sin which the Christian is required to reveal in confession,[7] it follows that our imaginary couple are no more bound to mention the true facts of their union in confession

---

[1] ' Nemo tenetur infamare se,' *Duct. Dub.* III. ii. 5, 16 (8).

[2] ' Nisi agatur de delicto ab ipsis commisso,' *Cod. Jur. Can.* 1743 (§1).

[3] *C.J.C.* cc. 5 ff., C. ii. q. 5 ; c. 1, C. xv. q. 5 ; cc. 4, 5, 6, X. v. 34 ; see also Lyndwood, V. 14.

[4] *S.T.* ii. 2, q. 69, a. 1, ad 2.

[5] *Theol. Mor.* iv. §§ 273 ff.

[6] Prümmer, ii. p. 244, with quotations there from Lehmkuhl, Noldin, etc.

[7] *S.T.* Suppl. q. 6, aa. 1, 2, and commonly. On the disputed question whether *doubtful* mortal sin must be confessed see Alph. Lig. vi. § 474, and authorities there.

than, on the principles we have just considered, they are in general. If the confessor enquired upon the point, and his enquiry was obviously directed to discovering whether the penitents were in all respects ' rightly disposed ' to receive absolution (of which fact the confessor is the sole judge),[1] they would no doubt be obliged to answer truly. Failing this, however, if they are genuinely convinced that they are doing no wrong, they may keep silence with a clear conscience.

It would seem, therefore, that if we are to sustain our conclusion that those in invincible error should make known their condition to responsible authority, even though it would otherwise remain undetected, we shall have to sustain it in the face of the entire weight of traditional canon law and moral theology. It will have to be sustained, again, in the face of the entire practice of the Church of England. Confession of mortal sin, though undoubtedly recommended in the Church of England, is certainly not laid down as a precept. The mediæval law, which still obtains in the Roman communion, has been abrogated for the Anglican by disuse, with the full consent of authority.[2] This clearly implies that it is left to the individual to decide whether he will or will not submit even those grave sins of which he is fully conscious to the tribunal and discipline of penance ; and that loyalty does not oblige him to do so. Still less, then, can he be required to submit to the same tribunal those problems in which, though he recognises his divergence from the Church, he is convinced of his own complete integrity.

Nevertheless it may be suggested that on this point Christian thought will perhaps advance to a new definition of the requirements of loyalty, and demand that earnest-minded members of the Church who are conscious of being in ' invincible error ' should, if they are doubtful whether they may remain members of the community, submit their case to the accredited representative of the community for decision. And though we have frankly admitted that this demand runs counter to the general verdict of the past, it receives no small support from the analogy of secular societies. ' No one would claim the right of being president of a Tariff Reform

---

[1] Gury, i. § 78.   [2] See further, *infra* pp. 279 f.

Club while desiring to propagate Free Trade.'[1]   If a member of a society which, among other things, stood emphatically for the total abolition of the use of intoxicants, habitually indulged in private in his glass of port and thought himself quite right in doing so, we should feel his position to be extraordinarily ambiguous.   And if he too were conscious of the ambiguity, but took no steps to obtain an authoritative decision on his case, we should undoubtedly hold that his inaction argued a defective sense of loyalty.

Or, again, a member of a Conservative Cabinet who was firmly convinced that Communism held out the only hope for national prosperity, but was prepared to remain in the Cabinet because a certain number of its measures seemed to him of a desirable character, would be doing no less than his duty in making the Prime Minister aware of the real state of his feelings.   The Prime Minister is, after all, the person finally reponsible, and he ought to have the opportunity of saying : 'A convinced Communist in a Conservative Government is not merely an anomaly, but a danger to Conservatism. However genuine you are in your convictions, however much you try to keep them wholly to yourself, however closely you associate yourself with many details of our programme, it cannot but happen that you will look at every suggestion from an angle very different from our own, and this is bound to affect our activities in a way we do not desire.'

If this be true, it would seem equally true that a bishop should be given the opportunity of saying to one of his clergy, if circumstances really demanded it : ' Though you try both honestly and successfully to keep (let us say) your disbelief in the bodily Resurrection of Christ to yourself, and though you actively sympathise with and forward the general programme of Church life and teaching in this diocese except on this one point, it is psychologically impossible for you so to isolate it that it will not permeate your entire activities and outlook.   You will grow more and more antipathetic to the Church and her purposes ; and imperceptible though this decline in sympathy be, both to yourself and others, it may at any moment result in very serious consequences. We ought therefore to look round for some means by which, without

[1] Figgis, *op cit.* pp. 102, 103.

publicity and without detriment and sacrifice to yourself, you may be enabled to retire from your present difficult position. You have deserved well of us, not least of all by the candour and sincerity with which you have made known the real state of your mind, and therefore we must show you every considera-tion.   We must both of us take time to see how best the result can be secured ; but I have no hesitation in saying that, as soon as such a thing is practicable on both sides, you must be relieved of your pastoral responsibility.'

The same consideration seems to apply without any differ-ence of principle to the layman.   In the case of the man and woman previously considered, the Church should be given the opportunity of deciding whether after all their ' error' on the marriage question, however conscientious, would not in time so influence their whole outlook as to make severance from the community inevitable.   That their case should be con-sidered in the most lenient way imaginable, that everything should be done to spare their feelings and safeguard their spiritual needs, goes without saying.   Nor have we as yet decided whether it would be the duty of the authority with whom the decision rested to require them to withdraw from communicant membership in the Church.   All we have suggested is that responsible authority should have the opportunity of making such a decision if the circumstances seem to require it.   And this suggestion, we must repeat, appears to go far beyond anything which could be required on the basis of traditional Christian thought or of contem-porary Anglican principles.   We must leave it, therefore, as a suggestion not without some plausibility on general grounds, but at present wholly unsupported by any authoritative utterance of the Church.

5. *Refusal of Communion*

Our last paragraph left us with still a problem.   What is the duty of the priest under whose notice there comes, either in the confessional or outside it, a grave case of ' invincible error ' on the part of one of those for whose spiritual welfare he is directly responsible ?   When, if ever, is he to warn them not to present themselves for communion; and when, if ever, should he refuse communion to them if they present themselves? Here we are bound to consider for a moment the problem of pastoral jurisdiction, and cannot altogether rid ourselves of technicalities. In spite of this the matter is so urgent, at least for the clergy, that we may perhaps be forgiven for treating it with some fulness.

Strictly speaking, the parish priest as such has no disciplinary jurisdiction. But as a confessor he has a definite commission to refuse absolution in such cases as seem to him to demand it; and this would carry with it the duty of warning those to whom absolution is denied to refrain from the Holy Communion until they have been absolved. Further, modern English canon law (if we may use such a phrase) seems to confer upon the minister of communion some right or duty of refusing it to ' notorious evil livers.' It will be simplest to consider this latter point first.

That communion is to be refused to the unbaptized and excommunicate is a universal rule, and need not further be discussed. That it is to be refused to those who, though baptized, are not ' willing and ready ' to be confirmed is a specifically Anglican law dating from Archbishop Peckham's time, and designed apparently to bring confirmation back from a general neglect into which it had fallen.[1] Under the old canon law a communicant could also be required to produce evidence that he had made his confession before presenting himself for communion;[2] but Lyndwood says that a bare affirmation is sufficient testimony,[3] and it may be assumed therefore that the fact of his presenting himself could be taken to imply that he had made his confession. There was some hesitation also about pressing the requirement of confirmation. Lyndwood takes the rule to apply to adults only, and holds that it need not be enforced if the fact that the person is unconfirmed is not generally known.[4] The rights of the parish priest in respect of refusing communion are therefore extremely limited, even in regard to these very definite requirements of Church membership.

[1] *Constitutions at Lambeth*, 1281, § 4; Gibson, p. 466; Wilkins, ii. p. 51; Johnson, *ad loc.*   [2] *Ibid.* § 1.
[3] *Provinciale*, III. xxiii. *verb.* ' sacramento'; cp.V. xvi. *verb.* ' vel episcopi.'
[4] *Ibid.* I. vi. *verb.* ' admittatur.'

So limited indeed are these rights, that communion may not be refused by a priest even to a penitent to whom he has personally refused absolution. In pre-Reformation times this rule only applied where communion was asked for publicly; if the 'penitent' presented himself privately he might be repelled. This is the position of St. Thomas,[1] as well as of the earlier canon law.[2] Later writers, like Alphonso Liguori,[3] saw clearly that what was at stake was not so much the possibility of ' scandal ' as the breach of the seal of the confession; and that therefore private refusal was just as much to be forbidden as public. To this principle there would appear to be no exception; and while of course it is universally held that a Christian who refuses to adapt his ways to those of the Church so that absolution will be possible is doing wrong in presenting himself for communion, it nevertheless remains the case that *if* he presents himself, the priest is bound to administer communion to him.

Where so much is certain, it seems increasingly difficult to justify the comparatively modern rubrics and canons which appear to give the curate complete discretion in repelling notorious public offenders from communion. This alleged modern right is based upon two rubrics in the Communion Office of 1549, and canons 26, 27, and 109 of 1604. The first rubric, as is well known, requires that if any ' open or notorious evil-liver,' or one ' who has done any wrong to his neighbours by word or deed so that the congregation be thereby offended,'

---

[1] *In Sent.* iv. d. 9, q. 1, a. 5; cp. *S.T.* iii. q. 80, a. 6, ad 3.

[2] *C.J.C.* c. 67, D. ii., *de cons.*, from Augustine; Lyndwood, III. xxiii. *verb.* ' confessum ' (on Peckham's Constitutions, 1281). Lyndwood gives four reasons for the rule in the matter of *public* request for the sacrament :— (a) breach of the seal, (b) need for public disciplinary process, (c) possibility of penitence of applicant—'quia Spiritus ubi vult spirat,' (d) scandal. Cp. also Hubert Walter's canons at Westminster, 1200, § 2 (Wilkins, i. p. 505; Johnson, *ad loc.*); Richard Marsh of Durham's canons, 1220 (Wilkins, i. p. 579; Johnson, *ut sup.*), and a canon of Richard of Sarum, 1223 (omitted by Wilkins, i. p. 599; quoted by Johnson). There is doubt of the text in all these cases owing to the confusion in MSS. between *petenti* and *penitenti*; but the true reading in each case should obviously be ' secreto ne detur communio eucharistiae *impenitenti*, sed publice et instanter *petenti* danda est, nisi publicum sit ejus delictum ' (*or*, ' dummodo occultum fuerit ejus delictum '). Johnson fails to understand this, and so makes nonsense of the passages.—Cp. also *C.J.C.* c. 2, X. i. 31, referred to below, p. 244, n. 2

[3] *Theol. Mor.* vi. §§ 50, 51, 246, 658.

signifies his intention of partaking of the Lord's Supper, 'the curate shall call him and advertise him, that in any wise he presume not to come to the Lord's table' until he has repented and made amends, or declared his full purpose of doing so. The second rubric requires the curate to 'use the same order' with 'those betwixt whom he perceiveth malice and hatred to reign.'

So far the only right conferred on the curate is that of admonition. But the rubric goes on at once to enjoin him 'not to suffer' impenitent persons of this character 'to be partakers of the Lord's table,' or 'not to admit' them to the Holy Communion, and the act involved is spoken of as 'repelling.' It is arguable that these phrases too must be interpreted as meaning no more than admonition, and so the Presbyterians who attended the Savoy Conference appear to have taken them, for they demanded that the minister should have full power to admit or repel communicants.[1] No alteration was made in the text of the rubric. But it is possible that the bishops intended the words 'admit,' 'repel' and the like to be taken in a fuller sense than before, since they added the clause providing for notice to be given at once to the ordinary by 'the minister so repelling'[2] —a clause which would be pointless if 'repelling' meant no more than private admonition.

Canon 26 forbids the minister 'in any wise to admit to the receiving of the Holy Communion any of his cure or flock which be openly known to live in sin notorious, without repentance,' and others of the same kind. Canon 27 enjoins that no minister shall 'wittingly administer the communion to any who refuse to kneel or to be present at public prayers;' or to any 'common and notorious depraver' of the Prayer Book, the sacraments, the Articles, the Ordinal or 'His Majesty's sovereign authority in causes ecclesiastical,' unless he acknowledges his repentance and promises not to offend again. A clause at the end of the canon requires the 'minister repelling' under the provisions of either canon to 'signify the cause thereof' to the ordinary 'upon complaint or being required by the ordinary,' and 'to obey his order and direction.'

This would seem to be clear enough Uncertainty arises,

---

[1] E. Cardwell, *Conferences*, p. 317.   [2] *Ibid.* p. 363.

however, from the fact that the principle thus laid down is
wholly foreign to the spirit of organised Christendom, and
gives to a person lacking disciplinary jurisdiction in the
external forum the right to impose virtual excommunication
without any formal examination of the case. Nothing
could be more subversive of established order and Christian
justice. Augustine had asserted as a universal rule : ' We
may not prohibit any man from communion, unless either
he have confessed his guilt of his own accord, or have been
cited and convicted either in a secular or in an ecclesiastical
court.'[1] The Extravagants of Gregory IX, in the obscure
but crucial canon *Si sacerdos*, forbade the priest to repel from
communion (' for even our Lord did not remove Judas from
communion ') unless the guilt of the offender could be proved
in court.[2] The later canonists (e.g. Lyndwood) tended to
interpret this law of occult guilt only, thus giving the priest
a limited measure of summary jurisdiction in cases of notorious
wrong-doing. But how limited it was may be seen from
Lyndwood's long and valuable discussion of the meaning
of ' notorious.'[3] Admission of guilt, or conviction by the
competent authority, confer ' notoriety ' upon a sin ; nor
need that which is admitted or proved before the court be
the actual sin itself, but such circumstances in which the law
invariably presumes that the sin has been committed.[4]
Apart from this, a sin can only be 'notorious ' if it is so
publicly committed that denial is impossible[5] ; that is, if
the offender has been caught *flagrante delicto*, as an assassin
might be, in the presence of many witnesses.

If, then, we interpret the rubrics and canons in accordance
with the old law on which they were based, there can be no
doubt that the curate's right to refuse communion on his own
initiative is to all intents and purposes confined to the cases
of persons who have been found guilty of an offence against
the Christian moral law either in a secular or in an ecclesiastical
court. This has been the accepted interpretation in the past

[1] *Serm.* cccli. (ed. Ben.) 4 (10).
[2] *C.J.C*, c. 2, X. i. 31 :—' nisi judicario ordine quis probare possit.'
[3] *Prov.* V. 15, *verb.* ' delicto notorio ' ; based on *C.J.C.* c. 7, X. iii. 2.
[4] ' Notorium praesumptionis.'
[5] ' Publica et famosa vox ex evidentia rei, quae nulla potest tergiver-
satione celare.'

four centuries. Thus Bishop Wilson, dealing with a case of the kind in the year 1721, gave as his decision : ' Forasmuch as the said Mr. Archdeacon did insist upon repelling from communion any person whom he in his conscience thought unworthy, notwithstanding he was often told of the evil consequence and tyranny of such a procedure, we do hereby declare that the said assertion is contrary to the rule of the Church in all ages ; and . . . we do order and require that neither the said Mr. Archdeacon nor any other minister do for the future presume to repel any persons from the Holy Sacrament whose crimes have not become notorious *either by their own confession, by presentment, or adjudged to be so by some sentence of law.'* [1] Bishop Andrewes wrote in his own prayer book a note alongside the rubric in question : ' Our law in England will not suffer the minister to judge any man a notorious offender but him who is convicted by some legal sentence.'* [2] Modern authorities wholly support these decisions.[3]

No doubt Canon 27 gives the priest the obvious right of refusing communion to those who present themselves with

[1] *Works* (Oxford, 1863), i. p. 462.

[2] *Ibid.* (Oxford, 1854), xi. (Minor Works) p. 151 ; cp. also R. Hooker, *Eccles. Polity*, VI. iv. 15, and the full consideration of the question in the Dean of Arches' Judgment (Sir. L. Dibdin), in Banister and Thompson, *Law Reports*, Probate (1908), p. 386.

[3] The following may be quoted :—A. J. Stephens, *Book of Common Prayer with Notes* (Ecclesiastical Historical Society), pp. 1066, 1070 : ' Nothing less than a confession in open court, or conviction by the sentence of the judge, amounts to *notorium juris*. . . . Until the fact has been established by the sentence of a temporal or ecclesiastical court of justice . . . or by his public confession, that a person is a notorious evil liver or offensive to the congregation, the law will presume him to be innocent, and the minister has no legal right to refuse the communion.' T. A. Lacey, *Church Law*, p. 25 : ' It does not appear that a priest may actually exclude such persons, or on his own responsibility withhold from them the sacraments if they present themselves. His authority extends only to ' repelling ' or warning them not to approach. No Christian may be deprived of the sacraments, save by sentence of excommunication pronounced by a duly constituted judge or regular process.' *Ibid.* pp. 223, 224 (on Canon 26) : ' The *admission* here spoken of is not clearly defined, and the curate might discharge his duty by warning such persons not to approach the Lord's Table.' (On Canon 27) : ' This jurisdiction is too doubtful, especially after this lapse of time, to be safely exercised, except perhaps . . . where a person presents himself for communion with openly expressed contempt for the prescription of the ritual.' To the same effect, Proctor and Frere, *History of Prayer Book*, p. 476.

open contempt of the sacrament, or in a condition, such as
that of intoxication, in which everyone present would
recognise that they were unfit to receive it. Such cases indeed
are ' notorious ' with that *notorium facti* which we have seen
to be expressly included in the canonical definition of
' notoriety.' No doubt also there are rare cases in which
the curate who takes justice into his own hands, and refuses
communion on his own initiative, will not be blamed by
loyal Churchmen, though he may be liable to proceedings in
a secular court. Beyond this, however, we must insist that
exclusion from communion is only legitimate under the conditions already mentioned. The open discipline of the Church
is in other hands than those of the parish priest. How does he
stand in relation to its private discipline in the confessional?

6. *Refusal of Absolution*

There can be no question that a confessor is empowered
to refuse absolution to a penitent who is not ' rightly disposed,' and that in traditional theory and practice no penitent
is regarded as rightly disposed who persists in a course of
action which his confessor, speaking as a responsible authority
of the Church, has told him to be wrong in the eyes of the
Church.[1] No doubt, also, it would be disloyal of such an
unabsolved penitent to present himself for communion,
though if he chose to do so, either contumaciously or with a
clear and convinced conscience, the priest would be bound
to minister to him.

So far all is clear; beyond this everything is difficult.
We meet once more with that standing problem of the Church
of England which provides the atmosphere for all our discussions, that her laws are dependent upon custom and disuse
far more than upon canonical enactment. This creates for
the individual priest a situation of almost overwhelming
difficulty. He is left to his own conscience to decide what is
and what is not required of the individual by his Church,
and consequently to decide on his own responsibility when

[1] *Rit. Rom.* ap. Tanquerey, i. p. 293 ; Gury-Ferreres, ii. § 626.

and when not to absolve.   It is noteworthy in the highest degree that the Church of Rome, which legislates freely upon every conceivable point, and consequently leaves little of importance to the uncertainties of custom, has long known that even so the burden is too heavy for the individual confessor, and has in operation a twofold machinery which is designed to lighten the weight materially.   On the one hand, by a system of 'reserved cases,' she has retained to the bishops, or their expert penitentiary delegates, the decision as to whether absolution shall or shall not be granted in certain matters of grave importance ;   and allows each bishop, after consulting his synod, to reserve cases of this kind to himself according to the peculiar needs of his own diocese.[1]   On the other hand, by the system of 'dispensations,' hard cases can be dealt with as they arise ;   and since most dispensations, though not all, are reserved to higher authority than the parish priest, it is provided that they also shall be dealt with by experts who from wide experience are enabled to compare case with case, and to act upon principle and not on rule-of-thumb.   Now that the practice of private confession has revived in the Church of England on a considerable scale, and shows no sign of diminishing, it seems natural to suggest that nothing is more needed among us than the elaboration of machinery of a similar kind.   The responsibility resting upon the Anglican confessor is infinitely greater than that of his Roman brother ;   and at present, at all events, the assistance afforded him by authority is infinitely less.

Nor is this the only reason why the reservation of cases and the appointment of expert penitentiary priests seem desirable.   The confessor after all may make mistakes in deciding what is contrary to the Church's law, and so by refusing absolution cause unnecessary and undeserved anguish to loyal Christians.   Indeed, the less official guidance there is, the more this is bound to happen.   The natural tendency of an earnest Christian is to be rigorist ;   the more he feels and is allowed to feel his own responsibility the more likely he is to demand more than ought to be demanded.   His practice may not always square with his theory ;   human sympathy will sometimes cause him to give absolution where

[1] *Cod. Jur. Can.* §§ 893 ff.

conscience bids him withhold it. Here the penitent will not
suffer, but the confessor will. He will have acted against
his own conscience, and whether he was right or wrong
in so doing, his conscience will suffer a permanent wound.
It is no exaggeration to say that the number of instances in
which one or other of these evil results occur in the Anglican
practice of the confessional is considerable ; and so simple
a remedy as that of reservation of serious cases to the bishop
and his official delegates is seriously overdue.

Regrettable though this state of things undoubtedly is,
it has to be faced. We must consider the responsibility of
the priest who in default of such authoritative assistance
has to make up his own mind in difficult questions of the
kind. In view of the circumstances just mentioned it is
often suggested that the duty of the Anglican confessor is
to absolve all penitents who are in ' good faith '—i.e. who are
conscientiously convinced that they are doing right—however
much he himself thinks that their course of action is contrary
to the rule of the Church. The suggestion is grounded upon
the fact that the Church of England has no apparent intention
of regulating any except the most obvious cases of sinfulness
(adultery, bigamy, theft and so forth), and therefore may be
supposed to leave everything else to the sole decision of the
individual conscience.

This theory, attractive though it is, can scarcely be admitted. From the merely social point of view the rationale
of penance would appear to be as follows. By mortal sin
(than which there is certainly no other *necessary* ' matter ' to
bring a Christian to sacramental confession) the offender has
put himself outside the pale of the Church ; in confession
he asks to be received back. It would obviously be wrong
to receive him back upon terms easier than those on which a
catechumen would be received for the first time into the
Church by baptism. Thus, to take an example from the
mission-field, if a catechumen who, on the most conscientious
grounds imaginable, refused to abandon polygamy were
resolutely refused baptism, it would be absurd to absolve
him after baptism if, even though on equally conscientious
grounds, he relapsed into and insisted on persevering in
polygamy. And this gives us a useful rough-and-ready test

to apply to such problems. The confessor can ask himself, ' If this penitent presented himself for baptism, with the same definite intention of persevering in the practices which I deprecate as he shows at present, should I conceive it to be my duty to baptize him ? ' If the answer to this question were ' No,' it would carry with it, *a fortiori*, a negative answer in the case of sacramental absolution. If, on the other hand, the answer in the problem of baptism is ' Yes,' it does not necessarily carry an affirmative corollary in the second case. The demands made by the Church upon a mature Christian may well be more' serious than her demands from a neophyte.[1]

---

[1] Objection may be taken to this conclusion by technical theologians on the grounds that the penitent, acting as he is in ' good faith ' or ' invincible error,' and with the full support of conscience, cannot be in mortal sin, and therefore is not by any stretch of imagination unworthy of full Church membership. This argument, however, distorts the truth. Clearly, as he is doing what conscience bids, he is guiltless before God, and his ' sin ' is purely ' material ' ; and on the strict basis of canonical requirements he is not bound to mention the fact of his conscientious divergence to anyone in authority, whether his confessor or another. But we have suggested that a higher conception of loyalty would require him to do so ; and in any case if he did do so, and learnt that the Church could not countenance the course of action he was pursuing, a wholly different state of affairs would result. For though the Church, in view of his obviously clear conscience, could not hold him morally guilty, this need not in itself mean that she was willing to retain him as a member so long as he persisted in his course of action. We cannot hold the conscientious heathen polygamist to be morally guilty—he knows no better, as we say—but we are certainly not prepared to tolerate his innocent polygamy within the Church. Further, the penitent who learnt that his course of action was contrary to the principles of the society, and yet pressed for absolution and communion, would *primâ facie* be acting in a disloyal manner ; and on *this* ground, as well as on the previous one, would be unable to claim absolution as an unquestionable right, so long as he persisted in the conduct to which the Church takes exception. See further, p. 271, n. 4 ; and Additional Note H., p. 395.

A confessor who failed to accept our conclusion would hold one of two positions. Either (a) he would be convinced that he was free (or even bound) to absolve in all cases of conscientious ' invincible error,' whatever the degree of divergence from the Church may be—in this case, his conviction being itself conscientious and invincible, he would have to follow conscience ; although, as suggested above (pp. 236-240), he would be bound, if the divergence were serious, to inform the bishop of his course of action, and to abide by the result. Or (b) he might be doubtful whether the arguments given above, though not altogether without relevance, carried the full weight given of the conclusion reached. In this case he would technically be in a state of ' doubt,' and the matter would have to be settled on the principles suggested in the next chapter. In accordance with those principles we should have to say that the question was one which involved a vital interest

We conclude, then, that occasions may sometimes arise when a confessor is bound to refuse absolution even to a penitent in good faith. The problem still remains, on what occasions will this extreme course be necessary? We may relegate to the next chapter all cases in which the confessor himself is in doubt as to the exact mind of the Church in the matter; problems of doubt have their own methods of solution which have not yet been discussed. For the present we confine ourselves to those clear-cut issues in which the confessor has no doubt whatever that the mind of the Church points emphatically towards one course, whilst the mind of the penitent is in all good conscience firmly set on pursuing the opposite course. We may revert to our question of the sincere but unmarried couple living together as husband and wife. The confessor is clear that it is a breach of the moral law for this to continue; the couple not only intend to persist in their union, but are also convinced that they are right in doing so. Cases similar in principle are continually arising, as every Anglican confessor knows, in connection with the use of contra-conceptives in marriage; a use which many genuine Christians regard as warrantable in certain instances, against an equally strong judgment of many others on the other side. Is it inevitable that the priest should in all such matters refuse absolution where he finds that the penitent's determination to persist is fixed and firm, whilst he himself is clear that the state of things is one which the Church does not allow?

Obviously the confessor must not refuse absolution till he has exhausted every other possible alternative. There may be a chance, if he thinks out his own position in the light of this conscientious pertinacity of good Christian people, that he has convinced himself too certainly of what he thought the Church demanded. There may be a chance, again, if he labours to express his own conviction in the most adequate terms and with carefully thought-out arguments, that the penitent may change his mind and admit the error—if it

(namely, the whole system of Church discipline), and that consequently he would not be justified in taking the benefit of the doubt. That is to say, if he admitted any relevance at all in the arguments in the text above, he would be bound to conform to the conclusion just as much as if he thought it definitely proved.

be an error—in his course of action. It is possible that if the case is referred to the bishop—as surely a difficult case should be wherever possible—the latter, acting perhaps on the advice of his experts, will relieve the confessor of responsibility and give a definite decision himself. We must assume that all these methods have been tried and have failed ; the clash of views is as final as before, and the bishop gives no ruling. Is the confessor then bound in the last resort to refuse absolution ?

Except in one respect, the whole verdict of the past would insist that his duty lay in refusal. But the exception is important. It is commonly agreed that a penitent in ' invincible error ' may sometimes be left in the dark as to the view which the Church takes of his condition, if enlightenment is certain to bring with it no change in his conduct, or to involve him in disgrace or scandal or be the cause of quarrels and friction.[1] The reasons for this principle, which confers upon the confessor a certain discretionary power of dispensation, are given as succinctly as anywhere in Schieler-Heusser's ' Theory and Practice of the Confessional.' 'As it is not allowable to expose one's neighbour to a danger to which it is anticipated that he will succumb, so the confessor must not expose a penitent to the danger of refusing to fulfil a duty by instructing him about it. He must rather leave the penitent in material sin (i.e. purely technical nonconformity), because a *peccatum formale* (deliberate transgression of a known principle of morality) outweighs all *peccata materialia*.'

The same book gives a clear summary of the limiting conditions within which alone this discretion may be exercised. In any case its use is to be strictly guarded. ' We must not easily conclude that the penitent would not obey after having learnt the truth.' Nor may it be employed ' where the ignorance of the penitent concerns the first principles of morality or the immediate conclusions deduced from them ; for such ignorance is either not actually existent, or will not be for long invincible, and is generally hurtful to the penitent. Especially urgent is the duty of admonishing the penitent when omitting to do so would confirm him in a sinful habit,

[1] Alph. Lig. vi. §§ 210, 610 ; Lehmkuhl, ii. §§ 444 f., pp. 321 ff. ; Schieler-Heusser, *Theory and Practice of the Confessional*, pp. 442 ff. ; *Duct. Dub.* i. 3, rule 8, and commonly.

which he would probably find great difficulty in overcoming later.' Again, ' admonition must be given when the ignorance touches the duty of giving up a gravely sinful immediate occasion (of sin), as such ignorance tends to the ruin of the penitent, by rendering easier the fall into formal sin. The penitent must (also) be admonished even when he is not disposed, if the confessor's silence were to bring harm to the community by scandal, for instance, to the faithful.' And finally, 'the confessor must admonish when, on account of special circumstances, his silence would be equivalent to a positively false answer.'

Important though this principle is, even when thus limited, it does not at first sight touch our problem of conscientious nonconformity. The ' invincible error ' referred to, in these passages at all events, is not that conscientious divergence from the ruling of the Church of which we have been speaking, but sheer ignorance (combined, of course, with conscientiousness) on the part of the penitent that the Church has ever spoken on the matter, or at all events that his circumstances are such as to place him in a state of technical or material sin. Thus the instances in which the principle is usually applied are, for example, where a patient in extremity of illness innocently desires an operation which the Church regards as unlawful ; [1] or where a marriage has taken place, to the knowledge of the confessor but not to that of the contracting parties, within the forbidden degrees ; [2] or where the penitent is unaware of the duty of restitution, but would not discharge it even if he knew of it. [3] Ignorance alone, and that in the strictest sense, would appear at first sight to be the only condition contemplated by this mitigating principle ; not conscientious divergence at all.

I have suggested elsewhere that Roman Catholic theology has been led into an inconsistency on this point by the

---

[1] Arregui, *Theol. Mor.* p. 136.

[2] So the extreme case in *Duct. Dub.* i. 3, rule 8 ; also referred to by Hall, *Cases of Conscience*, additional case 4.

[3] Alph. Lig. *ut. sup.*, and commonly. One of the objections urged against the principle is that if the penitent would not obey the ruling of the Church on hearing of it he cannot be *rite dispositus*. Liguori replies to this by pointing out that what the confessor has to consider is the ' present and actual ' disposition of the penitent, not his ' future and inferential ' disposition (*futura et interpretiva*). This is an important point, which should always be borne in mind in the practice of the confessional.

doctrine of infallibility.[1] In all other respects the two kinds
of ' invincible error '—i.e. sheer ignorance and conscientious
though deliberate divergence—are treated as identical, and
subordinated to the same rules. And, as we shall see,[2] the
principle is actually applied to conscientious divergence by
Roman Catholic writers in no less a matter than that of
birth-control. There seems no reason, therefore, why divergence of temperament or moral conviction should not be
treated, in the Church of England at all events, with the
same kindliness as divergence due to accident. This is not
to say that the confessor will be free to absolve any and
every penitent who with a clear conscience persists in a
course contrary to Christian principles. The limitations
already considered must apply equally in this case. But it
suggests that *sometimes* a priest may be in a position to
absolve, even though the penitent's conduct diverges
materially—and that on a question of primary importance—
from what he himself holds to be the Church's considered
rule of life. He will have before him a choice of evils. On
the one hand, if absolution is given, he will have connived
at something which the Church condemns, though in the
case in question it springs from a serious and conscientious
indisposition to conform. On the other, if absolution is
refused, grave spiritual harm may result to the penitent and
perhaps to others as well. And there we must leave the
matter for the moment, for the question of the choice of evils
will come before us in a later chapter.[3]

We may summarise the long and somewhat technical
discussion of this chapter in the following terms :—

(*a*) An 'invincible' conscience must always be obeyed, even
though it points in a direction wholly condemned by the Church.

(*b*) The Church has a right to say within what limits she
will tolerate conscientious divergence on the part of her
members ; she has also a right to remove from communion
those who, even though conscientiously, refuse conformity
beyond these limits.

(*c*) No conscientious dissentient, however final the issue

---

[1] *Ignorance, etc.*, pp. 45, 131 f.

[2] *Infra*, p. 298.

[3] Further possibilities of absolution in some cases of this kind are
considered, *infra*, pp. 299-301.

between himself and the Church may be, is bound by this fact alone to resign his membership until officially called upon by the Church to do so.   But it would be less than loyal for such a dissentient to withhold from the Church the opportunity of deciding whether in the circumstances it wished to retain him as a member.

(*d*) Where ' offenders ' are removed from communion the fact implies no necessary stigma ; the Church's judgment upon the case may be wrong.

(*e*) This discipline may be exercised either by open condemnation in a duly constituted tribunal, or privately by refusal of absolution in the confessional.

(*f*) Refusal of absolution is tantamount to exclusion from communion, but a priest has no right to refuse communion to anyone but a ' notorious evil-liver,' even though he knows him to be unabsolved.

(*g*) Normally it is the duty of the confessor to refuse absolution where he is convinced that the penitent is acting in a manner contrary to the mind of the Church, and proposes to continue in such action.   But in special circumstances it seems that, in the Church of England, he may absolve, even though the penitent is aware of the Church's condemnation of his conduct, and yet out of deference to conscience refuses to conform.   Here the confessor must be guided by the principles which determine cases of conflict of evils.

(*h*) To relieve confessors of the grave responsibilites which at present burden them in the Church of England, it is highly desirable that the most serious problems should be reserved to the decision of higher authority, failing clearer declaration of the mind of the Church in such matters.

CHAPTER VI

1. *The Doubts of Anglicans*

IN the early days of railways a popular ' Punch ' joke represented a railway guard looking into a non-smoking compartment full of vigorous smokers, and saying with a significant
and ingratiating smile : ' There are two important bye-laws
on this line, gentlemen. Passengers are forbidden to smoke
in non-smoking compartments ; and the Company's servants
are not allowed to receive gratuities.' We need not enquire
into the guard's morality, but it is obvious that his words
must have created a certain doubt in the passengers' minds
as to the absoluteness of the bye-laws in question, and it is
probable that on this particular occasion neither rule was
strictly observed. Here is a trivial example of a moral
problem that meets us frequently—the problem of *Doubt*.
A ' law ' or principle is alleged to exist ; it is certain, perhaps,
that it was at one time in force, or is still recognised and
obeyed in some branches of the Christian Church. But it
is doubtful whether (for example) it still has a claim on the
members of one particular communion, or in the special
circumstances of a given class or individual. What is the
right course of action in cases of the kind ?

A simple instance in the present conditions of the Church
of England is provided by the principle of fasting communion.
There are those who say that the fast before communion has
from time immemorial been the canonical rule of the Catholic
Church, and that there is no evidence that it has ever been
' abolished ' in the Church of England. Others, on the contrary, maintain that the practice has no basis either in Scripture or the Prayer Book ; that it is a survival of primitive
and mediæval times, when both social custom and contemporary ritual made its observance easy ; that it may be an
excellent custom for those who can practise it, but that

loyalty to the Church does not make it obligatory upon anyone to adopt it unless he feels or finds it to be of value to himself. Whatever may be our opinion about the arguments adduced, there is clearly something to be said both for and against the surreptitious cup of tea with which so many of us fortify ourselves against the rigours of an early service. If certainty could be reached—if it were clear either that loyalty to the Church of England involved conformity to the rule, even though individuals found it valueless or a trifle irksome ; or (on the other hand) that Anglicans were free to adopt or ignore it at discretion—there would be no problem. But so long as both positions are urged with emphasis, if not with vehemence, many earnest-minded churchmen feel that the rule is surrounded by a state of doubt. The question for them must be : ' What is my duty in these circumstances of doubt ? Ought I to conform, or am I free to take my own course in the matter, irrespective of the Church ? '

The case we have chosen is one where doubt arises as to the *authority* behind the ' law ' in question—has the rule of fasting communion a valid claim upon Anglicans by virtue of their Church membership ? Questions of promulgation, acceptance, use and disuse are all involved here ; but it would be wrong to think that these are the only conditions which may induce a state of legitimate doubt. There may be doubt as to the justice of a ' law ' in a particular case ; as to its applicability in that case ;[1] as to its interpretation ; as to the degree of urgency or necessity which may justify the individual in dispensing himself from it. This last case of ' doubt' approximates to a ' conflict of duties' of a type which we shall discuss more fully in the next chapter ; for ' urgency ' implies a danger of disaster which it is a man's duty to avoid if morally possible. Here we may consider mainly problems in which there is no conflict of duties, but only a conflict between a doubtful duty on the one hand, which conscience has no inclination to recognise unless it prove to be required by loyalty, and the natural but not necessarily very strong desire for freedom from vexatious interference on the other.

[1] I.e. *dubium facti* as distinct from *dubium juris*.

From this point of view cases of doubt resolve themselves, for members of the Church of England, into two classes. On the one hand are those in which some striking and obvious difference of principle is to be observed between modern Anglican usage and the usage either of the pre-Reformation Church or of other branches of the Church to-day. The difference may be due either to deliberate legislation by Anglican authority—as in the matters of clerical celibacy, the Latin liturgy and the disavowal of the papal claims ; or to customary disuse with the consent of authority—as with the regulations requiring fast and confession of mortal sin before communion. Where customary disuse and nothing more has determined the peculiarity of Anglicanism in any point, there is naturally enough every reason for hesitating to regard it as valid ; it is not always easy to determine whether the conditions required for valid custom have been satisfied. But only on a doctrine of Anglican infallibility which we have already disavowed could we maintain, even in the case of her official enactments, that permissions given by the Church of England counter to the preponderant verdict of Christendom are beyond question valid for conscience. It is perfectly legitimate to doubt their validity—not indeed on the grounds of lack of jurisdiction, or of an alleged ' Protestant ' atmosphere in official circles (both of these arguments we have considered and dismissed)—but on the obvious grounds that where two great branches of organised Christendom disagree there must be cause for doubt.

The second class of case is less commonly recognised, but it is in every respect equally important. Groups of Christians, as to whose sincerity we have no doubt, and whose intellectual ability we recognise even where we disagree from them, put forward from time to time demands that the Church should officially condemn some proposition or type of conduct of which they vehemently disapprove. Vivisection, betting and gambling, ' modernist views,' the use of intoxicants for any but purely medicinal purposes, have all been pilloried in this manner by enthusiasts, who invite an endorsement of their views by official action which would in the end— if we were logical in these matters—involve the penalty of exclusion against all who failed to conform. In so far as these prohibitions have not yet been canonically adopted by the Church, they cannot be thought of, even doubtfully, as a part of ecclesiastical law. But that is not the whole of the matter. They are strongly supported by the conscience of good Christians, who may be merely in advance of their age on these points. They are, we may say, customs in the making ; and custom voices the demands of corporate loyalty as surely as does promulgated law. So, for our purposes, a moral principle which is strongly urged by a not inconsiderable body of Church people—especially if representative of many different classes and points of view, and not unsupported by some at least of the most intelligent and saintly of contemporary Christians — is in somewhat the same condition as a law whose promulgation, acceptance, observance or application is in doubt. It has no *direct* claim upon any conscience which does not fully respond to it ; but has it an indirect claim by virtue of the all-important duty of loyalty ?

A similar difficulty arises in connection with other movements in the Church—movements which aim not at the suppression of a particular type of conduct regarded as sinful by their adherents, but at the introduction of a new duty into the Christian code. The League of Nations Union, the Sunday School movement, the Foreign Missionary Societies seem to be somewhat in this position. Groups of churchmen, not inconsiderable in number, and including many of the Church's most loyal and enthusiastic members, regard devotion to these or similar causes as wholly essential to true churchmanship ; anyone who shows himself callous, indifferent or captious appears to them to be in moral default on a matter of primary importance. What, then, should be the attitude of a Christian who, while seeing no vital objection to movements of this kind, can after conscientious thought summon up no real enthusiasm for them ? It is ' doubtful,' perhaps, whether they have a claim upon him. They have the approval of authority, but not in any canonical form ; and though they are widely supported it is not clear that the support is sufficient to justify the conclusion that the conscience of the Church has wholly endorsed or adopted them. What is our duty in the matter ? May we stand aside in a neutral isolation, neither blessing nor cursing ? Or does loyalty to our fellow-churchmen demand the more positive attitude of extending to them all the support we can—attending their meetings, subscribing to their funds, vindicating their intentions ? Aloofness towards an established and considered practice of the Church is—as we saw at an earlier stage—inconsistent with true loyalty ; at what point then, and on what grounds, does aloofness cease to be legitimate in respect of these unofficial 'Movements' ? At a time when enthusiasm is somewhat suspect and the attitude of friendly neutrality more than popular, it is not wholly idle to ask this question.

An easy solution of many of these problems would be for the Church at once to declare her official position towards them, affirming them either to be enjoined, forbidden or left open to the conscience of the individual to accept or reject. Some such action by authority may—on certain points at least—be expected within the next few generations. Our primary business is of course with the present ; yet we may remind ourselves that the process of codifying the principles to be recognised as authoritative is not without difficulty and danger. The difficulty is apparent to all ; the danger lies in the case with which all codification may lead to merely formal observance in the present, whilst binding the future down to a sterilising tradition whose value has disappeared.

Further, the special circumstances or the special genius of the Church of England has caused her in the last three centuries to look askance at codification, and to allow her members the relatively greater liberty to be found under the régime of free custom. It is too early to suggest that this new experiment in Christian constitutionalism is a failure, or that it should be abandoned in favour of wholesale legalism. It is not inconsistent with a desire for fuller authoritative guidance to ask for a little more time in which to experiment with the method of free ethical enquiry in combination with general loyalty to primitive and catholic tradition, before we acquiesce in the much more drastic step of codification. The latter may have to come, and within strict limits at all events is a much-needed undertaking ; but its dangers are so evident that they are not to be incurred until the ground has been prepared as carefully as possible by less formal methods.

In the meantime, with Anglicanism as it is, and in the

absence of any formularies of conduct comparable even to the simple doctrinal formularies which it retains and administers, problems of ' doubt ' must assume a larger importance, and touch a wider range of subjects, in our communion than elsewhere. Our immediate purpose must be to find how far the rules of procedure of traditional casuistry enable these problems to be solved on systematic and universal lines. If any satisfactory results can be achieved along these lines they will have the merit of introducing form and definition into the present uncertainties of Anglican ethics, without hurrying into the dangerous experiment of an authoritative and canonical code.

2. *The Benefit of the Doubt*

In the earlier stages of bridge-playing, the neophyte is sometimes tempted to adopt as his own the rule : ' When in doubt, play trumps.' Brief experience and the strictures of his partner soon convince him of its insufficiency. The amateur casuist has often been guilty of a similar mistake in the matter of ethics, taking as his guiding principle the rule, *In dubio pars tutior eligenda*—' When in doubt always take the safer course,' or, ' When in doubt obey the law.' [1] It is universally admitted that this principle—commonly called ' tutiorism '—is too rigorist for the moral life. It implies that no degree of doubt as to the validity or application of a given ' law ' can ever justify us in ignoring it. We may revert to the illustration of the guard and the non-smoking compartment which we used earlier. If the most ardent smoker in the carriage, though fully conscious of the virtual abrogation of the law by the guard's connivance, had nevertheless thrown his cigar out of the window and kept himself rigidly from smoking throughout the journey, whilst all his fellow-travellers took advantage of the tacit permission given to their tobacco, his action would have been no more than a

---

[1] Lip-service was paid to this principle by important mediæval authorities ; e.g. Innocent III :—' In dubiis via est eligenda tutior ' :—*C.J.C.* c. 5, X. v. 27 ; cp. c. 3, X. iv. 1 ; c. 12, X. v. 12 ; c. i. V. 11, *in Clem.* (' In iis quae animae salutem respiciunt, ad vitandos graves remorsus conscientiae pars securior est tenenda.') But often tutiorism meant no more than probabiliorism. *Infra* p. 263, n. 3.

misplaced and ostentatious piece of pedantry.   Or again, anyone of us who found the lawns of a public park dotted with
picnic parties, and the park-keepers looking on complacently
in spite of notices warning visitors to keep off the grass, might
reasonably draw the attention of the responsible authorities
to the surprising paradox involved, but could not fairly be
held bound not to trespass on the grass himself.

The instances just selected are trivial enough.   Moral
considerations scarcely enter into them at all ; the bye-laws
contravened are to all intents and purposes merely penal.
The rigorist method becomes more dangerous when it is
applied to morality.   Once allow that any ' law ' or principle
of conduct, however doubtful and by whomsoever stated, is
binding upon conscience—and nothing less than this is consistent with tutiorism—and, as Azpilcueta pointed out in the
seventeenth century, ' a thousand opinions held by the Church
as valid for salvation would be exploded ' in a moment.[1]
Any uneasy feeling—any ' causeless, perplexing, melancholy
scruple '—would become authoritative and ' stop a man in
the course of his duty.' [2]

No one has put this more frankly or fairly than Mr.
Shebbeare in an important article published some years ago.
' Tutiorism,' he writes, ' which is equivalent to saying :
When in doubt give way to your scruples—would often lead
to a cowardly desertion of duty.' [3]   A few pages further
on he adduces other arguments against the principle in
question.   ' The persons who most seek " direction " '—and
indeed, we may add, all persons who, whether they seek
' direction ' or not, give themselves up to serious enquiry
about specific points of morality—' are the persons of scrupulous conscience ; the tendency of the high-minded amateur
in moral theology is always and everywhere towards rigorism ;
and rigorism is the very worst of all possible systems for the
scrupulous.   Persistently to take the " safe side," persistently
to do more than one is sure that one is really bound to do,
persistently to give way to scruples which increase as they

---

[1] Azpilcueta (Navarrus), *In comm. d.* vii. *de poen.,* c. 4. 8, 64 ; cp. Alph.
Lig. vi. § 474, on confession of doubtful mortal sin.

[2] Baxter, *Christian Directory,* iv. c. 19, t. 3.

[3] *Church Quarterly Review,* July 1912 (vol. lxxiv. n. 148), p. 339.

K

are indulged—what surer road could be found towards physical breakdown ? And the same method which leads to physical overstrain in some, leads to moral reaction in others. The lapse into violent ill-temper of the man who feels that he has long been more forbearing than he was really bound to be, is a phenomenon familiar to every student of human nature. And it is far from being the most serious phenomenon of its class.' [1]

The argument may be put in an even more cogent form. 'When in doubt obey the law' means in effect, 'Do nothing rash or unusual unless you are absolutely and directly certain that you ought to do so.' It is the spirit of those who deny to conscience the right to say, 'You may'; the spirit of Gamaliel, who would not act without 'authority.' It is the spirit which would eliminate from life all ventures of faith, all risks of heroism, all generous though quixotic impulses, and reduce everything to one dead level of conformity. It is surprising to find no less a theologian than Harnack upholding this principle even at the present day, but his words are clear. He quotes as the principle of tutiorism : 'In cases of doubt all action is to be avoided,' and adds, 'This view alone is moral.' [2] Against this we may set the robust common-sense of John Sharp, that clear-thinking archbishop of the seventeenth century : 'It is a very idle thing for men to talk,' he says, 'that a man must do no action till all his Doubts be removed.' [3] We must not indeed do that which we fear may be wrong (and it is to allay such fears that moral theology has elaborated these rules about doubt) ; but we need not and ought not to delay action until we are certain that what we are to do is the one thing absolutely demanded of us in the circumstances. [4] There is a margin of 'allowable actions' in all the contingencies of life ; once we are clear that our intention lies within the sphere of the 'allowable' it may be better to go forward with it than to wait further for the 'necessary.'

---

[1] *Church Quarterly Review,* July 1912, pp. 344, 345.

[2] *History of Dogma* (E.T.), vii. p. 105 n.

[3] *Discourses concerning Conscience,* ii. (1685).

[4] Hence 'probabilism' is called not a 'direct' but a 'reflex' principle of certainty—it does not convince that an action is a duty, but does convince that it is *not* a sin. See *supra* c. 1 ('Indifferent Acts'), *infra* p. 266.

Rigorism, therefore, though it had the solid support of Cicero (in one at least of his moods) and Pliny,[1] was in the end rightly rejected by Christian experience, and even attained to the dignity of an anathema [2] in the eighteenth century. But it is easier to condemn the doctrine than to find anything to put in its place. Some formula is necessary which will allow us in all reasonable cases to take the benefit of the doubt. The middle ages gravitated towards the principle of allowing the benefit of the doubt in cases where there was more to be said against the validity of the ' law ' than in its favour. This principle, technically known as ' probabiliorism,'[3]

[1] Cicero, de Off. i. 9 (30), ' Bene praecipiunt qui vetant quicquam agere quod dubitas aequum sit an iniquum ; aequitas enim lucet ipsa per se, dubitatio significat cognitionem injuriae ' ; Pliny, Ep. i. 18, ' Illud cautissimi cujusque praeceptum :—quod dubitas ne feceris.'

[2] Prop. 3 damn. ab Alex. viii. (7th Dec. 1690), Denz.-Bann., No. 1293, ' Non licet sequi opinionem vel inter probabiles probabilissimam.'

[3] In pre-Reformation moral theology it is often not at all easy to distinguish between tutiorism and probabiliorism, or even between probabiliorism and probabilism pure and simple. Thus a writer may say, ' Take the safer course ' and mean either, ' In case of doubt always obey the law,' or ' In case of doubt always obey the law unless the arguments against it are the more probable ' (tutior here = probabilior). This confusion, due to the ambiguity of the word ' safer ' (according as it is contrasted with ' probable ' and ' more probable ' alike, or only with ' probable'), is pointed out by John Sharp, Archbishop of York, in the second of his pamphlets, Discourses concerning Conscience ; I do not know any other writer who grasped it so clearly.—On the other hand, until it was suggested by Medina that an opinion might be ' probable ' even where the possibility of a ' more probable ' opinion to the contrary was not ruled out, ' Take the probable course ' meant no more than ' Take the more probable course ' would mean later.—In general, however, it is clear (i,) that pre-Reformation writers saw the impossibility of tutiorism. The principal references are Augustine, de Fid. et Op. 19 (35) ; de Conjug. Adult. i. 25 (31), 26 (33) ; Ep. 47, ad Publ. (pass., but particularly c. 6, of the starving Christian who takes meat from an idol-temple :—' Either it is certain that the food was offered to an idol, or it is certain that it was not, or neither of these things is known. If it is certain [that it was], it is better to reject it with Christian fortitude. In either of the other two cases, it may be used for his necessity without any scruple ') ; Greg, Naz., Or. xxxix. 19 (' If there be any doubt, let charity prevail ') ; Lactant., Div. Inst. iii. 27 (' It is folly to obey doubtful precepts ') ; Aquinas, de Ver. q. 17, a. 3, ' Nullus ligatur per praeceptum aliquod nisi mediante scientia (sc. certa) ejus praecepti.'—Against the apparently tutiorist maxims of canon law (supra p. 260) may be set the Regulae Juris of Boniface viii. (in Sext. fin.), Nos. 11, 15, 30, 49, 57. (ii.) As Medina said, in so far as the probabilist question arose they were probabiliorist, e.g. Aquinas, Quodl. viii. a. 13 ; cf. references to Albertus Magnus, Sum. Tr. i. de hom. q. 70, a. 2 ; Antoninus, Sum. p. i. t. 3, c. 10, § 10, etc., in Prümmer, i. p. 207 ; Lehmkuhl, i. p. 67 ff. The extraordinary varia-

cannot indeed be allowed to stand alone. As also in the case of ' probabilism,' its use must be restricted to those problems only in which some vital interest is not at stake.[1] But it is not on these grounds that it has fallen into obsolescence. The difficulty with probabiliorism is simply that as a matter of practice it is impossible in most cases for the questioner or his adviser to sum up the arguments so fully and exactly as to enable him to decide on which side the balance of probability really lies. Least of all was such a course practicable in the hurry of the counter-Reformation, when moral theologians on the Roman side set themselves to re-capture the direction of conscience throughout Europe. What perhaps influenced the principal Jesuit theologians in abandoning probabiliorism was not so much (as is commonly supposed) the need of a rule which would enable them to give lax decisions, as of a rule which would give swift decisions. And such a rule could not be found in this careful weighing-up of the minutiæ of evidence and argument which went by the name of probabiliorism.

The moral theology of the Reformers held firmly to the mediæval rule, and Taylor, Perkins, Ames, Baldwin, Baxter [2] are probabiliorists to a man. This perhaps accounts to some extent for the decline of their influence, and the complete abandonment of moral theology outside the Roman Church at the beginning of the eighteenth century. The Jesuits, however, were not daunted by the difficulties of the situation. Laying hold of a rule originally proposed by the Dominican, Medina, they maintained as a principle that *whenever* the ' law ' was doubtful a Christian could take the benefit of

tions of Liguori at different periods of his life need not delay us. (iii.) They only allowed the ' safer ' course to be set aside where matters of vital importance (mortal sin) were not at stake (Aquinas, *Quodl.* ix. q. 7, a. 15; Antoninus, *ut sup.*; Sylvester Prierias, *Sum.*, s.v. ' Dubium,' § 2).—Soto, *de Just. et Jur.* iii. q. 6, a. 5, ad 4, admits probabilism as an abstract theory, but forbids its use in practice.

[1] *Infra* pp. 271 ff.

[2] The only Reformed theologian of note who appears to have had any leanings towards probabilism was Osiander, and he limits its scope as severely as do modern Roman Catholic writers. Taking probabilists in general he says of them that they change the words of the Psalm (xxv. 5) ' Lead me in Thy truth ' into ' Lead me in Thy probability.'—*Theol. Cas.* Intd., c. 3, §§ 104, 106.

the doubt and ignore it.[1] With an exegesis as erratic as
it was irreverent, they quoted Eve, David, the Archangel
Michael and even the Virgin Mary as scriptural warrant
for the rule [2]—ignoring the fact that, although Eve took
advantage of the doubt suggested by the serpent, she is
scarcely commended for it in the biblical record. This
principle—that a ' doubtful law does not oblige '—is in its
simplest form the rule of probabilism, which has brought
Roman Catholic moralism as a whole into such undeserved
disrepute. A ' probable opinion ' (which may be acted upon
in cases of doubt) is simply a ' reasonable doubt ' as to the
obligation of the law. The history of the controversies which
centred on probabilism has often been written,[3] and need
not be repeated here. All we need notice is that the system
owed its unenviable reputation to three causes, two of which
—the first and the third—patently undermined its ethical
value, whilst the second, though not in itself unreasonable,
was found to be small safeguard against the other two.

(I) The first objection to the principle that in all cases
of doubt the benefit of the doubt can be taken lies in the
obvious fact that—even more than with probabiliorism—
it needs serious and drastic limitation. There may be cases
in which it is unexceptionable—the smoking carriage and the
public park provide us with examples—but there are other
cases in which common-sense would reject it without a
moment's hesitation. If a doctor, for example, were to
omit any serious precaution before an operation on the
grounds that in the case in question he had reason to doubt
its strict necessity, we should hold him morally responsible
for any evil consequences that might ensue. Not even if
the balance of probability were strongly against the necessity

---

[1] Verbally admitted in the patristic period and middle ages, but probably with a probabiliorist application. See references in Alph. Lig. i.
§§ 64, 70, 77, 97.

[2] So Concina, *App. ad Theologiam*, iii. diss. 1, cap. 1 (reference to
Caramuel and Terillus) ; Osiander, *Theol. Cas.* Intd., c. 114 (from Bordonus).

[3] Döllinger-Reusch, *Geschichte der Moralstreitigkeiten* is of course the
fullest modern account. Its principal defect is that the authors' sympathy is wholly on the probabiliorist side (Concina, Gonzalez), and in
consequence they tend to ignore the important arguments advanced on
the side of probabilism. Thus Vasquez's crucial exposition of the case
for probabilism is scarcely alluded to.

of observing the precaution—not even, that is to say, on probabiliorist grounds—would his omission be condoned; and where he acted, as on general probabilist principles he would, upon a mere doubt, the same condemnation would hold with double strength. So glaring was this objection to the whole theory that prompt steps had to be taken by the reforming popes (Alexander VII, Innocent XI and Alexander VIII) to counter it.

(2) The second cause which brought probabilism into disrepute was the admission of ' purely external ' probability as a substitute for rational or ' internal ' probability. Internal probability means simply a doubt based upon personal consideration of the facts of the case ; external probability is a doubt mainly supported by—if not wholly based upon—the doubts of others. Where moralists of repute could be found to doubt or deny the validity of the ' law ' in question in sufficient numbers, there—it was held—the Christian was free to ignore it without further consideration. There is embodied here a principle which has no little support in common-sense. Not every man has the necessary equipment of sound casuistry, and if his doubts are to be relieved at all he will probably have to have recourse to authority in some form. But in matters of this kind the authority of the Church is obviously ambiguous—otherwise, to everyone who understood loyalty in the sense we have given to it, there would be no doubt. Hence a second type of authority is necessary—the authority of the expert ; and since even experts will disagree, it is better to fortify oneself with the opinions of several than with that of one alone. The experts may not be able to make clear to us the grounds on which they have reached and hold their conclusions, and therefore we shall not have a direct certainty or conviction of our own. But we shall have what theologians call a ' reflex ' certainty —a trustful confidence in the judgment of persons of greater insight and maturity than ourselves.

It is no doubt the child's method and the child's mentality to rest content with reflex convictions of this kind. But in questions of a practical character we continually rely upon the decisions of experts—of doctors, solicitors, bankers or business men. Such dependence upon experts in secular affairs is commonly adjudged not merely reasonable and expedient, but also right and necessary. It is a moral duty to consult a doctor in matters of health, or a banker in matters of investment, at all events if the welfare of others depends upon our health or income, and it would be morally wrong to omit such a precaution. But it is also morally unexception-able—provided always that we see no actual flaw in their advice—to rest content with it. It follows, therefore, that—*if* a man is of such a mentality that he cannot find the solution to his own moral problems (and if he could he would no longer be in doubt), and the circumstances demand immediate action—he is to be praised rather than blamed if he has recourse to experts, and prefers to act upon their considered judgment rather than upon the last impulse which crosses the troubled surface of his own mind.

Probabilism, however, at all events in its earlier stages, was not content to allow the Christian to depend upon one expert only. To make assurance doubly sure it insisted upon the concurrence of four or five,[1] though these of course were not necessarily consulted by the enquirer, but were quoted by his principal adviser in corroboration of his own opinion. Here was a real safeguard which the laxer moralists very soon threw away. But, quite apart from this perversion of the doctrine in practice, the fatal objection to any theory of the sufficiency of a consensus of ' external ' probability is just that it allows and even encourages men to remain at the mental level of children in moral problems. The expert is apt at all times to magnify his office, and if those who consult him are frail enough not to want to take trouble, the stage is set for an exhibition of dominance on the one side and passive receptivity on the other, all the more attrac-tive if (as is often the case) the result is to be a waiving and not a tightening of the ' law.' So the old Bishop of Barchester learnt to rely on Archdeacon Grantly as the ' one medicine in his pharmacopœa strong enough to touch even the gravest

---

[1] Where cases requiring particular knowledge were involved, one doctor of specially expert character could be taken as a guide. An old rule said that in doubt Augustine should be followed ' in subtle disputes and questions,' Jerome in matters of ' translation, history and interpre-tation,' Gregory the Great in ethics, Ambrose ' in sermons and judicial decisions.'—J. Altenstaig, *Lexicon Theologicum* (Lugd., 1561), s.v. ' opinio.'

disorder,' and for every problem of conscience had the unvarying prescription, ' The Archdeacon will set you quite right about that ; no one has got up all that so well as the Archdeacon.'[1] Experts are necessary when you cannot solve a problem for yourself ; they become a gross abuse if they encourage you not to attempt to solve your problems. The aim of moral theology, as of all other branches of theology, is to train men to freedom within the sphere of the Christian tradition ; and to allow them to be content with authority in any sphere of religion—to allow them to remain sheep when they have it in them to become shepherds— is the worst service that can be done both to them and to the Church. It is even true to say that ' within certain limits we should prefer a man to act wrongly on his own judgment than do what was objectively right on another's.'[2]

(3) The emphasis upon the sufficiency of external probability became therefore a danger whenever it absolved men from the duty of attempting to probe their own moral difficulties. It became a flagrant abuse when, for the concurrence of five or six authors of repute as guarantee of the ' probability ' of an opinion, there was substituted the sufficiency of one author only.[3] This is the third count in the indictment against historic probabilism. It is true of course that a mere counting of heads on either side of an argument does not decide the question of truth and falsehood. The one may be right where the many are wrong ; but the burden of proof lies with the one rather than the many. And where the enquirer is allowed to choose his own authority in each case[4] (as obviously he must be allowed, provided that he does not change his allegiance during the course of the case to suit his own interest),[5] the abuse becomes even more startling. Even ' authors of repute ' have their moral blind spots ;

---

[1] A. Trollope, The Warden, c. 3.

[2] H. Rashdall, Theory of Good and Evil, ii. p. 435.

[3] And even of any one modern author (' si liber sit alicujus junioris et moderni '), Prop. 27 damn. ab Alex. VII, 24th Sept. 1665 (Denz.-Bann., No. 1127). This laxity gave rise to Pascal's ejaculation : ' How useful it is to have many writers on moral theology.'

[4] ' The confessor must allow a penitent to follow any " probable " opinion even where his own is more probable '; Azpilcueta, Ench. Conf. 26, 4 ; Alph. Lig. vi. § 604, and commonly.

[5] Lehmkuhl, i. p. 88, and commonly.

and it is not very difficult to fortify one's own desire for freedom by finding an authority, severe enough in other respects, but eccentrically lax on the particular point in question. Where genuine experts disagree, the likelihood— though not the certainty—is that he who is in a minority of one on a particular point will be wrong on that particular point ; and it is a piece of mere hardihood to allow his opinion in such a case to be regarded as ' probable.'

We may acquit the Jesuits—as we said before—of any wide-spread intention of manufacturing lax opinions in order to make salvation cheap and accessible. Apparently grave laxity may be no more than the individual aberration of a faddist ; it may also be simply a recognition of the true solution of a difficulty in extreme or wholly abnormal cases. But, however well-intentioned its origin, it needs drastic safeguards ; and the late seventeenth and the eighteenth centuries were employed by serious-minded Roman Catholic writers, especially in France, in elaborating these safeguards for the general probabilist principle that in case of doubt we may take the benefit of the doubt.[1]

3. *Probabilism and its Safeguards*

We may review the two principal safeguards suggested for probabilism, and enquire whether they are sufficient to enable us to adopt the rule for our purposes.

(1) The doubt must be a genuine doubt ; not a passing fancy or prejudice.[2] The White Queen found it easy to believe half-a-dozen impossible things before breakfast ;

---

[1] It may further be urged against probabilism that it defeated its own end of simplification by over-burdening moral theology with nice distinctions and subdivisions. More than seventy new technical terms were put into currency during the course of the two centuries in which it was the centre of controversy; and though we may attribute this in the main to the exigencies of defending a hardly-pressed doctrine against rigorist attacks, we need not disagree with Concina (*App. ad Theol.* I. diss. iii. c. 12) that the result was to reduce ' theologia ' to ' battalogia.'

[2] *Prop.* 3 *damn. ab Inn. XI*, 2nd Mar. 1679, ' Dum probabilitate sive intrinseca sive extrinseca quantumvis tenui, modo a probabilitatis finibus non exeatur, confisi aliquid agimus, semper prudenter agimus ' (Denz.-Bann., No. 1153).

it is as easy, especially in the present ferment of opinion
in the Church of England, to summon up doubts about all
except perhaps the most absolute principles of conduct.
It is as necessary, therefore, to-day as it was in the seventeenth century, to insist that ' doubt ' must be strictly interpreted in such cases as are to allow of the benefit of the doubt.
In technical language there must at least be a ' probable '
opinion against the law in cases where it is proposed to waive
it—some fact or argument whose force even conscientious
consideration cannot weaken.   A real ambiguity in the
formulation of the law, the undoubted tolerance by authority
of its neglect, the definite exception from its operation of
certain categories of cases into which that under consideration
may reasonably be held to fall, the emergence of an important
fact which obviously never entered into the calculations of
those who formulated the law, nothing less than this would
appear to constitute a ' doubt ' in the technical sense. ' The
doubt,' as Father Rickaby says,[1] ' must not be a mere
negative doubt, or ignorance which cannot tell why it doubts ;
not a vague suspicion or sentimental impression that defies
all intellectual analysis ; not a mere subjective inability
to make up one's mind, but some counter-reason that admits
of positive statement, as we say, " in black and white." '

(2)   But even if we interpret ' doubt ' in a strict sense,
there will yet be genuinely doubtful cases in which the issue
at stake is too serious to allow the benefit of the doubt to
be taken.   One such case—that of the doctor and the operation
—we have already noticed.   No degree of probability that
sepsis would not supervene in any particular case could justify
him in neglecting to sterilize his instruments—he would be
bound in common morality to take the ' safer course.' Similarly it is a rule that no one may carry matches on his person
in the workings of a coal mine.   A visitor going down the
pit might have the strongest possible reasons for supposing
that the matches he carried would strike only on the box ;
he might resolve not in any circumstances to use one until
he reached the surface again ; and in this case it would be a
' probable opinion ' that the rule forbidding matches was

[1] *Moral Philosophy*, p. 156. See further Note D, ' Probable opinions,'
p. 383.

superfluous as far as he was concerned. Nevertheless, he would be guilty of a serious moral lapse if he failed to produce and set aside his matches before entering the workings ; for no due precautions can be superfluous where the lives of others are at stake. Considerations such as these led Pope Innocent XI in 1679 to limit the sphere within which ' probable opinions ' might legitimately be employed, and the benefit of the doubt taken, to cases in which no vital interest was concerned.[1] The limitation is without doubt necessary and salutary, and all modern writers enforce it strongly. ' Probabilism,' they lay down, ' may not be employed where a *certain* end has to be secured '—a ' certain ' end meaning an end which, if not in all circumstances, at all events in the circumstances of the case, has an undoubted claim to be respected, and will certainly be jeopardised by neglect of the ' law.' The ' certain ' ends, which no probable opinion (and even, for the probabiliorist, no ' more probable ' opinion) may allow us to ignore in any case in which they are relevant, are compendiously enumerated in all manuals of moral theology.[2]

(i.) First comes the *attainment of salvation*.[3] The phrase is not a popular one in modern usage ; it carries with it a tinge of selfish particularism which is probably better avoided. But the underlying meaning is clear and necessary enough. We cannot expect to ' attain salvation ' unless we are doing all in our power to make our character and actions conform to the pattern of Christ. If then a principle presented itself which obviously was concerned with the most fundamental matters in Christian morality—a principle whose abandonment by the Christian community as a whole [4] would clearly result in far-reaching and deplorable deviation from that Pattern— it would be one of which we might say that the ' attainment of salvation ' was bound up with it. And under

---

[1] *Propp. damn. ab Inn. XI*, 2nd March 1679, Nos. 1-3 (Denz.-Bann., Nos. 1151-1153). See also Note E, ' Limitations of Probabilism,' *infra* p. 387.

[2] This list from Tanquerey, ii. 221.

[3] *Prop. 4 damn. ab Inn. XI*, 1679 (Denz.-Bann., 1154).

[4] ' As a whole '—because it is an accepted principle that the *individual* (sc. heathen or heretic) may deviate very far from the Christian ideal and yet achieve salvation, provided he is in ' good faith,' or ' doing as much as he can.'—See *Ignorance, etc.*, cc. ii. and iii. ; *supra* p. 249 n. ; and *infra*, Additional Note H, ' Subjective and Objective Necessity,' p. 395.

the restrictions we have just considered, no mere doubt as
to its validity or applicability would justify him in waiving
conformity to it.   There are Christians, for example, who
have serious doubts about prayer.   Their own prayers seem
to them to be wholly without effect in their struggle against
temptation ; and they find it difficult, in addition, to attain
to any theory of prayer which will hold good against deter-
minist objections.   But prayer is obviously a matter which,
if necessary at all, directly concerns the whole moral life
in its most essential particulars.   No mere doubt as to its
utility or reasonableness can therefore exempt an earnest-
minded man from continuing at all events to try to pray.
Only if he were *certain* that prayer was useless in practice and
unjustifiable in theory would he have the moral right to
discontinue it.

(ii.) A second certain end to be secured is *the validity of the
sacraments*.[1]   It is better, of course, to administer or receive
a sacrament in a manner possibly invalid than not to administer or receive it at all ; and we must therefore interpret
this rule of cases in which valid administration is possible,
though perhaps more troublesome than the doubtful method.
It has been argued from time to time, for example, that
baptism with steam or snow is probably valid ; [2] and it
might be held that this was at least a probable opinion.
But it cannot be called *certain* ; and our restriction suggests,
what common-sense endorses, that the priest who on the
basis of this probable opinion neglected the obvious and
relatively easy precaution of melting the snow or condensing
the steam would be guilty of slackness and irreverence, if of
nothing more.

(iii.) The third 'certain' end is much more sweeping, and
its limits in consequence not so clearly defined.   A ' probable '
opinion may not be used where what is at stake is an ' important spiritual or temporal interest (whether our own or
another's) which justice or charity compels us to respect.'
The cases of the precaution before the operation, or the
visitor in the coal mine, are all we need for examples to bear

[1] *Prop.* 1 *damn. ab Inn. XI* (Denz.-Bann., 1151).

[2] Alph. Lig. vi. §§ 102-104.   On frozen wine for the Eucharist, *ib.*
vi. §§ 11, 207.

out fully the truth of this principle. In each case human life is at stake, and therefore no reasonable or normal precaution may be omitted, however unlikely its necessity may appear to be. Naturally enough, it is not always so easy to appreciate whether the ' interest ' at stake is sufficiently important to warrant our refusing to allow the benefit of the doubt, or whether it is one which we are bound to respect— which has an absolute claim upon us. Here, therefore, is a margin of uncertainty in which (as we have urged before) only a man who is himself accustomed to defer to moral claims has the right to be regarded as an authority.[1] But in general, as our examples will perhaps make clear, it is not so difficult to decide on these principles in what cases the benefit of the doubt may legitimately be taken ; and the result tends to confirm the opinion that, if strictly guarded in the various ways which history has endorsed, probabilism is a doctrine which accords with the verdict of common-sense and Christian prudence.

The importance of the two main safeguards we have arrived at—that the ' doubt ' must be a real and legitimate one, and that the ' benefit of the doubt ' may not be taken where what we may call vital interests are at stake—could be illustrated by countless instances. The inimitable opening scene of ' Sense and Sensibility,' in which Mrs. John Dashwood whittles away her husband's charitable intentions towards his mother and sister, not only shows how illegitimate doubts can insinuate themselves into conscience, but also exemplifies the taking of the benefit of the doubt where no doubt, however legitimate, could justify it. More striking even, because of the gravity of its theme, is the central incident of ' Romola.' Tito Melema, the pliable and self-seeking character round whom the story revolves, has good reason to suppose that his benefactor, Baldassare, is dead ; but the evidence is not final. Shall he, then, dissipate his patron's wealth in what will almost certainly prove to be a

---

[1] Sylvester Prierias (*Summa,* s.v. ' Dubium,' § 4) suggests that where there is ' doubt as to the character of a doubt ' the usual principles apply, e.g. if it were doubtful whether a doubtful law concerned a vital interest, we should still have to behave as though it did, in spite of the double doubt. There is a nicety of discrimination about this which makes criticism or discussion almost impossible. The point is not commonly reproduced.

vain search for him, or put it to his own private uses ? The doubt is in every sense legitimate. The opinion that the search will be fruitless is based not merely on 'probable,' but even on 'most probable' grounds ; and Tito takes advantage of it accordingly. But the 'outward law which the great heart of mankind makes for every individual man,' and its reflex, the 'inward shame which will exist even in the absence of the sympathetic impulses which need no law,' proclaim unhesitatingly that he has no real alternative but to go in search of his benefactor. Life is at stake, and a life whose preservation at all costs is a duty of gratitude ; no doubt, however reasonable, can avail to waive duty in such a case.[1]　Nevertheless, Tito takes the inexcusable step, ignores the claims of duty, and stifles conscience at the bidding of selfishness.

Three weeks later he receives convincing proof that Baldassare is alive. If duty had been clear before, it is even clearer now. Yet once again Tito evades it, this time by summoning up a whole host of illegitimate doubts, and convincing himself that in virtue of them he is exempted from his obligation. 'Certainly the florins were in a sense Baldassare's—in the narrow sense by which the right of possession is determined in ordinary affairs ; but in that larger and more radically natural view in which the world belongs to youth and strength, they were rather his who could extract the most pleasure out of them. That, he was conscious, was not the sentiment which the complicated play of human feelings had engendered in society. . . . But what was the sentiment of society ? A mere tangle of anomalous traditions and opinions that no wise man would take as a guide, except so far as his own comfort was concerned. . . . Any maxims that required a man to fling away the good that was needed to make existence sweet were only the lining of human selfishness turned outward ; they were made by men who wanted others to sacrifice themselves for their sake. . . . Could any philosophy prove to him that he was bound to care for another's suffering more than for his own ? '[2]　So the old legitimate doubts having been laid to rest by certainty, the new invalid doubts are invented to give a liberty which even the old doubts could

---

[1] G. Eliot, *Romola*, c. ix.　　　　　　　[2] *Ibid.* c. xi.

not justify ; and by sweeping away the double safeguard Tito is free to set conscience at defiance and enter the path which leads to his final downfall. It was against all analogous perversions of the true principle, *Lex dubia non obligat,* that the reforming popes set up their twofold restrictions.

4. *Fasting Communion—Confession—Clerical Celibacy*

Probabilism, as reformed and restricted by these means, offers us a working principle at all events with which to approach our doubts. Experiment alone will show whether its application produces results which the Christian conscience can endorse. The most obvious—though not necessarily the most serious—cases of doubt for Anglicans are those in which a principle strongly affirmed by the rest of western Catholicism, and formerly affirmed by canonical authority in the Church of England, is to-day disregarded in the latter communion. We have accepted the claim made in the English Articles that a particular or national Church has the right to re-interpret or revise for itself principles hitherto held in common with other branches of the Church ; and have seen reason to hold that this right cannot strictly be limited to what are commonly called ' purely ceremonial ' matters. But we have repeatedly insisted upon the fact that the existence of the right does not guarantee infallibility in its exercise. Where, then, an Anglican is seriously disturbed as to the differences between England and Rome, and does not know to which discipline to conform, we cannot reassure him by saying ' Of course the Church of England must be right.' His doubt is perfectly valid and reasonable. He may prefer Anglicanism *as a whole* to Rome, but he can perfectly well hesitate to accept the Anglican rule (which is almost always a permission to do something which Rome forbids) in any particular case in which it runs counter to that of Rome.

As the principal ground for doubt in these cases is simply the fact of the difference between the two communions, it matters little whether the Anglican variation is the result of canonical enactment or customary disuse. The fact that Anglicanism has rejected a rule is quite enough in itself to

make it genuinely doubtful, whichever form the rejection
may, in fact, have taken ; and the individual is free to take
the benefit of the doubt unless some vital interest is at
stake.   The crux of the enquiry therefore must always
be whether such an interest is jeopardised by the Anglican
permission or not ; and each case must be treated on its
merits in accordance with the answer given in the particular
matter at issue.

The method can be most simply illustrated by an examination of three problems concerned with order or discipline, in
which it is at least probable that no vital interest is concerned.
It may of course be said that all disciplinary divergences between England and Rome imperil the cause of reunion, and
that this is beyond all question a matter of vital importance.
But to this it is reasonable to reply that the only *vital* point at
issue between England and Rome is that of the papal claims;
and that variations on minor points of discipline would matter
little if this fundamental stumbling-block to reunion were
removed.

Before attacking these three problems, however, we must
deal with a consideration which, it may be supposed, dominates a good deal of discussion on points of this character.
It appears often to be assumed that purely ' human,' ' ecclesiastical ' or ' ceremonial ' ordinances are matters of no moral
significance.   They do not seem to bear upon any of the
great Christian principles of justice, benevolence, truthfulness and the like.   In consequence many of their detractors
speak of them as matters of indifference, to be adopted or
disregarded at. the pure whim of the Christian ; whilst some
at least of their champions make no attempt to defend them
on any other grounds than that the Church has ordained
them—as though they were merely vexatious and meaningless commands, designed to no purpose except to elicit blind
and unquestioning obedience.   It cannot be too strongly
asserted that this assumption, in either or both of its forms,
is wholly unwarranted.   If we have admitted an admixture
of human promulgation even in the most ' divine ' of moral
laws, we must at all events be prepared to admit an element
of the divine—a bearing upon the requirements of genuine
moral behaviour—in the most human or ' ecclesiastical ' of

laws ; and if such an element can be elicited, it is of profound importance that it should be set in the forefront of any apologia that is made. Counsel is never more darkened than when that which can be vindicated on rational grounds is championed on wholly or almost wholly irrational ones.

Thus of fasting communion, for example, it might reasonably be said as follows. Fasting—the moderate discipline of natural appetites—has an obvious moral value, recognised as much by psychologists as by ecclesiastics. It makes for that ' organic hardihood ' which William James set out as one of the conditions of the highest character. Christianity has used it to that end, and has in the past given it an additional specialised function in emphasising the solemnity of her distinctive sacraments. Baptism,[1] confirmation,[2] ordination [3] were all preceded by a fast. It is perhaps a small matter, and yet it is after all possible that a man or woman who deliberately and for no good reason rejects such an opportunity and occasion of self-discipline before the solemn act of receiving Holy Communion is one who regards religion, if not morality as well, as something to be embraced only if it does not interfere with comfort. From this point of view the fast before communion might reasonably be presented as a simple and natural piece of self-discipline, all the more significant in that it calls to mind the reverence and solemnity with which the sacrament should be invested in a Christian's eyes. The argument would carry different weight with different minds, but at least no one could say any longer that the practice it was designed to support was of an entirely non-moral character. The same consideration applies with even greater force to the other two ecclesiastical problems which, with that of fasting communion, we propose to consider.

(1) *Fasting Communion.*—The fast before communion is undoubtedly a practice of great antiquity and universality,[4] to which the pre-Reformation English Church never wavered in her allegiance.[5] It has never been officially abrogated by English canonical enactment, and can be supported by

[1] *Did.* vii. 4 ; Justin, *Apol.* i. 61.
[2] *C.J.C.* c. 6, D. v., *de consecr.*
[3] *C.J.C.* c. 4, D. lxxv., from Leo, *Ep.* lxxix.
[4] E.g. Augustine, *Ep.* cxviii. ad Jan. ; *C.J.C.* c. 54, D. ii., *de consecr.*
[5] E.g. Const. Sudbury (1378), § 4 (Wilkins, iii. p. 135).

reasonable argument, as we have just seen, as a laudable practice. It is not therefore a wholly negligible principle ; it is no mere scruple or fancy that calls for its consideration. On the other hand, for an Anglican its obligation is extremely doubtful. Within the Church of England it has most certainly been abrogated by legitimate custom ; the arguments sometimes used to invalidate this conclusion (as that the Church of England has no right to waive, either by enactment or desuetude, an ecumenical custom ; or that the mediæval canon law is still binding in the English Church) have been considered and dismissed at an earlier stage [1] By the operation of custom, and with the full consent of authority, the Church of England offers her members complete freedom in the matter. But is she right in doing so ? Can they, without disloyalty to the Church *as a whole*, avail themselves of that freedom ? The law of fasting communion is at least doubtful for us ; but may we take the benefit of the doubt ?

The point to consider, as was suggested a moment ago, is simply whether any matter of vital interest is involved. Where a purely ecclesiastical law is concerned, this can only be the case if the obligation involved is admittedly a ' grave ' one ; that is, if it is concerned with a weighty question of behaviour, to whose gravity attention is drawn in suitable and explicit language, and whose observance is made a serious matter of loyalty by the competent lawgiver.[2] It is true that the Church of Rome still asserts the law of fasting communion to be of such a character. But recent legislation, even in that Church itself, has widely extended the possibility of dispensation from it in cases not merely of urgent necessity but even of moderate inconvenience,[3] thus reducing materially the likelihood of its general spiritual necessity. The conclusion seems inevitable. The law is frankly doubtful for the Anglican. It affects no matter of vital importance. Beyond all question no conceivable obligation of loyalty

---

[1] *Supra* pp. 89-97. [2] Suarez, *de Legg.* iv. 18.

[3] *Cod. Jur. Can.* 858, § 2 ; *A.S.S.* xxxix. 603, 604 (1906) ; *A.S.S.* xl. 344 (1907)—of invalids ; *A.A.S.* xv. 151, 152 (1923)—of priests whose duty requires them to duplicate, or to celebrate at a late hour of the morning. In urgent cases of this character, the ordinary may dispense from the rule to the extent of allowing liquid nourishment to be taken ; in less urgent cases the matter is to be referred to the Congregation of the Sacred Office.

could require him to conform to the mediæval and Roman practice.

But the implications of this conclusion must be noticed. They absolutely prohibit the Anglican priest from refusing communion to non-fasting communicants, or the Anglican confessor from refusing absolution on the same grounds.[1] As far as the direct requirements of loyalty are concerned, the Anglican is perfectly free to ignore the practice of the fast before communion. But this does not mean that he is free to put the matter altogether out of his mind without further consideration. The practice has a vast weight of Christian experience in its support. To a large extent both psychology and religion suggest that, for those who are able to conform, it offers opportunities of self-discipline not lightly to be ignored. It cannot be demanded of all as a matter of loyalty ; but it may well be a duty for many— perhaps for the majority of normal Christians—as a practice essential to their personal advancement in spiritual and moral strength.

We have a perfect right to insist upon these considerations with emphasis, and to urge that the individual Christian is shirking a moral task of real importance if he does not face and answer for himself the question—' Though loyalty does not demand of me that I should fast before my communions, is not the practice a duty imposed by the needs of my developing spiritual life ? ' In answering this question he would be bound to consider such matters as physical health, opportunity and the like. But if no serious obstacle presented itself in these respects, it is more than possible that the fast before communion, though not an obligation of loyalty, would reveal itself to him as a duty demanded by the general sustenance of his Christian zeal and earnestness.

(2) *Confession of Mortal Sin before Communion.*—Much the same considerations seem to apply to the problem of confession of mortal sin before communion. Here again is an ecclesiastical law of long-standing fully recognised by

---

[1] Unless, of course, despite all that can be said on the other side, the priest is ' invincibly ' certain that the law is essential to salvation. It is inconceivable that any sane person should take this view ; but if he did, his action would still be limited by the considerations below, p. 283.

the pre-Reformation Church of England,[1] and still enforced in the Roman communion,[2] which modern English authority and custom have allowed to lapse into almost complete disuse. So far we are on common ground with the fast before communion. Differences however appear at two points. In the first place, the Exhortation in the English Communion Office enjoins the duty of confession before communion upon all who are unable by means of self-examination and direct confession to God, ' with full purpose of amendment,' to secure a full trust in God's mercy and a quiet conscience. In the second place, a number of Roman Catholic authorities regard the practice as established by divine law,[3] and therefore as essential to salvation;[4] an opinion partially at least borne out by the established rule that not even the Pope can dispense from it. Azpilcueta, Caietan, and among modern authorities Noldin, dispute this opinion, it is true. But their hesitations are of no practical importance, since it is universally held that the practice is obligatory *sub gravi* by virtue of the Tridentine decrees, and consequently a matter of vital importance.[5]

How far, if at all, do these differences from the previous case affect the problem? An Anglican whose conscience bade him observe the rule, whatever his Church said about it, would of course be in no difficulty; nor would an Anglican who had no scruples in accepting the English position. Our concern is with the Anglican who, while recognising that a great deal could be said in favour of the nullity of the rule in his communion, is not wholly convinced on the point. For him it is still a rule, though—in virtue of the relative cogency of the Anglican position—a definitely doubtful rule.

---

[1] E.g. *Lib. Leg. Eccl.*, ascr. Theodulph, A.D. 994 (c. 44, Wilkins, i. p. 281); Council of Eynsham, A.D. 1009 (can. 17, *ibid.* i. p. 289); Council of Durham, A.D. 1220 (*ibid.* i. p. 577); Const. of Abp. Peckham, A.D. 1281 (c. 1, *ibid.* ii. p. 52).

[2] Conc. Trid. *Sess.* xiii., *Decret.* c. 7; *can.* 1 (Denz.-Bann, Nos. 880, 893), based on 1 Cor. xi. 28, thereafter commonly.

[3] Alph. Lig. vi. § 256, and authors there quoted. Cp. Prümmer, iii. pp. 140, 141.

[4] Tanquerey, ii. pp. 131-151, on the divine law :—' Lex evangelica complectitur . . . praecepta quae servare necesse est ut vitam aeternam consequamur.'

[5] Prümmer, iii. p. 141.

But, although doubtful, it is a rule whose observance those who support it regard as vitally important, and consequently it would seem to be wrong for anyone who hesitated to regard it as definitely abrogated to take (or allow) the benefit of the doubt and ignore it. What, then, is the doubtful conscience to decide in the matter?

Once again, we must beware of regarding the question as a trivial matter of 'mere ceremonial.' The problem again involves the conditions of worthy approach to the central Christian sacrament. 'I am not convinced,' it might well be said, 'that a man has made such preparation for receiving the sacrament as the law of reverence demands, if—after conscious mortal sin—he fails to add sacramental confession to such repentance as in other ways he has shown. And voluntary irreverence in such a matter is surely a very grave offence—it is, in other words, the adoption of an attitude towards God which may undermine the foundations of the whole moral life.' We need not stop either to justify or to rebut such a position; but we must recognise that it appears to make it imperative for any one who holds it to insist upon conformity as a condition of communion.

At the same time, we have the right (and indeed the duty too) to press for the grounds on which the waverer thinks it possible that the matter is one in which a vital interest is at stake. He must elect either for 'external' or 'internal' probability. His 'external' ground can only be that the Roman communion asserts the practice to be essential; and he must then be prepared to give his reasons for accepting Roman authority on this head when—by virtue of his very position as an Anglican—he rejects it in matters of even more fundamental importance. His only refuge from this dilemma will be that of 'internal' probability; he accepts the Roman statement *not* because it is a Roman statement, but because he himself thinks it possible that the practice in question is essential to full moral progress. And he must be willing to accept the word 'essential' in its fullest implications, as meaning not merely 'conducive' or 'helpful' to morality, nor essential for certain persons or at a particular epoch only, but as a *sine quâ non* of the moral life for the Church as a whole. Only if he means 'essential' in this latter sense can he say that a general abandonment of the practice would perhaps jeopardise the fundamental well-being of the Church, and so be justified in treating the rule as one which even doubt will not allow us to disregard.

The point is at once so important and yet so involved that it would be well to illustrate it further. For centuries it was unanimously held—with what justification we need not ask—that the monastic life was an 'easier,' 'better' or 'more certain' way of attaining salvation than the secular. But the Church never allowed this conviction to carry with it the conclusion that all men must take monastic vows. There was no doubt that salvation *could* (with greater difficulty) be attained in the secular life, and that, in consequence, to remain 'in the world' was legitimate to the Christian, whether layman or priest. Thus the principle seems clearly established that if two courses both lead to the same goal, we are not bound in all cases to take the easier or safer of them, even though the goal is one which *must* be reached. The most ardent champions of monasticism were not prepared to say, 'It is possible that only the monastic life leads to salvation,' or 'It is possible that the secular life is a *cul-de-sac* which can never reach salvation;' and unless they were prepared to subscribe to these two propositions they were not in a position to preach or enforce the universal obligation of monastic vows.

The parallel may be strictly applied. An Anglican priest may think the practice of confession of mortal sin before communion an easier, better, more helpful method of reaching the goal of the Christian life than its neglect. But unless he is prepared to go further and say, 'It is possible that this practice is so vital to the Christian life that its abandonment, even by the considered judgment of the whole Church, would result in the gravest moral deterioration,' he has no right whatever to preach its universal obligation, or to make it an irreducible condition of communion. He may commend it with all the eloquence and zeal at his disposal, provided that he indicates the non-authoritative character of his teaching, but he is going beyond all catholic principles if he insists upon it.[1]

[1] The conclusion carries with it identical implications for the individual as in the preceding case. *Supra*, p. 279.

But even if the priest is prepared to accept the word 'essential' in all its implications, as we have just expressed them, he is still not free to attempt to *enforce* the practice in question.   Before doing so he would be bound to consider *first*, whether his ordination vows did not prohibit his making a demand so plainly in excess of anything required by contemporary usage ; and *second*, whether the obvious disturbance of the doctrinal and ritual unity and constitutional stability of the Church involved in his action would not outweigh in gravity any good results which might come from his nonconformity.   Thus, even in the unlikely event of his being able conscientiously to settle the question of his ordination vows in his own favour, he would still be faced by a 'conflict of evils' of the kind to be discussed in the next chapter.

With all this in view, it seems that only in the rarest possible instances will it be legitimate for a priest to enforce demands not required by the established usages of the body to which he has promised allegiance.   Still more stringent would this conclusion be where that which he defied was not merely an established usage (or disuse), but a canonical and unambiguous formula authoritatively declared to be still in vigour.   Here, so far from being free to *enforce* his demands, he would be obliged, as was indicated on a previous page,[1] to consider very carefully the question of his ordination vows before beginning even to *teach* in a sense contrary to the formula.[2]   And in either case, if what has previously been said holds good,[3] he would be bound to take immediate steps to inform his bishop of his contemplated course of action ; as also to defer to the decision of the Church if she offered him the alternatives of silence or resignation.

(3) *Clerical Celibacy.*—Mid-way between the two cases just considered comes the problem of clerical celibacy, which first of all drew attention to this whole question of ' doubt ' in our original discussion of loyalty.   As with fasting com-

---

[1] *Supra* p. 230.

[2] If the formula involved a genuine ambiguity (whether recognised or not) it would of course be legitimate for him to expose the fact and advocate his own interpretation until the matter was authoritatively settled in one sense or the other ; but *not* to attempt to enforce any demand in excess of ordinary usage.

[3] *Supra* pp. 234-240.

munion and confession before communion, the principle that a clerk in major orders may not marry (or re-marry), and that (conversely) marriage is an ' irregularity' (impediment) to Holy Orders, is of very great antiquity, fully maintained— in its first branch—by the Eastern Churches, and in both branches by the Church of Rome. It is generally held to be of graver obligation than the fast before communion ; on the other hand, in contrast to the confession of mortal sin, no one has ever suggested that it is anything more than an obligation of human or ecclesiastical law.[1] Rare instances of official dispensation from it for priests and deacons are known to have occurred even in the Roman communion, as for example in the case of clergy who married during the ecclesiastical chaos of Henry VIII's reign, or of the French Revolution.[2] Indeed, comparatively recent papal legislation allows to bishops,[3] and even to priests,[4] the power of giving a dispensation in this matter *in articulo mortis* to deacons and their accomplices who have been guilty of the offence. Of priests the strongest thing that can be said is that they are ' scarcely ever' allowed to marry, although for bishops a dispensation is never given.[5] Furthermore, though Holy Orders are an annulling impediment to matrimony, this is only the case if at the time of ordination the candidate was clearly aware that the obligation of celibacy was annexed to his new condition ;[6] and the obligation itself is based not entirely upon the ecclesiastical law which requires it, but also upon the vow of celibacy annexed by implication to major orders in the Roman Church.

On all these grounds, therefore, we must conclude that the duty of clerical celibacy (apart from the special question of a vow of celibacy) is regarded by the Roman Church as in itself less urgent than that of confession of mortal sin before communion. The Anglican, therefore, who is disposed

---

[1] *S.T.* ii. 2, q. 88, a.11, and commonly.

[2] Migne-André, *Dictionnaire du Droit Canon* (Paris, 1862), i. 1146; Prümmer, iii. p. 582; Lehmkuhl, ii. p. 534; Tanq, i, 595.

[3] Leo XIII (1888); Prümmer, iii. pp. 578, 582; Lehmkuhl, ii. p. 566.

[4] Pius X (1909); *ibid.*

[5] Prümmer, *ut sup.*

[6] As, of course, in the Roman communion he always would be— Prümmer, iii. 579 f.; Lehmkuhl, ii. p. 434.

to think that the language of Article XXXII does not entirely relieve him of the duty of considering the problem, has even less reason in this case than in the former for holding that conformity to the Roman rule is incumbent upon him. The same argument may be pressed as before.   Unless he is prepared to admit as a reasonable possibility that the marriage of clergy, even if deliberately allowed in all branches of the Church, would produce irretrievable moral disaster, he has no cause on grounds of loyalty to think himself bound, and no right to think other clergy bound, to remain celibate.

This, again, does not imply that on other grounds, peculiar to his own case, a priest might not quite rightly conclude that God meant him to remain celibate, just as a married layman might on other grounds quite reasonably conclude that marriage made it impossible for him to be ordained. But in neither case does loyalty demand the conclusion, or indeed affect the question at all.   Loyalty, however, does impose an obligation in this case, which was not in the same measure operative in either of the previous two.   *There* the abrogation of the mediæval rule in the English Church was the work of custom ;   *here* it is the result of deliberate canonical enactment.   Custom has in the abstract the same rights of abrogation as law ;   but ordination vows do not demand of us the same punctiliousness in the observance of the customs as in the observance of the canons of our Church. It might be in some slight degree excusable for a priest or confessor to teach, though not to insist upon, the universal obligation of fast or confession before communion even in the face of the Anglican disuse of those practices, though we have suggested that it could be only *justified* by a conscientious conviction that they were perhaps universally necessary to salvation.   But it would be almost if not quite inexcusable for him even to teach, and still more to attempt to enforce, the obligation of clerical celibacy in the face of the unequivocal language of the English Article.   And even if he brought himself to believe this course permissible in spite of his ordination vows, he would be bound as in those other two problems to consider the inevitable conflict of evils involved, and to submit the matter to the bishop, before taking action.

The same conclusion, in all its stringency, must hold good whenever a minister makes up his mind to teach doctrines, or initiate practices, which run counter to the explicit statements of the Anglican formularies, in so far as those statements are officially declared to be still in full vigour.

5. *The Papal Claims*

The last three cases have dealt with minor doubts caused principally by the divergence between Anglicanism and Rome. The major doubt—that as to the validity of the Anglican rejection of the papal claims—must next come into question. Once again the discussion centres round the problem, Is any matter of vital importance involved? But here the restriction, that the benefit of the doubt may not be taken in such cases, is urged against the Anglican with what at first sight seems conclusive effect. Among the lax propositions condemned by Innocent XI in 1679 is one to the effect that ' an infidel who refuses belief on the grounds of a less probable opinion will be forgiven his infidelity.' [1] It is only fair to the Jesuits to notice (surprising though it may seem when their position as the ' active squad ' [2] of the papacy is taken into account) that they were the authors of this liberal opinion, and explicitly took it to mean that ' a Protestant might stay in his own religion even if he thought Romanism was more probably, or even most probably, the true faith.' [3] The doctrine was, however, rightly condemned; and on this condemnation is based the general restriction that probabilism may not be used where salvation is at stake. This is applied by Fr. Slater [4] as follows : ' The law which makes the attainment of the end obligatory makes it also obligatory to use safe means, not merely probable means,

---

[1] *Prop. damn.*, etc., No. 4 ; Denz.-Bann., 1154, ' Ab infidelitate excusabitur infidelis non credens, ductus opinione minus probabili.'

[2] Harnack, *History of Dogma* (E.T.), vii. p. 103.

[3] Döllinger-Reusch, pp. 110, 111. The German writers give the Jesuits singularly little credit for this amazing piece of broad-mindedness. Bremond, *Histoire du Sentiment Religieux*, i. p. 414 (with special reference to Bonal, the Franciscan) recognises the full significance of this triumph of humanism over dogma.

[4] *Cases of Conscience*, i. 55.

to attain it. And so an Anglican who thinks that Anglicanism is probably the true form of Christianity is not justified in exposing his salvation to risk by remaining an Anglican.'

We may put this in a simpler form. ' There is no salvation outside the true Church,' says the Roman controversialist ; and having thus nailed his flag to the mast he continues: ' You doubt the truth of this statement ? You think it a trifle uncertain ? Quite so, I do not ask you to admit any- thing whatever that you are not honestly prepared to admit. But note that your doubt, uncertainty, hesitation does not protect you in this matter. If the law I have stated is even *possibly* true, it affects a vital interest ; and in such a case neither probabilism nor common-sense exempts you from the duty of conformity.' The argument seems logical and cogent, and would appear to carry its conclusion with it. At first sight our reformed probabilism seems to lead us direct to Rome. But as a matter of fact the whole train of reasoning is based on a curious misuse of words due in origin to conventional politeness alone. When we say to an opponent, ' I doubt the truth of your statement,' we may mean simply, ' I am not convinced by what you urge on its behalf.' But the same form of words serves the purpose of a polite but none the less emphatic denial ; it may mean, ' I deny your statement *in toto*, but in deference to the courtesies of discussion I veil my denial under the decent euphemism of doubt.' To ' doubt ' a statement in the strict sense of the word implies at least to admit the *possibility* of its truth ; but in the controversial usage dictated by politeness to ' doubt ' a statement is tantamount to ' denying ' it.

And it is surely in *this* sense, and not in the sense insinuated by Fr. Slater, that all Anglicans ' doubt ' the Roman claims. In so far as those claims carry with them the principle that unconditional submission to the papal jurisdiction is of the essence of Christianity, the ' doubt ' we express can only be interpreted as involving a polite but final denial. When we admit our ' uncertainty ' as to the truth in question, we in fact assert its absolute falsity. If we allow it to be said that we ' think that Anglicanism is probably the true form of Christianity,' we imply at the very least that we believe Anglicanism (involving, as it does, the rejection of the papal claims in any form in which they would be recognised by modern Rome) to be *without doubt* one of the true forms of Christianity, and perhaps that we think it to be *probably* the truest form at present in existence. The 'probably' qualifies an implied 'truest,' not the spoken 'true.' 'No salvation outside the Church of Rome' is not a 'doubtful' truth to the Anglican. It is an undoubted falsehood; and with the recognition of this fact the whole ambitious argument based on the equivocal phrases just considered collapses like a house of cards.

We may press to its full the argument from the 'religious' and the 'secular' lives used in a previous case. An Anglican may hold many different views about the Roman claims. He may think that membership in the Roman Church is the better or easier way of achieving salvation; or that the chair of Peter is entitled to a 'primacy of honour'; or that in a reunited Church the Pope should have the same 'primacy of jurisdiction' as the Head of a College has among the Fellows; or that 'by divine providence' he has exercised in the past, should exercise in the present, and may again exercise in the future, a similar primacy. But none of these positions, whether held as 'possible,' 'probable' or 'certain,' carries with it the vestige of an obligation *per se* to join the Church of Rome of to-day, which claims a wholly different position in Christendom; any more than the stoutest champions of monasticism could for a moment assert an obligation *per se* on any Christian to take monastic vows.

Fr. Slater's argument, therefore, does not affect the question unless we are prepared to admit that Anglicanism, and all other non-Roman forms of Christianity into the bargain, might be in this or some other vital respect wholly contradictory of the true ideal of Christian polity, whilst Rome (conversely) might in all of them be right. Even so the argument is ineffective. Our choice still lies only between a number of communions any or all of which might prove (so far as we know) to be wholly debarred from leading their members to salvation. And if, where either of two courses is 'safe,' we are not bound in all circumstances to take the 'safer,' still less are we bound to take the 'safer' course (if the word can be used at all in this connection) where all possible courses are admittedly 'unsafe.' But enough has been said for our immediate purposes. Fr. Slater's argument is valid only for an Anglican who is certain that the Roman communion provides all the conditions necessary for salvation, whilst doubting whether the Church of England does the same. And how many such Anglicans are there ? [1]

It might, however, be said, ' I agree that submission to Rome is not a *sine quâ non* of salvation, and on these grounds there is no reason why I should secede from Anglicanism. But it is doubtful whether the reunion of Christendom will ever be attained apart from our acceptance of the Roman claims, and that reunion is a matter of vital importance. Does not this make it incumbent upon me, if not to join the Church of Rome here and now, at all events to urge the acceptance of those claims upon the Church of England ? '

The argument brings us face to face with the ambiguity of the phrase ' the papal claims.' If it means the traditional

[1] Certain minor points in connection with this discussion may here be noticed : (*a*) The argument deals with objective conditions only. As before, there may be subjective circumstances in any individual case which make it obligatory for an individual to take the ' safer ' of two ' safe ' courses. Thus a Christian might quite conceivably be under the moral obligation of entering the religious life, for reasons of which we have no knowledge, whilst fully admitting the general ' safety ' or legitimacy of the secular life. Similarly, an Anglican might be morally convinced—on what grounds it does not matter—that to become a Roman Catholic was the *only safe* course *for him*, whilst not convinced that Anglicanism was ' objectively ' or universally ' unsafe.' But in either case, the obligation arises not from the greater ' safety ' of the course preferred, but from considerations distinctive of the particular case. The instance therefore would have no bearing whatever upon our conclusion, which is concerned wholly with the obligation of the law ' nulla salus extra ecclesiam ' *per se* in cases where it is alleged to be possibly true, but not certain. (*b*) An Anglican might say, ' I pass no judgment on the Roman claim in general ; such matters are too deep for me. But I think it *possible* that I myself cannot achieve salvation as an Anglican, whereas I might as a Roman. Doesn't this carry with it the obligation to join the Church of Rome ? ' This position merely reintroduces the whole argument in a subjective form. We should have to ask, ' Are you *certain* that you will achieve salvation as a Roman ? ' If he replied in the negative (as surely he would) his position would simply be, ' I may lose salvation either as an Anglican or (though this is less likely) as a Roman : I may achieve it either as an Anglican or (though this is more likely) as a Roman.' As before, there is no obligation on him to take the more likely course (merely because *it is the more likely*), else every pre-Reformation Christian would have been a monk. (*c*) In so far as Fr. Slater's argument is valid, the opposite view is equally valid, viz., ' An Anglican who thinks that Romanism is probably the true form of Christianity is not justified in exposing his salvation to risk by becoming a Roman.' In either case there is, in fact, a suppressed premiss (in the first, ' Rome is safe, anyhow ' ; in the second ' Anglicanism is safe, anyhow ') ; and it is upon the truth or otherwise of these respective premisses that the argument really depends.

' Nulla salus extra ecclesiam,' as interpreted by Rome, then
it is a flat denial of a fundamental truth about the Christian
polity ; and nothing whatever could justify an Anglican
who held it to be false either in acting as though it were true
himself or in urging its acceptance upon others. If the phrase
had any of the other meanings we have suggested, it might
reasonably be held that a priest would not be false to his
ordination vows in laying emphasis upon them and urging
their acceptance ; but neither he nor any other could be
required to leave the Church of England for the Church of
Rome on that account. The reunion of Christendom will
never be achieved on the basis of what is untrue ; and so long
as ' ecclesia ' means the Roman communion, and no more,
the phrase ' nulla salus,' so far from uniting Christians, is the
primary cause of their unhappy divisions.

6. ' Birth-Control '

The last four problems have all involved questions of
a semi-ecclesiastical character ; and despite our repeated
suggestion that so-called ' ecclesiastical ' problems may be
none the less ' moral ' as well, there will be those who view
all four with a certain impatience, as being unworthy of the
attention of a serious Christian. The problem of ' birth-
control ' takes us into the fully ' moral ' sphere, and involves
new and interesting questions of general application. It does
not, however, take us altogether out of the ' ecclesiastical '
sphere, for various branches of the Christian Church have
expressed themselves with emphasis on the subject. It is a
question therefore which, as matters stand to-day, a churchman cannot consider altogether out of relation to the factor of
loyalty. He may indeed ask, ' What ought to be the attitude
of the Church in this matter ? ' But the more immediate
question is, ' What ought to be the attitude of the Christian
or his confessor in the matter, the attitude of the Church
being actually what it is ? ' At the present moment the
problem is not one which is left wholly to the decision of
the individual conscience by the Church ; such a problem
will be provided for us by our next and final case of doubt.

Practices analogous to the modern use of contraceptives (' venena sterilitatis ') were condemned as long ago as St. Augustine's time ; and the condemnation is repeatedly enforced, e.g., by Peter Lombard.[1] St. Thomas states a principle on which the prohibition both of *coitus interruptus* and of the use of contraceptives can be based, and regards it as pertaining unequivocally to the ' natural law.'[2] It is possible that in this he was unconsciously guilty of some confusion of thought ;[3] but the point is not important for our present purpose. In the Roman communion the principle has apparently been wholly unchallenged ; the condemnation of all forms of ' birth-control ' was repeatedly reiterated in the nineteenth century ; and the duty of teaching against it repeatedly imposed upon parish priests and confessors.[4]

In the Church of England, however, this ' traditional ' view has within recent years been vehemently challenged. It is sometimes suggested that the movement for a repeal of the prohibition against birth-control by the Church is due to the greater stringency of modern economic conditions, or to the fact that a new sense of the value of the mother's life has made a maximum interpretation of the command to ' increase and multiply ' untenable. Neither of these suggestions, however, is borne out by the facts. Arguments such as those of the danger attending another confinement, or of the necessity of limiting the number of children imposed by inadequate incomes, were well known and fully discussed as long ago as the fifteenth century.[5] No doubt there are novelties in the modern situation which must be taken into account, and some of them at least appeal to motives which every one will respect. Thus, while it is beyond question true that the use of contraceptives is often merely the outcome of a selfish desire for personal comfort and relative affluence on the part of husband and wife, combined with a defective sense of citizenship, there are better and more Christian arguments in support of the

---

[1] Aug., *De Nupt. et Con.* i. 15 ; Pet. Lomb., *Sent.* iv. d. 31.

[2] *C. Gent.* iii. 122 ; *S.T.* ii. 2, q. 154, a. 1.

[3] I hope to take another opportunity of dealing with St. Thomas's apparent ambiguities and confusion in this matter.

[4] Replies of S. Off., May 21, 1851 ; April 19, 1853 ; March 30, 1889; of S. Pen., March 10, 1886 ; November 13, 1901 ; September 2, 1904.

[5] Gabriel Biel († 1495), *Summa in Sent.*, iv, d. 31, q. 1.

practice ; and some of these have a force to-day which they lacked in the past. Within the last hundred years, for example, the Christian world has gained an appreciation of the value in God's sight, as well as in man's, of the happiness of children, which can without exaggeration be called an ethical discovery of incalculable importance. We may, indeed, think it misguided to attempt to promote this end by limiting families to one or two children, but the underlying motive is beyond criticism. Again, the change in the position of women which the last half-century has witnessed, and which has resulted in the throwing open of practically every profession to women on equal terms with men, has led to a natural, proper, and wholly Christian demand that the wife should not be forced, by the exigencies of married life, to abandon all the activities in which she found her interests and occupation before marriage. Once more, it may be argued that this demand is not in itself of such outstanding importance as to justify family limitation by methods of ' birth-control ' ; but at least we must admit that those who take the contrary view are serious-minded people whose opinions deserve an impartial and sympathetic hearing.

It is not surprising, therefore, in face of these facts, that Anglicanism hesitates to endorse what we have called the ' traditional,' or ' Roman Catholic,' view. In the Lambeth Conference of 1908, the bishops denounced the use of contraceptives in the strongest possible terms, and ' earnestly called upon all Christian people to discountenance the use of all artificial means of restriction as demoralising to character and hostile to national welfare.' [1] In many respects this attitude was perpetuated by the Conference of 1920, which ' regarded with grave concern the spread in modern society of theories and practices hostile to the family,' and ' uttered an emphatic warning against the use of unnatural means for the avoidance of conception, together with the grave dangers—physical, moral, and religious—thereby incurred, and against the evils with which the extension of such use threatens the race.' [2] At first sight this appears definite enough. But, as I have

---

[1] *Lambeth Conference Report*, 1908, Resolution 41, p. 56. Cp. also the Encyclical Letter, p. 38, and the Report of the Committee, pp. 144-147.

[2] *Lambeth Conference Report*, 1920, Resolution 68, p. 44.

pointed out elsewhere,[1] the context of these sentences imports into them an element of ambiguity which would be absent if they stood alone, and in particular the resolution represents the Conference as ' declining to lay down rules which will meet the needs of every abnormal case.' It seems natural, therefore, to regard the resolution, despite its ' emphatic warning,' as having opened a door for the legitimate employment of contraceptives in exceptional circumstances.

In 1930, the Lambeth Conference produced two resolutions (Nos. 13 and 15) on the subject. Neither of the two was very happily phrased ;[2] but the second, though passed by a majority vote only, made it perfectly clear that the bishops who voted for it were not prepared to condemn the use of contraceptives in every case. The crucial words are these : ' Where there is a clearly felt moral obligation to limit or avoid parenthood . . . and where there is a morally sound reason for avoiding complete abstinence, the Conference agrees that other methods may be used.'[3] The Report of the Committee of the Conference which dealt with this question by way of preliminary discussion was even more explicit : ' There exist moral situations,' it said,[4] ' which may make it obligatory to use other methods (than that of abstinence).'

It seems unnecessary to discuss in detail the resolution and Report from which we have just quoted. The successive qualifications introduced throughout the passage in question prove that the signatories were very far from endorsing ' birth-control ' in any and every case ; indeed, it might well be inferred from much of the language used that they held the number of cases in which it could be treated as legitimate to be very small indeed. The point of vital importance is that nearly two hundred bishops, meeting on a solemn occasion, gave it as their considered opinion that the use of contraceptives could not be regarded as in all circumstances unlawful.

Enough has been said to show that an Anglican has good reason to doubt whether the universal condemnation of ' birth-control ' in the Roman communion is paralleled by

[1] *Theology*, August 1925, p. 82 ; and also in the first edition of the present book, pp. 292, 293. As this resolution may now be supposed to be superseded by that of 1930, it seems unnecessary to discuss it in detail.

[2] See my criticism in detail in the *Church Quarterly Review*, October 1930, pp. 96–110.

[3] *Report*, p. 43.   [4] *Ibid.*, p. 91.

L

as absolute an obligation in the Church of England. On the other hand, the principle involved is one which beyond all question is intimately bound up with fundamental issues. The mere fact of doubt, therefore, cannot possibly in this case, any more than in others,[1] carry with it the benefit of the doubt. The Anglican layman or confessor would seem as much bound to conform—in spite of the Lambeth resolutions —as his Roman brother. It is understood, of course, as usual, that if his conscience unequivocally sanctioned the practice of ' birth-control,' and the tests of invincibility were satisfied, he would be free to follow his conscience, though he could not insist upon receiving absolution if he made the matter known in confession. With this type of conscience we are not now dealing ; our business is with those who, while desiring to do all that loyalty demands of them, are genuinely in a fog as regards the whole matter—not least of all because of the ambiguities of the resolution already mentioned.

We may tabulate the various possible points of view somewhat as follows :—

(a) An Anglican who conscientiously held the traditional doctrine, with its absolute condemnation of the practice, to be the true one (and the case can certainly be argued with a great deal of cogency) could not of course be compelled to accept the bishops' standpoint. As in previous cases, he would have the complete right to preach his own doctrine, and we must add, if a confessor, to refuse absolution to any penitent who admitted the practice and refused to abandon it, provided that he gave the Church the opportunity of declaring his rigorism excessive if she so desired, and were prepared to resign his official position if constitutionally called upon to do so.

At the same time, an Anglican who held this rigorist view would be forced—in this matter, as in that of confession before communion—to consider the grounds on which he held it. No more than before could he appeal to the bare authority of the Roman Church on this point, when on others (as for example that of the papal claims) he held himself justified in rejecting it. He might, however, base his position on the same ' internal ' grounds as those of Rome, that the practices

[1] Cp. *supra*, pp. 270–275.

condemned were ' against the law of nature,' or (as the 1920 resolution says) employed ' unnatural means.' The former of these two phrases would really be an appeal to an ultimate intuition of the inherent wrongness of the practice, as to which, if it were held ' invincibly,' nothing more could be said. The second phrase is highly ambiguous. It may be no more than a similar appeal to intuition ; but if it is more than this it appears to involve a curious confusion of thought. Is ' unnatural ' the same as ' artificial ' ; and if so, is all ' artificial ' interference with the processes of nature—all control of those processes by the methods of science—to be adjudged immoral ? Or is it only *this* process which may not be so controlled or modified ? And if so, why is ' artificial ' (i.e. scientific) control debarred from coming to the aid of natural control (i.e. complete abstinence) in this matter alone?

The point need not detain us, interesting though it is. The difficulties of maintaining an argument along these lines commonly throw the controversy into other channels. The prohibition of ' birth-control ' *in toto* seems likely in the future to draw most of its strength from the possibilities of grave incontinence and swift moral deterioration which the practice opens up to the individual, and the great social evils which might follow in consequence from anything like official con-donation, even in the hardest of hard cases. This argument is profoundly impressive. It provides convincing ground for the assertion that no responsible Christian communion could ever extend its tolerance to the use of contraceptives as a normal and unquestionable practice. But, if the argu-ment is advanced on behalf of *complete* prohibition, it brings up an important question of principle. At first sight nothing would seem more obvious than that the Church should forbid all her members, without qualification, to employ any practice whose social consequences seem likely to be disastrous. And yet as a matter of history such total prohibition of practices simply and solely on the ground of public inexpediency appears rarely, if ever, to have been countenanced.

There are at least two obvious examples of this to hand. Gambling and ' drink,' as we euphemistically call it, are both of them sources of untold social evil. Nor is the argument for the permission of either of them in rare cases in any degree so weighty as in the corresponding case of birth-control. Setting aside the use of alcohol for medicinal purposes, little more than a moderate degree of gaiety and exhilaration (which for the time being, and to put the case at its strongest, we may call ' innocent ') would be lost if every good Christian gave up both ' drinking ' and betting ; and the temporary psychical lacuna (if we may so call it) created by the abandonment of the practices would soon be filled. There are indeed modern movements which demand that the Church should incorporate ' Thou shalt not drink,' and ' Thou shalt not bet,' as explicitly in her moral code as ' Thou shalt not steal,' or ' Thou shalt not commit adultery.'[1] But, on the whole, organised Christendom is slow to respond, and even so both appeals come curiously late in the day. When practices which admittedly do an infinite amount of harm could be prohibited with little more than temporary inconvenience to a minority, it is strange that the Church should be so reluctant to take the step of prohibiting them.

The question opens up an interesting historical problem which deserves fuller investigation than it has ever received. It would appear that the Church has never prohibited any practice, however dangerous to society, unless convinced of its immorality on other grounds than those of its social effects. Such a conviction, in each case, is ultimately of the character known as intuitive. Like all intuitions, it may be right or wrong ; all Christians alike need not share in it ; and it is certainly subject to the possibility of revision. It is even arguable that in some cases, especially where the practice is prohibited on the grounds that it is covered by a prior and wider intuition, the chain of argument binding it to the intuition supposed to justify its condemnation is what psychologists call a ' rationalisation '—an argument devised to support a conviction already there. In such cases the original ground of the conviction, however little its supporters knew it, may quite possibly have been the general inexpediency of the practice ; [2] but it has never been the sole ground alleged for it.

---

[1] Without any implication, of course, that the four are of equal gravity.

[2] See further *infra*, pp. 329 ff. Often enough, of course, the intuition has taken the form, ' This is forbidden in Scripture and therefore must be wrong in itself.'

At all events, if we examine the various ' sins ' condemned as wrong in all cases by the Church, we find that, though sometimes *we* can see no reason for the condemnation except the (to us) eminently reasonable one of general inexpediency, Christian thought *as a whole* has never been content with this ground alone. Theft, murder, suicide, adultery, polygamy—in every case it has been supposed that the law of God prohibited them either directly or by implication, apart from their consequences. The condemnation of ' usury,' in its legitimate form of interest on capital, as well as in its illegitimate forms, was bound up with the conviction that barren metal cannot by nature breed. And the prohibition of birth-control in the Roman communion, as we have seen, is explicitly based upon a conviction that the practice is contrary to the natural law ; a conviction for which support is found in the passages from St. Thomas Aquinas already mentioned.

We may not share the intuitions which animated our predecessors in their condemnation of practices deplored by us on grounds of general expediency alone. But we have not to look very far to find their reason for insisting that, without such an intuition of its inherent wrongness, nothing is to be condemned in all cases and in all its forms, however grave the argument from expediency may be. It carries us back to the two first moral principles of the gospel message—that the Christian law is a law of liberty ; and that the individual conscience should as far as possible be trained to autonomy and a capacity for self-legislation. The multiplication of general prohibitions, beyond the barest minimum required by respect for what was supposed to be known of the absolute moral law, would be fatal to both these ideals. It would bind a quasi-Mosaic yoke upon the faithful ; and it would limit rather than expand their capabilities for moral autonomy. Few things are more impressive than the manner in which—in obedience, we must believe, to this unconscious and unexpressed tendency—the Church has consistently held its hand and resisted the temptation to prohibit practices, however dangerous in character, against which no more than general inexpediency could be urged. Only where an intuition was current that the practice, apart from all questions of consequences, was wrong in itself, might a writ of general prohibition run.

This self-denying ordinance which the Church seems to have respected even in her most legalistic periods has therefore a fundamentally and indeed peculiarly Christian origin. We can scarcely hold ourselves free to insist upon a greater stringency of codification. If this is so, certain consequences immediately follow. Only those (and there are very few of them) who hold the use of alcohol to be wrong in all cases, however ' temperate ' or ' innocent,' are entitled to demand that it should be wholly prohibited to Christian people by the Church. Only those who have a similar conviction can make a similar demand in the matter of betting and gambling. And if we are to be loyal to these fundamental principles of Christian thought and experience, we cannot insist that *in no case whatever* (however menacing and disastrous) may contraceptives be used, unless we have a clear conviction on other grounds than those of social expediency that the practice is wholly wrong.

Considerations such as these emphasise the difficulty of maintaining the total condemnation of birth-control in all cases. But the practical question still remains. What is the confessor to do who, on whatever grounds, is absolutely and conscientiously convinced that ' birth-control ' is wholly wrong ? Must he refuse absolution in every case, however poignant, in which the ' penitent ' refuses to give up the practice ? That terrible conclusion does not immediately follow. If he accepted the arguments we put forward in favour of the occasional absolution of penitents in invincible error on a single point, who show themselves rightly disposed in general,[1] the confessor might from time to time mitigate the rigour of his position by this means ; and this, as a matter of fact, is the course adumbrated by numerous Roman Catholic authorities of distinction.[2] Again, since we are

---

[1] *Supra*, p. 253.

[2] So explicitly Génicot (*Theologiæ Moralis Institutiones* (Brussels, 1909), ii. p. 568—quoted, *Theology*, Dec. 1930, p. 307) ; slightly less explicitly Lehmkuhl, ii. p. 614 ; Arregui, *Summarium Theol. Mor.*, p. 518 ; Tanquerey, i. supplementum, p. 25 ; J. A. McHugh and C. J. Callan, *Moral Theology* (1930), ii. p. 606 ; H. Merkelbach, *Summa Theol. Mor.* (1933), iii. p. 932 ; H. Davis, *Moral and Pastoral Theology* (1935), iv. p. 261.

dealing with an intermittent practice (call it sinful if you will) and not an habitual state of sin, it would be legitimate to treat certain cases (e.g. those in which the penitent normally tried to maintain absolute continence) as ' relapses,' and to give absolution on signs of moral distress being forthcoming. Or, again, where a penitent was unaware of the ' rule ' in question, he might be left in his invincible ignorance on the ground that he would not alter his conduct even if he knew of the rule.[1] Opinions will differ, no doubt, as to the propriety of these suggestions. But failing some such mitigation of the strict canons of discipline, absolution would have to be withheld until the penitent showed a willingness to conform.

(*b*) It may of course be said that if a confessor were genuinely convinced of the inherent wrongness of the practice in all cases of its occurrence, he could not conscientiously permit himself to absolve any penitent who refused to abandon it, however much the actual letter of the moral case-law allowed it. To do so would be an act of moral weakness and logical inconsistency. This may be so ; the question of inconsistency and compromise is one to which we shall come in the next chapter. But the same argument does not apply to a second attitude which may very well be taken up towards our problem. There are many Anglicans, clergy and laity alike, who find themselves in a genuine condition of doubt in regard to it. Attracted on the one hand by the outspoken and challenging directness of the Roman position, but not deaf, on the other, to the arguments which can be advanced on behalf of the bishops' opinion, they find it impossible to advance further towards any definite conclusion of their own. For them the actual condemnation of the practice in every case is of course ' doubtful,' but it is not directly negatived. And it is doubtful in the main for the very reason that they are aware of instances in which to insist upon abstention from the use of contraceptives would appear to lead directly to the most disastrous consequences for the persons concerned.

Nevertheless, though doubtful, the matter obviously

---

[1] *Supra*, p. 251. This is undoubtedly the view of the ' less explicit ' authorities mentioned in the preceding note.

touches a vital interest ; and therefore in general the benefit of the doubt may not be taken. The doubtful confessor is so far in the same position as the confessor who assents without hesitation to the Roman Catholic view. But though this is so *in general*, in those particular cases which chiefly give rise to the doubt, circumstances may make it both legitimate and logical to take advantage of the mitigations just suggested, and extend the benefit of absolution to persons so situated. For one who held to the full rigour of the condemnation, relaxations of this character might appear conscientiously impossible ; but to a conscience in doubt on the point, the knowledge that such a course was allowed by the admitted principles of moral theology where circumstances warranted it (i.e. where the penitent's error is genuinely ' invincible,' or where he is struggling to eliminate the use of contraceptives as far as it is humanly possible) would come as a real relief. Without forcing himself to a decision on the main issue before he was able to see his way clearly, the confessor would still be in a position to deal with the problems that came before him, free from the constant fear of binding upon his penitents a burden which God never intended them to bear. Humanity demands that such relief should be available both for confessor and penitent ; and, if the arguments we have used on the subject carry conviction, moral theology does not refuse what humanity requires.

(c) Curiously enough, it is the Anglican who finds himself whole-heartedly endorsing the bishops' decision as expressed in the 1930 resolution, who is in the greatest practical difficulty. The resolution, in fact, says either too much or too little. It tells us that the ' primary and obvious method ' of family limitation is that of ' complete abstinence ' (curiously enough, no reason for this view is advanced either in the resolution itself, or in the Report of the Committee concerned, where the same phrase is used) ; and emphasises that only ' where there is a morally sound reason for avoiding complete abstinence ' may ' other methods ' be employed. But who is to decide whether there is such a ' morally sound reason for avoiding complete abstinence ' ? The resolution does not say ; yet, the more the matter is considered, the less possible does it become to regard with equanimity the prospect of any half-instructed, lukewarm, comfort-loving pair of Anglicans deciding the matter for themselves, with the bare dogmatic statement of the resolution, that complete abstinence is the ' primary and obvious ' method of family-limitation, as the sole argument on behalf of a principle against which will be thrown into the balance the full weight of the most passionate and insistent of human impulses. If this is to happen unchecked, it is as certain as anything can very well be that only the most conscientious and loyal of Church-people will ever regard themselves as morally prohibited from employing the ' other methods ' which the resolution mentions. The remainder will unhesitatingly take advantage of the permission extended by the resolution only to those who have a ' morally sound reason for avoiding complete abstinence.' Thus the result of the resolution will be to encourage a practice which the bishops undoubtedly regard as no more than a second-best, and which, as every parish priest is only too well aware, stands in no need of adventitious stimulus. Liberty of conscience is among the greatest of Christian privileges ; but there are some prices too high to be paid for it.

Considerations of this kind do not, indeed, entitle us to assume that in this matter the bishops did not propose to leave the decision wholly to the individual. But it can at all events be asserted that many of those who unhesitatingly accept the general intention of the resolution would view any such prospect with considerable alarm. But who is to decide, if not the individual ? The matter so clearly concerns the moral atmosphere of the Church as a society, that she might well claim some right for her accredited representatives to be heard whenever the problem arises. Indeed, if there is any type of problem in which the machinery of ' reserved ' cases and official penitentiary advisers [1] is urgently needed, this surely is a problem of the kind. Decision is rarely a question of such immediate urgency that there would not be time for the expert to be consulted ; and the variety of rulings which must arise from leaving the matter to individual confessors will be so great as to make some superior control eminently

[1] *Supra*, p. 247.

desirable. No proposal to create such machinery, however, has ever been put forward by authority ; and to most Anglicans the suggestion will appear incompatible with the distinctive genius of their Church. If, then, on the one hand, we dare not contemplate leaving the question wholly to the decision of the individual Christian, whilst on the other the provision of elaborate penitential machinery is neither congenial nor practicable, only one conclusion remains open. We should attempt to persuade the conscience of the Church of England that in a matter of such urgency her members should at least take the opinion of responsible authority before making their decisions, and should discipline themselves not lightly to disregard such opinions if and when they have been ascertained.

In support of this view we can at least quote certain phrases from the Report of the Committee to which allusion has already been made. It is true that the Report says that ' each couple must decide for themselves as in the sight of God ' ; but this statement may mean no more than that every Christian has at once the duty and the right of making all moral questions a matter of personal enquiry and—if conscience achieves certainty—of personal decision. On the other hand we are told emphatically that in ' all these matters of sex self-deception is all too easy ' ; and that ' if perplexed in mind,' ' competent advice, both medical and spiritual,' should be taken.[1] An Anglican, therefore, who finds himself in general and conscientious agreement with the bishops' resolution, and moreover accepts our corollary that the matter is too serious to be left to the decision of the individual, would have good reason for maintaining that no one is morally free to employ methods of birth-control in matrimony until he has received the sanction of the Church for his own particular case. If he were himself a priest and confessor he would be bound to undertake the burden of decision in such cases as were brought to his notice ; though he would of course be free—subject always to the rule of secrecy in this matter, whether in the confessional or outside it—to take advice upon the exact circumstances of each particular

[1] *Lambeth Conference Report* (1930), pp. 92, 91.

case.[1] The general principles on which he would consider the matter would be those governing the ' conflicts of evils ' with which the next chapter will deal. He would weigh the evil of ' permission ' against that of rigorism, and decide for whichever seemed the lesser of the two, in full assurance that the problem admitted of no other method of solution.

We must consider for a moment the criticisms and objections to which our conclusions might be subjected :—

(1) It may be said that we have done no more than endorse the present attitude of the Church of England in the matter in all its diversities, and have suggested no remedy. In part this is true ; and if so, to those who trust the Church of England, it is evidence that Anglican good sense endorses the reformed probabilism upon which we are working, and would confidently allow it to be applied in other cases where the decisions of conscience remain doubtful. Furthermore, our business throughout these chapters is with the Church of England as it is, and the problems that arise therefrom ; and in this matter the resolution of the 1930 Lambeth Conference, which has throughout been the basis of our discussion, is the most recent and authoritative document to which we can appeal. But it is not true that no suggestions for improving the situation have been put forward. In the first place, we suggest that it is the duty of all those who follow the bishops' leading—and it may be supposed their number is not inconsiderable—to urge that in a matter of such importance no one should trust his own judgment very far, and that the most loyal course is to refer to a representative of the Church (not necessarily of course the priest of the enquirer's own parish) for a ruling. In the second place, we can express the hope that methods of some kind may be devised—perhaps diocese by diocese as circumstances allow—to lighten the very heavy burden which otherwise must rest wholly on the individual priest alone. If these two suggestions were to commend themselves to the Church of England as a whole, one small step would have been taken to rescue us from the difficulties of the present situation.

[1] In this way (especially if the bishops extended a measure of encouragement) an informal system of penitentiary advice might in time be built up which would to some extent lighten the burden at present wholly resting upon the individual confessor.

If, further, it be urged that the suggestions put forward assume a far more extensive use of the confessional in the Church of England than is the case at present, or is likely to be the case within any measurable period, we may reply that they would be equally to the point if sacramental confession were wholly unknown. Many, no doubt, will feel that the confessional is the only appropriate place in which official decisions of this character should be given. But a priest is still the accredited representative of the Church, whether people consult him in confession or not ; and wherever he gives his rulings—in the vestry or the nave or the study or elsewhere—they are still the Church's rulings. So long as the enquirer's identity is kept an inviolable secret, the method or occasion of dealing with the case is relatively unimportant so far as the actual decision is concerned.

(2) It may be alleged that to require of devout Christians that they should in all cases submit their decision in this matter to authority is to put them at a disadvantage as compared with lax and worldly persons, whether nominally Christian or not. So much, of course, is true. But the same can be said of all moral principles. The earnest-minded are always at a disadvantage as compared with the lax or unscrupulous. If then the cause were grave enough (as the discussions raised by the question certainly imply it to be) no objection o n this head could be taken to the suggestions outlined above.

(3) Again it may be said that our clergy are not as a whole competent to give wise decisions in this matter. To this it might with reason be replied that they are a great deal more competent than the vast majority of immature lads and girls among their parishioners who rush into matrimony so light-heartedly, and a great deal more serious-minded than the ordinary comfort-loving couple. Defective regulation is at least better than no regulation at all. It is true, of course, that years of systematic training are needed in this matter of all others for the handling of individual cases aright, and that little has been done officially to put the clergy in the way of viewing the problem in its wider aspects and with full realisation of its pitfalls. Here, of course, the need for

diocesan advisers, with whom would have to be associated one or more medical men to advise upon the aspect of the problem which comes specially within their sphere, is overwhelming. But in default of such bodies of advisers it is true even at the present day that no diocese—indeed, no city of any size—is without some clergy whose qualifications equip them beyond all question to speak with real authority on the subject. The layman or the inexperienced confessor would not have to look very far for a ruling which he could safely follow.

(4) It may, however, be alleged that the English layman, so far from being in the habit of making his confession, is unlikely to be willing to submit questions of this kind to his clergy under any conditions whatever. Even if this be true, things will be in no worse case than they are at present by reason of our urging him to do so. That the matter is serious, everyone agrees. That it is one in which the pressure of instinct is peculiarly hard to resist, is obvious. That every ' permission ' given or taken is fraught with far-reaching results both for the individual and society, need not further be argued. The Prayer Book clearly contemplates it as right that churchmen in spiritual and moral difficulties should lay their troubles before a ' discreet and learned minister of God's word ; ' we do no more than suggest that in such a difficult problem as this it is a matter of obligation, for all but those who have clear conscientious convictions of their own in the matter, to deal with it along the lines which the Prayer Book advises. And if it be too late, at this time of day, to appeal to the Prayer Book as a determinant of loyalty, is there anything left to which we can appeal ?

(5) Finally it may be urged that we have nowhere dealt with the question : What *ought* the Church to hold as true about this whole matter of birth-control ? Or, in other words, what ought we to think about the Lambeth resolution ? It is doubtful whether anything of value can be said further on this question. The arguments on all sides have been too fully canvassed in the public press and pamphlets in the last few years for any consideration of importance to have been overlooked. The material for a decision is already before every individual ; and even if he says, ' I cannot decide

the matter,' this is in itself a decision to leave it undecided for no one else can decide for him. There are indeed three possible decisions, and three only, and they are those we have given in paragraphs (*a*), (*b*) and (*c*) respectively; paragraph (*b*) representing the decision of the person who decides that he cannot decide. In general, we have argued, it is immaterial whether a man holds (*a*) or (*b*). The only question is, does he hold (*c*) or not ? And as to this one straightforward enquiry is enough. Can he conceive of any definite case, actual or imaginary (so long as it is within the bounds of credibility), in which the use of contraceptives in marriage could morally be endorsed ? If so, his position is that of paragraph (*c*), and his conduct is to be determined accordingly. If not, his position is expressed by paragraphs (*a*) or (*b*), and for practical purposes it does not matter which of the two expresses it more exactly. In either case he is bound to treat the condemnation of the practice as in fact universal and absolute ; and any exceptions he makes must be made, if at all, within the very narrow limits of possible mitigation to which we have drawn attention.

7. *Betting and Gambling* [1]

The problem of betting and gambling, and of the proper behaviour of the Christian towards them, takes us almost entirely out of the region of loyalty. In general the attitude of the Church has been to regard betting as a thing indifferent.[2]

[1] No substantial difference in meaning is usually recognised between ' betting' and 'gambling.' But the words are not wholly synonymous. It is more natural to use the former where what is designated is (*a*) a wager between two definite persons ; (*b*) a single definite event or series of definite operations, rather than a continuous practice ; (*c*) a wager in which the chances are determinate either absolutely or within certain clear limits, and the risks not excessive ; (*d*) a deliberate and even unemotional wager as distinct from a ' feverish ' speculation. Where one or more of these characteristics are notably absent, the operation seems more fitly to be called a ' gamble.' The two words are commonly used together, as in the titles of Canon Charles' and Canon Green's books, and in the text above, to indicate that transactions of all these different kinds can be treated together, and that the words may in essence be treated as interchangeable. An instance in which Canon Green uses ' gambling ' in a specialised sense in which it is not interchangeable with ' betting ' is quoted on page 314.

[2] Any manual of moral theology will provide the necessary references. Canon Belton gives a useful summary of traditional teaching on the subject in his *Present Day Problems of Christian Morals*, c. 5.

The practice can of course be horribly abused and indulged in to excess, and misuse and excess are naturally enough forbidden in this as in all other indifferent matters. Still, with this proviso, betting is treated in traditional theology as ' allowable.' There is nothing praiseworthy in it, but on the other hand a Christian cannot be blamed for indulging in it in strict moderation. It is in all respects analogous with what we euphemistically call the question of ' drink.' A Christian may ' drink,' but he must never ' drink ' to excess ; so he may bet, but he must not bet to excess.

Thus if conscience asks : ' May I back horses or play cards for money ? ' the first point settled is that loyalty to the Church does not forbid it. It forbids anything resembling that unhealthy, excessive gambling which palpably harms both spiritual and temporal interests ; beyond this it leaves the matter open to the individual to decide. In deciding it he would have to ask himself just the same questions as in the parallel case of ' drink ' :—' Can I afford it? Is it enfeebling my will ? Is it making demands on my time ? Am I in danger of developing a " craving " for it ? Is my example encouraging others, more liable to temptation in this matter, to indulge in it to excess ? ' All these questions conscience would have to weigh and answer before it would be justified in concluding, ' You may take part in " moderate " or " innocent " betting ' ; and even then it would have to set very definite limits as to time, circumstances and amounts. But it would not have to ask, ' Does loyalty to the Church forbid it ? ' for the answer to that question is quite obviously ' No.'

On the highest plane of Christian morality, however, we may have slight hesitations about the conclusion just reached. Many Christians, among them men of the highest piety for whose judgment we have the sincerest respect, hold that all betting and gambling is ' wrong in itself,' and consequently that no Christian ought to indulge in it even to the slightest degree. The natural sequel to this position is the demand that the Church should officially declare gambling to be wrong, and that the Christian who persists in it should be liable to censure in the external forum and refusal of absolution in the internal. Perhaps, with that inherent Anglican distaste for formulated law which conditions all our problems, they would not press their demands to this conclusion; but that is a detail. What is more than a detail is this :—Here, we may say, is a possible 'custom' in the making; does not loyalty demand that we should conform to it ?

We must distinguish at this point between custom in the making and custom come to its own. Where custom has come to its own, it is the duty of the Christian—out of loyalty if for no other reason—to conform to it unless he has a genuinely conscientious objection in the matter. We may instance, for example, the support of foreign missions, contribution to diocesan funds, the maintenance of Sunday schools and the like as customs which have come to their own, and from which consequently no loyal churchman, unless conscientiously convinced that the activities involved were mischievous or malignant, could withhold adherence. Similarly with frequency of communion. The Anglican formularies only insist upon communion thrice in the year. But the custom of more frequent communion (let us say once a month as a minimum) is firmly established; and it would be less than loyalty to shelter behind the older canonical minimum and disregard the newer customary one. But the demand that all betting and gambling should be treated as forbidden is not on all fours with these established customs. It has not yet made its footing good; and therefore ecclesiastical loyalty alone cannot be said to demand conformity to it in every case.

What loyalty does demand is that every Christian should consider the matter seriously, both as regards his own personal practice and as regards the attitude which it is desirable that the Church should take up. It is not every fad or fancy that gains momentary currency of which as much could be said. Life is too brief for the exploration of every avenue which chance wayfarers commend to our notice. But here is a matter about which men to whom we pay great and well-deserved respect feel seriously, and it is less than duty, either to them or to the Church to which we all belong, that we should contemptuously ignore that which they take so deeply to heart. It may be that they will prove right, and that their view will in the end commend itself to the conscience of the Church. If so, we shall have much with which to reproach ourselves, in that we despised the day of small things and withheld support from the movement in its infancy, not on any solid grounds of doubt or dissent, but through the merest callous indifference. The reproach will in itself provide a measure of the offence.

The problem of gambling, therefore, gives us an instance of a moral question which at all times—but particularly in the present state of opinion in the Church of England—every loyal member of the body is called upon to consider seriously. Is it ' wrong in itself ' ? Is it wholly inexpedient ? Is it of doubtful legitimacy ? And finally, what may be inferred as to the proper attitude of the Christian towards it ? These four enquiries provide the setting for discussion of the problem ; and the setting is the same for every general question with which Christian ethics has to deal, once the primary matter of the demands of loyalty has been settled. The discussion, therefore, is of importance not merely in this particular example of gambling, but as a norm for many other discussions of a similar character which the moralist must face.

(1) *Is gambling ' wrong in itself ' ?*—' The wagering of money on an uncertain event,' or ' the determination of the ownership of property by an appeal to chance,' is often spoken of as a thing which is ' wrong in itself ' or ' inherently sinful.' This implies of course that no Christian may indulge in it, except perhaps where something equally wrong in itself, and of greater urgency, could be avoided by this means alone. The phrase ' wrong in itself,' or ' inherently sinful,' has met us before, and we shall have to deal with it again at a more appropriate point.[1] Here we may ignore the difficulties involved in it, and ask simply, ' If there are any types of behaviour which are inherently sinful, is gambling one of them ? ' For the answer ' Yes ' to be maintained, it would have to be alleged either that it rested upon a primary intuition which persisted after all argument and enquiry ; or that gambling was evidently an instance of the breach of a principle as to which a primary intuition of similar character was universally current.

[1] *Infra* pp. 328-331.

In all moral questions an appeal to the phraseology employed by ordinary serious-minded Christians is, though never final, of considerable value. Such an appeal is possible in the present case. A thing which is regarded as inherently sinful or wrong in itself can never be 'abused' or 'indulged in to excess.' You cannot abuse what is already and in itself an abuse. We do not speak of an 'abuse of' or 'over-indulgence in' adultery, or dishonesty, or cruelty, or drunkenness, because these things are themselves excesses or abuses. On the other hand, it is possible to speak of excessive indulgence in theatre-going, or of an abuse of alcohol; and this implies that both theatre-going and alcohol have their legitimate if limited uses. Now the rules about wagers current among quite serious-minded people—'Never play cards for money for high stakes,' 'There is nothing wrong in a shilling on a horse' and the like—imply quite clearly that betting and gambling can be indulged in to excess, and that this is a very different matter from their indulgence within strict limits. This suggests that the practice is not in the same category with adultery, dishonesty, cruelty or drunkenness. It is something which can be abused, and therefore is not wrong in itself.

This argument from popular phraseology, frail though it is, warns us at least that we must not accept too uncritically the statement that 'betting is always wrong.' Its supporters must be pressed to give their reasons, and to answer the possible objections that may be raised. To raise these objections and press for these reasons is always an ungrateful and unpopular task. In the present case it is particularly distasteful, because some of those who must thus be questioned are men to whom as scholars, moralists and guides of souls the Church owes more than she can hope to repay. Again, if in the end, though for different reasons, we arrive at conclusions virtually identical with theirs, our questioning may appear no more than a misplaced and misguided pleasantry, altogether remote from the exigencies of practical life. Nevertheless, nothing is lost by serious enquiry. If nothing emerges of importance for the immediate problem of gambling, something may be gained in experience of method which will be of value in other problems where the issues are even more obscure.

The opponents of gambling in any and all of its forms reject the validity of the appeal to popular phraseology. The rejection is not always convincing. To the argument, ' Gambling only does harm when indulged in to excess,' Canon Peter Green merely replies, 'Any great moral question can be made to look ridiculous by trivialities.' [1] But we cannot insist upon the verdict of popular opinion—even in serious Christian circles—against them. This question may be just one of those in which the Holy Spirit is still guiding the Church to higher truth ; and what our view ought to be upon the matter cannot safely be inferred from what it is at present. For their own part, again, the opponents of gambling do not take refuge in a mere intuition of the form, ' Every Christian can see for himself that the practice is wrong.' They attempt to show that gambling involves the breach of some Christian law as to whose finality everyone is agreed.

Thus Canon Charles writes [2]:—' To decide the ownership of property by an appeal to chance . . . cannot be other than an immoral action. . . . It is based upon the repudiation of all reason, and so translates its devotees into the region of the arbitrary and irrational, and creates in them such a degree of unnatural excitement as to inhibit the natural checks of the reason on such extravagances.' It is clear, of course, that to decide the ownership of property by an appeal to chance is *often* immoral, and produces the results which Dr. Charles mentions. Nor is it denied that gambling (which is such an appeal and decision) is often immoral and attended by those results. But this is not the writer's contention. Indeed, if it were the only truth that could be reached on the matter, it would be fatal to his contention. It would lead only to the conclusion, ' Gambling is often immoral,' and would leave the door open to exactly the type of discussion which Canon Charles would closure—the discussion as to when gambling is immoral and when it is not. Hence his universal law : ' To decide the ownership of property by an appeal to chance *cannot be other* than an immoral action '—must be immoral, in fact, in any circumstances whatever.

Now in this form the generalisation simply cannot be

---

[1] *Betting and Gambling* (1924), p. 56.
[2] *Gambling and Betting* (1924), p. 31.

sustained. Not only have we no intuition which supports it, but we can envisage cases in which the appeal to chance is the only way of escape from an intolerable dilemma about possession. Hecato's old problem of the plank in the shipwreck is a case in point, though an extreme case. If two mariners clung to the plank, and it were certain that both would drown unless one sacrificed his life for the other, and if, further, each took the heroic line of insisting on sacrificing himself, the only moral solution which would prevent the loss of both lives would be an appeal to chance. In the circumstances they would of course find it difficult to ' toss up ' (though with two explorers who have only enough water left to sustain life for one, such a course would be possible) ; but unless they agreed upon some other similar expedient, both would perish. And everyone would agree that the sacrifice of two lives where one could perhaps be saved would be wrong—or, if agreement is not general on this point, we have merely to amend our imaginary circumstances and entrust the voyagers jointly with a message which must be delivered at all costs, to secure universal support. If this line of argument is to be maintained by the opponents of gambling, they will be compelled to define limits within which the appeal to chance is illegitimate for the determination of ownership ; and show that gambling in all its forms, however innocuous in common opinion, falls wholly within those limits.

More commonly, however, the attack is developed along the lines that gambling is an attempt to ' get something for nothing.' [1] Here two questions have to be asked. Is the attempt to get something for nothing in all cases illegitimate ? And if so, is gambling such an attempt ? Both statements seem to be at least doubtful. When I ask a stranger to tell me the time, when I swear a friend to secrecy as to my actions, I am getting something for nothing ; but in itself there is nothing wrong with either action. It may of course be replied that in these circumstances I am not really getting something for nothing, because I tacitly agree to do as much

---

[1] So Green, *op. cit.* p. 53. The author adds, ' Can we do this to the glory of God ? Is not the use of time and money in such a way a denial of the doctrine of stewardship ? Betting is a sin against God '—p. 57 (hence gambling is a sin against one's neighbour) ; Charles, *op. cit.* p. 30.

for the other person (or for other members of the same society) should occasion demand it. 'And this no doubt is true, but it brings up our second question at once. Is it not equally true that gambling in its essence is *not* an attempt to get something for nothing, because in every case of betting and gambling *something* is given in return for whatever is gained ?

In essence gambling is a contract by which in certain circumstances I can claim something from another, in return for which I give him the right, in other circumstances, to claim something from me. To confer a right upon another by contract, for however short a period and with whatever limitations, is certainly to give him *something*; it endows him conditionally with a claim upon ourselves which he did not possess before. We may hope no doubt that circumstances (i.e. the issue of the race, or whatever the event may be about which the wager is made) will make it impossible for him ever to substantiate his claim; but even so we have given him a measure of right against ourselves and our property, and that is a definite ' something.' It is true that the terms of the contract make it impossible that both of us should benefit materially when settling-time comes, but material benefits are not the only benefits for which cash-payment can legitimately be made. If I win the bet it is arguable that the interest and excitement it has given him, even when his material loss is set against it, warrants his paying me as a ' just price ' the amount of the bet—whose cash value to me may have been considerably off-set, as a matter of fact, by the fear that I might lose.

In any case a contract which eventually results in a disproportionate material gain to one party or the other need not be immoral in principle. A life insurance policy or an option on the purchase of a house are instances in point. If I buy for fifty pounds the sole right to make an offer for the house within a week, I may at the end of the period be in a position to make no offer, or only an inadequate one. In either case my fifty pounds is gone, and I have nothing to show for it. On the other hand, by giving me the option, the vendor certainly gains the fifty pounds, but during the period of the option he may lose an immediate offer for the property

far greater than any he is likely to get at any other time.
Each party to the contract stands to gain and each to lose
materially by it, as circumstances (over which neither perhaps
has any control, and which may therefore fitly be called
' chance ') eventually fall out.

To this it may be replied that in the case of the option it
is not certain that either party will lose thereby.   Both may
as a matter of fact be satisfied'; whereas in the case of the bet
it is certain that one of them *must* lose.   This again is true,
but the circumstances of the case alone can decide whether the
loss is of sufficient importance to affect the morality of the
contract.   The immaterial benefits on either side would have
to be weighed up before this could be said ; and it is at all
events possible that they would prove so considerable (in
the shape of the pleasure and interest involved in the bet)
that the incident of a slight material benefit on one side and
a slight material loss on the other could not affect the general
innocence of the contract.   In assessing the ' just price,' as
St. Thomas told us, a trifling addition or subtraction either
way makes no difference ; and in some bets at least the
material loss or gain is not more than a trifling matter of this
kind.

It would seem that the only ground on which it could be
alleged that betting and gambling is wrong in itself must be
that the ' excitement,' ' interest ' or ' pleasure ' involved is
in all cases of an immoral character.   This again is ground
taken up by Canon Green. ' Gambling,' he writes, ' is
unquestionably injurious to character. . . . Does any man
want his pretty daughter, whom he is proud of, to marry a
gambler ? ' [1]   The answer expected is obvious.   Yet it may
be suggested that here the writer is using the words ' gambling'
and ' gambler ' in a new sense ; and that if he were not
doing so the question would be a dangerous one for his
cause.   Throughout his work Canon Green has used ' gambling,' with ' betting ' as its equivalent, to cover all cases of
whatever kind ' whereby the transfer of something of value
from one to another is made dependent upon an uncertain
event.' [2] But the word ' gambler ' in the question just cited
is obviously used of a person wholly devoted to backing horses,

---

[1] *Op. cit.* p. 54.   [2] *Ib.* p. 17.

or playing cards for high stakes—a person whose whole life is wrapped up in the pursuit. On any other supposition the question becomes absurd. No man would mind his 'pretty daughter' marrying an eligible and comfortably situated husband who once a week played bridge at the club for sixpence a hundred, or put half-a-sovereign annually into a Derby sweepstake. Nor is it possible to say that 'gambling' to this limited extent is *unquestionably* injurious to character. Yet by Canon Green's own definition, this *is* gambling, and the person concerned is a 'gambler.' In the sentence we are quoting the writer is obviously speaking not of betting and gambling in themselves, but of feverish betting and gambling, or betting and gambling to excess. And as far as this is concerned every Christian conscience will give him unhesitating support ; our only reservation is that the evil of a practice indulged in to excess can be no evidence as to the morality or immorality of that practice considered in itself.

The last few paragraphs have played the unhappy part of devil's advocate against the too-sweeping condemnation of betting in all its forms. They suggest at least that the condemnation, or at all events the grounds which have so far been alleged for it, are invalid. It has been irksome to examine and criticise the opinions of writers whose moral earnestness and practical experience are beyond all question, and we have yet to show that anything has been gained by it. In the meantime the next question is one on which happily there can be no general disagreement, though some doubt may still remain as to the consequences to be deduced from it.

(2) *Is gambling wholly inexpedient ?*—No one can deny the dangerous and indeed disastrous influence of gambling in every class of society. The evidence adduced in the exhaustive parliamentary enquiries of recent times,[1] and endorsed by Canon Green in the book from which we have been quoting, is too strong for any unbiassed reader to be in two minds about it. If he is still unconvinced, half-an-hour's conversation with an experienced parish priest should

---

[1] So *Reports of Select Committee of House of Lords on Betting*, 1901, 1902 ; *Report of Select Committee on Betting Duty*, 1923—all published as parliamentary papers.

suffice to remove the last vestiges of doubt. Gambling is as dangerously subversive both of the temporal and of the moral well-being of society as any practice well can be. No degree of emphasis upon this point can be excessive, and all Christians must thank Canon Green and Canon Charles for the forcible manner in which they have driven it home. What duties, then, does this truth impose upon the Church and the individual ?

That it does not authorise the Church as a whole to prohibit Christians by direct command from all kinds of betting and gambling—whether the prohibition be enforced by the logical sanctions of censure and ultimate exclusion or no— is an inference from the discussion in the last case which cannot well be avoided. If the only argument against them is the inexpediency of their consequences, then gambling and betting must *in themselves* be called legitimate for the Christian. But we recall that the mere stamping of a practice as ' legitimate in itself ' does not by any means make it legitimate for every possible Christian on every possible occasion. It does not necessarily legitimatise it even for any actual Christian on any actual occasion. The admitted facts about gambling are that it may become a serious danger to the individual, and that even if it does not, his indulgence in it contributes, by example, to the maintenance of a grave menace to society, and may in addition create ' scandal,' and lead weaker characters into a rapid course of moral deterioration. If any practice can be called ' wholly inexpedient,' this surely must deserve the title. Granted the truth of this, it is clear that the Christian has need to consider his position very seriously before he holds himself free to bet or wager even in moderation.

(3) This answers the second and third questions. We come therefore to the fourth, *What may be inferred as to the proper attitude of the Christian towards this employment of his money ?*—On the one hand is the admitted fact of its grave social inexpediency ; on the other, the fact that there is little to be said on behalf of betting and gambling, even in respect of the stimulus they afford to social intercourse and healthy amusement. ' Drink ' and the use of contraceptives may or may not be greater dangers to society ; but the

former has certainly its very definite beneficial uses, and there are hard cases which make an almost irresistible claim on behalf of occasional permission for the latter. Where teetotalism or abstention from contraceptives for the sake of social purity come into conflict with the need for alcohol in a case of physical exhaustion, or the possible permission of birth-control in a genuinely hard matrimonial case, the problem becomes one of a ' conflict of evils,' of a character which will receive fuller treatment in the next chapter. But gambling is very rarely involved in a conflict of evils. The ' evil ' incurred by refusing to indulge in it can hardly be more than infinitesimal ; whilst the evils attendant upon the practice are very real and serious. The conflict (if such it deserves to be called) would be at best that of a pigmy with a giant.

It seems to follow that the Christian is bound to ask himself questions such as the following :—' Am I certain that no moral danger either to myself or to my immediate neighbours and friends is involved in my gambling ? ' ' Am I certain that it will bring no " scandal " to the Church ? ' ' Am I morally convinced that my example will contribute nothing to the maintenance of a practice admittedly dangerous to society as a whole ? ' If these questions were answered in the affirmative, he would be free to bet and wager within the strict limits imposed by the ideal of moderation. If no affirmative answer could be reached, the case remains one of doubt ; and as the matter is one of vital interest to the well-being of society, both temporal and moral, it is clearly a case in which the benefit of the doubt could not be taken.

The conclusion of the matter appears to be this. The position that betting and gambling are ' wrong in themselves ' is supported by arguments too problematic to be convincing. The admitted fact of its general inexpediency alone does not warrant the Church or the Christian in stamping it as wholly forbidden. But in spite of these admissions, the questions which conscience would have to answer satisfactorily before it could assume a freedom to bet, even within strict limits, are so searching that only very rarely would it seem possible for the Christian to hold himself or to be held free from serious blame if he indulged in the practice.[1] Even if the moral danger to himself were negligible, the inexpediency of his giving an example in the matter is very great ; and there is little positive benefit to be derived from the practice to counterbalance this inexpediency. By a different route we appear to have reached the same practical conclusion as that of those opponents of gambling who hold it to be wrong in itself. And if so we may reasonably be asked whether it was either wise or necessary to scrutinise their arguments so captiously. The old advice to state conclusions, but to be silent as to the grounds on which they are reached, emerges with double force. Surely, it may be said, if two parties agree upon a matter of practical policy, it is mere folly and worse to quarrel about the grounds upon which it is to be advocated ?

Attractive though this criticism is, it does not commend itself for long. Nothing is more disastrous than to advance a good cause by bad arguments, for the unmasking of a fallacy in the argument only too often throws discredit upon the cause. In connection with working lads and men it is quite clear that their usual objection—' There's nothing wrong in having a shilling on a horse if you can afford it,' or ' A shilling on a race gives me as much pleasure as the same amount spent at the pictures '—cannot be met by the assertion that to put a shilling on a horse is wrong ' in itself,' whilst visiting the cinema is only wrong ' in excess.' If the common-sense of mankind is any test at all of truth, the truth is on their side. There *is* nothing wrong in itself in having *one* shilling on *one* horse when you can afford it. What is wrong is having many shillings on many horses when you cannot afford it ; especially if it rapidly ministers to a passion for barren excitement and depraved company, or encourages others of lower moral fibre to their ruin. And this is likely to be *so* wrong in almost every case that we can confidently expect the force of the argument to appeal to every sensitive conscience. The unconscientious may be dragooned into decency for a time by emphatic denunciation of their habits as ' wholly wrong.' But they will lend a ready ear to every argument,

---

[1] The corollaries of this for the confessor are similar to those drawn in the previous case, *supra* pp. 299-301.

whether sophistical or genuine, which weakens the force of dogmatic condemnation ; and the last state is only too likely to be worse than the first.   If an intuition is ultimate and unverifiable nothing more remains to be said : but if it is to be supported by argument, it is of the first importance that the argument should be as far beyond the suspicion of invalidity as human enquiry can make it.

CHAPTER VII

1. *Duty and Desire*

To the last type of problem which we have to consider the
name of 'divided loyalties' is often given, though we might
also speak of it as the 'ethics of compromise.' In such
problems conscience hangs perplexed between two courses,
weighty arguments being available for and against either
course. Instances of the kind have already met us in the
progress of our argument, and we have reserved their fuller
discussion to this point. The problem of birth-control
presents itself in this form for those who, on the one hand,
regard encouragement of the practice as an almost unmitigated
evil, but on the other look for some means of making allow-
ances in hard cases. The confessor who is prepared to
absolve in a case of 'invincible error' [1] has to decide on what
occasions the resultant weakening of discipline is outweighed
by the good to be secured for the penitent. But problems
of the kind are innumerable. A sense of vocation may call
a young man to the mission field, a sense of his parents'
dependence upon him may suggest that his duty lies at home.
As a citizen a craftsman may feel impelled to oppose a strike
which loyalty to his trade-union demands of him that he
should support. Patriotism may urge a man to fight for his
country in a cause which conscience (perhaps supported by
the dominant feeling of his Church) cannot wholly endorse.
The solidarity of his political party may seem to demand
of him silence upon a point of policy against which on all
other grounds he feels himself bound to protest. Veracity
bids him tell the truth in answer to a particular question
put to him, though a truthful answer or even silence may
appear to involve innocent persons in disaster. The classical

[1] *Supra* p. 253.

case of Jeanie Deans in ' The Heart of Midlothian ' is known to everyone ; so is the classical problem of the murderer who asks a son whether his father is in the house. A not dissimilar problem is that set by General Dunlop Swinton in his story of ' The Green Curve '—that of the commander who has to choose between surrendering a key-position to the enemy and expelling a vast non-combatant population to meet certain death. All these problems belong in the main to one type, and if Christian reflection upon practical morality avails anything it should at least have produced some hint of the right lines along which to look for a solution.

These cases of ' perplexity,' as they are called, have at least one distinguishing characteristic in common with cases of ' doubt ' which marks them off from problems of ' error.' In cases of error, properly envisaged, there is no question before conscience on the main issue ; so far as that is concerned the man is assured of the course he must take. The only question that arises is a subordinate one. What is to happen thereafter ? Is he bound to resign his membership of the society to which he belongs if in some important respect he differs from it ?—But in problems of doubt and perplexity conscience is not certain but *uncertain*. In ' doubtful ' cases we hesitate between obeying and ignoring a principle which has indeed some support in authority, but no final support in conscience. In cases of perplexity we have to choose between *two* alternatives for and against each of which much can be urged. So though ' doubt ' and ' perplexity ' are both distinguishable from error, they also differ from one another, for in ' doubtful ' cases—or those of them at least which admit the principle of the *lex dubia*—there is little to be said on behalf of either alternative ; in cases of perplexity there is much to be said against both.[1] Perplexity, in other words, is doubt taken to its extremest limit.[2]

Whenever, then, we find ourselves called upon to choose

[1] So Leibnitz in a curious little essay *de Casibus Perplexis in Jure* : ' In perplexo pars invenit utraque causas, in dubio stricte dicto neutra.' Where the doubt concerns a matter of vital importance there is little to be said on behalf of ' liberty ' except what can be said for liberty in general ; these cases are distinguished from perplexity therefore by the fact that little can be said on *one* side, whilst in perplexity much can be said on *both*.

[2] See further Additional Note F, ' Doubt and Perplexity,' p. 388.

between two alternatives, each of which, if adopted, is bound to produce remorse, unhappiness, distress or evil either to ourselves or to persons for whose well-being we feel a degree of responsibility, we have what in technical theology is called a problem of perplexity. At first sight we may be surprised that so trifling a word is used of matters often involving the deepest anxiety and anguish. But the word ' perplexity ' is one of those whose meaning has been enfeebled by course of time. As originally used by Gregory the Great for these problems, in a curious and fanciful exposition of Job xl. 17,[1] it had a terrible and adequate connotation—it meant ' entanglement in Satan's net.' The devil has so entrapped us—perhaps through no fault of our own—that we can see no course of action open which will not involve us in deep and perhaps lifelong regret or remorse. ' The arguments of his suggestions,' Gregory writes, ' are wrapped together (" perplexa ") by complicated devices, so as to make many sin in such a way that if they wish to escape one sin they cannot do it without being entangled in another sin.' Taken in its original meaning, therefore, the word is only too expressive of the heart-rending character of many problems of this kind.

It is sometimes suggested (as, for example, in much of Jeremy Taylor's discussion of the subject [2]) that problems of perplexity can be subdivided into three classes, according as the choice lies between two ' evils,' between two ' sins,' or between an ' evil ' on the one hand and a ' sin ' on the other. Thus the commander who had to solve the problem of surrendering his fortress or sending the non-combatants

---

[1] *Moral in Hiob.* xxxii. 20 (35). The instances given by Gregory are those of the guilty secret, the unjust command and the repentant simonist who cannot give up his position without spiritual detriment to his flock. Another case is given in viii. 6 (9)—a conflict between humility and zeal. Alexander of Hales defines ' perplexitas ' as ' inevitabilitas peccandi ' (*Summa*, ii. q. 121, m. 4) and adds further instances. St. Thomas appears to suggest that perplexity is impossible (*S.T.* i. 2, q. 19, a. 6, ad 3 ; cp. ii. 2, q. 62, obj. 2 ; iii. q. 64, a. 6, obj. 3). What he really means is that the *right* choice will not, in the circumstances, be sinful, and that the man is wrong in thinking that it will. This of course is true, but it is impossible to harmonise it with his other doctrine (*supra* p. 193) that a lie is always a sin, though often only a venial sin. Leibnitz (*op. cit.*) compares ' perplexitas ' to the Gordian knot.

[2] *Duct. Dub.* i. 5, rule 8.

to almost certain death would be said to be perplexed between two 'evils.' On the other hand a man who had taken a solemn oath to conceal a criminal secret, would have to choose between two sins—either the sin of betraying a secret he had promised to keep, or the sin of being accessory to a crime. Jeanie Deans, again, on this theory, would have to choose between a 'sin' and an 'evil'—on the one hand the lie, on the other hand her sister's death. The purpose of such classifications is clearly to simplify our problem by ruling out from the beginning any perplexity in conflicts between a 'sin' and an 'evil,' on the ground that no manner of 'evil,' however great, ought ever to justify a 'sin.' Thus Cardinal Newman, in a passage to which W. E. H. Lecky frequently alludes, asserts [1]: 'The Church holds that it were better for sun and moon to drop from heaven, for the earth to fail, or for all the many millions who are upon it to die of starvation in extremest agony, than that one soul—I will not say should be lost—but should commit one venial sin, should tell one wilful untruth though it harmed no one, or steal one poor farthing without excuse.'

This simple distinction between 'sins' and 'evils' is however not merely misleading but actually dangerous. It ignores the obvious truth that to allow any 'evil' to take place without good cause is itself a 'sin,' and may be a very gross and heinous sin. 'Our own duties to men's bodies,' says Richard Baxter,[2] 'are to be numbered among spiritual things.' The prevention of evil, in other words, is not only a desirable thing, it is also, other things being equal, an imperative duty. Even where the evil threatens the person himself who can prevent it, or those who are dear to him, the fact that its prevention is desirable [3] to him does not make it any the less a duty.

This is a point of such importance that we may consider

---

[1] *Anglican Difficulties*, p. 190, quoted Lecky, *Map of Life*, p. 88 and elsewhere. For the principle cp. Leibnitz, *op. cit.*: 'Si ex jure res decidi *potest*, sequitur quod decidi ex eo etiam *debeat*; quia ad subsidaria remedia non nisi cum necesse est confugiendum est.'

[2] *Christian Directory*, ii. 9.

[3] 'Desirable' here and throughout this chapter is used in the sense of 'actually desired,' which is indeed the only sense in which it can be contrasted with 'duty'; for if 'desirable' meant 'ought to be desired' the word would in itself be expressing a duty pure and simple.

it a little further. Conscience, in these cases of perplexity, hovers anxiously between two alternatives ; but often enough the man himself has leanings to one side more than to the other. He does not know which is the right course of action, and he would like to do what is right ; but he *does* know which of the two he would like to discover to be right. He does not know, perhaps, whether it will be right to save his father's life by a lie to the murderer ; but he does know how earnestly he wishes that this might prove to be the right thing to do. Not all cases of perplexity are cases of this kind ; frequently there are desires or fears which pull at the heart in both directions. But enough of these cases exist to make them a special and peculiarly difficult class.

It is often suggested that we should ignore altogether our desires or interests in matters of this kind and concentrate wholly upon the question of right and wrong ; the rule is even propounded that it is always safe to choose the course opposed to our dominant interest of the moment. Sometimes this rule is put in the form, ' Be sure that your motive is right, and never mind the consequences.' But this distinction between motive and consequence is confusing—for every motive is a desire for some consequence, even if it be no more than the doing of ' that which is right and reasonable as such ; ' and in any case we cannot divest ourselves of responsibility for the consequences of our actions. What the phrase really means is, ' Do not waive a principle which you generally accept as binding, in favour of one whose claim, in any particular circumstances, is bound up with consequences which appeal to your immediate desires.' There is an element of truth in these contentions. As we have had occasion to notice before, desires are imperious and deceitful things ; they can easily stifle the voice of conscience or pervert its judgments. It is wise always to be on our guard against them, and to hesitate long before concluding that what is desired at any moment is also right. At such times the tests of invincibility, previously alluded to, should certainly be applied, and applied rigorously, before we decide that to gratify a desire is justifiable.

But beyond this point it is un-Christian to suspect all desires of being evil. Desires spring ultimately from those hidden impulses of our nature which we inherited at birth ; and none but the most Calvinistic of theologians would dare to say that all such impulses were wholly bad. Desires, again, are evoked by objects or consequences which present themselves as being within our grasp—often material in character, but sometimes spiritual ; and while it would verge on a blasphemous scepticism to suspect all our spiritual desires (including, let us say, the desire for the moral well-being of a loved child) of immoral selfishness, it is less than Christian to envelope even our material desires in the same suspicion. For the thing desired owes its being in the end to God, and so does the man who desires it—and who dare say that either of these creations of God is wholly evil ?

It is surely more Christian and more reasonable to say that, while often enough we desire what is wrong or evil or harmful, what makes it wrong or evil or harmful is not as a rule the thing itself nor the desire for it, but the fact that it is desired to excess, or at the wrong moment, or in preference to other objects which are more worthy of desire. St. Paul was not ashamed even to desire death, but he recognised that there were other objects to be attained which had a prior claim on his allegiance. And if we were to make a catalogue of things which the man of ordinary moral sensibility regards as desirable, expedient, pleasant or useful—even if they were in most cases matters of purely temporal well-being—we should recognise that to desire and pursue them is only wrong if it supersedes or crushes out other desires of more cardinal worth and importance. Friendship, recreation, home and family life, good health, a comfortable income— it is untrue to the spirit of Christ to call any of these things utterly evil. To desire them and pursue them only becomes unlawful if other things which lie even nearer to the heart of Christ, and for which He Himself was content to sacrifice home, friendship, comfort, material well-being, even life itself, are crowded out of view.[1]

[1] Cp. Thamin, *Un Problème Moral*, 321, 322 : ' Expediency and duty are so closely interwoven that it is easy to discover, with a little analysis, some interest concealed even in the strictest determination of duty ; and some trace of good motive, *alambiquée et sophistiquée*, even in the most sinister piece of policy. . . . There is always some interest on the side of duty ; may there not therefore be some duty always on the side of self-interest ? '
M

We may, however, state the case on behalf of desire more strongly still. Other things being equal—that is to say, if higher claims do not intervene at the moment or in perpetuity—it is actually a duty to promote the material well-being, not only of others, but also of ourselves. To desire or work for anything of material value to ourselves with such passionate enthusiasm that we blunt our sensibilities in regard to our own spiritual development, is obviously to sink to the level of the merely 'carnal' man. Similarly, if the pursuit of personal well-being—even though it be of a spiritual order—blinds us to the needs and claims of others, our life is becoming 'selfish'; and 'carnal-mindedness' and 'selfishness' are equally un-Christian. Fortunately, however, it is easy for the sensitive conscience to discern and guard against these dangers; and, so long as they are guarded against, the pursuit of the desirable—even though of a wholly material kind—is the pursuit of something which can be used with effect both for 'spiritual' and for 'unselfish' purposes. Within these limits, therefore, the pursuit of the desirable is a duty; and even though it is desired for its own sake and without conscious reference to 'spiritual' ends, it is not on that account to be adjudged sinful. The fact that a thing, however material, is desired by a conscientious Christian, so far from proving that it is wrong to pursue it, goes far, therefore, to prove that it is right to do so. To say this does not in any way lessen our respect for temperance as a Christian virtue, or asceticism as a Christian vocation. Temperance is for all Christian people, and asceticism for some, just one of those 'higher claims' of which we have spoken; and the fact that a thing is desired cannot tell us *how much* it ought to be desired, or what other claims it has the right to supersede.

While, therefore, we must always be on our guard against the pressure of desire, it is not true that to aim at things which we desire is necessarily a sin, or can never be a duty. 'In so far as the sense of duty is made to contrast with joy and happiness, it is a false antagonism.'[1] If, for example, truthfulness can ever be waived at the instance of a higher claim, and if for a moment we grant that to save a father's

---

[1] J. A. Hadfield, *Psychology and Morals*, p. 93.

life is such a claim, it would be our duty to use this means of saving his life ; and the fact that we *wanted* to save it would not make it any the less a duty. The desirable and the praiseworthy are not necessarily opposed to one another ; and to do what one wants to do, if it is a duty, need not be selfish. Indeed, what we desire to do may sometimes be so necessary for the well-being of others that it is our duty to do it even if we cannot avoʳd selfishness in the doing. If by becoming Prime Minister a man could certainly save his country from serious disaster, it would still be his duty to take the position, though his motive might be nothing else than personal ambition. And in a sense, because it was his duty, the action would be praiseworthy ; though we should at best have the very faintest of faint praise for it. Such a case is no doubt an extreme one ; but we should not hesitate to praise him if he were at all events trying to stifle his personal ambitions, even though he met with comparatively little success in the attempt.[1]

The opposition between ' duty ' and 'desire ' is no more than the opposition between ' sin ' and 'evil ' reduced to its most plausible form. It follows therefore that it may be dangerously misleading to speak of any particular case of perplexity as involving the conflict of a ' sin ' with an ' evil,' or of ' duty ' with ' desire ' ; for not to avoid an ' evil ' where it can legitimately be avoided is in itself ' sinful,' and the pursuit of the ' desirable ' within the proper limits is a ' duty.' We can speak of perplexities, if we will, as conflicts between two ' sins,' though even this phrase is question-begging and is better avoided.[2] It is safer to regard them as conflicts between two ' duties,' two ' claims ' or two ' principles of morality ' ; or conversely as between two ' desirable results ' or two ' evils.' Any of these phrases will meet our purposes, and for all practical purposes they are identical ; for the achievement of a ' desirable result ' (or, what comes to the same thing, the avoidance of an ' evil ') is itself, as we have seen, a duty ; and remains a duty until some higher claim intervenes.

[1] The matter is further considered in Additional Note F, ' Doubt and Perplexity,' p. 395. Cp. H. Sidgwick, *Method of Ethics*, p. 201.

[2] Because, as we have previously noted (*supra* pp. 193, 194), the right course in *any* given set of circumstances cannot be sinful.

2. *Conflict of Evils*

To the argument of the last paragraph it will at once be replied, in language with which we are already familiar :— Surely there are some things which no Christian would ever do, however desirable the consequences might be—even though they involved the spiritual well-being of myriads of others? [1] It is unthinkable that a Christian minister should attempt to propagate the Gospel by means of a lie ; or should commit simony to secure preferment, even though by his promotion he may do infinite good to the souls of others. Nor should we allow that bigamy is morally right in any case, however desirable the probable consequences would appear to be. Few occasions can be imagined on which it could be a man's duty deliberately to intoxicate himself to the point

---

[1] These would be the sins which St. Thomas calls 'mortalia ex genere suo' (i. 2, q. 72, a. 2),—*always* mortal, whatever extenuating circumstances (e.g. excellence of motive) other than sheer lack of volition might be alleged. The assertion of such a category of sins which are always mortal without exception is a well-known crux in St. Thomas ; for he does not allow sin to be 'mortal' except from a motive of hostility towards God and goodness ('deordinatio animae usque ad aversionem ab ultimo fine, scilicet Deo,' *ib*. a. 5), and it is at least arguable that he has not proved that any 'peccatum' must *always* involve such a motive. The matter is well discussed by W. H. V. Reade, *Moral Theology of Dante's Inferno*, pp. 177–201 ; he comes to the conclusion that St. Thomas' problem is really due to a lack of vocabulary. St. Thomas teaches that 'there are some *peccata* which a man cannot *will* to perform without proving that he has renounced the *ultimus finis* and made himself worthy of damnation ; a correspondence between certain outward acts and certain inward states of will must as a rule be assumed (p. 194). . . . What St. Thomas requires (if it were possible) is a philosophical language in which the names of *peccata*, while expressing the specific character and *materia* of each sin (i.e. the external act), will also connote a definite kind of *dispositio* in the agent, so that there can be no question of a discrepancy between inward and outward *gravitas*.' This however would not meet the case unless a new term were thus formed for *every* sin, as *any* sin may become mortal (however venial it normally is) if the necessary *deordinatio* accompanies it (q. 88, a. 1). St. Thomas himself stultifies his own category of sins mortal *ex genere* by saying, e.g., of *acedia* that though it is of this category, any particular case of *acedia* is only mortal when manifested 'in perfection' (ii. 2, q. 35, a. 3). Thus even sins which are mortal *ex genere* are not mortal in every case ; they may be venial or pardonable, if not actually allowable, if committed 'in imperfection' only. In effect this amounts to saying that no 'sin' is absolutely and invariably mortal—in every case the circumstances must be taken into account. The class of sins mortal *ex genere* is merely a rough and ready guide as to what sins usually connote a sinful disposition, and has no scientific value.

of complete insensibility. We can fairly say that the duty of truthfulness, again, must outweigh everything except perhaps the gravest possible disasters on the other side; and this will limit severely the number of cases in which it is lawful even to contemplate the possibility of divergence from the truth. It may conceivably be right to lie to save a father's life, and at least the question deserves consideration; but it cannot often be right to lie to save a twopenny stamp.

Again, the duty of providing for one's family is clearly more urgent than that of choosing the profession most suited to one's natural gifts; and we could scarcely praise any man for leaving his children to the casual support of chance philanthropists in order to pursue a vocation in which his highest talents might be exercised for the benefit of mankind. Similarly—if we assume for a moment that stealing is sometimes pardonable—the mere motive of obedience to a parent's command could never justify a child in a theft, however slight; nor would it ever be right to withhold payment of a just debt in order to give to charitable purposes. In cases of this kind, our objector would conclude, there is surely a conflict between a ' sin ' which is wholly or almost wholly forbidden, and an alternative ' evil ' which it is indeed our duty to avoid if possible, but only by legitimate means?

At this point we must resume a discussion upon which we have twice already trenched. We admitted, at an earlier stage,[1] that the conscience both of individuals and of the Christian community has always thought of certain moral principles as principles to which no considerations of expediency, but only the claim of a ' higher ' principle (if such a principle could be found), could justify us in making exception. Voluntarily to disobey any such principle would be, as we say, ' wrong in itself,' or ' inherently sinful.' The conscience of Christendom, we further saw, has drawn a clear distinction between things ' wrong in themselves ' and things ' disastrous in their consequences,' and has emphasised that distinction by refusing to condemn *in toto* any class of action, however clearly it appertained to the second of these categories, unless it was clearly perceived to belong also to the first. Utilitarian philosophers, with anthropologists and

---

[1] *Supra* c. ii. pp. 72-78 ; c. vi. pp. 297, 309.

psychologists of certain schools of thought, combine to hint that in this matter the Christian conscience has been the victim of an illusion. As a fact, they suggest, it has been the experience of the disastrous consequences involved, and nothing else, which has all unconsciously led men to classify certain things as ' wrong in themselves,' in order to enforce by the sanctity of an *a priori* dogma the inexpediency of certain types of conduct. Thus they

> ' deduce you chastity
> Or shame, from just the fact that at the first
> Whoso embraced a woman in the field
> Threw club down and forewent his brains beside ;
> So stood a ready victim in the reach
> Of any brother-savage, club in hand.
> Hence saw the use of going out of sight
> In wood or cave to prosecute his loves.' [1]

Fortunately our purpose does not require us to enter the mazes of this problem. It is enough to remind ourselves that, where such principles are unanimously held, they have a claim which no one can morally disregard save at the bidding of an invincible conscience. On the other hand we recognise that—even if the utilitarian or evolutionist hypothesis be non-suited—such intuitions or quasi-intuitions of the ' inherent sinfulness ' of types of conduct are not necessarily infallible. In actual fact they have constantly been revised and re-stated ; whilst the accident that any one of them has not so far been modified by the conscience of Christendom cannot be taken as final evidence that it can never be so modified.

Furthermore, when any such principle of alleged immutability is involved in a serious problem of perplexity—when, for example, to obey the claims of truthfulness would involve a whole community in disaster—this very fact alone suggests strongly that it has been too rigidly formulated in the first instance   We are bound to begin our inquiry in such cases with the question, ' Can we show reason why the principle, either as originally stated or with some degree of mitigation, should have this final claim to preference over all other principles (whether of duty or of desirability) that can be put

---

[1] Browning, *Bishop Blougram's Apology.*

forward ? ' If, after exhaustive investigation of the principle by application to circumstances of widely different kinds, we find our original conviction of its primacy unimpaired—or find that, stated in a modified and more accurate form, it still retains the same ultimate primacy—we must abide by this conclusion. In every problem into which it enters, to ignore it will be a ' sin ' which no compensating advantage on the other side can exonerate from blame.

But the number of clearly-defined principles, of which it can be said that *in no conceivable circumstances* may the breach of them be thought of as in any degree allowable, must at the best be very small. Indeed, if we followed out this line of thought to the end (as has rarely been done in Christian ethics), there could strictly speaking be only *one* such principle. For if any principle had an inalienable right to be observed, *every* other principle would have to be waived if the two came into conflict in a given case. It is only because such conflicts between primary moral principles are in most cases almost inconceivable that we are able to speak loosely of a *number* of laws whose breach would be ' wrong in itself.' But the conception *is* a loose one ; and this is the reason why it is dangerous to assume, except as a last resort, that any given case of perplexity is a conflict between ' sin ' and ' evil.'

As a general rule, and apart from certain very specific sins (such as adultery), which, by virtue of that un-philosophical use of language to which we have just alluded, we can without hesitation call ' wrong in themselves,' we shall not be able to say more of any principle or claim than that it is of obligation ' normally,' or ' in ordinary circum-stances,' or ' in almost every case,' or ' in every case except that of extreme necessity.' Such limitations of legitimate exceptions to a minimum of cases are, no doubt, extremely valuable ; but they do not in themselves foreclose the question. There is always the possibility that the principle under discussion is opposed by a claim—which may perhaps appear primarily as a claim of desirability or expedience—so urgent that the case is not covered by the normal rule. We shall have a conflict between two ' claims ' or two ' evils,' and though one of these may normally have the right to prior consideration, we shall yet have to decide whether the case in question is not so abnormal as to constitute an exception to the rule. The more the general priority of one of the claims is recognised, the less likely it will be that in any particular case an exception should be made. But unless the prority is made absolute, the *possibility* of an exception is not wholly ruled out ; and we have still to find which claim in the particular circumstances is the higher, or which evil the lesser.

For that of course is the only solution in cases where the perplexity can legitimately be thought of—as it almost always can—as a conflict between two claims or two evils. It is the common-sense rule—' Of two evils choose the least,' or ' Of two claims choose the higher.' It is as old as Aristotle,[1] and Cicero endorses it emphatically.[2] But it is also the solution of the Church : it was officially stated as long ago as the 8th Council of Toledo in 653 A.D.[3] We must notice its apparent kinship to another principle which Christian thought from St. Paul onwards has unhesitatingly rejected—the principle of ' Let us do evil that good may follow,' or ' The end justifies the means.' It is hard at first sight to see the distinction between the two rules, though clearly the first

---

[1] *Eth. Nic.* ii. 9. 4, τὰ ἐλάχιστα ληπτέον τῶν κακῶν.

[2] *de Off.* iii. 28 (102), 'Minima de malis eligenda.' Gregory the Great of course enforces it : ' He who is encircled by walls on every side and tries to escape, throws himself down where the wall is lowest,' *Mor. in Hiob.* xxxii. 20 (35). Other instances of this commonplace will be found in Alex. Halens, *Summa*, ii. q. 121, m. 4, a. 2 ; Aquinas, *S.T.* ii. 2, q. 104, a. 5 in corp. ; W. Perkins, *Treatise on Conscience*, c. 2 ; J. Taylor, *Duct. Dub.* I. v., rule 8 : ' Where we cannot avoid as much as we should, we must avoid as much as we can ; ' Sanderson, *De Obl. Conscientiae Praelect.*, ii. 17, 18, 19 : though of diplomacy and compromise in general he says, ' Away with this insane theology from our schools, our pulpits, our hearts ; ' R. Baxter, *Christian Directory*, ii. c. 9 : ' Great and heinous sins may be endured in families to avoid a greater hurt, and because there is no other means to cure them. For instance, a wife may be guilty of heinous pride ' (later he adds, ' so proud that she will go mad or disturb her husband and his family by rage if her pride be not gratified by some sinful fashions, curiosities or excesses ') ' and the husband be necessitated to bear it ; not so far as not to reprove it, but so far as not to correct her, much less cure her. . . . A man may silently bear the sins of a wife, or other inferior (*sic*), without reproof or urging them to amend, in case that reproof hath been tried to the utmost and it is evident by full experience that it is like to do a great deal more harm than good ; ' F. Baldwin, *de Consc.* I. i. ; J. A. Osiander, *Theol. Cas.* i. Intr., c. 2, n. 52.

[3] Can. 2.

is mere common-sense, whilst the second opens the doors to the worst laxities of a degraded casuistry. But there is a distinction, and that a vital one. The first principle implies that we are shut up to an absolute choice between the two evils ; no other alternative is possible, no other open ; one or other must be chosen. ' The end justifies the means,' on the other hand, carries no such implication. It is open to all kinds of misuse ; it might for example be used to justify an evil ' means '—that is, a means commonly recognised as wholly unlawful or at all events as supremely inexpedient— where a good means was equally available. For in most normal circumstances there *is* available some other alternative, which though perhaps in no way a happy one, is at all events possible and free from any such flagrant violation of first principles. ' I must steal or starve,' for example, is not an inevitable alternative in modern England, whatever be the truth of more disturbed parts of the world. The English poor law system is not ideal, yet it does at least provide an inculpable way of escape from the dilemma in question.

Similarly, the vicar's wife, whom ' Punch ' represented as saying in reference to the Church rebuilding fund, ' As all honest means have failed, we must try a bazaar,' was choosing the wrong way out of her perplexity—assuming always the inherent immorality or supreme inexpediency of bazaars. It is usually impossible to exhaust ' honest means ' so lightly. A great many problems of perplexity may be eased by recog- nising that the moment for final choice has not yet come ; there still remain expedients, unpleasant enough no doubt, but at least unquestionably legitimate. But indefinite post- ponement is scarcely possible ; we must prepare to face the clear-cut dilemma sooner or later. And we are brought back to the difficulty that the principle ' Of two evils choose the least ' is of little value as it stands ; for in any given case we have still to decide *which* is the least evil of the two in question.

Even the scholastic attempt to classify ' law ' in the descending grades of natural, revealed, ecclesiastical and civil, is of little use here, except as telling us that in ordinary cases a ' law ' of higher rank in the hierarchy should take precedence of a 'law' of lower rank. Such a classification is easy and valid enough.[1] There can be no doubt that duties are of different degrees of urgency—to save a life is more important than to keep a social appointment, though the latter is, in general, a duty. But no such classification helps very much when we come to problems of real urgency. What we need to know is whether the case before us is one in which the 'ordinary' rule of procedure still holds good or not ; and that no classification can tell us. Thus a man should ordinarily, no doubt, vote for the political party in which he believes. But many exceptions can be made to the rule, as for example where the candidate is a person of grossly immoral character. What, then, is to be said of Herbert Spencer's case of the tenant farmer who may be ejected from his farm if he votes on the opposite side to his landlord ?[2] Here there are not merely two principles at issue as to which it is difficult to say that one takes general precedence of the other—the State before the family, or the family before the State ; there is also uncertainty as to whether the action contemplated—whichever it be—will be a serious infringement of the claims of the opposing principle. To vote against your party *may* not, as a matter of fact, make the slightest difference to the election on this occasion ; on the other hand, to vote against your landlord *may* not involve the ruin of your family. Everything appears to be enveloped in a fog of possibilities, uncertainties and guess-work ; and even if we could say *in general* which of the two duties is the higher, it would not carry with it any final solution of the particular problem.

The same conclusion must be granted in the case of another casuistical rule which has wide support, and which both Sanderson and Jeremy Taylor put forward.[3] It is the principle that, other things being equal, 'negative precepts take precedence of positive.' Where a principle of morality normally falls into the shape of 'Thou shalt not,' it should

---

[1] Instances will be found in Jowett, *Introduction to Philebus* (in *The Works of Plato Translated*, vol. iv.) ; Martineau, *Types of Ethical Theory*, ii. p. 40 ; Janet, *Morale*, p. 369. The difficulties involved are well brought out by Thamin, *op. cit.* pp. 326-327.

[2] H. Spencer, *Data of Ethics* (1884), p. 267.

[3] *de Obl. Consc. Prael.* ii. 17-19 ; *Duct. Dub.* I. v., rule 8, § 35.

commonly be obeyed in preference to an alternative ' Thou shalt.' This rule, though it is no more than a rough and ready test, will sometimes be found of use. Negative commands are always more definite than positive ones, for they draw a line between certain clearly-designated types of action and ourselves, and say in effect, ' Never admit these into your life.' For this reason it has happened that practical moral instruction is always more rife in statement of what is to be avoided than of what is to be embraced, and that in regard to the principles of greatest urgency it prefers a negative form. ' Thou shalt not steal ' is clear and concise ; the corresponding positive form (' Always be honest ') is vaguer and less effective. But every negative rule has a positive counterpart. It is somewhat of an accident that it has gained currency in the one form and not in the other— ' Every negative is founded on a positive,' as St. Thomas says.[1] If it should happen that a child were brought up on the two rules (among others) ' Never omit your prayers ' and ' Always save life if you can,' the strict application of our principle would result in his leaving a sick man to die rather than neglect his prayers to attend to him.

The attempt, therefore, to grade our principles of conduct into ' higher and lower claims,' or ' greater and lesser evils,' or ' positive and negative precepts,' proves neither very hopeful nor very fruitful. Yet it is not without importance that we should examine each such claim and try to give it a general position in our hierarchy of duties. Reflections of this kind serve one purpose of great value. They help to stiffen the moral fibre both of the individual and of society. If a man can be brought to reflect upon his character and circumstances ; to select those principles which, viewed in an impartial and serious-minded atmosphere, seem to him most worthy of his constant and devoted allegiance ; and then resolve never to set them aside except at the call of some greater moral urgency, the effort will make of him a more reliable, consistent, honourable and unselfish person than he would otherwise be, and in cases of perplexity he will have less doubt than others as to the direction in which his true duty lies. And if many men could be brought to take

[1] *S.T.* i. 2, q. 72, a. 6.

the same steps, the results upon the society in which they moved would be considerable. Standards would be raised; intercourse purified; many problems of apparent 'perplexity' would cease to arise, or if they arose would be clearly seen not to be problems at all. We may not be able to solve problems of perplexity; but by stimulating thought of this character we can certainly reduce both their number and their burden.

The difficulties we have been considering might be illustrated by many different examples. Two cases in which the attempt has been made to stamp a practice as a 'sin' to which no exception could possibly be allowed have been already considered—the case of 'birth-control' and the case of gambling. In the latter instance we found ourselves forced to conclude that the arguments on which it was alleged that all gambling was wrong in itself were fallacious; in the former case we found that the crux of the problem turned on the meaning of the word 'unnatural.' But in both cases it was obvious that a fallacy in the *a priori* argument for the condemnation of the practice did not end the discussion—the argument from grave social inexpediency had still to be met and considered. As regards gambling, it appeared that so little was to be said on behalf of the practice in any individual case that it would rarely be possible for the Christian to consider himself free to indulge in it on the grounds that to do so was the 'lesser evil.' With birth-control the case was different; circumstances might arise (so at least many moralists would hold) in which relaxation of the principle in a particular instance might conceivably prove the right course in spite of the argument from general expediency. To illustrate the situation further we may examine two more problems—the first that of 'lying,' the second that of a 'general strike'—in which attempts have been made to foreclose the issue by some such principle as that lying, or striking, is 'wrong in itself,' and therefore never allowable.

Our method must be to examine the principle thus presented, as we did in the previous cases of gambling and birth-control; and consider whether in the form as stated, or in some mitigated form, it can be upheld. If it can, the problem is one of a 'sin' against an 'evil,' and no further discussion is needed. But if the best conclusion we can reach is simply that the lie, or the general strike, is only allowable ' in cases of extreme urgency ' (or some such formula) we are still within the realm of conflicts between ' evil ' and ' evil,' or ' claim ' and ' claim.' It remains only to ask whether any method can be devised to discover when the urgency is sufficiently extreme, or the circumstances sufficiently abnormal, to justify us in preferring a generally lower claim to a generally higher one ; or to enable us on principle to select for obedience one of two claims of approximately equal rank.

3. *Problems of Truthfulness*

A lie, as we noticed in a previous chapter, is obviously the utterance of something which the speaker believes to be untrue—for the question as to whether it is *actually* true or not no more affects its sinfulness (if it is sinful) than the accident that it occasionally produces happy results. It is the intention of representing the facts as other than they are conceived to be by the speaker which is of cardinal importance. It is sometimes suggested that ' the intention to deceive ' should be included in the definition, and some casuists diverted their energies from more urgent subjects to consider whether—on this basis—any man could ever be said to lie to himself.[1] The problem is of theoretical interest only. No one could misrepresent the facts as he conceived them without *some* hope of deceiving ; but whether that hope should be included in the ' essence ' of the lie, or (as St. Thomas decided [2]) in its ' perfection,' is of no importance. Again we need not stop to observe that lying is possible by other channels of expression as well as speech. Gesture, glance and even on occasion silence may equally well be employed to misrepresent the facts. One thing, however, it is important to notice—that concealment of truth is quite a different thing from lying, and has its own series of problems. There are many occasions on which it is certainly

---

[1] E.g. de Lugo, *de Fide*, iv. 11.—Is ' Every day and in every way I am getting better and better ' a lie to oneself ?

[2] *S.T.* ii. 2, q. 110. a. 1, ad 3.

allowable, and may be a duty, to conceal the truth, but the problem will still arise, as an entirely distinct issue, 'Granted that I *may* (or *ought*) to conceal the truth on this occasion, may I do so by means of a lie ? '

Moralists have at all times been attracted by the principle that in no circumstances whatever is any conscious attempt to misrepresent facts allowable ; and that consequently lying is a ' sin ' which no opposite evil can justify us in committing. St. Augustine, as we have seen, is the champion of this rigorism ; Kant followed him with equal emphasis.[1] Traditional catholicism, we suggested, has never faced the full difficulty of maintaining this position ; partly because the subterfuge of equivocation was normally found to be available ; partly because, while refusing to regard any lie as sinless or allowable, it has freely treated many lies as ' venial ' or pardonable. The distinction is a nice one, and common-sense suggests very forcibly that in this matter it is unreal as well. Not only do we agree that many conventional expressions which are not strictly true are free from blame ; there are also occasions when the ordinary decencies of society demand the use of an impromptu euphemism. ' Not at home,' as a social convention, has its critics ; but their criticism is directed wholly towards the effect the phrase may have upon the servant who is told to use it, or the child who overhears it and knows it to be in the strict sense untrue.[2] If misunderstandings of this kind could be avoided, the usage would scarcely be criticised. Less tolerable is the advertising ' puff '—' The most remarkable novel of the year,' or ' Unrivalled in excellence,' or ' A real bargain.' But even this is harmless enough— for no one would stake his life upon its truth ; and it is regarded in the main as no more than a regrettable, if pardonable, eccentricity of salesmanship.

But the problem goes far deeper than this. Professional secrets at all events must be guarded at all costs—the secrets of the confessor, the statesman or the doctor ; and sometimes the mere refusal to answer a question will be tantamount to a

---

[1] See the tract *On a supposed right to tell lies from benevolent motives*, in Abbott, *Kant's Theory of Ethics*, p. 361 ; and cp. *supra* pp. 188-192.

[2] An interesting example will be found in E. V. Lucas, *Landmarks*, c. 3.

revelation of the secret. Only a direct denial of the truth will preserve the truth from discovery ; is it then allowable ? Cases again are commonly adduced in which it seems at least an open question whether a lie is not the lesser evil of two alternatives—the case of the murderer with an axe (a credulous murderer, no doubt, if he fails to suspect the lie) who enquires whether your father is in the house ; the case of the lunatic whose life can be saved only by lying to him ; the case of the dying mother who enquires after her dead child ; the case of an innocent life which only a lie can save from a tyrant, a pirate or a miscarriage of justice. And further—whatever be our judgment on these cases—it is easy to imagine both occasions on which veracity is apparently wholly unmeritorious, and also occasions on which a lie is apparently at least as noble and praiseworthy as the truth.

Imagine, for example, a person with a shameful secret to conceal, threatened by two blackmailers. The first, who knows of the secret, says, ' Give me a thousand pounds, or I will reveal such-and-such a shocking truth about you.' The second, not knowing of the secret, but having gained some other hold over his victim, says, ' Give me a thousand pounds, or I will tell such-and-such a shocking lie about you.' The first blackmailer could perfectly well have invented a lie to suit his purpose, but if we think of him as one who (like Matilda's aunt, in Mr. Belloc's ' Cautionary Tale ')

' from his earliest youth
Had had a strict regard for truth,'

it is at least possible that he would reject the idea of blackmail by means of a lie, whereas he does not hesitate to black-mail by means of the truth. Yet it scarcely seems that this curious scruple, however genuine it may be, in any way lessens his guilt. He contemplates one sin only—that of blackmail, and rejects the other, that of lying ; whilst the second blackmailer is prepared to commit both ; but the immorality of both appears to be identical. It may be urged that in the circumstances the blackmail is so heinous an offence that the additional act of lying is relatively insignificant. But even so it is curious that we have a case in which the choice between truth and lying seems indifferent—in which the lie, if it is told, appears to add nothing to the wickedness of the agent.

However this may be—and we need not deny that a case of sorts might perhaps be made out for the moral superiority of the truthful blackmailer—there are certainly 'noble' lies which to all ordinary seeming are as praiseworthy as the truth. John Inglesant's heroic attempt to save King Charles' honour, at the cost both of veracity and of his own reputation and freedom, is an obvious example from fiction. The well-known instance of the British officer, himself an atheist, who refused to save his life from his Mohammedan captors by abjuring Christianity, lest it should bring the British name into discredit, may be set alongside it. In the latter case the speaker might no doubt have said, ' I am as a matter of fact an atheist, and on those grounds I regard Christianity as not only wholly untrue but also a deplorable error. But as by " Christianity " I imagine that you imply not merely a particular set of doctrines, but the whole system of life, ideals and civilisation of which (whether I like it or not) I am as much a product as my fellow countrymen ; and as I cannot in the present circumstances abjure the one without, in my opinion, showing myself disloyal to the other, I refuse to do what you require.' Such a declaration (if it had been heard out to the end) would have been strictly true, and as ' noble ' and effective as the lie that was actually told.[1] The captive might, again, have refused to answer altogether. But in either case, would anything have been gained that was not gained by the lie ; and can either alternative be regarded as in any way more estimable or laudable than the lie ? Does the lie detract in the smallest measure from the nobility of the action, or taint even in the slightest degree an otherwise amazing piece of heroism ? Indeed was not the lie the most effective gesture in the circumstances ? And if so, have we not again a case in which there is no difference between lying and telling the truth ?

[1] Technically perhaps, no lie was involved in the assertion ' I refuse to abjure Christianity.' Virtually, however, a lie was implied, as the only possible construction that could be put upon it by the captors would be ' I refuse to abjure Christianity because I am a Christian.'

We have then some ground for concluding that the misrepresentation of the real (or supposed) facts cannot in every case be condemned out of hand as sinful. It may be impossible to secure agreement on this point; and further argument would probably be fruitless. But even those who refuse to accept this conclusion introduce what is, in effect, a very similar qualification, when they allow that some lies, though 'sinful,' are in essence venial or excusable. The problem for Christian casuistry is so to express these judgments as not to open the door to laxity of every degree. There are special reasons—reasons peculiar to the problem in question—why we should hesitate long before admitting the moral justifiability of any lie, even the most apparently heroic. A lie, in the first place, is often such an easy thing to tell with impunity, that considerations of expediency and self-interest—of what will happen if it be 'found out'—do not help to reinforce our desire to resist temptation so much in this matter as in others. Again, even if we do not admit Bacon's contention [1] that there is something radically pleasant and attractive in lying, the absolute 'Thou shalt not lie' has so continually been, and must so continually be, qualified in one way or another that the whole principle has become enveloped in a cloud of doubt. There is obviously something ambiguous about it, but what that 'something' is no one is quite prepared to say. For these reasons it is *prima facie* more likely that men will lie than steal or murder—let us say—for self-interest. While, therefore, we recognise that self-interest and duty may sometimes point in the same direction, and that a naturally desirable action, or one which is prompted in the main by family affection, maternal solicitude or the like, need be none the worse for that, it is when these sentiments appear to move us in the direction of a lie that we have most to be on our guard. The claims of truthfulness in any given case will find few other motives high or low to second them; whilst opposed to them will be every specious argument that sentiment can devise. T. H. Green clearly envisaged this fact in the hypothetical advice

[1] *Essay* I. The idea is as old as Lucian's *Philopseudes*. Cp. also the barber in *Romola* (c. 3): 'Truth is a riddle for eyes and wit to discover, which it were a mere spoiling of sport for the tongue to betray.'

he imagined himself to be giving to Jeanie Deans in the classical problem of ' The Heart of Midlothian.' [1]

There is a further reason why Christian thought rightly regards any lie with suspicion, and hesitates to admit its legitimacy. There are some acts which more than others throw a flood of light upon the moral condition of their agents. You may see a man drinking beer, but the fact does not in itself suggest that he is an habitual drunkard. You may observe him reading a novel or seated in a theatre, but it does not follow that he is an incorrigible idler. But if you hear him lie—particularly if he lies with conviction—you suspect at once that he is habitually careless about truth. It is not easy to assign any reason for this curious difference in the value of acts as evidence of their agent's character; but it would seem to depend in the main upon the known habits of contemporary society in each case. In a society of drunkards you would readily suspect everyone who had recourse to the bottle of being a toper; in a moderately sober society the same suspicion is slow in arising. And because the modern conscience is on the whole sluggish in this matter of truthfulness, a lie is only too often the sign of general unreliability.

Exceptions will arise of course, where the known habits or character of the individual outweigh the evidence of his spoken truth or falsehood; and this consideration throws some light upon our two puzzling cases of the truthful blackmailer and the unflinching atheist. The reason, for instance, why we tend to regard the truthful blackmailer as no better than the lying blackmailer is that we cannot conceive anyone who would willingly be guilty of blackmail as having any real regard for truth. If his truthfulness is not wholly hypocritical, it must be wholly conventional. A man so indifferent in general to moral issues can scarcely be genuinely sensitive on this single point. And, on the other hand, in the case of the officer who would not abjure the religion in which he did not believe, we feel convinced that one so fully alive to the highest demands of the situation in which he found himself could not be the victim of levity in regard to truth and falsehood. In either case the problem of their

[1] *Prolegomena to Ethics,* p. 380.

regard for truth is definitely settled, and that in a direction contradicting the face-value of the evidence, by enquiry into the full conditions of the act.

In general, however, and apart from particular exceptions of this kind, we regard all lies with abhorrence, because they suggest only too strongly that the man who utters them is habitually indifferent to truth. Furthermore—and here the sin of lying is analogous to all other sins—indulgence breeds habit ; and every lie is dangerous in this respect also, that it may tend to make its speaker more careless about truth. And yet, as we have seen, it is universally agreed that some lies are pardonable, if not actually allowable. Can we then discover some essential factor or factors in the lies which are commonly condemned which are absent in the lies which are universally condoned ? If so we shall be some way towards determining what it is about lies which makes them immoral, and shall be in a position to say that where these factors are absent—though at no other time—it is at least possible that the ' lie ' is blameless.

4. Lies, Pardonable and Unpardonable

There will be those, of course, who object to this form of enquiry. They will say, with Augustine, ' I am convinced that all lies are wrong. I can give no reason for this convic-tion ; it is a primary intuition about which nothing more can be said.'[1] But if they draw even the slightest distinction, between ' less pardonable ' and ' more pardonable ' lies, it must be based upon the presence or absence of just such factors as those of which we are in search. For this reason we may fitly vary the terms of our enquiry and ask, ' What lies are pardonable, and what are not ? '—recognising at the same time that those who do not feel themselves tied to the Augustinian tradition will in some cases prefer the word ' blameless,' or even ' laudable,' to the word ' pardonable.' And certain conclusions at once emerge. A lie inspired by a wholly ' carnal ' or wholly ' selfish ' end could hardly ever be condoned. Again, no merely trivial purpose could condone

---

[1] For a modern exposition of the Augustinian position, see *infra*, Additional Note G, pp. 399 ff.

a lie, apart from the recognised conventions of polite society, or those 'jocose' lies in which the discovery of the deception follows so closely upon the deception itself—and is so essential to the harmlessness of the joke—that for practical purposes there is no deception at all. The certainty that the lie would involve suffering, distress or injustice would be additional *prima facie* evidence against its legitimacy. More important, however, is the fact that no lie which disturbs to any extent the general atmosphere of trust and confidence which alone makes civilised intercourse possible, is easily pardoned. 'I must not cause that declarations in general should find no credit.' [1]

This disturbance may result from a lie in one or both of two ways. Sometimes its effect is confined to the two persons immediately involved—it destroys all confidence between them, but spreads no further. At other times, the lie will in addition reflect upon the trustworthiness of the Church, nation, class or profession to which the speaker belongs, and so imperil the moral credit of that society, causing it to forfeit the respect and fair dealing of others. And it appears that, other things being equal, the more a lie tends to produce either or both of these two results, the nearer it comes to being classed in ordinary judgments as 'a sin' which no alternative 'evil' can justify —the greater the urgency required to make it venial, if it can be so called at all. For a penitent to discover that his confessor had lied to him, for example, would be so serious a thing that scarcely any degree of 'urgency' could condone the lie. It would destroy a relationship of peculiar confidence and sanctity, and would cast a slur upon the whole priesthood

But cases arise in which, by open or tacit consent between the parties, it is agreed beforehand that a particular lie, or lies of a particular type, shall not be allowed to affect their relationship in either of these ways. This is true of those conventional phrases or decent euphemisms to which we have alluded ; though an inexperienced person—a young footman or a child—not being aware of the convention, might still regard the duty of truthfulness as binding. It is true, again, in the case of war. Not indeed that civilised inter-

---

[1] Kant, *op. cit.* (Abbott, p. 362).

course is altogether at an end between the contesting parties. They still look forward to a resumption of full international relations when their particular dispute is settled. Consequently the degree to which stratagem and deceit are allowed is strictly limited by a tacit convention between them; and if either side violates this convention—as would happen if it advanced its machine-guns under cover of the Red Cross, or of a white flag—it cannot plead the exigencies of war as its excuse. But within the limits of convention, deceit is regarded as legitimate. It will not redound to the discredit of the general who employs it, or to that of his country, nor will it embitter or disillusion his opponent.

A similar situation arises where the deceit can never be discovered. Here also the condition of mutual confidence will not be violated in either way. This would appear to excuse a benevolent lie to a lunatic (we recall Jeremy Taylor's case of the 'fellow dressed as an angel'), to a sick man in delirium, or to a person at the point of death. An interesting side-issue here is the problem whether a deceitful *promise*, equally well-intentioned, is equally pardonable. Would it be right for example for a son, in order to ease the last moments of his dying mother, to promise something which he never intended to perform, and would certainly not have undertaken in any other circumstances owing to its wholly inexpedient or unjust character? The question derives its acuteness partly from the special sanctity we attach to death-bed appeals, partly from the peculiar nature of a promise. Vows and oaths present similar difficulties, but we cannot discuss them here. It is enough to suggest that where discovery is impossible (as distinct from merely unlikely) one of the principal arguments against mendacity disappears.

In cases such as these we cannot indeed say without drastic qualification that any lie or deceit is excusable. An aimless lie would still be blameworthy; a selfish, malicious or unjust lie would still be base; a notorious lie might lead others astray. But if real evil can be avoided by the lie it is at least possible that the good which might accrue would outweigh not only the scandal caused to bystanders, if there are any, but also the harm done to the speaker's character either by the act of lying, or even by the indulgence of selfishness. And if other motives besides selfishness were operative, or if his purpose were wholly unselfish, the lie would be by so much the more relatively if not absolutely blameless. At all events in the cases in question, the normal arguments for truthfulness no longer enter into consideration ; we have something more akin to a choice between two evils than to one between an evil and a sin.

The problem becomes more difficult where the normal confidence between persons would be shaken by the lie in one or other of the two ways mentioned, though not in both. It might for instance cause a private rupture between the two persons primarily concerned, without having any repercussion upon society or any class of society as a whole. Here we are bound to confess that only a high degree of ' evil ' to be avoided would excuse the lie. We may take the case of the sick mother who asks her husband for news of her sick son, the latter, to the husband's knowledge, but not to the mother's, being already dead. If the ' lie that cures ' is told, and succeeds in its purpose, its falsehood will be manifest. It will not redound to the discredit of society as a whole, but it might result in deep-rooted unhappiness in the family—the wife resenting that her husband should treat her as a child and suspecting him of screening her from knowledge of unpleasant facts at other times ; the husband, once he has begun to shield her from the truth, gradually removing her further and further from his real thoughts and anxieties.

Substitute a doctor for the husband, and the balance is changed. A reasonable patient would recognise that it is a doctor's business to save life wherever possible. She might be grieved that he thought her too frail to bear the truth ; but her outlook on life would not be seriously altered, nor would the reputation either of the particular doctor or of the medical profession suffer. Substitute a priest for the doctor, and once more the balance changes. A priest's business is with the soul rather than with the body, and among the spiritual results which he is specially bound to consider and promote is exactly that respect for veracity which we regard as essential to human intercourse. His lie would not merely suggest that he—although peculiarly commissioned to safe-guard the credit of truthfulness—was careless to its claims ; it might also lower the dignity of truthfulness itself in the estimation of the sufferer, so that her own regard for it would be lessened both in theory and in practice. Probably we cannot go further than this in general consideration of the problem. In every case a further adjustment of balance would be necessary in view of the distinctive mentality of the patient, and the exact relationship existing between her and the speaker. Enough has been said, however, to suggest that the ' good ' which might be secured by the lie would have to be off-set by a possibly high degree of resultant ' evil ' too. In most cases nothing less than the moral certainty that death would follow the shock of hearing the truth would justify us in readily regarding the lie as venial.

In other cases, the lie, while making no difference in the relationship between the persons concerned, might involve society as a whole, or one particular class or branch of society, in discredit and danger. This brings us at last to the classical problem of the lie to the pirate. Discussion of it by the great casuists has often been confused, both by their regard-ing a broken or lying promise as more heinous than a simple lie, and by treating a mental reservation or equivocation as less heinous. Busenbaum, for example, the Jesuit of some-what lax opinions on whom Liguori based his ' Moral Theology,' says that a promise made to a pirate or robber holds good ' unless you remembered to use an equivocation ' in making it.[1] Sanderson[2] considers merely the promise made with mental reservation, and is more at pains to condemn reservations as such than to discuss the case. Joseph Hall[3] investigates the promise on oath only, and holds it to be inviolable because ' once we have interested God in a business it is dangerous not to be punctual in the performance.' ' If therefore a bold thiefe,' he writes, ' taking

[1] Alph. Lig. iii. § 174. ' Si oblitus sis uti aequivocatione.' To his credit Liguori, in expanding and discussing the decision, omits this clause —a fact which is wholly unnoticed by Meyrick (Moral Theology of Ch. of Rome, p. 45), who criticises him severely and undeservedly on the point. Liguori held that the promise would be binding in foro interno.

[2] de Obl. Jur. (Jacobson, p. 198).

[3] Cases of Conscience, Dec. i., case 8.

you at an advantage have set his dagger to your brest, and
with big oaths threatened to stab you, unless you promise
and sware to give him an hundred pounds to be left on such
a day in such a place for him, I see not how, if you be able,
you can dispence with the performance.' But, following St.
Thomas[1] and others, he suggests that you are not without
redress. ' The help is (which is well suggested by *Lessius*)
that nothing hinders why you may not, when you have done,
call for it back againe, as unjustly extorted.   And truly
we are beholding to the Jesuits for so much of a reale equivocation.' If, however, you promise also not to denounce the
pirate, ' you are bound to be silent in this act ; but withall
if you find that your silence may be prejudiciall to the
publique good, for that you perceive the licentiousnesse of
the offender proceeds (and it is like so to do) to the like
mischiefe unto others, you ought, though not to accuse him
for the fact done to you, yet to give warning to some in
authority to have a vigilant eye upon so leud a person, for the
prevention of any further villainy.' [2]

Setting these complications on one side, it is clear that a
lie to a pirate cannot rupture the normal relations between
him and his victim. These have been sufficiently and indeed
finally broken by the pirate himself. He is an Ishmaelite
with his hand against every man, and every man's hand
against him. He has declared his intention of associating
with his fellows upon a basis wholly different from that of
ordinary civilised intercourse. Certainly his victim—unless
like St. John the Apostle he is set upon reclaiming him to
an upright life—will have no further intention of associating
with him on any terms whatever ; except perhaps as a member
of a society bent upon his extermination. So far as their
mutual intercourse is concerned, therefore, the lie is wholly
unimportant. But there is still intercourse of a sort between
the pirate and society. By trusting his victim he shows that

---

[1] *S.T.* ii. 2, q. 89, a. 7, ad 3.
[2] With this may be compared the established rule that if a priest learns
in the confessional that his ' penitent ' intends to do harm to a third person,
and cannot dissuade him from it, he may hint to the intended victim that he
is in some danger, though he must do this without running any risk that the
identity of the ' penitent' is guessed. *C.J.C.* c. 2, X. i. 31 ; Alex. Halens,
Summa, ii. q. 121, m. 4, a. 3 ; Lyndwood, V. 16, verb. ' confessum.'

he does not expect society as a whole to treat him with complete unscrupulosity, and is prepared to make some slight concession in return. If he believes his victim's lie and on the faith of it releases him, discovery of its falsehood will (as Whewell[1] pointed out) involve other members of the liar's caste or society, who may fall into the pirate's hands, in very serious consequences. In representing those whose spokesman (even though unwillingly) he must be held to be as holding a lower standard of morality than in fact they actually hold, the liar has not only lowered their credit, but has also lessened such small chances of fair dealing at the pirate's hands as they might otherwise have had. And in doing this without their consent he has inflicted an injustice upon them which it is hard to condone.

This consideration however would appear to be inoperative if the lie availed to secure time for a rescue party to arrive, and put a stop to the pirate's career of aggression. We have assumed that one main reason for not lying to him is that the lie may lower the credit of society as a whole, and so aggravate his tendency to lawlessness. But if immediately after the lie has been told he is certain to be captured, he will have no chance of executing reprisals upon other members of society. Not that *any* lie will necessarily be excusable even in these circumstances. If the motive is merely selfish or cowardly, it will of course stamp the act as selfish and cowardly too, even though the result might still be in the best interests of society. If on the other hand it envisaged any other consideration, as for example the possibility of ridding society of a pest, or saving the life of a third person, it would be so much the less blameworthy. If, again, the effect on the speaker's character were likely to be seriously harmful, the lie would be hard to condone ; if no such consequence were to be feared it would help to make it venial.

In the palmy days of theology, progress was made by someone less cautious than the rest proposing a thesis, which was then subjected to discussion and criticism. The argument of the preceding paragraphs, which may appear all too cold and calculating, is no more than such a tentative thesis, open for anyone to criticise as he will. One such

[1] *Elements of Morality*, i. p. 174.

criticism, however, can be dealt with at once. It is commonly said that everyone has a right to the truth ; and it may be alleged that this simple piece of natural justice has here been wholly ignored. This is true enough ; but is the doctrine of a universal right to the truth so simple or so just ? There are many truths, secrets for example, to which few of us have any right at all. The axiom must at least be amended into the form : ' Everyone has a right not to be deceived.' In this form it is more specious, until we realise that it is no more than another version of ' Never lie to anyone,' and that even those who endorse this principle most strongly have always found it necessary to add, ' But some lies are readily pardonable.'   In this form the axiom will hold good, but it is no longer any criticism of our argument. It allows us to consider in *what* circumstances deceit is pardonable. We may have defined our circumstances wrongly—that is only too possible—but nothing in the principle just alleged makes it wrong of us to have attempted to define them. Even Baxter, who held as strongly as anyone the doctrine that a lie was a ' sin ' against which no ' evil ' could be balanced,[1] wavered in his allegiance when he considered the case of the pirate. ' If King and nobles were in a ship,' he writes,[2] ' which would be taken and all destroyed by pirates unless I told a lie and said they are other persons ; if I were equally in doubt which course to take, to lie or not (though sin have more evil than all our lives have good), yet a sinful omitting to save their lives is a greater evil than a sinful telling of a lie.' The argument is obscure, for the simple reason that Baxter's resolution to regard all lies as sin has forced him to present it in the form of a conflict between two sins. But the conclusion is obvious, and it is the same as ours. There will be occasions in life when—whether a lie be ' always a sin ' or no—it will be virtually blameless ; and the business of casuistry is to discover of what kind those occasions may be. The method suggested may be condemned as ' utilitarian ' ; but what other method could there be ?

---

[1] *Christian Directory*, I. iii. 19. ' The lives of many may not be saved by a lie.'   Cp. *ib*. 14, ' We must not sin for the accomplishment of any good whatever.'
[2] *Ib*. I. iii. 6.

It is therefore along lines such as these that we may deal with the problems connected with lying, whether we hold that a lie is ' always wrong ' or no. The case of the murderer with the axe is analogous to that of the pirate ; the gravity of the lie turns in the main on the likelihood of its aggravating the murderer's activity against society, and on the possibility of securing his apprehension before he commits further acts of the same character. Where, however, the force from which we think to escape or to save another does not threaten immediate danger to life and limb, so that other alternatives still remain open, the evils incident to every lie would seem to forbid deceit except perhaps as a last resort. Nor would it seem often, if ever, admissible to meet fraud in business or industry with counter-fraud or lies. Such action would only tend to poison for ever a well already tainted ; and the history of industry in the last century offers countless examples of the social ruin caused by such selfish and dishonest methods of short-sighted expediency.

The case of Jeanie Deans remains more difficult ; not least of all because the dénouement of the novel weights the scales on the side of truthfulness by providing a happy though unexpected issue to the whole tragic situation. Had Scott allowed Effie to be executed as the result of her sister's truthfulness, the problem would have been presented in its true colours. Much can be said in extenuation or even in strong support of the lie. Its falsity could never have been discovered ; it is this fact as much as any other which makes the problem so acute. Nor would injustice have been done by it—Effie was as innocent of the alleged murder of her child in actual fact as she was in Jeanie's mind. And yet we may doubt whether any serious-minded Christian could really have advised Jeanie to lie in cold blood. Unless we are to base this conclusion on a mere sentiment, the reason for it must be sought in the peculiar sanctity of the relationship which would have been violated by the lie—a relationship between the individual and the society to which she owed everything in life. This relationship would be violated, even though society remained unconscious of the fact ; and that on an occasion when society, in exchange for the protection and sustenance it had given throughout

life, rightfully and formally demanded a truthful answer
to its question.

If ever a ' right to the truth ' could be validly pleaded, it
must surely be in circumstances of this kind. But if we
continue to avoid the idea of ' rights to the truth ' and consider the circumstances alone, it is certain that the violation
in question could not fail to have a terrible effect at least
upon the speaker's character, and that by virtue of the special
relationship so violated. In the case of one less conscientious
and pure-hearted than Jeanie Deans it would perhaps merely
have strengthened that tendency to postpone the claims of
society to all other claims which is of the essence of disloyalty.
This would have been terrible enough, for disloyalty in an
unconscientious person snaps the last link which binds him,
and all who take their cue from him, to any moral obligations
at all. In the case of Jeanie herself it would have resulted
in lifelong distress, questioning and shame, leading perhaps
to a morbid self-hatred which would have made her life
unbearable to herself and useless to others. The same
result, it may be said, would have occurred had she told
the truth and her sister been put to death. This may be so ;
yet there is at least one difference. If the truth were told,
Jeanie could turn for comfort and sympathy in her distress
of mind to any member of society who recognised the claims
of loyalty ; in the case of the lie she could appeal for consolation to no one but Effie. And if Effie were a person of her
sister's own moral calibre she would be the first to repudiate
the lie told on her account—indeed, she would never have
permitted it to be told. But the Effie of the novel is a weak
and colourless woman who could do little to support Jeanie
in her distress. The probable result of the lie would therefore
be to save the life of a somewhat ineffective person, and at
the same time to destroy the moral efficiency of a character
of real value to society. Effie's life has indeed a claim to
sympathy ; but an even greater claim is that of Jeanie's soul.

Unless, therefore, we choose to foreclose the issue, and
say bluntly either that society in this case has an undeniable
right to the truth, or Effie to the lie that would save her life
—and whichever of these positions we chose to adopt we
should have no answer to those who championed the opposite

conclusion—we must attempt to argue from the probable consequences in some such way as this.   Here the amateur casuist is at a disadvantage.   He cannot rival Scott in fertility of imagination, and therefore any attempt of his to construct alternative endings to the story will be weak and uninspiring as compared with the original.   The author, in fact, has told us either too much or too little to make any other solution but his own a possible one.   If he had given the bare facts of the problem and asked, ' What should Jeanie have done ? ' without telling us what she did do and how it all turned out for the best, we should have had an open field for discussion, as we have, for example, in Frank Stockton's problem of ' The Lady and the Tiger.'   If, again, he had written two further alternative endings to his story, in one of which Jeanie still told the truth but failed to secure the reprieve, whilst in the other she lied and saved Effie's life ; and had traced out in each of them—as only he could do—the sequel of the choice for all the persons concerned, we should be in a similar but even better position.   As it is, in attempting to estimate the best action in the circumstances, we have to pit our puny imaginations against Scott's whole genius, to create for comparison other issues to the story than the one which he has made so vivid

Our instances have given us some, at least, of the factors whose presence tends to make a lie wholly inadmissible. If its effect will be to render the speaker more indifferent either to truthfulness or to loyalty, or to violate the mutual confidence between himself and the person to whom the lie is told, or between the latter and society, or between society and the liar, nothing but the highest possible degree of urgency could make it pardonable.   Where the probability of evil consequences in any or all of these respects is slight or negligible, whilst real evil of other kinds could be averted by the lie, we are still within the realm of conflict, and have to look further for some principle on which to weigh up the evil on either side.   The discussion may appear to have been almost fruitless ; at best it has only served to reduce somewhat the area within which a lie, however well-intentioned, can be called venial.   But even this is something.   If a man can say ' Within such and such limits alone can the possibility of lying ever be condoned—outside them a lie is a " sin " which no " evil " can counterbalance '—he has at least one anchor which will hold in the storm of temptation. The temptation to lie usually comes with startling suddenness, and an immutable rule is of immense value. ' Ofttimes the case is so sudden that no enquiry can be made, and therefore I confess that a Christian should know which sins are greatest and to be most avoided.' [1] The Christian has still to be ' cautious and watchful amid the reefs and inlets, the shallows and straits ' [2] of the moral life ; but it is all to the good that he should have charted and buoyed some at least of the rocks in that difficult sea.

5. *General Strikes*

In the case of a general strike, as in the case of lying, we find moralists, politicians and apologists who attempt to force it into the popular but misleading shape of a ' sin ' versus an ' evil,' or some kindred formula, and thereby to foreclose the issue. Here, however, this method of argument cuts both ways. On the one hand we meet with a doctrine which exculpates the striker altogether by saying that a man always has the right not to work if he prefers it. This is only another way of saying that loyalty to the community never demands that men should work, and that cessation of work cannot therefore be a sin against the community ; or that a strike can never be a sin. The issue therefore is thus presented as one between a duty to the trade-union on the one hand, and a complete absence of any contrary duty to society on the other ; with the corollary that no consideration for the well-being of society can ever form a moral objection to a strike—expediency alone need be considered.

On the other hand it is asserted that workers engaged in occupations immediately essential to the maintenance of life have no right to withhold their services at any time, at all events in such a way as seriously and directly to threaten the supply of the commodity upon whose production they

[1] Baxter, *op. cit.* i. 3, 6.   [2] Tertullian, *de Idol.* 24.

are normally engaged ; and that a strike of such workers is a ' sin ' which no ' evil ' attendant upon their conditions of employment can justify. Or it is urged that an attempt to use the starvation of the populace to force a government to concede something which it has decided, after consideration, not to concede, is an 'attack on the constitution,' with the implication that such an attack is entirely or almost entirely immoral.[1] It will deepen our appreciation of the care with which problems of perplexity must be approached if we spend a few moments in considering these allegations.

Has a man, in the first place, an absolute right to withhold his work from society ? It is to be assumed of course that he exists during his period of absence from work upon private means or savings previously accumulated, and does not claim the right of being supported in voluntary idleness. Even so, the position is only of doubtful validity. We should certainly blame a great artist, musician or statesman who withdrew into a life of cultured and selfish ease before his period of active work could reasonably be thought to have ended. He would be depriving the community of a factor of value to its full life and well-being, and that to no purpose except the gratification of mere self-interest. And it seems unjust to allow to the manual worker a moral privilege in this respect which is refused to the genius. What applies to one type of worker must surely apply to all.

A second consideration tends to reinforce our doubt as to the validity of this alleged right to refuse work. During the period of idleness the ' striker '—be he artist or artisan— is living as a rule upon savings accumulated from his past wages, whether in trade-union funds or otherwise. The fair determination of wages is even at the present day regarded as a matter of communal interest only to the slightest of degrees. But in so far as society tolerates, approves and in some small measure legislates that each man should have

---

[1] The recent general strike (May 1926) was also held to be illegal, as inducing workmen to break their contracts of employment without notice. This of course was true ; and a breach of contract is no doubt immoral as well as illegal. But the point had, and has, nothing to do with the question of the morality of strikes as such ; and those who hold the positions stated above would still condemn a ' general ' strike root and branch, even though every striker worked his full period of notice before he downed tools.

an income in excess of his immediate needs, it seems clear
that the motive which underlies such tolerance, approval or
legislation is not that of giving him an opportunity to retire
from work while his efficiency is still unimpaired, but rather
that of enabling him to provide for sickness, old age and the
requirements of family life, or to surround himself with the
comfort and amenities appropriate to that efficiency. If,
then, he uses such savings as he has to enable him to cease
work on insufficient grounds or before his normal time of
retirement comes, it is arguable that he is guilty of an abuse
—though not perhaps, in an ordinary and isolated case,
a serious abuse—of the tolerance and approval which society
has conferred upon his opportunities of saving. Thus the
right to refuse work at all times and on any grounds—however
trivial—appears to be a right to which no man can lay claim.
Honest work is normally a duty towards society.

But whatever be the truth of such arguments—and they
are perhaps too slender to be pressed unduly—it is clear
that even a right of individuals to withhold their work at will
(if such a right exists) would not in itself confer upon all
the workers in a given trade, or in many trades together,
the right to strike in unison on a given day. What is permissible in the case of an individual may become a dangerous
conspiracy if adopted as a corporate measure by many.
And here we may conveniently pass over to the arguments
on the other side. Can it be said, either that *no* body of
workmen has the right to strike, or that—even if the right
is allowed and recognised in certain trades—it cannot
exist in such key industries as mining, transport or food
supply ?

The legitimacy of strikes as such is not denied by modern
moral theologians : and popular opinion regards them as
generally allowable at all events in what may be called
' non-essential ' or ' luxury ' occupations. If the makers of
pearl buttons for dress-waistcoats struck for higher wages,
no one would brand them forthwith as engaged in an immoral
conspiracy. And under contemporary conditions it would
seem impossible to deny the same moral right to workers in
' necessary ' industries such as the railways or the mines,
even though actual legislation penalises strikes in some

public utility concerns. No doubt society could and ought to devise machinery whereby workers of these categories could claim redress for their grievances, real or imaginary, in a less drastic but no less effective manner than by a strike; for it is obviously more important in every way to avoid strikes in these occupations than in the 'luxury' trades. Until such machinery is devised, however, no one can morally deny to the worker in the 'necessary' industry a method of bargaining held legitimate in 'unnecessary' industries.

Against this it may be said that in none but the most extreme of imaginable cases could a strike of the police or of the army be condoned; and that industries which secure and maintain the life of the community, such as the railways and mines, should rank on the same plane as occupations which secure its peace and order. There is however this difference. A miner or a railwayman enters his profession not so much through direct choice as through necessity, heredity or local conditions; he has therefore some right to protest if he finds that the conditions under which he is forced to labour are too onerous. The soldier and policeman, on the other hand, enter theirs of their own free and deliberate initiative, and at a later age, and are by so much the more supposed to have considered, approved of and consented to the conditions of their employment before adopting it.

Again, the direct purpose of army and police service is the maintenance of peace and order, and no one who enters either service can be for a moment ignorant of the fact. But the lad who goes on the railway or down the pit scarcely realises that he is entering an industry of integral importance to the national life. Thus, whatever may be thought of the position of the leaders of a strike in the respective cases under consideration, the position of the rank and file is wholly different. The soldier or the policeman must realise in full from the first moment of his enlistment the effect that strike action on the part of himself and his colleagues will have on the community, and must be thought, tacitly at all events, to have surrendered at his enlistment any claim to strike if dissatisfied, whilst the miner and the railwayman

N

are in a wholly different position in this respect. If they
strike, they do indeed menace the well-being of the community directly. But when they entered the industry this
possible result of a strike had never occurred to them because
they had never considered its relation to the national life,
and therefore they cannot be thought to have waived any
rights they may have had by accepting employment of this
character. Or if its significance had occurred to them, it
may still be the case that sheer necessity made it impossible
for them to find any other employment not so conditioned ;
and on this account we should be compelled to allow them some
degree of privilege which we should rightly refuse to the
forces of the Crown.

If the ' solidarity ' of the working classes is a fact of any
moral significance at all, ' sympathetic ' strikes in themselves
must be as valid as any other form of strike. Indeed there
is no strike which is not to some slight degree sympathetic.
There are always at least a few highly-paid and highly-placed
strikers who withhold their labour for no personal benefit,
but in support of less fortunate workers in the same industry.
But when a sympathetic strike becomes a general strike,
and so aims a direct blow at the heart of the community,
can it be condemned either in itself or on the grounds that it
is ' unconstitutional ' ? We have admitted the legitimacy
of strikes in general, and have allowed this legitimacy even
in the case of ' necessary ' industries. This of course does not
mean that *every* strike is lawful ; it means only that we can
see no justifiable moral reason for condemning all strikes
without qualification. The legitimacy of any particular
strike must depend on the urgency and reality of the grievance
which caused it ; for even the most innocuous strike is to
some extent an ' evil ' to society and therefore to be avoided
unless due cause can be shown. But gravity of cause will
proportionately weigh against gravity of ' evil ' resulting,
and sufficient ' injustice ' to the workers even in one particular trade might conceivably justify a general strike whose
purpose was to secure justice. We are in the realm of conflict
of evils once more. Nor do we seem to be out of that realm
even if it be proved that a strike is ' unconstitutional ' ;
for even a rebellion, though unconstitutional in principle, may

sometimes be a praiseworthy thing because the lesser of two evils.[1]

It is difficult, if not impossible, to fix a point at which a general strike becomes an attack on the constitution. Strictly speaking, unconstitutional action must be action calculated either to overthrow a government and to take over some or all of its functions by methods foreign to the constitution (i.e. methods other than defeat in the Houses of Parliament or at the polls), or to alter the constitution by such alien methods. And it is doubtful whether any general strike not specifically directed to these ends can be called unconstitutional. If the grievance which lies at the root of the strike is a constitutional one (as for example some alleged injustice in the franchise), and the government of the day, after considering it, has refused redress, the strike might for a moment be thought unconstitutional, as attempting to force an extension of the franchise and so to alter the constitution, by means other than parliamentary legislation. Yet even this is doubtful, for the purpose of the strike is not to seize the ballot-boxes and forcibly to put in them the voting-papers of the unfranchised, but to induce the government to take the necessary legislative action. It is certainly an abnormal method of inducement; but that in itself does not make it unconstitutional. It may be an illegal method if it transcends the limit of strike-action laid down by Act of Parliament. It may employ expedients of doubtful morality, just as the use of bribery, slander or physical terrorism would commonly be thought immoral ways of securing a minister's resignation. But while we can see a distinction between 'moral' and 'immoral,' 'legal' and 'illegal,' 'customary' and 'abnormal' methods of attempting to influence a government, these are very different from the distinction alleged between constitutional and unconstitutional methods. It would seem wiser and better that the appeal to 'constitutionalism' should be abandoned in discussions of this character. On what grounds is the physical pressure of mob-violence to be regarded as 'unconstitutional,' if the

[1] Cp. *S.T.* ii. 2, q. 42, a. 2, ad 3—'Perturbatio regiminis tyrannici non habet rationem seditionis;' cp. R. L. Poole, *Mediæval Thought and Learning*, pp. 202 ff.; *Some Principles*, p. 187.

financial pressure of capitalists or the propagandist pressure of newspapers are exempt from the same condemnation ?

It would appear then that striking cannot be treated as wholly wrong in itself. Like war, it is an ' evil ' ; and one only to be employed at the instance of very grave ' evils ' which menace or operate on the other side. To attempt by a general strike to force the government (which is the representative in such matters of the whole community) to change its considered mind upon a *chose jugée* is a grave menace to the community which nothing but the gravest cause can justify. A still more serious course of action is to continue such a strike after the government has proclaimed a state of emergency, and called upon all loyal persons to return to their work to avert the danger to society. Such action constitutes what may without doubt be termed a war on the community ; but Christianity does not condemn either this war or any other war as immoral out of hand. A war must have a just and proportionately grave cause, and without such a cause is immoral. But when the cause is sufficiently grave, neither war, rebellion nor striking need be anything more than the lesser of two evils.

If support were needed for what has been said, it could easily be derived from theologians of the highest repute. It is certainly the doctrine of modern Roman Catholicism. In Leo XIII's famous encyclical ' Rerum Novarum,' which laid down the principle that a man's wages ' must be sufficient to enable him to maintain his wife and children in reasonable comfort,' [1] occurs a passage on strikes. ' When work-people have recourse to a strike,' the Pope says, ' it is frequently because the hours of labour are too long, or the work too hard, or because they consider their wages insufficient. The grave inconvenience of this not uncommon occurrence should be obviated by public remedial measures. . . . The laws should be beforehand and prevent these troubles arising ; they should lend their influence and authority to the removal in good time of the causes which lead to conflicts between masters and those whom they employ.' [2] This, it must be

---

[1] *Encyclical Letter of Pope Leo XIII on the Condition of Labour* (Official Translation, Dublin, 1891), p. 35.

[2] *Ib.* p. 30.

admitted, is not absolutely explicit ; but no such criticism can be brought against Cardinal Manning's interpretation of it. Manning had already emphasised the 'rights of labour to self-protection' in a pamphlet which attracted a good deal of attention,[1] and he greeted the encyclical in the following words :—

'A man has a right and an absolute liberty to work for such wages as he thinks just, and to refuse to work for less. Men have both the right and liberty to unite with others of the same trade or craft, and to demand a just wage for their labour. If this just wage is refused, he (sic) has both right and liberty to refuse to work—that is to strike. Leo XIII fully recognises this liberty. So long as the cause is just, the right to strike is undeniable. He is free to work or not.' 'On the liberty to strike,' Manning repeats, 'Leo XIII is explicit. . . . A strike is like war. If for just cause a strike is right and inevitable it is a healthful constraint imposed upon the despotism of capital.'[2] True, there is no mention here of a general strike, but once the principle of combination has been admitted, it seems merely a question of degree if the combination is extended beyond the same trade or craft within which the Cardinal allows it.

It follows, therefore, that the most we can say even of a general strike is that it is a war on the community, and that such a war, like other wars, is justifiable if the grounds for waging it are sufficiently grave. We may indeed doubt whether, under modern conditions, the worst grievances of any existent body of workmen approximate even remotely to such a degree of gravity as would justify 'war' on the scale of a general strike. Nevertheless the problem of strikes, in so far as it concerns moral theology, is again a problem of choice between two 'evils' or two 'loyalties' or two 'claims.' It falls into the same rank as that of most problems of perplexity. Even though we say that *normally* the urgent need of the community should take precedence of the urgent need of one body of workmen or another, we have no material

---

[1] H. E. Manning, *Rights and Dignity of Labour* (London, 1887).
[2] H. E. Manning, *Leo XIII on the Condition of Labour*, reprinted from 'Dublin Review,' July 1891, pp. 13, 15. See also Prümmer, *Theol. Mor.* ii. p. 307.

for deciding in a given case whether we are still within the bounds of the ' normal.' We have to decide between two ' evils,' but how are we to say which of the two is the least ?

6. *The Ethics of Compromise*

The entire progress of our argument—indeed, it may be said, the whole object of casuistry in history—has been to reduce to their smallest numbers the problems in which a final choice between two grave evils is the only possible solution. The number of legitimate expedients which have presented themselves is not insignificant, and the test-cases to which they can be submitted on the whole justify them at the bar of Christian moral sense. Thus the large number of cases, in which the rigorist would demand the resignation of a ' dissentient ' Christian from the body of which he is a member, shrinks on inspection to those rare instances in which the body itself demands his resignation. The rigorism of private refusal of absolution is, in a similar manner, mitigated by the doctrine of invincible error—to some degree, at least, even in authorised Roman Catholic moral theology, and perhaps further if the logic of the position be fully carried out. ' Always take the safe course ' is reduced by probabilism, in its least exceptionable form, to those cases only where vital interests are at stake. Inspection of principles which at first sight prove intractable—' Thou shalt not lie,' for example—results in the discovery that only in certain circumstances do they retain anything like their absolute rigidity. In all these ways problem after problem may be removed from the sphere of that final and exacting dilemma in which one of two grave ' evils ' has necessarily to be embraced.

At the same time, certain questions have accumulated in the course of our survey which do not appear amenable to any of these methods of treatment. For many the question of birth-control is of this character. The choice involved in the ' Green Curve ' is another instance ; so is the Jeanie Deans problem. ' Measure for Measure ' provides a Shakespearian parallel. We may add to them the perplexity of the patriotic trade-unionist on the declaration of a general strike. In these cases and others like them the clear-cut choice between two evils would appear to be inevitable. Yet there is a chance that in some of them at least it might be deferred —perhaps for a time only—perhaps also for such a length of time as would allow of some new factor to intervene and make the final choice unnecessary. And it is to be considered whether—when such a deferring of the issue is possible—it can be held legitimate ; and, if so, upon what terms ?

Jeanie Deans could not defer her decision beyond a certain moment ; but in a sense the trade-unionist can. He may be obliged to cease work at his particular trade, and that, no doubt, he will feel to be unpatriotic. But if he enrols himself as a special constable, or enlists for the maintenance of food-supplies, is he not doing a better thing than if he remains wholly inactive ? He is at least giving patriotism some share of its due as against sectional trade-loyalty, even if on the other hand he is subordinating patriotism to trade-loyalty by joining in the strike. By this means he certainly postpones, in some sense, the final agony of choosing definitely between the two. The confessor who reconciles it with his conscience temporarily to condone birth-control in a particular case, whilst maintaining its prohibition in general, makes a similar attempt to serve two masters. When an issue is deferred by such expedients, how are we to judge of it ? Is it the double disloyalty of Mr. Facing-Both-Ways, or is it an effort at the highest and most difficult solution in sight ? Or are there conditions and principles to determine the occasions on which it is right and legitimate, as distinct from those when it is wholly to be deprecated ? If such conditions can be found, they will help to reduce yet further the number of cases in which one evil out of two must inevitably be embraced.

Such a deferring of the issue may be termed a compromise. It is of the essence of a compromise, so understood, that it is not intended to last in perpetuity. Many apparent compromises have indeed lasted for years, if not for centuries ; but that is in the main an accident either of fact or of terminology. It is an accident of fact when, by a lowering of moral insight, those who accept the compromise fail to see that neither of the two contesting claims is thereby satisfied ; in such a case the compromise endures until someone of more single vision or higher moral sensibility denounces it for what it really is. It is an accident of terminology when what we call a compromise is in reality a solution, in which both contestants come to discover full satisfaction of all their legitimate claims. But the purpose of a compromise, as distinct from a solution or conciliation, is merely to stave off the evil day in the hope that some *deus ex machina* will emerge to avert its threatened catastrophe. The miner who volunteers for railway-service during a general strike does so not through any weakening of his desire to see the strike achieve its purpose, but in the hope that something will 'turn up' to bring about that achievement before the full rigours of strike-action have to be applied and suffered. In the meantime he thinks it right to mitigate those rigours by his own effort as much as he can. The mine-owner who subscribes to strikers' relief funds on a similar occasion is animated by a similar hope. He is strengthening his opponents' hands, but without any purpose of strengthening their artillery. The issue may sooner or later have to come to a head. But as long as that possibility can be delayed it is worth while to delay it, for in the meantime there may be a change of sentiment or situation which will render the final clash abortive.

As a matter of fact, every strike—and indeed almost every war—is itself a compromise of this character. Neither contestant exercises his possible strength to the full ; even ' frightfulness ' has its limits. Each plays to some slight extent into his opponents' hands. Thereby the struggle is in all probability prolonged ; but its tension is lessened, and an irrevocable breach between the combatants avoided. A strike is civil war in its most gentlemanly form ; a war between civilised nations never sinks to the depths of barbarism. The real issue in a strike is ' civil war or submission'; in a war— ' frightfulness or defeat ' ; but the hope of those who initiate them is that experience of some lesser measure of suffering will induce their opponents to come to terms before the final issue has to be faced. The compromise selected is never intended to endure ; if it fails to produce some means of evading the issue, then the issue must come. A country or continent cannot be subjected to armed camps for ever. Either the cause of contention must be removed, or the armies will move from camp to battlefield.

So when Jeremy Taylor says that ' fooleries and weak usages are suffered in some Churches rather than by reforming them make the ignorant people think all religion is indifferent,' [1] or discusses the age-long problem of the wife who knows not whether to connive at her husband's infidelities,[2] he does not suggest that either of the connivances in question, however long it may in fact last, can in essence be anything more than a temporary measure. In the end, the ' fooleries ' must be banished or approved. The wife's ' connivance,' after a certain point is reached, will become consent—though the point at which this occurs is not necessarily reached as early as an outside observer might suppose. Connivance remains connivance only as long as the alternative of separation from the husband is held in reserve as a practical possibility. Once that alternative is effectively abandoned the compromise is ended, and ended perhaps in the worst of all possible ways, by surrendering to one of the two ' evils ' involved without duly facing it.

Here we have perhaps the most obvious danger of compromise—its tendency to harden imperceptibly into an acceptance of one of the two alternatives between which it was intended to mediate. Without any definite act of decision conscience gives up its neutrality, and finds that by secession to the side of one of the contesting claims it has conferred upon it a bloodless victory. The side embraced may happen —as Browning showed in the ' Statue and the Bust '— to be that which the world would call the ' right side ' ; but that lightens the blame only to the slightest degree. In any case a moral issue has been evaded ; a judgment of conscience which should have been reached deliberately has gone by default.

One of the dangers of compromise is thus clearly indicated —it allows conscience to burke an issue by imperceptibly surrendering to one of the parties to the case. We cannot say that, where this danger becomes a reality, it will always

---

[1] *Duct. Dub.* I. v. 8, § 5.   [2] *Ib.* § 6.

be on the side either of the greater or of the lesser moral evil that conscience ranges itself. In actual fact, it will probably be on the side of the *status quo ante*, whether that side be the better or the worse of the two ; mere inertia will rule the day. In any case it is clear that no compromise, no deferring of the issue, can morally be allowed to continue once a drift of this character has begun ; and this gives us a condition to be stringently observed. The compromise, such as it was, has failed of its purpose ; we only lose in moral integrity by keeping up the fiction longer. So in the recent general strike (which by its deliberate half-measures was obviously a compromise in itself), once the drift towards patriotism (if the expression may be allowed) had fairly set in, the strike-leaders took not merely the most logical but also the most moral course in declaring it at an end. By this means the real issue was brought to the fore once more, and was seen to have been neither settled nor even eased by the strike. The latter, both in method and in purpose, had been a compromise, whose only value might have been to clear the stage for some change of heart or fortunes which would have prevented the real issue—the danger of a long-drawn-out coal stoppage—coming to a head.

In the moral life this danger incident to compromise is very real. Connivance, as we have suggested, not only appears to observers identical with consent ; it actually merges into consent, while enabling the conscience which contrives it to delude itself that no consent has yet been given. A second danger of compromise is equally grave, and if allowed to realise itself, equally disastrous. The purpose of compromise is to avoid if possible, and at all events to lessen, the tension of the ultimate choice. In so doing the choice is postponed, and for a sensitive soul the agony of deliberation is prolonged ; so much so that it may prove worse in the end than the immediate acceptance of the choice. When the choice is inevitable—as with a visit to the dentist, or the breaking-off of a bad habit—it is of course folly and worse to put it off. Such postponement is mere procrastination, and not compromise ; for compromise always contemplates a reasonable possibility that the situation may change before the final choice is forced upon conscience. Even within its legitimate limits, however, compromise as a remedy may be worse than the disease. A war of attrition lessens the daily casualty list; but in the long run it may be no more prudent than shock-tactics, and infinitely more expensive.

Where so much can be urged against delay by compromise, it is only natural to ask whether a policy so fraught with danger is moral at all. In the world's vocabulary, ' compromise ' has as bad a sound as ' casuistry.' So far from rendering to God and Caesar their respective dues, it seems to play their claims off against one another, and so attempts to serve both God and mammon. That is how the world judges it in the abstract; and in the abstract the world is always rigorist. But the issue is unfairly stated. We are not dealing with conflicts between God and mammon, between a ' sin ' and an ' evil '—if we were, the accusation would be valid, for ' the disciples of the absolute may never compromise.' [1] We are dealing with conflicts between ' claim ' and ' claim,' each recognised as valid, or between ' evil ' and ' evil,' each recognised as evil. That being so, we are surely right in extending to their utmost limits what Stevenson calls ' the invaluable minutes in which the wheels of life run before us, and we can divert them with a touch to one side or the other.' [2]

It has to be remembered that the choice between two ' evils ' is equally a choice between two ' claims.' There is a claim upon us to avoid any evil which conscience does not call us to embrace. So long as the choice is genuinely postponed but no more, some tribute is paid to both claims, and either claim can in the end be wholly satisfied, though of course at the expense of the other. Further, there is always a chance that something may intervene to enable us to satisfy both claims, or to remove one of them wholly from the problem. But once the choice is made, one claim—as to which we opine that it had at least as much validity as the other—is finally set aside; a wrong has been done to it which cannot be righted. Despite the dangers of compromise, despite the evil name it has, it may nevertheless

[1] J. Morley, *Compromise* (1888), quoted, *New English Dictionary*, s.v.
[2] *The Ebb-Tide*, c. 8.

prove better and wiser to delay the issue rather than to force it.

The problem of compromise has not attracted the notice it deserves, but in so far as moralists have considered it they support this view. ' So long as two claims can be observed concurrently, they should be observed,' writes Alexander of Hales ; [1] ' when they prove finally incompatible, the greater claim must be embraced.' This is not wholly relevant, for we are dealing with cases in which it seems impossible to decide as to the greater claim or lesser evil ; but so far as it goes it bears out the plea for postponement as long as it is morally possible. Baxter is more exactly to the point— ' There is a great deal of difference,' he writes,[2] ' between omitting the substance of a duty for ever, and the de- laying it, or altering the time and place and manner.' Leibnitz,[3] in the same way, quotes a ' common opinion ' in favour of delaying decision as long as possible, and gives it full approval provided always that circumstances allow of it.

The limits to be set to compromise are clearly indicated by the dangers that beset it. On the one hand the moral tension must not be gravely diminished ; the case must be treated as still *sub judice*. As soon as compromise begins to act as a salve to conscience, or allows the problem to be set aside with a mental label ' for reference only,' it is on the point of merging into consent to one claim or the other, and evading the duty of deciding between the two by a resolute act of will. If conscience begins to be content with the com- promise, it becomes necessary to revive the whole question in its full intensity, and ask whether this contentment is anything more than moral indolence. But, on the other hand, the moral tension must not be gravely increased, for that would defeat the principal end which the compromise had in view, and intensify perplexity of conscience almost if not quite to the breaking-point. If these conditions are observed, we need not be too anxious about the duration of a com- promise ; its limits are set by psychological and moral rather than by temporal calculations.

---

[1] *Summa*, ii. q. 121, m. 4, a. 2.   [2] *Christian Directory*, i. 3, rule 12.
[3] *De Cas. Perplex. in Jure*, vii.

7. *Commercial Honesty*

We may illustrate what has been said by considering one of the most poignant cases of perplexity which can arise— that of the petty dishonesties forced upon a salesman by an unscrupulous employer, with the alternative of dismissal and almost certain unemployment if he refuses to be accessory to them. No doubt there are degrees of connivance in such matters. A typist required to produce fifty copies of a letter beginning, 'Yours is the only complaint we have ever had about the quality of our goods,' is only in very small measure a party to the dishonesty involved ; but even so we should scarcely encourage her to remain in her employment without concern. No doubt also business methods have improved since M. Thamin wrote : ' In business, more than anywhere else, little lies seem allowable and even necessary. Deception becomes an art, and even a merit, as though there were open war between salesman and customer. . . . Shopkeepers ought to be warned that lies are neither a part of their profession, nor wholly blameless as far as it is concerned.'[1] The poetical efforts of Flurton Fraley, 'the great American poet,' and his fellow versifiers, may not have been without effect even on this side of the Atlantic, though it is to be feared that the lines are not yet ' pasted up in half the offices of the country ' :—

> ' All of us know that money talks throughout our glorious nation,
> But money whispers low compared to business reputation ;
> Pull off no slick nor crooked deal, for pennies or for dollars—
> God, think of all the trade you'll lose if just one sucker hollers.'[2]

But however this may be, even if a single case remained of commercial dishonesty forced upon an honest employé, it would be serious enough ; and where the health, nourishment and education of a family depend wholly upon the salesman's continuous employment the proportions assumed by the problem are very grave indeed.

---

[1] R. Thamin, *Un Problème Morale*, p. 74.

[2] T. H. Stribling, *Fombombo*, c. xvii. Mr. Stribling's novels are particularly fertile in genuine problems of conscience and interesting ethical types.

The problem, moreover, is one in which compromise is almost fatally easy. The injustice caused by each ' little lie ' is often so trifling as to be negligible ; it is only as a series that they assume any noticeable bulk. It is therefore painfully tempting to put off the decision from day to day. The ' custom of the trade ' can be cited in defence, or the proverb, ' Caveat emptor ' ; or the frank tolerance extended to advertisement exaggeration of almost every kind and degree. In such cases, surely, it is prudery to call a ' little lie ' a sin, or to say that no counter-balancing ' evil ' to be avoided thereby will condone it ? For under modern conditions the ' evil ' in question is very real ; it is difficult to overestimate the horrors of un-employment for a conscientious man charged with domestic responsibilities. Everything points towards postponement of the final decision as the right course in the circumstances, not *sine die* perhaps, but at all events for the moment.

Much, therefore, can be urged in extenuation of the shop-assistant's lie. He is not a principal, but only an agent, and in a sense not even a free agent. If, further, we could say of him that apart from a direct refusal to lie he were doing all in his power to produce a reform in the methods of the particular shop in which he was engaged, and of the trade in general (as, for example, by getting his trade-union to interest itself in the matter) ; and that by reason of his abhorrence of lies he had adopted a standard of rigorous veracity in all other relationships of life, we should have made out as strong a case on his behalf as could be made. But would it be strong enough to justify him, as a Christian, in remaining in his employment with an untroubled conscience ?

It seems certain that it would not. But it seems equally certain that the reasons in favour of his leaving his employ-ment—provided that all or most of the conditions above mentioned were fulfilled—would not be strong enough to oblige him to leave it, or run the risk of dismissal, immediately and without foresight for the future. Circumstances can be imagined in which even that drastic course might be his duty. But, in general, if his heart were honestly set upon breaking with his unhappy environment, he would be entitled to time. It would even be his duty to take time—time to make last appeals for reform, time to enlist friends on his behalf, time at least to search for other openings. And—again provided the conditions mentioned were in being—few of us would dare to limit that time too strictly. The compromise must surely be allowed to continue if necessary, at all events for such period as the moral tension of conscience is not relaxed.

So long as a man thus situated does not become a moral Micawber—complacently accepting the present on the off-chance of a miracle 'turning up' to release him from his dilemma; so long as he is genuinely eager to bring the unhappy state in which he labours to an end; so long as any reasonable hope of averting a catastrophe by honest means remains—so long (provided always that grave injustice is not being done to any particular individual) he should be allowed, and probably even advised, to postpone his final decision. But here the duty of avoiding the second danger demands consideration. The course proposed, it might be objected, will do nothing to rescue the man from his distressing moral situation; the continual strain of telling the lie he hates must wear him out even more than the drastic action of resigning his position. In some cases at least, this will be so; and no doubt if the distress seemed likely to produce even more tragic consequences than might ensue from the loss of his situation, it would be his duty to choose the latter as the lesser evil. But till this limit is reached the compromise, in that form in which it cannot be confused with any consent to the lie, is perhaps the right course of action in the circumstances.

It may be objected that this conclusion is hopelessly lax, and allows dishonesty to be practised unchecked. Such an objection overlooks the conditions we have mentioned. We can indeed assert without hesitation that no genuine compromise could very well last for long and at the same time safeguard these conditions. Either complacency will steadily set in, or the tension will prove intolerable; in either case there is a clear sign that the compromise must be terminated and the choice taken. But for such time as the compromise is both genuine and tolerable—be it for days only, or weeks or months—it may be countenanced. It still leaves a door open for a solution less tragic than the choice which may have to come ; and in so doing may be a factor for greater good than any which impulsive action could produce.

But it may further be urged that, in the case in question, the man is an accessory to acts of dishonesty the whole time that the compromise lasts, and that nothing can justify this. This objection can only be sustained on a legalistic basis which esteems sins of act as invariably worse than sins of thought or desire. It is to condemn a compromise which allows an 'evil' to be committed in action, but to permit compromises which allow it to be entertained in thought. The distinction is an unreal one. Every compromise is a temporary refusal to exclude here and now from possibility an ' evil ' which ultimately may have to be excluded (at the cost, of course, of another ' evil ' which will have to be suffered in its stead), and it matters little whether the ' evil ' so allowed is committed in outward act or no. On the basis of pagan ethics we might have to judge differently ; but in the Christian scheme even to entertain an ' evil ' in thought unnecessarily is so heinous, that to put it into act unwillingly, and for the sole purpose of avoiding what may be an even greater ' evil,' can scarcely be more immoral.

And, again, the distinction between ' thought ' and ' act ' is not as clear cut as it appears at first sight. An evil entertained in thought is in most cases an evil committed in act as well. A man will hesitate for months and years before he takes the final step which makes him a missionary or a pastor of souls ; and we do not blame him if the hesitation is genuinely forced on him by grave family difficulties. But all the time he is not merely contemplating the possibility of ' evil ' in thought, he is also committing an injustice towards those whom his hesitation is depriving of his services. Either all postponement of grave moral decisions must be condemned, or all must be allowed within the limits we have accepted as valid.

It has already been suggested that no genuine compromise or postponement of decision can last for long. For this reason it is unnecessary to labour the point that a moral crisis must not be measured by days and hours. Even in the case of the salesman it would be an extreme of rigorism to insist that he must decide his problem, and take his action, within twenty-four hours of the moment when conscience first awoke to its gravity. Nor need we insist that it must be settled within a week or a fortnight, or any other determinate period. The moral limitations of compromise will determine the period and force a decision soon enough. The business of the moralist, therefore, is to ensure that these limitations are duly recognised, and allow them to fix the time, rather than to fix an arbitrary limit himself.

If the circumstances of a legitimate compromise do not themselves cry, ' Choose ye this day,' the moralist need not utter the challenge for them. It is for him to insist that the choice must still be regarded as impending, but to allow conscience to weigh the alternatives for so long as it is able to do so without too great a strain, and without acquiescing inertly in one or other of them as accident decides. If this conclusion is true, it is of importance in more than one of the difficulties with which we have been faced. Many of them are created by the modern fluidity of opinion on grave moral subjects in the Church of England. Where the Church itself cannot declare its mind we dare not force the individual to a hasty decision. He must be allowed to pay deference to two conflicting claims so long as he retains a real sense of the rigours of the conflict, and yet is not in danger of succumbing morally under its weight. In the process he may discover at length that one of the two has for him a stronger claim than the other ; then he is bound to decide for it, and that at all costs. Or the Church may come to a clearer view in the matter, and this will relieve him of the burden of decision. Or new factors of unexpected character may emerge to lessen the weight of the problem. In no case of earnest perplexity will compromise prove easily tolerable ; but if it is more tolerable than the strain of decision, and circumstances do not insist upon immediate choice, something may be gained by postponement.

On these grounds, therefore, the deliberate inconsistency of moral persons can sometimes be excused. Such inconsistencies, based on high ethical grounds, are more frequent than we often recognise. The confessor who holds on the one hand that to permit a particular practice even in an individual case must normally constitute a grave threat to the moral order, and yet, on the other hand—and on equally conscientious grounds—cannot bring himself to refuse absolution in one particular instance, deserves more than sympathy in the crisis of conscience through which he is passing. He is entitled to our respect and approval, not merely if he weighs the matter long and carefully before deciding finally which claim of the two to recognise ; but also if, in the meantime, he actually pays tribute to both claims by asserting his principle with full emphasis on the one hand, and on the other by allowing himself (after taking all due measures to avoid ' scandal ') to absolve not once only but repeatedly. Such inconsistency on a lower moral plane, or practised lightheartedly, would deserve the frankest condemnation as the worst conceivable form of hypocrisy or moral cowardice. But in the region of grave conflicts of evils in which we are moving, it may be an even higher form of self-sacrificing thought and love than a final decision either way. The test is always the same :—if the moral earnestness of the crisis is maintained there is a genuine compromise, as painful in its own way as the final decision would be. ' They also serve who only stand and wait ' ; and a moral compromise, nobly undertaken and bravely endured, may enshrine a greater devotion of service and of faith than a reckless embracing of one alternative, even though the world calls the latter heroic and the former merely base.

' Giving people time,' it has been well said,[1] ' not quickly taking them at their word ; not closing up the account, or forcing a complex matter to a speedy issue ; not insisting that men must mean all that their words or even their deeds imply ; . . . is not this the bearing which we may learn from our Saviour ? . . . Giving people time ;—it is, I think, one of the best ways of taking in one of the hardest tasks— the task of being at once loyal to truth, and gentle to those who are denying and opposing it. . . . Who can measure the responsibility of trying to force on the decision, to presume the issue ? . . . A great responsibility plainly rests upon us

[1] F. Paget, Sermon on ' Forbearance,' in *Studies in the Christian Character*, pp. 179 ff.

if we will not give men time ; time to develop and learn in whatever way they can ; time to reconsider things and by God's grace to repent ; time to find their way in life, and feel its discipline, and do themselves justice.' And if we may give time, may we not also take time for ourselves, when decisions are difficult and grave issues hang upon them ?

8. *Conclusion*

Compromise, conceived under the conditions suggested in the last few paragraphs, is the final defence which the Christian can raise against the threat of those grave decisions between two serious evils which moral theology calls perplexities. In many of them circumstances force the decision so suddenly that no compromise at all, however moral, is possible ; in all the rest (unless some new factor intervenes) the conditions under which alone it can be held legitimate will themselves allow it to endure only a very short time. Ultimately we are forced back to cases where a decision has to be reached between two evils, and conscience is utterly unable to decide which of the two is the lesser. All that has preceded has availed at best merely to reduce the number of the cases ; nothing can avail to reduce their poignancy.

It must frankly be admitted that in such cases no adaptation of the principle of the ' lesser evil ' or the ' greater claim ' can be proposed which will guarantee a solution. It is impossible—even with the fullest human knowledge of the case—to understand all the consequences, good and evil, which will follow the adoption of either alternative, and therefore no balance can be struck between the two. The common utilitarian assumption that it is a simple matter to decide where the ' greatest happiness of the greatest possible number ' lies—even if happiness be taken in its crudest form of physical pleasure—is wholly wide of the mark. The consequences of any action continue to all eternity ; neither good nor bad can be summed in such a way as to make effective moral accountancy possible. And if this is so it seems that we have reached a point at which the whole ambitious structure of moral theology is revealed as a complete futility. Every man must decide for himself according to his own estimate of conditions and consequences ; and no one can decide for him or impugn the decision to which he comes.

Perhaps this is the end of the matter after all. Yet it may be suggested that we are wrong in thinking that no one is more qualified than his neighbour to give a decision in such cases. On an earlier page it was indicated that three conditions are necessary for the solution of problems of conscience—sound rules of procedure, alertness of intelligence and imagination, and earnestness of moral purpose. On the last of these three we ventured to lay particular stress ; but important though it is in all types of problem it reaches its highest importance in this matter of perplexity. A just estimate of ' claims ' or of ' evils ' can only be formed by those who have in practice most devotedly given themselves to the recognition of such claims, or to the exhibition of Christian fortitude against such evils. Mere theorists or partisans will always be at a loss. Duties must be made at home in the heart before their relative importance can be estimated ; and they can only be made at home in the heart by being made at home in life as well.

It follows, for example, that in the case of the perplexity caused by a general strike for the patriotic trade-unionist, neither the ardent patriot who has no sense of the legitimate aspirations of labour, nor the ardent unionist who is deaf to the calls of any wider society, nor the recluse or idler who has none of these interests at heart, has either the character or the right to claim that any decision to which he may come is in any real sense valid for conscience. If he or any other attempts to judge of the matter on a moral basis, his first step must be to obtain the experience and the disposition which will enable him to enter with sympathy into the inner meaning of the claims on either side. This is not the work of a moment ; it is therefore the duty of the Christian to prepare for the problems of the future—which can at least with some degree of certainty be anticipated—by a deliberate, devoted and prayerful effort to extend his range of sympathies in every direction. Such men, when the crisis comes, will be able to speak with authority from a heart neither blinded by passion, warped by prejudice, disqualified by ignorance nor hardened by traditionalism. Their voices will carry far in spite of the noise of conflict ; they will bring relief to many whose consciences are over-burdened by the gravity of the choice which presents itself, and will point a clear path to those who are groping to find what is right. Casuistry is a science necessary for human life ; but when it comes to grips with its hardest problems it will only succeed if it is directed by sympathy, strengthened by self-discipline and enlightened by prayer. So equipped, it may not always, perhaps, be able to satisfy the minds of men that its conclusions are valid and well-grounded ; but we can scarcely doubt that in the judgment of God its mistakes (if mistakes they are) will secure ready pardon.

ADDITIONAL NOTES

NOTE A.

Definition of Conscience (see page 3).

It is well known that the Franciscans (e.g. Alexander of Hales and Bonaventura) tended to locate conscience in the emotional side of human nature (see H. T. Simar, *Die Lehre vom Wesen des Gewissens in der Scholastik des XIII Jahrhunderts*, Friburg, 1885, pp. 7-25, for a full account). The Dominican tradition, on the other hand, as exemplified by St. Thomas, is so clear that conscience is simply 'the mind passing moral judgments' that its definitions are directed to making clear not so much the *fact* of these judgments, as the *manner* in which they are reached. Hence, as is well known, St. Thomas follows an old tradition which distinguishes two elements in what we should call 'conscience'—the *synderesis*, or intuitive grasp of first principles or standards by which alone moral comparisons can be made; and the *conscientia*, or process of applying these first principles in estimating the rightness and wrongness of particular actions. The former he describes as 'a law of our mind, in as far as it contains the first principles of the law of nature' ('lex intellectus nostri, inquantum est habitus continens praecepta legis naturalis, quae sunt prima operum humanorum,' *S.T.* i. 2, q. 94, a. 1, ad 2); or an 'innate habitual possession of the first principles of action, which are the natural principles of the law of nature' ('habitus naturalis principiorum operabilium, quae sunt naturalia principia juris naturalis'—*de Ver.* xvi. 1). It is the dominant factor in the judgments of conscience, and so may aptly be termed, as Jerome suggested, a 'spark' of the divine mind. 'Conscience' strictly so-called is the 'application' of this knowledge of the first principles to particular acts to decide whether they are right or wrong (*S.T.* i. q. 79, a. 13; i. 2. q. 19, a. 5; *de Ver.* xviii. 1); and the process is wholly akin to that of scientific discovery or

379

judgment (*de Ver.* ut sup.). Again the laws of conscience (i.e. of the 'synderesis') resemble the statutes of the civil power (i. 2, q. 96, a. 4, objj. 1, 2), and its method of applying them to a particular case is comparable to the process by which a jury arrives at its verdict and a judge gives sentence (ii. 2, q. 67, a. 2, ad 4). The whole matter is treated from the intellectual side.

St. Thomas' disciples in all branches of the Church followed his line of thought. Roman Catholic writers echo his definition with merely verbal changes. William Ames, the great Calvinist moralist, calls conscience ' a man's judgment concerning himself, as regards his subjection to the judgment of God,' and begins his treatise with the words : ' I call conscience "judgment" to indicate that it is a function of the mind and not of the will . . . for all the actions which are assigned to conscience in Scripture appertain to some power or faculty of reason.' Baldwin, his Lutheran contemporary, after noticing the Franciscan tendency to locate conscience in the conative side of the soul, elects firmly for the Thomist theory: ' Conscience,' he says, ' is an operative faculty of the mind which applies those moral principles (*principia actionum*) implanted in us either by the light of nature or the light of Scripture to some action, of which reason declares that we ought or ought not to do, or to have done it.' [1] Among Anglicans, Sanderson defines conscience as ' a faculty or habit of the practical understanding by which the mind of man, by the use of reason or argument, applies the light which it has to particular moral actions.' [2] Jeremy Taylor, in an effort to be precise, loses himself in verbosity ; but his drift is clearly the same as that of the rest : ' Conscience is the mind of a man governed by a rule, and measured by the proportions of good or evil, in order to practice, viz., to conduct all our relations and all our intercourse between God, our neighbour, and ourselves ; that is, in all moral actions.' [3]

This is the consistent English tradition, in spite of the deviation of the sentimentalist school which has been considered in the text. Bishop Butler, though he had affinities with the ' moral sense ' view, may sum the whole matter up for us : ' There is a principle of reflection in men by which they distinguish between, approve, and disapprove their own actions. The mind can take a view of what passes within itself, its propensions, aversions,

---

[1] F. Baldwin, *de Casibus Conscientiae*, i. 3

[2] R. Sanderson, *Of Conscience and Human Law*, i. 13 (Lewis' translation, 1722, revised by Bishop Christopher Wordsworth).

[3] *Duct. Dub.* i. 1. Note that all the four writers just quoted accept the distinction between *conscientia* and *synderesis*, without making any particular use of it.

passions, affections, as respecting *such objects*, and in *such degrees* ; and of the several actions consequent thereupon. In this survey it approves of one, disapproves of another, and towards a third is affected in neither of these ways, but is quite indifferent. This principle in man, by which he approves or disapproves his heart, temper and actions, is conscience.'[1] And again, ' There is a superior principle of reflection or conscience in every man, which distinguishes between the internal principles of his heart as well as his external actions ; which passes judgment upon himself and them ; pronounces determinately some actions to be in themselves just, right, good, and others to be in themselves evil, wrong, unjust.'[2] Two modern definitions are : ' That in me which says, " I ought " or " I ought not " ' (F. D. Maurice, *The Conscience*, p. 31) ; ' The mind occupied with moral phenomena ' (J. H. Hyslop, in Hastings' *Encyclopedia of Religion and Ethics*, s.v. ' *Conscience* ').

For a further note on *Synderesis*, cp. *Some Principles of Moral Theology*, p. 178, and on the pre-mediæval conception of conscience, *Ignorance, etc.*, p. 4.

NOTE B.

Two Modern Views of Casuistry (see page 125).

Two modern discussions of casuistry deserve notice. Frederick Denison Maurice, on his appointment as Knightbridge Professor at Cambridge, revived the old title of the Chair (Casuistry and Moral Theology), and his first course of lectures was published under the title of ' The Conscience : Lectures on Casuistry.' Maurice professes himself to sympathise with the aspirations of the casuist ; but he seems to mean little more by this than that ethical definitions should not be reached *a priori*, but only in relation to the verdicts of actual consciences reflecting upon concrete situations. He shows little understanding of anything that can be called casuistical method ; he quotes almost entirely from Jeremy Taylor alone, and then only such passages as lend themselves most readily to criticism. There is in fact little of casuistry in the book, and the sub-title is a complete misnomer.

Very much more important is Mr. Bradley's attack on casuistry.

[1] *Serm. I.*   [2] *Serm. II.*

Dr. Rashdall's criticism of it is well-known (*Theory of Good and Evil*, ii. pp. 420 ff.) ; but one or two further points may be noticed. Mr. Bradley's condemnation of casuistry is partly due to his conviction that it is ' not the business of moral philosophy to tell us what in particular we are to do ' (*Ethical Studies*, p. 174)— a statement with which we need not quarrel, as we are concerned rather with moral theology. But it also depends on a judgment of fact that *reflection* has no place in the solution of moral problems. ' That which tells us what is right or wrong in particular cases is not reflection but intuition.' In a footnote is added, '"Intuitive" is here used as the opposite of "reflective" or "discursive," "intuition" as the opposite of "reasoning" or "explicit inferring." If the reader dislike the word, he may substitute " perception " or " sense " if he will.' ' We know what is right in a particular case by what we may call an immediate judgment or intuitive subsumption.' ' Moral judgments are not discursive ' (*ib.* 175, 176). What is meant by a ' discursive ' judgment, or ' inference,' is given in another footnote : the non-discursive or intuitive judgment ' does not look to the right or left, and considering the case from all its sides, consciously subsume under one principle ' (p. 178). This however is true only of the *ordinary* moral judgment ; in difficult cases apparently reflective judgments are necessary : ' In practical morality no doubt we *may* reflect on our principles, but I think it is not too much to say that we *never* do so, *except where we have come upon a difficulty of particular application* ' (p. 176,—the last sentence not italicised in the original). ' If the current notion that moral philosophy has to tell you what to do is well-founded, then casuistry, so far as I can see, at once follows, or should follow ' (p. 178). But does it not follow equally in any case where intuitive judgments fail, and still we have to decide what to do ? In the last two passages the necessity of casuistry is apparently admitted ; it is strangely inconsistent therefore that Mr. Bradley adds almost immediately (p. 179)—' Collisions (of duties) must take place, and here there is no guide whatever but the intuitive judgment of oneself or others.'

How far the writer is thinking of debased casuistry only appears from the following (p. 178) : ' The casuist must have little ingenuity if there is anything he fails to justify or condemn according to his order. And the vice of casuistry is that, attempting to decide the particulars of morality by the deductions of the reflective understanding, it at once degenerates into finding a good reason for what you mean to do. You have principles of all sorts and the case has all sorts of sides ; *which* side is the essential side and which principle is *the* principle *here*, rests in the end on your mere private choice ; and that is determined by heaven knows what. . . . Hence the necessary immorality and ruinous effects of practical casuistry.' Apart from the fact that no attempt is made to prove that this effect is *necessary*, it is also clear that exactly the same criticism might be passed upon ' intuitionism.' That too *can* become a matter of ' private choice determined by heaven knows what ' if it shows itself as a ' vice ' ; and in such cases we might say that it decides to do ' what it means to do,' without even finding a good reason for it. Joseph Surface, ' the man of sentiment,' is a classical example of the ' vice' of intuitionism. Mr. Bradley safeguards his intuitionism from this line of attack by a host of limitations which amount to no more than saying that ' it presupposes the morality of the community and is subject to the approval thereof ' (p. 180), i.e. that only the intuitions of the morally earnest man can be accepted as validly moral. But if similar safeguards were allowed by him in the matter of casuistry, the latter would be as unexceptionable as the former.

NOTE D.

Probable Opinions (see p. 270).

It may be as well to consider at rather greater length the limitations in the use of ' probable opinions' in cases of doubt. St. Thomas clearly recognised a difference between ' doubt ' and ' opinion.' ' Doubt' is a complete suspension of judgment ; ' suspicion' has a tendency, based on a ' slight sign' only, to adhere to one alternative rather than another ; ' opinion' is an adherence to one alternative, though ' with the fear (i.e. on probable

grounds) that the other may be true.'[1] It would strictly follow
from this that if the arguments against the validity of a law—
so far from creating an *opinion* against it—are not even sufficient
to induce that complete suspension of the mind which St. Thomas
calls 'doubt,' we have not reached conditions under which it
is legitimate even to contemplate the possibility of waiving the
law. This, however, would mean that there must be at least as
strong arguments against the law as on its side (equiprobabilism)[2]
before we can contemplate its abrogation in our particular case.
Such a rule has the same defects as probabiliorism, that it involves a nicety of moral accountancy for which the human mind
has commonly neither the time nor the capacity. It seems
enough, therefore, to say that to constitute practical doubt there
must after full consideration remain at least enough argument
against the law to reduce our adherence to it to an 'opinion,' by
creating a definite, reasoned and solid 'fear' that it may be invalid, even though strict investigation might show that there was
slightly more to be said on the side of the law than against it.
If, however, even casual inspection showed that there was
a *good deal more* to be said for the law than against it, we
could not honestly say that there was probability on the side
of the doubt.

It is in this sense that the original probabilist maxim—'We
may use a probable opinion even though the contrary be more
probable '[3]—must be understood; i.e. we may take the benefit
of the doubt even where the arguments in favour of the law
might conceivably be stronger than those against it. The practical
emphasis is upon the genuineness and solidity of the 'probability'
required to excuse, not upon the possibility of the counter-arguments
being weightier. So Medina says quite definitely, 'For an opinion
to be probable it is not enough that specious reasons can be adduced
on its side, nor that it should have champions and defenders—
any error might be adjudged probable at that rate. It must be

---

[1] *S.T.* i. q. 79, a. 9, ad 4 ; ii. 2, q. 2, a. 1 in corp. ; cp. *de Ver.* xiv. a. 1.
The classification is a commonplace ; Lyndwood (v. 15) knows an ascending
scale of *six* degrees of certainty : doubt, suspicion, opinion, presumption,
belief, certainty.

[2] Equiprobabilism does not allow the benefit of the doubt to be taken
(as the name would seem to imply) in *all* cases where the arguments against
the law are as good as those for it, but only in cases where the doubt concerns
the promulgation of a new law as distinct from the cessation of a law known
to have been promulgated. Its basis is not so much *equal probability*
as the principle 'melior est conditio possidentis'; see, e.g., Tanquerey, ii.
233.

[3] So Medina, *in Prim. Sec.* q. 19, a. 6, fin. 'Si est opinio probabilis
licitum est eam sequi, licet opinio opposita sit probabilior.'

asserted by wise men and confirmed by the best arguments.'[1] But given an opinion of this latter kind it is ' safe and sure and free from danger,' and you need not ' torture ' yourself with the abstract possibility that knowledge more definite than you can attain to in the matter might show the contrary opinion to be more probable.[2] What Medina asserts is, in fact, that if an opinion is solidly probable the bare possibility that it might in the end prove less probable than its opposite need not deter us from acting upon it. He does not assert, as his imitators and disciples undoubtedly did (thus challenging anti-probabilist controversy), that any opinion could be probable in the face of *known* arguments of greater weight to the contrary. Indeed the whole tenour of his discussion suggests that he would have accepted the view that we *could* not have a probable opinion *in the face of more probable arguments to the contrary known to us* : though we can have a probable opinion in the face of possible, but so far unknown, ' more probable ' opinions to the contrary.

There is no reason to suppose that Medina would have hesitated to adopt as his test of a probable opinion (or, as we have said, a ' valid ' doubt) the conditions which his first great critic Comitolus propounded as necessary to create a ' more probable ' opinion : that its authors must be wise, upright, impartial and experienced in matters of the type in question ; that where authorities of this kind are found on both sides the opinion which the greater number of them support must be chosen; and that the arguments in favour of the opinion must be the ' more urgent ' and based on reason rather than on custom and authority.[3] Modern probabilists are of the same mind in the matter. Lehmkuhl repeatedly asserts that ' light and trivial doubts ' cannot possibly create a valid doubt,[4] and deals at great length with the canonical principles

[1] ' Opinio non dicitur probabilis ex eo quod in ejus favorem afferantur rationes apparentes et quod habeat assertores et defensores (nam isto pacto omnes errores essent opiniones probabiles) ; sed ea opinio probabilis est, quam asserunt viri sapientes et confirmant optima argumenta.'

[2] ' Opposita sententia (i.e. probabiliorismus) cruciat animos timoratos ; nam semper opporteret *inquirere* quaenam sit opinio probabilior, quod timorati viri numquam faciunt.'

[3] ' Opinioni illi palma danda est quae rationem consuetudini auctoritatique praeponit,' P. Comitolus, S.J. († 1626), *Responsa Moralia* (1609), V.q. 15. The noticeable appeal to reason against authority is strictly limited by the proposition that reason must agree with the divine will, which is ' announced by Scripture, the Councils, the traditions of Christ and the Apostles, the customs of the Church, the laws and mandates of the Pope, the unanimous voice and agreement of the Fathers and Doctors, *et Theologorum in gymnasiis disceptantium conspiratio et consentio.'* This is an appeal to reason, but to reason in leading strings.

[4] E.g. i. p. 82.

which must be applied for the strict determination of valid doubt and probability.[1] Tanquerey requires that there should be some 'really grave argument or authority' in support of the doubt, whose gravity is unimpaired even after the opposing arguments have been inspected;[2] nor will he admit that the consensus of five or six grave theologians can create such probability so long as there remains against them any really serious argument which they have failed to meet.[3]

Why, then, it may be asked, should probabilists insist that genuine doubt can exist, and can justify in waiving the law, in the face of a more probable opinion upholding observance of the law ('relicto probabiliori')? At first sight this seems a mere defiant verbal flourish—how could an opinion or doubt be as much as probable if there were 'more probable' arguments on the other side? One reason for the paradox we have already seen : the more probable arguments which may be discounted are not the *known* but the *unknown* arguments for the law. Once you have a reasonable and weighty doubt you need not become involved in the interminable discussions which would be necessary to weigh up the balance of probability on either side. But another reason—equally practical—dominates Vasquez's exposition of the matter (*in Prim. Sec.* disp. 62, c. 1). In any case of doubt, the 'more probable' opinion for a man must *be the opinion which he himself holds;* he would not hold it otherwise. If then this opinion (and we must remember that it is an opinion only, not a certainty) is on the side of the law, is he bound to follow it? We are once again in the sphere of amateur rigorism, or scrupulosity ; though the man has now not a *formed principle* that *all* doubtful laws must be obeyed (tutiorism), but only a strong *feeling* that *this* particular law should be obeyed. The answer is clearly as before, 'You are not bound to obey the law on a mere opinion that it may be binding, if there are sound reasons for suggesting that it is not binding, e.g. if responsible people agree in holding that it is not.' This is important ; for often enough where all is doubtful it is better to listen to the words of the prudent and experienced than to act upon a slight preponderance of inclination in the opposite direction of one's own. But the legitimacy of such a course (which we all admit) would not be officially allowed unless Medina's sentence, or something akin to it, were endorsed as satisfactory.

[1] *Ib.* pp. 82 ff.; cp. *Some Principles of Moral Theology*, pp 195 ff.
[2] Tanq. ii. p. 235.
[3] *Ib.* p 238, from Alph. Lig. i. § 82.

NOTE E.

Limitations of Probabilism (see page 271).

The limitations imposed by Innocent XI on the use of probabilism were not wholly unrecognised even by the most convinced probabilists, including some of the laxest Jesuits. Even the notorious Escobar had limited the use of probable opinions to cases in which no danger threatens which prudence, justice or charity bids us avoid [1]—a fact which Pascal entirely failed to observe and which consequently vitiates all his strictures. Diana, equally notorious ('Agnus Dei qui tollit peccata mundi,' Caramuel blasphemously called him), was far less circumspect—he allowed the medical man to use a less probable opinion *relicto probabiliori*, though even he hesitated to allow the benefit of the doubt where sacraments are concerned. [2] Vasquez, the first systematic probabilist, on the other hand, insists upon the safer course being taken where there is danger of a breach of the natural law or of charity, or in the case of the sacraments ; nor will he allow a judge or doctor to act upon a probable opinion where grave consequences are involved. [3] Suarez forbids the use of probabilism where justice or charity are at stake. [4] But no doubt the absence of authoritative decisions on the point led to great laxity.

The limitation is sometimes expressed in Roman Catholic manuals by a technical phrase which requires explanation. Probabilism, we are told, is allowed only where the question at issue is that of the mere ' legality or illegality ' [5] of the action concerned ; it does not touch its ' validity.' What is meant by this rule is as follows. Doubt in each case concerns one law or principle in particular, and can therefore only exempt us from the

---

[1] *Liber Theol. Moral.* (1644), Prooem. Exam. iii. C. 3.

[2] *Res. Mor.* p. ii. tr. xiii. res. 2, 7; p. iv. tr. iv. res. 4.   Diana died in 1663.

[3] *in Prim. Sec.* disp. 62, c. 6 ; 63, cc. 2, 3 ; 64, cc. 2, 4.   The restriction as to the judge is confined to the final Court of Appeal. Disp. 64, c. 1, is an interesting discussion as to whether a lawyer may prosecute on a ' probable opinion' of a man's guilt, or may defend him, when he believes him to be guilty, on a ' probable' opinion of his innocence.   Vasquez takes a highly reasonable view—it is the lawyer's business to give a true exposition of the evidence and arguments on his side of the case, and to leave the decision to judge and jury.

[4] *de Bon. et Mal.* disp. xii. sect. 6, § 10.

[5] ' De solo licito.'

duty of obeying that law ; it cannot exempt us from the claims of other laws pointing in the same direction as to which we have no doubt. An illustration will make this clear. It is usual in warehouses in which explosives or combustibles are stored for the owners to display a notice forbidding smoking or the striking of matches. A tourist who strolled into such a warehouse and found the notice partially defaced, or torn down, might reasonably doubt whether the management insisted upon its observance. Probabilism would at first sight suggest that it was ' licit ' for him to light his pipe, and that he owed no duty to refrain to an owner who allowed his warnings to lapse in this way. This conclusion would be fair enough ; to the owner as the person who regulated behaviour in the warehouse he would no longer owe obedience in this respect. But to the owner as the possessor of valuable property in the warehouse, and to the lives of those who worked in and about it, he would still owe a duty which the mere defacement of the warning could in no way abrogate. He could not be blamed for disobeying a notice which had been allowed to lapse into illegibility ; and in so far as this notice was concerned it would be ' licit ' for him to strike the match. But he could and would be blamed for disobeying the dictates of common sense, humanity and justice ; and the state of the notice would in this respect provide him with no excuse.

NOTE F.

Doubt and Perplexity (see page 321).

The distinction between ' doubt ' and ' perplexity ' is recognised clearly by all important Roman Catholic writers. So Liguori (i. § 10) : ' Conscience is perplexed when a man is so placed between two precepts that he thinks himself bound to sin whichever he obeys. E.g., A can save B's life by perjury in a law-court ; he is tortured on the one hand by the precept of religion forbidding perjury, on the other (though in error) by the precept of charity towards one's neighbour, and cannot decide what to do.' (The ' though in error ' does not affect the case, as the error is presumably invincible.) In his discussion of the ' doubtful ' conscience, on the other hand, Liguori assumes tacitly that there is only one ' law ' in question (ib. § 26). Lehmkuhl (i. p. 45) says, ' A special kind of doubt (" singulare dubium ") is presented by the

perplexed conscience, when a man thinks himself bound to sin whichever of two alternatives he chooses ("quando ex utraque parte homo
putat peccatum instare").' Tanquerey (ii. p. 210) : 'Sometimes a
person finding himself placed between two precepts thinks he is
bound to sin whichever he chooses—then we speak of a perplexed
conscience.' The distinction is clearly indicated by the fear of sin
in taking *either* alternative ; for in cases of doubt there is normally
no 'sin' (i.e. no breach of precept) in obeying the law ; the only
question is whether I am *obliged* to obey the law in this case.

The rule of the 'lesser evil' or the 'greater claim' (e.g.
Liguori, *loc. cit.*) is invariably given for cases of perplexity, thus
further marking the distinction between 'perplexity' and 'doubt.'
But curiously enough the writers seem not to notice the
number of genuine cases of perplexity which arise in life, and
tend to treat every problem which presents itself as a problem
of 'doubt' along probabilist, probabiliorist or equiprobabilist
lines. Sylvester, for instance (*s.v.*), treats *perplexitas* as a mere
synonym for *dubium*. It is not to be denied that cases of perplexity *can* all be so treated, and that great simplification results
therefrom. Either of the two 'precepts' involved can be treated
as the substantive one as to which there is 'doubt' ; and usually
the tendency of desire, noticed in the text above (p. 324), to
incline a man in the direction of one of them, makes it easy and
natural to regard the other in this light.

But the practice would appear to be illegitimate, and that for
two reasons. (1) In the first place, it weights the balance unfairly against the duty to which desire also points. It enhances
the tendency to regard desires as sinful, and consequently to
ignore the fact that duties, which we desire to perform for some
reason other than that they are duties, may nevertheless still be
duties (*supra* p. 326). A curious example of this may be found
in Fr. Slater's ' Moral Theology,' i. 68 f.: 'A young man '—so the
author propounds the case—' has promised to marry a girl
somewhat his inferior in social position ; they are satisfied that
the union would be a happy one for both, but the young man's
parents will not hear of the thing and strictly forbid him to see
the girl again. Must he obey his parents, or may he obey his
inclinations and keep his promise ? ' This method of stating the
question suggests that it is a conflict between duty (obedience to
parents) and desire (the ' inclination ' to marry)—the desire being
sufficiently marked to make the duty slightly doubtful. As a
matter of fact, however, the ' inclinations ' have nothing to do
with the problem. It is a clear case of a conflict of duties—the

duty of obedience to parents, and the duty of fidelity to a promise; and as such it is not affected in the least by the consideration that the young man's inclinations are engaged on one side or the other. It would be precisely the same problem if his inclinations were on the side of obedience and not on the side of marriage; for the question on which side they are does not affect the relative merits of the two duties as duties.

So completely is this ignored by the hypothetical advisers to whom Fr. Slater leads the young man that not one of them mentions the fact that the keeping of a promise is a duty. ' A probabiliorist would tell him that he must obey his parents . . . unless the opinion that he may ' (not ' *must*,' which would be required if the duty of keeping the promise were taken into consideration) 'marry the girl in spite of the prohibition is distinctly more probable. An equiprobabilist would say that he may ' (again ' *may*,' not ' must') 'marry the girl if the weight of opinion is fairly equal on either side. A probabilist would maintain that he may marry her if there is a solidly probable opinion which favours that course.'

It will be seen at once that this mode of presenting the problem alters its balance completely.[1] Because inclination is on the side of keeping the promise the latter is no longer regarded as a duty; and we are left with only one duty in question, that of filial obedience. The scales are heavily weighted therefore on this side; the young man has to show cause why he should even consider the possibility of disobedience, and the cause adduced is that of his desire to contract a marriage which he considers to be a ' happy one for both'; whilst the more important cause— that he has given a promise—is relegated to the background. The problem in fact is a genuine problem of ' perplexity ' and not one of 'doubt' at all, and so must be treated not on the principle of ' probabilism ' but on the principle of the ' lesser evil ' or the ' greater claim.' Only if the duty of obeying parents were normally regarded as more compelling than that of keeping promises could the latter be cancelled out for practical purposes, leaving the problem in the form of a general duty (obedience) which the circumstances of the case made doubtful. Fr. Slater's treatment of the case as one of ' doubt ' means in practice that it is less likely that a verdict in favour of marriage will be given

---

[1] Fr. Slater's presentation would be unexceptionable if the problem ran: ' A young man wants (but has not promised) to marry a girl, etc.' But this is quite a different problem; the adoption of the wrong method has led the writer to confuse the two. We may compare the way in which Fr. Slater secured his position in the matter of the papal claims by treating as a problem of doubt what is, in almost every case, a problem of a choice between two courses either of which may be ' safe' or ' unsafe'—*i.e.* once more, a problem of perplexity (*supra*, pp. 286 ff).

than if the case is treated as one of 'perplexity' between two claims of normally more or less equal importance. It simplifies the problem of course, but if the distinction drawn above between doubt and perplexity is valid, it is clear that it is a matter of more than theoretical importance to treat it in its proper category.

(2) In the second place, if the matter is strictly considered, the practice of treating cases of 'perplexity' as cases of 'doubt' would often make decision impossible. If a conflict between two 'precepts,' A and B, is to be treated as a conflict between a precept which circumstances (i.e. the intervention of the other precept) make doubtful and the natural desire for freedom, common fairness demands that the problem should be considered *both* from the point of view of precept A as the doubtful one *and* from that of precept B. And if both precepts were concerned with matters of vital importance the restrictions previously noticed would come into play, and we should still be bound to conclude (on investigating A) that A must be obeyed, and (on investigating B) that B also must be obeyed.

It would seem right, therefore, to insist that the distinction between 'doubt' and 'perplexity,' and the respective rules applicable in either case, is one of practical importance ; and that in every problem it is necessary to consider into which of the two categories it most naturally falls.

If, however, all problems of 'doubt' and 'perplexity' are to be treated under one category, it would seem wiser (as I suggested in *Some Principles*, pp. 192, 193) to treat them all as cases of 'perplexity.' On the one hand, if the doubt, though solid, is no more than a doubt (i.e. if the opinion in favour of the law is more than a scruple) the law has in the abstract some value as a regulative principle (hence the usual anti-probabilist argument that the rule of *Lex dubia non obligat* is not morally certain (Tanq. ii. 230 ; Prüm. i. 211). And on the other hand, even if nothing more than a desire for freedom suggests the possibility of disregarding a 'doubtful' law, freedom itself is a Christian privilege, and the assertion of freedom as against bondage, where nothing of greater urgency intervenes, *may* be a Christian duty. This is not to say that it is wrong to obey a law even when conscience declares it need not be obeyed ; our study of indifferent acts (*supra* pp. 38-52) forbids such a conclusion. But it is to suggest that such obedience will not always be (as traditional theology suggests it is, even though the opposite course is blameless too) the *safer*, or wholly blameless course. All problems of doubt (i.e. of law against freedom) *could* therefore be treated as problems

O 2

of perplexity—conflicts between a law which, though doubtful, has *some* bearing upon the case in question, and the law which makes the assertion of freedom a duty where no more pressing duty intervenes.

Such a treatment is advocated by the system of ' Compensationism,' or of ' sufficient reason,' which a section of modern Roman Catholic moralists prefer to probabilism and even to probabiliorism. Accounts of it will be found in Tanquerey, ii. 239–241 ; Prümmer, i. 204. In brief the system is as follows : We must estimate, on the one hand, the degree of applicability of the 'doubtful' law to the case, on the other hand the reasons which suggest exemption ; if on comparison these reasons seem ' sufficient ' to justify an exemption, it can be made, but not otherwise. ' Pensanda est gravitas legis et probabilitas opinionis oppositae. Quo gravior est lex et quo probabilior est ejus obligatio in casu actuali, eo major requiritur causa excusans.' The argument against so treating questions of doubt would be that in many cases it would elaborate a wholly trivial problem, easily decided on probabilist lines, into a crisis of conscientious scruples.

It would appear the wisest course, therefore, to leave 'doubt' and ' perplexity ' as two different categories of problem, and not to attempt for the sake of an unreal simplification to reduce either to a mode of the other.

NOTE G

A Roman Catholic Moralist on Lying (see pp. 193-195, 338-343).

One of the fullest modern Roman Catholic discussions of the problem of lying is that of Fr. A. Vermeersch (' de Mendacio et Necessitatibus Commercii Humani ') in ' Gregorianum,' January and July 1920. The outlook is singularly fair and balanced ; thus although the writer would not agree with the position adopted in the text above, that a lie may sometimes be the lesser of two evils and consequently blameless (*supra* pp. 193, 341), he frankly admits that there is both mediæval and post-Tridentine Roman authority for the doctrine (' Gregorianum,' 1920, pp. 26, 27).

Fr. Vermeersch himself holds firmly to the Augustinian-Thomist position that every lie is sinful, though the sin involved may often be slight (' malitia mendacii genere levis est . . . mendacium ergo mortale non erit, nisi ex accedente circumstantiâ vel odii unde profisciscatur, vel damni quod inferat, vel obligatonis dicendi quam violet '—*ib.* p. 36). This view, with its corollary that, though many lies will be pardonable (and, indeed, not necessary matter for confession), *no* lie can be blameless, we have found it necessary to question (*supra, locc. citt.*) ; and we have suggested further that the theory as a whole only survives (as commonly among Roman moralists) because of a series of expedients by which large classes of misrepresentations can be taken out of the category of ' lying ' altogether.

These expedients, of which we have given a few examples (*supra* pp. 124 f.), Fr. Vermeersch enumerates fully (*op. cit.* pp. 444-460). Quite naturally and rightly he finds himself out of sympathy with the majority of them, except in their most innocuous forms. His own solution, however, is not without difficulty. Starting from the admitted fact that actors and writers of fiction are not guilty of lying when engaged in their professions, because they are speaking ' ex ore alieno,' or not pretending to reveal ' their own mind,' he concludes that *whenever the circumstances of the case suggest that the speaker may not be revealing his own mind,* he cannot be held guilty of lying, though he may, of course, be guilty of other sins by reason of his misrepresentation.[1] ' So the husband who denies his adultery, or the criminal who denies his crime, is excused from the guilt of lying . . . because his answers objectively mean *either* " I did not do it " or " I do not propose to confess it." And this is not " contrary to his mind."
. . . When St Francis replied to the pursuers of a fugitive, " He did not pass this way " . . . the answer in itself involved the ambiguity :—either " He did not pass " or " I am not going to betray him." So when a doctor encourages a sick patient, he leaves it ambiguous whether he is speaking his mind or merely concealing the gravity of the illness.' [2]

Fr. Vermeersch rightly refuses to allow the speaker voluntarily to confirm his statement by corroborative assertions ; this would remove the ambiguity created by the equivocal circumstances. Again he says, ' Ambiguitatis usus ne fiat nisi necessarius ; nec necessarius existimetur qui solo amore proprio vel vani honoris ratione imperetur ' (p. 472). Even so, however, the theory, if we

---

[1] 'Si ita res se habent, quotiescumque ex adjunctis rationabiliter colligitur, exteriora verba non dici ab aliquo qui mentem suam communicat, aberit, cum ipsa locutione, copia mendacii, et quotiescumque idem dubitabitur, aderit vera et propria ambiguitas sermonis, quae ipsa, eâ quam supra diximus ratione, mendacium excludit,' *op. cit.* p. 462.

[2] *Ib.* pp. 462, 463 ; later (p. 470) he says, ' The sick person has evidence, in the very fact of her illness, for doubting the sincerity of the speaker.'

have rightly interpreted it, is somewhat disconcerting. On purely abstract grounds it seems to involve more fallacies than one. From the fact that the actor, *indubitably* speaking ' ex ore alieno,' is not guilty of lying, we cannot argue to the conclusion that the same is true of all persons speaking in circumstances which make it only *doubtful* whether they are speaking ' suam mentem.' Nor can it be said that ambiguity of expression and ambiguity of circumstance are morally identical. We may grant Fr. Vermeersch's premise that a genuine ambiguity—that is, an expression which is at least as capable naturally of a true interpretation as a false one (e.g., ' Aio te, Aiacidem, Romanos vincere posse ')—is not in itself a lie, though circumstances (such as the overwhelming evidence of the context) may convert it into something very like one. But, once again, we cannot argue from this to the conclusion that what would normally be called a lie (i.e., a statement which is naturally capable only of an interpretation false to the facts as the speaker conceives them) can be converted by its circumstances into an ambiguity. In either case the argument leading to the conclusion requires very full and careful statement before it can be accepted as valid.

Again, the theory seems to involve the curious corollary that a person known to be an habitual liar cannot be guilty of lying (though his misrepresentations may, of course, involve all sorts of other sins) : the circumstance that he lies habitually must, on Fr. Vermeersch's showing, make *all* his utterances ' ambiguous ' —' quae ipsa mendacium excludit.' Finally, we observe that lies are rarely uttered except in ambiguous circumstances—i.e., where the liar has something to gain by his misrepresentations ; and that therefore, whenever such circumstances can reasonably be suspected—i.e., whenever it is reasonable to suppose that he stands to gain by misrepresentation—his utterance, however sinful in other respects, must be adjudged ' not a lie.' In fact, the lower the view we take of human nature, the fewer ' lies ' there will be in the world.

Fr. Vermeersch has another expedient for ' concealing the things we ought, or desire, to conceal, without lies or verbal jugglery ' (p. 464) This is the *enigma*. The stage-manager who knows the theatre to be on fire can get rid of his audience quietly by telling them that one of the actresses has suddenly fallen ill ; and this is no lie but an enigma, because ' as soon as they get out of the theatre the audience will understand what the manager really meant by his enigma of the actress ' (p. 470). By these two devices it will be seen that the writer is enabled to treat as blameless

all those misrepresentations which common sense would natur
ally hold to be blameless. The doubt which arises is whether
his theory would not also exempt from the blame of lying (though
not necessarily from blame on other accounts) a great many
misrepresentations which sound common-sense would unhesitatingly stamp as glaringly mendacious ; and so (with those
classical forms of evasion which the writer himself reprobates)
lend itself to that debased form of casuistry which, while maintaining the letter of the law, eviscerates its spirit. Unless we have
wholly mistaken Fr. Vermeersch's meaning, his article does not
carry with it the conviction that the right way to defend the
blamelessness of some misrepresentations is not to say (as we
have done above) that a lie, though a lie, may sometimes be the
lesser of two evils, and on that account free from sin.

NOTE H.

Objective and Subjective Necessity for Salvation (see pp. 249, 271,
282, 285, 288).

The interpretation of the phrase ' necessary to the attainment
of salvation ' involves a certain ambiguity. We must draw a
clear distinction between what is *subjectively* and what is *objectively* necessary to salvation. *Subjectively*—that is, in the case
of any given individual—it is an accepted principle of moral
theology that nothing more is necessary to salvation than explicit belief in God as a ' rewarder,' together with moral ' good
faith '—i.e. living up to the ' best that one knows.' This was fully
established as the result of the discussions of the fate of the
virtuous heathen and heretics to which I drew attention in
Ignorance, Faith and Conformity, c. iii. (cp. also *ibid.*, c. iv., p. 121 ;
c. v. p. 161), and is merely an elaboration of the principle that
' an invincibly erroneous conscience excuses.'

At the same time it would be absurd for the Church, on the
basis of this position, to abandon her insistence upon distinctively
Christian truths and moral principles and say, ' Since a believer
in God needs nothing but a clear conscience to secure his salvation, we may safely leave him to the mercy of that conscience

without further instruction or discipline.' Apart from the revelation in Christ embodied in those truths and principles, human
frailty (we may fairly say) would suffer such a deterioration
of conscience that ultimately it might relapse into total inactivity, and moral distinctions fall into complete oblivion.
Some objective form of discipline must be necessary to secure—not
salvation *in this or that instance* (which is dependent upon ' good
faith ' alone)—but the continuance of the conditions which make
salvation generally possible. This is even more obvious if we
adopt some such phrase as ' leading the full moral life ' as a
preferable altêrnative to ' the attainment of salvation ' ; for ' good
faith ' and ' the full moral life ' (i.e. ' the best I *know* ' and ' the
best I *might* know ') are two very different things. It is to such
objective principles (whatever they may be) that moralists are
referring when they speak of ' laws necessary to the attainment
of salvation,' and refuse to allow the benefit of the doubt to be
taken in regard to them.

When, therefore, in regard to any principle (such as that of
fasting communion, clerical celibacy, communion with Rome, or
the like) the casuist asks, ' Is it necessary to the attainment of
salvation ? ' he does not mean, ' Is it necessary in this or any
other particular case ? ' The answer to that question must
depend wholly on the state of the individual conscience ; and—
if this were the meaning to be attached to the question—where
conscience invincibly declared the principle to be unnecessary,
the individual would be free to take the benefit of the doubt in
genuinely doubtful cases without considering the question of
loyalty, and the confessor would be bound to give absolution—two
conclusions we have rejected. For even an invincible conscience,
though it demands obedience and excuses from sin, does not give
to its possessor the *right* to claim the full privileges of Church
membership (*supra*, pp. 218, 225, 249) any more than it gives the
confessor the right or duty to confer absolution (pp. 248, 249).

What the question means is, ' Is this principle one whose
abandonment, even by the considered judgment of the whole
Church, would result in such widespread deterioration of conscience and behaviour as to make the full moral life generally
impossible ? ' If the answer to this question were ' Yes ' (as we
may suppose, for example, it would be for a Roman moralist in
the matter of the papal claim to unconditional supremacy *jure
divino*, for all Romans and some Anglicans in that of ' birth-
control,' or for all Christians in that of monogamy) the benefit
of the doubt could not be allowed in any case. If the answer

were ' No,' the benefit of the doubt might be taken in cases of genuine doubt. If no certain answer could be given (i.e. if there were a doubt as to the character of the doubt ; cp. p. 273 n.) l am prepared to err on the rigorist side and to say that the benefit of the doubt must still be refused.

INDEX

I.—AUTHORS

II. SUBJECTS

PRINTED BY J. AND J. GRAY, EDINBURGH